DESIGN YOUR DESTINY

11 ESSENTIAL STEPS TO BUILDING AND SELLING A COMPANY

DAVID GOWANS

What would your life look like if
you knew you could not fail?

About the Author

David Gowans is a proven entrepreneur with a successful business history. His purpose now is to help other entrepreneurs and business leaders across the world to build their business to a level where they can either sell or exit and enjoy freedom of time and money.

Having already started a business from scratch, built it successfully and then sold it, David has an advantage over other Business Mentors who may only be working with theory. Under his leadership, his old company was polled as one of the fastest growing companies in the country and won business awards based on their excellent people development philosophies. David's motto was to "reward those who do the work" and he firmly believed in incentivising staff to perform well, then they could share in the Company's success. This worked well and proved very successful. So much so, that David retired from work way earlier than he could ever have imagined as a kid growing up in the tough streets of Glasgow.

Now, his lifestyle is to travel to new countries, mostly by yacht, whilst working on new business ventures, and providing expert mentoring sessions to clients across the world.

The Proof is in the Pudding

Unlike many other coaches or mentors, David learned most things in business by actually being successful at them. The proof is in the pudding as they say, and being semi-retired at a young age is a fantastic achievement. David provides clients with real life experience and advice learned from his success in business, and how he managed to be free from life's constraints way before his 40th birthday.

Today, David's main focus is to share this knowledge and advice. His purpose is to bring more awareness to people so that they can have the confidence and direction to make big changes in their lives. David believes that society puts too much pressure on people, builds fears and limits the belief system of people at an early age. Then people seem to be trapped in this life cycle and generally live an unhealthy and stressful life, work until beyond pension age, and then at the end, they regret not taking action earlier in life. David's mission is to help people question their current situation, and challenge them to have more belief that they can make big changes and make their world a better place.

Contents

Introduction

Freedom.

That's what's driven me my whole life. Everything I've done, whether knowingly or not, was pushing me or pulling me towards greater freedom. For me business offered that opportunity – a way to design my own destiny and create enough wealth so I could travel the world and help other entrepreneurs fulfil their own dreams.

Gone are the days of getting a job with a company after school or university and receiving a gold watch from that same company after 40 years of service. Those opportunities simply don't exist anymore. Plus, they are not what people want anymore. Business is no longer seen as something other people do – reserved for corporate renegades like Sir Richard Branson. Small and medium-sized businesses are now the backbone of the global economy as more and more people turn away from the 9 – 5 grind to seek out a better work/life balance, more money and more freedom.

Technology is also allowing us to re-invent the way we work, how we work and where we work while also opening up new markets and greater opportunity. Today I regularly 'work' while sailing in the Mediterranean or exploring a new country. All I need is my laptop and a good internet connection. But, I'm not alone. Entrepreneurs with this mindset are popping up all over the world. We don't need to be shackled to an office or work cubicle – we can be anywhere.

More and more of us are questioning the 'system'. Why do we have to work in a job we don't really enjoy for 40 years, constantly looking forward to a few measly weeks holiday a year amongst an ocean of stress? All for a modest salary and retirement when we are too tired to enjoy it. What a life!

I think it is this grim realisation that is nudging more people into business in an effort to design their own destiny. And it's not just the 'natural entrepreneurs' who started their first business at 10 years old, all sorts of people are taking the leap of faith and backing themselves.

The problem is business is not easy. We've all heard the stark statistics of how many businesses fail. We've all met people with a great idea, who are still talking about the same great idea ten years later. Or perhaps we know someone who ended up going into business for themselves after an unexpected redundancy. Some, like me, are driven by a desire for something more – more freedom, more adventure, the ability to test themselves or to make more money. There are as many different types of people in business as there are businesses themselves. So, what separates success from failure? What is the difference that makes the difference? Is there some special recipe or secret sauce that can guarantee success?

I think there is. Or at least there are 11 essential steps that need to be taken to radically improve your chances. And it is those steps, once taken and mastered, that allowed me and my two business partners to build a specialist electrical contracting business from scratch and sell it for millions of pounds just seven years later. Together, we grew the business to a turnover of £14 million, employing 300 people.

During that time, we made our fair share of mistakes but we also learned some powerful insights that can make the journey easier, more enjoyable and much more lucrative for you. Using my own experiences, and those of other successful entrepreneurs, I've been able to distil the lessons I learnt to offer a road map for others so they can create the business they want and use that business to fund their dreams.

There is no doubt that business comes in all shapes and sizes, offering an infinite array of products and services, but when you can step back and appreciate the structures and processes that create great, saleable businesses then a great deal of the mystery disappears.

As entrepreneurs, it can be incredibly difficult to see the wood for the trees inside our own business. Often, we are so consumed by the immediate problems or the biggest issue 'right now' that we can forget to stay focused on the bigger picture. Or, worse, we never really get clear on what that bigger picture actually is.

Too many people go into business bursting with enthusiasm and excitement but without any real plan. Perhaps leaving a job they didn't like. Perhaps it was too stressful or they hated the boss and were convinced they could do a better job themselves. Or maybe they wanted to cut back on the relentless long hours or just wanted to make more money. Whatever the catalyst, they launch themselves whole-heartedly into the new venture. Exhilarated to have left the old situation behind and excited about what they can create in the new one. Of course, these transitions rarely go to plan. Often, it's not long before they are even more stressed, working even longer hours and possibly making even less money than they left behind. And when it does go well, there seems to be a lack of time to live your life as you imagined the freedom of being your own boss would give you. And there certainly isn't enough time to create a compelling vision that will help navigate challenging times.

Like most business people I learnt the hard way but that doesn't mean you have to.

This book is the 'must know' information and advice that you will need to transform your business from something that earns you a salary and gives you something to do to providing you with the lifestyle you have always dreamt of. Today, I have to pinch myself at my lifestyle. Since selling up I've travelled and lived in Brazil, visited the Amazon, backpacked around the Caribbean and Central America, cycled in Africa, sailed the Greek Islands, driven around the Turkish coast, taken a campervan around the Scottish Islands, learned salsa in Cuba, made city breaks to fabulous European cities and ticked off many other destinations that I had dreamt of. I've learned to sail and have visited some amazing places, I've taken time to learn how to live a nutritious and healthy lifestyle and I'm fitter and happier than I've ever been. My business created that possibility for me and it can deliver whatever you dream of too.

This book is designed for entrepreneurs who are already running a business or thinking of creating a new start up. If your dreams of business success seem to be getting buried under an endless 'to-do list', or you find yourself working harder than you've ever worked but are still not seeing the financial rewards, if you've forgotten what your kids look like or feel trapped by your business then this book is for you. Even if you don't have any intention to sell your business, it will provide important guidance and information that will help you run a successful organisation, ready for sale or ready to hand over to a management team should you want to.

And that's real freedom.

Step One:

Begin with the End in Mind

This idea is one of Stephen Covey's *7 Habits of Highly Effective People* and relates to the importance of being clear on what you are trying to achieve – right from the start.

There are two parts to this in the context of starting or building a business. First you have to tap into your own personal 'Why'. What's driving you to create the business or build the business in the first place? The second is about your exit strategy so that you are clear about what you are trying to create and what your end goal is.

Both are critical to consider sooner rather than later and are essential for different reasons.

Start with Why
In his book *Start with Why,* author Simon Sinek explores the first idea as a driving force for any

business. Too often we are really good at knowing what we do or what we make or sell and how we operate but the why is lost amongst the day to day operation of the business. And yet it is the why that gets us out of bed in the morning. It's the why that helps to push us through challenging times and without a clear appreciation of that driver it can be too easy to quit or decide to go back to the workforce. Building a successful and profitable business takes time, especially if the business is labour intensive. Managing people is notoriously challenging. It's not easy and it will drain you of energy. You may find it almost impossible to detach yourself from the business and no matter where you are or who you are with you will always be thinking about the business. It means long hours, hard decisions and challenging cash flow from time to time. The best way to stay focused during those times is to know your why and engage and connect with the extra reserves that can be made available when you are clear on your why or driving motivation.

To paraphrase, Austrian neurologist and psychiatrist Viktor Frankl, "When you know your 'why' you can endure almost any how". And he would know – he endured a concentration camp during the Second World War because he was determined to survive and write his book on psychology, which he did.

So, what's your why?

Have you ever thought why you are in business or why you wanted a business in the first place? Take a moment to really consider why you want to go into business or why you started the business you are already in. What is your end game? Do you even have one? Are you simply looking for a business that replaces your job and provides an income or are you looking to grow the company and sell it? Was your motivation redundancy or were you just desperate to get away from an irritating boss or from excessive stress and crazy work hours?

The challenge with those drivers is that they are 'away from' motivators. Human beings tend to be driven toward something or away from something else. Being motivated to get away from a job we hate is great for the initial departure and start-up of the business but it won't get you very far after that! Once you are out of the old situation your motivation may dry up or you simply replace your old irritating boss with new irritating clients and that could be disastrous.

What you need to run alongside any 'away from' motivation is a compelling personal vision of what you want from your life. Something that pulls you toward a better future. Something that makes you happy and excited – by just thinking about it.

My dream was to be free to travel the world whenever I wanted and to be wherever I wanted – all the time! Not long before I started my business, I had taken a year away from work to backpack around the world and I'd had the most amazing experiences of my life. I had joined an unofficial club and I had well and truly caught the travelling bug. Once I returned all I cared about was finding a way to be able to make that travelling lifestyle my way of life. For the first time, I witnessed the law of attraction in action. I'd read about it and heard other people's stories but I'd never really experienced it myself. Looking back, I think it hadn't shown itself in my life before because I'd never wanted anything badly enough before! Now I did – I wanted to travel and find a way to make that a reality.

When the opportunity to create a new business came unexpectedly I grabbed it with both hands. The travelling experience had given me a new more relaxed outlook on life and I also had a compelling vision of what I wanted the business to deliver so I was able to turn that opportunity into reality. From that day on, I was crystal clear that the business was a vehicle to provide me with the financial freedom to be able to travel the world forever. And it happened!

There were so many times in the start-up and development of the business that I could easily have thrown in the towel but even in the darkest most challenging times I was able to reconnect to my travelling dream, remember the experiences I'd enjoyed and why I was creating the business, and was able to push through to better times. If I hadn't found my 'why' I'm not sure I would have stayed the course.

Quiet Reflection

I recommend that you take yourself away for a few hours or even a couple of days and really map out what you want for your life. As I am writing this book, I am sitting at an idyllic spot on the east coast of the Isle of Skye in the Scottish Highlands. I'm sitting in my 1971 classic Volkswagen campervan overlooking the sea and spectacular scenery to the mainland. This is what inspires me and doing something similar might help you to work out your main objectives in life.

Obviously, building a business is hard work. It's often long hours and a significant amount of stress. It's critical therefore that you set out on your business building journey in an area that you are passionate about. It will make the work necessary for success more interesting, inspiring and exciting. Quiet reflection up-front can help you to assess whether your idea for a business is right for you as well as what you are trying to achieve from that business. Finding what you're passionate about is the key. You need to know who you are at your core, what drives you and where your interests and aptitudes lie. I found meditation really helpful. Before you can identify your true passion, you need to understand who you really are, your true self. Regular meditation allowed me to figure out what dreams and aspirations were mine and not follow what society says. We are conditioned by a whole host of inputs about what success looks like and what we should aspire to but this conditioning doesn't normally ring true to our core essence. It was only when I discovered travelling that I could differentiate between what really made me happy and what other people thought should make me happy. People can live their whole lives making decisions on a false belief or external expectation given to them (subconsciously) by their parents, teachers, peers, society or the media. Make sure that your personal vision is true to you. In terms of what it is you are trying to achieve and why, and also how excited and passionate you are about the business you are considering using as a vehicle to achieve those objectives. You need to like and enjoy the work and the industry you enter otherwise the business building stage will be unnecessarily tough.

Getting clearer on who you are and what really drives you will make a huge difference at this stage. Really take the time to consider who you are and what you really want out of life. Once you are clearer.... Dream big!

If you knew you could not fail what would your life look like?

Imagine your business is a huge success – you've sold it for millions – what are you doing? Where are you living? What experiences are you enjoying? Who are you with? What have you bought? It's always nice to consider what extravagance you may indulge in once you've made it – a gorgeous car or an amazing wardrobe. When we sold our business for millions I certainly treated myself and those close to me. I bought a top of the range Range Rover, a nice powerboat, the Breitling watch that I always wanted, new designer clothes and all the gadgets of the day.

But, I would caution you to think beyond how much money you want to make and the material possessions it will allow you to buy. Instead look beyond money and to the experiences and the lifestyle that money will allow you to enjoy. Possessions are nice but they only ever bring short-lived happiness. Even when we own beautiful things human nature means that we normalise them. In other words, the first rush of adrenaline and joy we experience driving the Aston Martin becomes commonplace and humdrum after a while. If you are not careful with the ego, before long you will want the new model or a more expensive car, and the cycle continues.

In fact, researchers from Princeton University have proven that money doesn't buy happiness. Clearly, not having enough money can have its hardships but using Gallup data for almost half a million people in America, the study demonstrated that 'enough' is actually about $75,000 (about £58,000). Once this magical threshold had been reached the happiness benefits from money and possessions taper off entirely.

Focus on the type of lifestyle you want, where you want to live, who you will spend time with, where you will go and who you will be. What new adventures will you enjoy? What experiences will you have? These are the things that can really ignite our passions and motivations and help us achieve our dreams

In his landmark book, *Think and Grow Rich*, possibly the most famous personal development book ever written, author Napoleon Hill talks about this idea as your 'definite major purpose'. He writes, *"truly thoughts are things, and powerful things at that, when they are mixed with definiteness of purpose, persistence, and a burning desire for their translation into riches, or other material objects."*

Everything is Created Twice

The reason a strong compelling vision is so critical to success is because everything is created twice. First in the mind and then in reality. Knowing what you want from life and holding that positive vision in your thoughts at all times not only motivates you and provides inspiration when the going gets tough but it also activates the Law of Attraction. When we are clear about what we want it's almost like a message goes out into the universe about our desires and the universe then conspires to bring that vision about.

This may sound like new-age hippy bullshit but I've experienced it myself enough times to know there is something to it. Once I was focused on finding a way to give me the freedom and money to travel, a strange sequence of unexpected events occurred that led to the opportunity to start the business. I honestly believe that my getting clear on what I really wanted orchestrated that opportunity.

Part of the reason for this is actually biological. There is a part of our brain, called the Reticular Activating System (RAS) that has a number of functions including information filtration. We are bombarded with information via our five senses – especially now in the modern world of constant connectivity. If we were to become consciously aware of everything we would go crazy. It's too much – complete sensory overload. To prevent this the RAS limits what we are aware of or pay attention to by deleting what's not relevant based on our thoughts, beliefs, attitudes, goals etc.

Most of us have experienced the RAS in action although we probably didn't realise it. Have you ever decided to buy a new car for example? You want a change and decide to buy a red Audi – you don't see many of them on the roads. You drive the car out of the showroom and overnight all you notice is other red Audi's – every man and his dog is driving that car! That's your RAS. Actually, the cars were always there but before you brought the car into your conscious awareness as something you wanted your brain ignored their presence and you didn't notice them.

Think of the RAS as the editor of a major newspaper – there are thousands of stories vying for attention but it's the editor that decides what goes on the front page. You need to establish your goals and visions as a front-page story so that you can attract the necessary people, events and opportunities into your life to bring about the second creation – making it a reality.

Our thoughts are incredibly powerful. And whilst this idea has appeared in personal development literature for decades it's now being verified by science and academic research.

Physicist Dr William Tiller of Stanford University has conducted many studies which demonstrate a connection between intention, thought and outcome. In one of his most famous, he instructed four people skilled in meditation to focus on an electronic box with the intention of increasing the pH by one point. The electronic boxes together with control boxes were then placed six inches from separate samples of water taken from the same source. It's worth pointing out that increasing the pH in the human body by one point would cause death so this is not something that is particularly easy or statistically probable (less than one thousand to one chance of happening naturally). And yet, the boxes that had focused mental energy directed toward them did indeed alter the pH of the water.

From his research Tiller concluded that, "From these studies and more like them, it can be seen that belief fuels expectations and expectations, in turn, marshal intention at both unconscious and conscious levels to fulfil expectations." According to Tiller, "We are running the holodeck. It has such flexibility that anything you can imagine, it will create for you. Your intention causes this thing to materialise once you're conscious enough and you learn how to use your intentionality."

In short – what we focus on and think about matters. Knowing what we want to achieve and holding that in mind as a magnet matters. The holodeck reference Tiller makes relates to Star Trek. In the sci-fi classic, crew of the USS Enterprise could enter the holodeck and chose to experience any alternative simulated reality. A necessary respite when everyone they met was trying to kill them! The point is – we have that same capability. We are literally dialling up our own reality – either by accident through the unhelpful and negative thoughts that consume us or by taking charge of that process to focus on what we want rather than what we don't want.

And remember Tiller is not some fringe crackpot – he's a highly respected Stanford physicist. And, he's not alone. Philosopher and theologian Dr Miceal

Ledwith puts it this way, "reality is not solid, it's mostly empty space and whatever solidity it has seems more to resemble a hologram picture rather than solid harsh reality. It's a shimmering reality that seems to be very susceptible to the power of thought". He goes on to suggest, "We are creating our own reality every day, though we find that very hard to accept – there's nothing more exquisitely pleasant than to blame somebody else for the way we are. It's her fault or it's his fault; it's the system; it's God; it's my parents... Whatever way we observe the world around us is what comes back to us."

There is now irrefutable evidence that what we think about on a habitual basis impacts what we experience. Just take a moment to allow that to sink in...

Are you focused on the negative side of life and what you want to avoid or are you focused on the positive side and what you want to attract? We tend to create what we focus on – hence why it's so crucial to have a clear positive picture to ensure we are creating the life we want rather than constantly re-creating the thing we are trying to get away from!

Having your vision written down is also important. In a famous study of Yale University students, researchers found that only three percent had written goals with plans for their achievement. Twenty years later researchers interviewed the surviving graduates and found that those three percent were worth more financially than the entire 97 percent combined.

Exit Strategy

Having discovered what your personal 'why' is, the second part of beginning with the end in mind is to consider your exit strategy for the business. It might sound strange to think about exiting your business before you've even started it or perhaps you're already knee deep in your business and all you can think about is the crisis unfolding right now. All of that is normal and logical but you need to stop.

In order to get anywhere you need to know two things. Where you are right now and where you want to go. When starting a business most of us are really good at the first part and pay limited, if any, attention to the second. But if you don't know where you are going then you will just get in motion and you could end up in a completely different and unwelcome place. Without exception, the business leaders that I have mentored who are in the biggest pickle are the ones who are not clear about their destination. Instead they jumped in feet first and have been swimming like crazy ever since – often treading water for years!

Perhaps you want to sell your business for a big fat profit and live off the proceeds. Maybe you would rather hand the business over to a management team and draw an income from your hard work. Or perhaps, more likely, you've never even considered what your end game is.

This is a mistake and the sooner you rectify it the better. Always aim to sell your business or reach a point where you *could* sell the business and step back with confidence if you wanted to. Whether you choose to sell will be up to you but if you don't start the business with that objective you will almost certainly waste a huge amount of time and money having to backtrack if you decide to sell further down the line. If you don't plan to sell, it's likely that you will grow and develop your business organically. This is fine, but it often means that you don't do proper due diligence around the business, don't institute written policies and procedures that would actually make that business run better and make it more valuable to a potential buyer. If you 'fly by the seat of your pants' for years and then decide to sell you will have to implement all that rigour in order to get the business to a point that you even *could* sell it.

If you want to retire at some stage then planning your exit is as important as running the business profitably. And having your final goal or lifestyle aspirations in the front of your mind at all times is key to pushing you to make the right decisions along the way.

Exit planning is something you should be doing years before you actually hand over the keys of your business. You should create a vision of what you want to happen in the business (more on this in the next step), how big it will be, how many employees it will have, the geographical locations it will operate in, the types of customers you will have, the financial results, and what it will be worth. A clear understanding of this will help you to create a strategy of how you will actually make that vision a reality. You are effectively designing your business's destiny so that it can facilitate your own destiny.

A good exit plan will help to drive your company to greater success. Understanding your plan will ensure you make the right decisions and, even more importantly, let go of the things that are not important. Getting involved in the trivia is something that too many business leaders do. It causes undue stress and consumes too much time that should have been allocated to running the business effectively. Knowing your exit plan will keep you focused on the priorities and get you to your goal a lot quicker.

Using a business mentor is an excellent way to build your exit strategy. Rather than trying to learn things the hard way, you can tap into their wealth of experience and set a robust strategy safe in the knowledge that it works. The great thing about business is you don't need to re-invent the wheel all the time and you don't always have to make your own mistakes. Business success is a well-trodden path – find someone you can trust as your guide so they can help you avoid the pitfalls. In fact, using a good mentor throughout my own business journey was one of the smartest business decisions I ever made.

If you are looking for a great mentor make sure they have actually led a business to sale and exit rather than someone who deals only in theory. Working with a fellow entrepreneur who understands the position you are in and the pressures you are under is always the best route (see my website www.davidgowans.com).

Even if you decide not to sell, the business you will create as a result of assuming you will sell will be stronger, more productive, more efficient and more valuable than the one you create with no end in sight. The last thing you want is to build the business, decide you want to retire and then find out that the business is actually not in a saleable condition. Or worse, fall ill and be in the position that you *need* to sell. Without the right exit strategy you may be forced to take considerably less than you hoped. The market may change, this more than ever is a real threat so being prepared and having a strong, functional saleable business as early as possible is always the smart play.

Buyers want to buy a business that will operate profitably without the founder. Often businesses are successful because of the force of a founder's personality but a buyer wants assurances that the business will still function well and efficiently once that personality has left the building. Building a management team is therefore critical to a successful exit strategy. A strong team will generate new ideas and energy, and will help you to build your business faster. It also provides a potential buyer in the form of a management buy-out.

Getting the right people also creates a layer of staff who can take responsibility and be accountable for their element of the business. It also allows you to delegate more effectively so you can get on with the task of building the business.

When we built our exit strategy, I found that I was not enjoying running the business much as I was getting too bogged down in the day to day activities. By building a good management team, and letting go of many of the tasks that held me back, I had more time to focus on what was important. I believe business leaders should be focusing 80 percent of their time on strategy, and looking for the next opportunity to take the business to the next level. When I learned this, and put it into practice, I started to step back and enjoy the role of business leader much more. I allowed the management team to get on with what they were good at and had been trained on, and I focused on the high-level elements only, and got back to my entrepreneurial ways of thinking of new ideas. But before you can get to this level, you need to build up the business and then free up your time.

In addition, business leaders who have already started planning their exit route tend not to get as stressed. They know the end goal is to make themselves redundant so they have already passed on the responsibilities to their management team. They have a belief that they will be ready to leave the business when the opportunity comes, knowing that they have a strong team in place who will continue to run the business into the future.

Everything that starts comes to an end. That's life – endless cycles. At some stage, you will need to leave your business. Doing it under your own terms is a lot better than being forced to do it from unfortunate circumstances or outside pressures.

Having a good exit plan means that you can prevent being put in a 'need to sell' situation and not being prepared for it. It gives you much more control over the outcome and will ultimately increase the value of the business. It will also help to minimise any threats from outside influences by having a well-run and adaptable business. And if you are approached by a trade buyer then you will be in a strong position to negotiate a better deal if you wish to sell. Some business owners may never want to sell up, but there is always the possibility that someone comes along and makes an offer they can't refuse.

That's actually what happened to us. We were approached by a large multi-national company who wanted a foothold in the UK. Because we had set the business up properly from the start and implemented strong policies and procedures it was ready for sale and we were able to negotiate a great price.

It goes without saying, but you need to keep your exit plan confidential. Don't ever share with your staff that you are building the business to sell it so you can disappear to the Caribbean! It's not good for morale. Employees get nervous, and so too do suppliers and customers.

Creating your exit strategy will be bespoke to you and there is plenty of useful information later in the book that will help you to identify the key points for your exit strategy. In summary you should be answering some of these questions:

- Why do I want to sell the business?
- Who will I sell it to? What type of companies would buy my business?
- When will I sell it?
- What value do I want for the business?
- What size will my business be?
- How many and what types of customers will I have?
- What geographical areas will we be operating from/in?
- What will my role be when I want to sell?
- What will I do after I sell?

Know where you are heading with your exit strategy but keep the detail to yourself. Once you are clear and you know what a saleable business looks like, just put it aside and focus on creating and building *that* business. Focus on the core operations, what you are good at. Otherwise, you will have created nothing from which you can exit!

Step Two:

Structure and Foundations

Once you are clear on your personal why and your exit strategy it's important to ensure that the foundations and structure of your company are fit for purpose and ready for growth.

As an entrepreneur, you may already have a decent sized business, busy dealing with the inevitable growing pains of your venture. If so you might be looking for some inspiration about what to do next. I remember that feeling well – being unsure of the best way forward after two years of relatively fast growth.

Or you may be reading this as you consider starting a business, or perhaps you are only still in the very early stages of your new enterprise. Either way, it's important to understand the different types of business structures so you can make the right choice now for your future exit strategy.

It is always preferable to make sure the administrative and legal side of things is done properly from the outset. Even if you have already started the business or it's several years old, it's always wise to go back and check exactly what type of business you've created and make sure all your ducks are in a row as soon as possible. It can be a difficult and expensive process to fix it later on. Tax also plays a big part and you want to make sure that when you exit the business, you do not incur a hefty capital gains tax bill when you could have avoided it if you had structured the business correctly from the start.

Types of Business

Too often when an entrepreneur is starting a business the excitement and enthusiasm is focused on just getting it going. We will jump into action without necessarily thinking too much about the legal structure of the business or the type of business we are creating. This is especially common for people who are keen to strike out on their own.

There are however several ways to create a business in the UK. Some readers will of course know this but I thought it worthwhile writing a little about it. The most common start-up structures are:

- Sole Trader
- Partnership
- Limited Company

Sole Trader

When deciding to create your own business you would probably consider setting it up as a sole trader or a sole proprietor. It is one of the most popular business types for 'one-man band' operations because it is very easy to set up. You as the sole trader retain full control and ownership. You own all the assets of the business and any profits made. On the flip side, you are also responsible for all the debts and liabilities the business accrues.

A sole trader is expected to register as self-employed with HM Revenue & Customs and will be required to submit an annual self-assessment, but generally speaking their accounting requirements are less onerous than those of a limited company and your accounts are private.

Although easy to establish there are significant drawbacks to setting up your business as a sole trader. The biggest drawback is around liability. As a sole trader, the business is not a separate legal entity to you as an individual. This means that if the business gets into debt or the business is sued then you are personally liable. Worst case you could lose your own personal assets such as a home or your savings.

In addition, because the business is not legally separate from you as an individual you will pay income tax in much the same way as an employed person does. The only difference is that an employed person pays tax on their gross income whereas a sole

39

trader would deduct business expenses and pay tax on what's left. However, if you have visions of creating a business that makes more than around £45,000 a year profit, you will be taxed as 40 percent for anything you make over that figure, rising to 45 per cent if the profit exceeds £150,000. Of course, tax rates and rules change and you should always check what they are when you are starting your business.

As a sole trader, it can also be harder to access finance to grow and expand the business.

If you plan to sell the business one day and retire then the sole trader route is almost certainly not the best business vehicle for you, as the business is effectively 'you'.

Partnership

A partnership is the business structure often chosen when two or more people go into business together but don't particularly want to set up a formal company. It's always wise to create a formal agreement between the partners to set out the terms of the partnership.

The biggest drawback to an ordinary partnership is the same as a sole trader – the business is not a separate legal entity. Instead, the individual partners are effectively viewed as two or more sole traders doing business together. Each partner is viewed as self-employed and pays tax on this basis on their share of the profits. The partnership itself and each individual partner must make annual self-assessment returns to HMRC, and the Partnership must keep records showing business income and expenses.

Partners share the decision making, any profits the business makes and also any debt the business accrues. If the business runs into trouble both partners' personal assets may also be at risk. Also, as there is no legal entity, once the partners retire, die or move on, the business ceases to exist.

There is another type of partnership that exists as a half way point between forming a limited company and running an ordinary partnership. Known as a limited liability partnership (LLP), this ensures that the individual partners are not personally responsible for the debt the business accrues. The partners still share the running of the business in the same way as partners in an ordinary partnership, but avoid the personal risk to their own finances in the same way as shareholders in a limited company avoid personal liability. The other main difference is that limited liability partnerships must be registered with Companies House.

Again, if you are planning to create a profitable business that you could sell at some future point then an ordinary partnership is also probably not the best vehicle. If you are setting the business up with partners then an LLP could be an option but it's more likely that a limited company would be more appropriate.

41

Limited Company

When it comes to limited companies it's easy to assume that they are only appropriate for big companies or for businesses where there are multiple partners. However, changes in UK law mean that a single founder can create a limited company and own 100 percent of the shares. Alternatively, one or more partners can form a limited company by registering the business with Companies House (UK registrar of companies) as 'limited by shares' or 'limited by guarantee'. When a company is 'limited by shares' they are owned by one or more shareholders and managed by one or more directors. Limited by guarantee companies are owned by one or more guarantors and managed by one or more directors. The same person can be the owner and director, so you can set up a company by yourself or with other people. Each partner (or shareholder/member) is then allocated shares in the company. If they are equal partners then the shares are equal, if there is a less active partner then the share allocation may be altered to reflect that.

There are many advantages of forming a limited company over the other forms of business. For a start, the business becomes its own legal entity which means that it will survive beyond the life of the business partners. This is very important if you have an exit strategy that involves selling the business.

As a sole trader or ordinary partnership, as profits increase you will be subject to higher personal tax rates. However, if you set up a limited company from the outset the business will pay corporation tax of around 20 per cent, making it much more tax efficient.

A limited company is completely separate from its owners, it can enter into contracts in its own name and is responsible for its own actions, finances and liabilities. The owners of a company are protected by 'limited liability', which means they are only responsible for business debts up to the value of their investments or what they guarantee to the company.

Obviously, it's always wise to speak to a professional about your plans so they can help you make the right decision but if you plan to create a business that you can one day sell then a limited company is almost always the best option. It's more formal and you will have to disclose more information which will be in the public domain, but for most businesses the advantages outweigh the disadvantages significantly.

As a result, we will focus on the limited company business structure throughout the book.

Ensuring that your business has been formed under the correct structure is essential. It may feel a little dull and you may be tempted to skip on past and worry about that once you are established and successful – but that would be a mistake. Taking time to really consider what you are trying to achieve and your long-term exit strategy should naturally direct you to one form of business over another.

When I started my business, I was really clear that I was looking to create a vehicle that could give me the financial freedom I wanted. The only way to do that was to think big from the start.

Formal Business Documentation for Limited Company
As the Limited Company is the preferred business structure, we will quickly run through the documentation you need.

Companies are 'incorporated' to form an entity with a separate legal personality. Once incorporated, under the Companies Act 2006, a company is required to have two constitutional documents:

1. A *Memorandum of Association* – often referred to as just the Memorandum - which records the fact that the initial founder(s) wish to form a company and agree to become its members. This is the document that officially sets up the business. The Memorandum cannot be amended; and

2. *Articles of Association* – often referred to as just the Articles – which are essentially a contract between the company and its members, setting the legally binding rules for the company, including the framework

for decisions, ownership and control. The articles explain who owns what type of shares and the members' associated rights.

In addition to the Articles, which is a public document, the shareholders may also enter into a Shareholders' Agreement. This document is not public and can drill into more detail on corporate governance and ownership. The Shareholders' Agreement provides more detail on all the various shareholders and their voting rights.

All shareholders have rights. Generally, over 50 percent shareholding gives you the control of the day-to-day decision making of the business, but whether you can put the business up for sale without other shareholders consent will depend on how much over 50 percent you own. If you have 75 percent or more of the shareholding then you have the right to liquidate the business or put it up for sale, but you do not have the ability to force the remaining shareholders to sell any of their shares. Only when you own 90 percent of the shareholding or more can you force minority shareholders to sell.

If you already have a limited company set up, it's always wise to go back and check the Memorandum and Articles of Association to make sure you actually have the authority to sell the company.

When setting up a business, especially with friends, family or colleagues, it can be easy to assume that the positive relationship will continue but many a business has been torn apart because of souring relationships. A fully considered and well drafted Shareholders' Agreement can act as a safeguard and give you and your fellow shareholders more protection against these types of scenarios so you can protect the business, your respective investment in the business and the relationships.

A good Shareholder Agreement should include as a minimum:

- Shareholders' rights and obligations - including provision to prevent unwanted third parties acquiring shares and how a shareholder can sell shares. Also, any provision for protection of those with smaller shareholdings and what their rights are.
- How the company will be run – including appointing, removing and paying directors, how company business will be decided, how large capital outlays will be decided upon, what management information will be provided to shareholders (depending on type of shareholding), banking arrangements and any financial obligations.
- Treatment of dividends – distributed or reinvested.
- Any conflicts of interest.
- Dispute resolution procedures.

Whatever the legal structure of your company, make sure you start off on a legally sound footing. If you have already started your business, go back and check all these issues to ensure you have the correct shareholding and shareholders' rights. I've seen many companies that were not correctly administered. The people running those companies didn't actually have as much power as they thought they had because of incorrect share type allocations. Make sure everything is in order and you get the advice of a good solicitor. Many small businesses are formed by an accountant, without the input of a solicitor. This is not always wise as the accountant may not have the legal background to know the detail required regarding share issue when there are several parties involved.

Anticipate the Due Diligence Process
When you decide to sell your business, you will encounter the due diligence process. But what does due diligence actually mean?

Due Diligence is the in-depth process of allowing your potential buyer to investigate your business before purchase. We will cover this in a lot more detail in step ten when you are in the process of selling, however it's always best to start a business with due diligence in mind. That way you know what you need to get right to increase the eventual value of your business which can make the selling process faster, easier and more lucrative.

The Mini Due Diligence

A good practice or habit to get into is to *anticipate* the due diligence process by performing a mini due diligence on your company at least once every year. Find the skeletons in the closet now, and get rid of them. Address any potential problems. Search for them well in advance of when you may intend to sell. If you don't then a potential buyer will almost certainly find them and use any problems as leverage to negotiate a lower sale price. Or worse, the buyer may pull out of a deal because of something that you could have prevented. Conducting an annual mini due diligence will ensure your business is robust and secure, it will be better run and more efficient as a result. It will also make it easier to sell and when the buyer institutes their own due diligence process you will have all the answers and evidence to hand. Having all your ducks in a row will put you in the strongest possible position when it comes to completing the sale.

Use a typical lever arch folder that is a different colour from your normal filing folders. Ours was called the 'Yellow Folder' and it contained all the relevant information on the company including copies of important documents.

Every year the business partners would take a weekend away to conduct a mini due diligence exercise. Although we were all well in control of the business, there were times that this process highlighted issues that we didn't even know existed and would probably never have known until we were looking to sell. They would have undoubtedly caused legal issues, delayed the sale or reduced the price. Thankfully, because of the mini due diligence, we were alerted to it before the sale and could complete the necessary paperwork to solve the problem. As a result, the mini due diligence process was a massive help.

Top due diligence areas to look at
When you have a potential buyer for your business, and have agreed a price and the sale conditions – that's the easy part. The buyer will then send in his professional advisors or solicitors and corporate accountants who will conduct a very detailed assessment of the information you have already provided to verify that what you said you are selling is actually what you are selling.

The main areas the due diligence team will be looking at are:

1. **Finances.** Are the accounts well managed and maintained, including a list of assets? They will be particularly interested in any large outstanding debts and order book value.
2. **Litigation.** Are there any current or potential disputes? These may be employee, customer, supplier or other forms of legal disputes. If so, what is the potential cost?

3. **Warranties.** Many businesses will provide warranties on their products and services. Are there any potential warranty claims?

4. **Intellectual Property Rights (IPR)/Patents.** Does your company properly own the IPR, patents, copyright on products/services? If patents are involved then do you have them properly protected? If not, a buyer may not be interested if the correct patent/IPR is not in place.

5. **Management Information Systems (MIS).** Are all policies and procedures in place? Have they been adequately communicated to all employees? This includes management information and reporting systems, computer software and web domain registration.

6. **Human Resources (HR).** Are all your personnel records up to date? Do you have employment contracts for all employees, including pension provisions in accordance with employment law? Do your employees have the appropriate qualifications to do their job? Are there any current or potential HR disputes with current or old employees? Do you have staff members who are off sick a lot – if so you may need to performance manage them?

7. **Health & Safety.** Ensure all health & safety policies are in place. If your business employs

a number of people then you should be maintaining records of any accidents or incidents. You should conduct regular reviews of your H&S procedures.

Risk Matrix

An ongoing exercise that will help you to maintain focus on these important areas is to create a 'Risk Matrix'. This will identify potential problems in all areas of the business so you can look at ways to mitigate the risk. Ideally you are looking to close down the risk completely or find solutions to reduce the potential impact should the worst happen.

You should include the high-level risk analysis at your monthly board meetings, and conduct risk meetings at least every quarter where your top team looks at the potential issues and solutions.

Look internally and externally – seek to pre-empt any problems so that you can plan for their contingency.

Stay Focused on Building a Great Business

Once you have set up the correct business structure or perhaps re-assessed your business structure and moved to something more suitable – focus on the business.

Whilst it's essential to set up the business properly from the start and have an exit strategy, there is still a long way to go before the business is ready for sale. You still need to do the hard work and build that saleable business.

When a potential buyer sees your business, you want to ensure that they have a great first impression. For example, we made our business 'look bigger' and more corporate than it actually was for a time. We changed our name to include 'Group' and updated our website to represent our aspirations and vision before we had achieved them.

Conversely, if your business is disorganised, premises are falling apart, staff are unhelpful and your documentation is a mess, then any potential buyer could be put off. They would be pretty sure that if that's how things look at first glance, there is sure to be even deeper problems once they take a closer look.

You may have a business that you consider to be a gold mine, but unless things are properly structured and on a stable foundation, most buyers will be put off or at the very least they will use that disarray to negotiate you down on price.

Remember, you never get a second chance to make a first impression.

Step Three

Vision: Values, Purpose and Mission

Taking time out to connect to your vision for the company can seem like something that only appears in text books or only relevant for very large organisations. If I'm honest I never took it that seriously until I read a fantastic book called *Beyond Entrepreneurship* by Jim Collins and William Lazier. Many of the techniques that I used in building my business, and share in this chapter, are adapted from their work.

The Importance of Vision
It is impossible to build a great company without an effective and authentic leadership style. And that begins with you. Your people may follow what you say, but they will definitely follow what you do. If you are not being yourself or trying to present a front for others, seeking to appear as something that you are not, people soon pick up on this and it can lead to

inconsistency and confusion. Neither is helpful in developing a profitable, efficient business.

As a leader, your number one responsibility is to create a clear vision for the company and to secure a shared commitment to that vision and encourage its vigorous pursuit.

But what exactly is the vision, and how do you even start to create one?

Essentially the vision is a clear picture of the business you want to create with as much detail as possible. If you don't know where you want to go, then how will you ever get there? Worse still you are likely to arrive somewhere else you didn't intend to be. Often, the nudge towards taking this step seriously emerges when we come to terms with the fact that the status quo is untenable. Perhaps your enthusiasm for the venture is waning as you find yourself working even longer hours without necessarily making more money. Perhaps 'taking it easy' seems further away than ever.

I still remember coming across an inspiring article that really changed our business. I studied the principles and we put them into practice and I was astounded at how much our business improved. The business looked and felt more professional, had a clear focus on where we wanted it to go, and the people were more motivated because they could appreciate what we were trying to create and were inspired by that vision. Consequently, performance increased dramatically. It was the single best thing that we ever did as business leaders.

The article I'm referring to relates to the **Collins Porras Vision Framework.** Jim Collins and Jerry I. Porras state that there is a significant similarity between the companies that enjoy enduring success. They all have a core purpose and core values that remain fixed while the strategies and practices endlessly adapt to a changing world. In other words, their 'why' never changes but their 'how' adapts to the business environment. Vision provides guidance about what to preserve and what to change. Their prescriptive vision framework adds clarity and rigour to the vague and fuzzy vision concepts that exist in many organisations today. The framework has two principal parts: 'core ideology' and 'envisioned future'. Core ideology combines an organisation's core values and core purpose. It's the glue that holds a company together as it grows and changes. The second component of the vision framework is the envisioned future. First, a company must identify bold stretch goals; then it should articulate vivid descriptions of what it will mean to achieve them.

Below I'll explain these principles which we took on-board when designing the destiny of our business.

Setting the Vision

Instilling your business with a lasting corporate vision is a challenging yet necessary task. When you consider any great organisation that has lasted throughout the years, you will find that it owes its resilience to the power of its beliefs and how its people adopt those beliefs.

In 2011 Steve Jobs famously declared that Apple was about "technology married with liberal arts, married with the humanities, that yields us the results that make our heart sing." Tim Cook, who took over from Jobs that same year shied away from such bold vision statements until 2016. In the closing remarks of an Apple developers conference in San Francisco Cook stated, **"At Apple, we believe technology should lift humanity and enrich people's lives in all the ways people want to experience it".**

That's compelling.

A shared vision creates teamwork, cohesion and a sense of community – just look at the loyal, passionate community around Apple. It creates the foundation for your company to grow without having to depend on a few key senior team members. If you set the vision well, your employees will buy into that vision making the business stronger. This approach means that staff turnover is lower because everyone in the business is connected to the shared future vision. And, if you do lose people because of unforeseen issues then you can always replace them with other people who already know 'The Way'.

In essence, according to Collins and Porras, a good vision consists of:

1. Core Values and Beliefs
2. Purpose
3. Mission

Core Values and Beliefs

The starting point for creating your vision is to establish your core values and beliefs, otherwise considered as the company's guiding philosophy. These are the fundamental motivating principles of the organisation. They will be present when making decisions in the business; in fact, they will be present when anyone makes any decision in the business. They will be evident in your actions and woven into your corporate policies.

The core values and beliefs of your business must be an absolutely authentic extension of your own core values and beliefs – what you value, feel and believe in your gut. As such they come from within *you*. You can't just make them up because they sound nice or because you think it's what your customers or staff want to hear. If you do they will come across as inauthentic nonsense. One of the most famous examples of this type of corporate tripe could be seen in the Enron corporate vision and values statements which proclaimed Respect, Integrity, Communication, and Excellence. Respect included the following detail, "We treat others as we would like to be treated ourselves. We do not tolerate abusive or disrespectful treatment. Ruthlessness, callousness, and arrogance don't belong here." Clearly the Enron traders didn't get the memo when tapes emerged of them saying, "Burn baby burn. That's a beautiful thing" as forest fires shut down a major transmission line into California, cutting power supplies and raising prices.

The core values and beliefs have to mean something and reflect the things that you as the founder (or founders) hold dear. They should mirror how you live your life, what you feel is important and what you value. There is no point developing a business that forces you to sell your soul and feel terrible about how you've achieved success. Your core values and beliefs need to be authentic, and establishing them requires that you look deeper inside yourself to consider what inspires you and makes you tick.

Actions speak louder than words, and it is your day-to-day actions that will help to illuminate what your core values and beliefs are. If you have business partners with a substantial share in your company then you should perform this exercise together and agree what they are collectively.

To establish the core values of our company, I arranged an off-site workshop with my two business partners, and we spent the next 12 hours defining what it was that was most important to us as individuals and how that would play out in the way we did business.

In order to figure out what Zappos core values were CEO Tony Hsieh sent an email to partners, managers and influencers and asked them, "please email me four or five values that you live by (or want to live by) that define who you are or who you want to be... (do not cc everyone)... each value should be one word or at most a short phrase (but ideally one word)... please email me the values that are significant and meaningful to you personally, not necessarily having anything to do with the company's values."

The resulting input was consolidated to create a working version of Zappos 10 core values and beliefs which was then road tested with managers against employees and ex-employees. Managers were asked for suggestions, additions, subtractions, or other feedback. In particular, they were asked to think about any employees that the manager thought represented the Zappos culture well, and whether what they liked about those employees was covered by the 10 proposed core values. Managers were also asked to think about any employees that they didn't think represented Zappos well, and whether the reason behind it was due to them not representing one or more of the core values.

The final version, listed below, was then tested with employees, fine-tuned and rolled out. Zappos 10 core values and the beliefs the company lives by are:

1. Deliver WOW through service.
2. Embrace and drive change.
3. Create fun and a little weirdness.
4. Be adventurous, creative and open-minded.
5. Pursue growth and learning.
6. Build open and honest relationships with communication.
7. Build a positive team and family spirit.
8. Do more with less.
9. Be passionate and determined.
10. Be humble.

When you set your company up based on your and your partners' values you will come across as authentic and your employees, customers and suppliers will be more likely to buy into that ethos and the business.

Another example, to give you some ideas of what core values looks like is sports giants Adidas...

Performance
Sport is the foundation for all we do and executional excellence is a core value of our Group.

Passion

Passion is at the heart of our company. We are continuously moving forward, innovating, and improving.

Integrity

We are honest, open, ethical, and fair. People trust us to adhere to our word.

Diversity

We know it takes people with different ideas, strengths, interests and cultural backgrounds to make our company succeed. We encourage healthy debate and differences of opinion.

Purpose

Next is the purpose of your company. Why does it exist?

This should be an outgrowth of the core values and beliefs and dovetail with them giving a sense of meaning to the work that will drive the business forward. When everyone in the business buys into the values and they are used as a way of aiding the recruitment process then everyone, not just the founders, derive a sense of fulfilment and meaning from the business which will make a huge difference to success. Purpose is a motivational driver, helping people to ask more of themselves because there is a meaningful reason beyond just making a profit or earning a living.

Be careful not to fall into the trap of thinking that the purpose of your company is to make lots of money for the shareholders or for you as the founder. A powerful purpose is never just about money. Ask yourself - who benefits from the services or products of your company, and how does it affect your local or wider community?

You should be able to explain clearly what the purpose of your company is, in one or two sentences. It should quickly and clearly convey the message of why your company exists and how it impacts the community and business environment it operates in. It should be enduring – broad enough to encapsulate the essence of the business while allowing it to adapt to changing market conditions.

Though brief and concise the statement of purpose includes identification of a company's core purpose and focus, its intended direction in the marketplace, and of the various business facets that funnel those things into actual business practice and transactions. It should define how a company's philosophy will be translated into daily actions in policy and standards of conduct and of operation. Good ones make us feel something.

Greg Ellis, former CEO and managing director of REA Group, said his company's purpose was "to make the property process simple, efficient, and stress free for people buying and selling a property." Not only does this statement of purpose emphasise the importance of serving customers and understanding their needs but also puts managers and employees *in customers' shoes*. It says, "This is what we're doing for *someone else*." And it is motivational because it connects with the heart as well as the head. It also directs action. If everyone is bought into that philosophy then it will direct the decision they make and ensure there is an authentic demonstration of that purpose. For example, employees can ask themselves "Is what I am about to do or is this decision going to make the property process simple, efficient and stress free for the customer or not?"

Other strong examples include the financial services company ING whose purpose is "Empowering people to stay a step ahead in life and in business". Kellogg Food Company's purpose is "Nourishing families so they can flourish and thrive". And finally, insurance company IAG's purpose is "To help people manage risk and recover from the hardship of unexpected loss".

When creating a statement of purpose for your company find a way to express the organisation's impact on the lives of customers or clients — whomever you're trying to serve. Make them feel it.

Purpose Exercise

Drilling down into what your purpose really is can be achieved by repeatedly asking 'why'. This helps to break it down and get to the real purpose. So, whatever answer you get for why you are in business ask why that is important. Once you get a new answer ask why that is important and keep going until you get to the heart of your purpose.

Another useful tip is to think about why your business is important from your customer's point of view. What customer needs are you meeting? Consider why your business should continue to exist and what would be lost if it were to disappear. Also, avoid vague statements.

Mission

Defining your mission is the third part of the vision puzzle – and it's the fun part. This is the creation of a clear and compelling overall goal – a BHAG (Big, Hairy, Audacious Goal) together with a specific timeframe for its completion. This is what will be plastered on your walls and what your people will be striving to achieve. It should emotionally connect to the people who belong to your organisation.

A mission statement should be a stretch outcome – it should be a mission! Something that won't be easy but will be worthwhile. It needs to be something that will seem unrealistic to many but that you know can be achieved.

I believe that nothing is impossible, it just hasn't been done yet. Before Roger Bannister ran a mile in under four minutes on 6th May 1954, the conventional wisdom was it couldn't be done – it was beyond the bounds of human capability. And yet, once the belief that it was impossible was broken by Bannister, the record was broken again just 46 days later. The last time I looked, the record stood at 3 minutes 43 seconds!

Like these runners with their goal in sight, a good Mission Statement has a finish line. It translates values and purpose into an energising, highly focused goal. It is crisp, clean, bold, and exhilarating. People should 'get it' right away.

There are three main types of mission:

- Targeting: setting a clear target.
- Common Enemy: focusing on beating a competitor or taking the underdog position, which can be inspiring. For a while Pepsi's mission was to "Beat Coke!"
- Role Model: Comparing your organisation to another you admire. Your mission may be to be the 'Apple' of your industry.

Whatever approach you take the result should be a compelling statement or paragraph for the future vision of the company. This could be a five-year vision or a three-year vision but it must have a specific timeframe as to when it will be achieved. Remember building a business strategy is a little like climbing a mountain. When you start your ascent, you don't think about trekking up the whole mountain immediately. You take it in stages. You start your mission at the bottom and work your way up. The completion of each stage is a separate goal toward the overall goal of reaching the top.

This is the same with your business. Your goal is to ascend the mountain, achieve success and exit profitably on your terms, but first you need to set goals of completing each stage safely while protecting and building on what you've already achieved.

The biggest challenge with specified missions is what happens to motivation once you arrive. However, a strong, specified mission is always more powerful than a mission without a dated end goal. You can always set a new one when you arrive – just make the next one a little harder.

Pulling it all Together

Write it down. Bring everything you come up with together into a written document that details the core values and beliefs, purpose and mission for your business. Writing it down forces a level of rigour to the process and delivers a greater sense of accountability to what you've said you and your business want to achieve.

The potency of writing things down was demonstrated by psychologist Professor Richard Wiseman who conducted two large studies into the psychology of motivation involving 5,000 participants from around the world. Participants were tracked for between six months and a year as they attempted to achieve a wide range of goals. By the end of the experiment only 10 percent had achieved what they set out to achieve. Of those 10 percent, ALL had written down their goals and broken them down into a series of sub-goals that created a road map into the future. Wiseman also found that the successful people in the study stayed focused on the benefits that they would gain from the achievement, told other people about their aspirations which were concrete, specific and time-bound.

Share your vision with your people so you can get buy-in from all employees, especially the management team. Where possible involve key people and allow them to contribute. Consider using the Zappos model and get input and feedback along the way so that you end up with a written values, purpose and mission that resonates with your people as well as you and your business partners. Human beings are much more connected to and committed to something they had a hand in creating.

Vision is the big picture stuff – it's incredibly important but tends to be trivialised or dismissed as something nice but unnecessary. It can feel a little touchy-feely, especially to a left brain logical type person. BUT – it is absolutely vital to set the tone and direction of travel for the business. If done well and inclusively it can directly influence decision making and how the nuts and bolts of the business come together.

A Word on Strategy

Wiseman's study showed that those who had drilled into their goals and created sub-goals and timelines were much more likely to succeed than those who only had the big picture. So, while the vision is critical the strategy of how that vision will be executed is every bit as important. The reality of business is that vision without strategy is about as useless as strategy without vision.

Once you know where you are heading, why you are heading there, and what you plan to achieve by a given time, you can start to break that down into a strategy that will guide the journey and turn the vision into reality.

There are four basic principles to consider for setting an effective strategy. They are:

1. Ensure that the strategy descends directly from your vision. This is the 'how to' part of executing that vision so it must be linked to a very clear idea of what you are trying to do.

2. The strategy must leverage the strengths and unique capabilities of your company (where possible also mitigating any inherent weaknesses). Focus on what you are good at.

3. The strategy must be realistic so take into account internal and external constraints or other factors.

4. Always set strategy with the input and participation of the people who will be charged with making it happen. Too much strategy is created at the top without any input from the people on the coal face who are often much more likely to know if it's possible or not!

The Strategic Process

Start with the vision document you created that outlines the core values and beliefs, statement of purpose and mission statement. These are your navigational documents and should be front and centre in the strategy process. Think of these documents as the coordinates of the mountain you are choosing to climb.

Next you must conduct an internal assessment of the company's capabilities. This is similar to assessing the climbing skills and resources of your expedition team.

The three component parts of an internal assessment are:

1. Strengths and weaknesses: What are the primary business capabilities and blind spots? Consider asking key personnel to anonymously submit the top three on each

side. Ask trusted advisors for input or any
mentors you call on for support.

2. Resources: What resources do you have to
help achieve your vision? Think about cash,
access to capital, materials, production
capacity and people.

3. Innovation and new ideas: What access do
you currently have to your people's input
and insights? How can you access everyone's
very best thinking and suggestions? What
new ideas and innovations are bubbling up
in product development etc?

After that, you should conduct an external
assessment of the market, competitors, economy and
trends etc. Continuing the mountain climbing theme
this is like studying the weather reports and assessing
what the other climbers are doing.

There are seven components of a good external
assessment:

1. Industry or market trends: How large is the
market? How segmented is it? Is it growing
or stagnating? What are customers telling
you about their evolving needs? Are you
addressing them?

2. Technology trends: Is there any disruptive
tech on the horizon that could influence or

change your business? Is there any tech that could improve your proposition? Could new tech improve your efficiency?

3. Competitor assessment: Who are your major competition? Are there new threats? What do they do particularly well? What are their weaknesses for possible exploitation? Do you have a differentiated position?

4. Social and regulatory environment: Are there any changes to society or regulatory changes that could impact your business?

5. Macro-economy and demographics: How strong is the overall economy? Are there any threats politically that could destabilise the economy? Are there any changes to demographics entering the workforce that could impact your business?

6. International threats and opportunities: Is there turmoil in export markets? Volatility in exchange rates that could impact you now or in the future? Any new markets emerging?

7. Overall threats and opportunities: Anything else you might have missed from the above. Again, consider asking key personnel to anonymously list the top three opportunities and top three threats.

Once you have this information you can make key decisions about how you intend to achieve your mission in light of the new information you've uncovered. This is about choosing the best route up your mountain.

Each business is different but you are going to need strategy for these basic areas as a minimum:

- Products or services strategy: looking at product line, manufacturing or service strategy etc.
- Customers strategy: looking at who your customers are and how you intend to reach them.
- Financial Strategy: cash flow, pricing strategy etc.
- HR strategy: looking at your people.
- Infrastructure strategy: looking at premises, plant, equipment etc.

Your strategic decisions should therefore come out of your vision and your internal and external assessment. These are the detailed directional guides as to how you will climb that mountain.

Starting and building a business can feel overwhelming at times but the vision and strategy can remove a great deal of the stress because it gives you a map.

"You don't eat an elephant whole" ... Break it down.

Step Four

You and Your People

If your business has a number of employees, and you are committed to creating a successful business that you can sell to fund your desired lifestyle, then you must be a good leader.

When we think of leadership, most of us think of the larger than life characters like Sir Richard Branson, Steve Jobs or Elon Musk but there are many different types of leadership style. There is no best leadership approach. It all comes down to being authentically you and running the business in a way that is comfortable to you.

Gandhi would have looked stupid trying to imitate Winston Churchill and vice versa. Plus, what made both such inspirational leaders was that they both embodied who they were as human beings. Gandhi's soft-spoken gentleness flew in the face of British colonial rule but was extremely effective in achieving his goal of getting the British out of India. Churchill was the very embodiment of the British Bulldog – exactly what was required to inspire resolve and win the war.

Be yourself. There is a caveat to this however – you need to know that as the top person in your company your style will set the tone for the entire organisation. Like it or not, your behaviour will affect the attitude and behaviour of all those working under your direction. Therefore, it's wise to seek to temper your most destructive tendencies.

Instead, be the best role model you can be. And look after your people.

Reward Those Who Do the Work

One motto I learned early in my career that really stuck with me was, 'Reward those who do the work'. We knew from the very start of running our business that if we looked after our employees, they would look after the business. And that doesn't just mean looking after them financially – it means treating them fairly and rewarding those that actually do the work!

Time and time again, research has shown that money is not the main motivator for employees. In a meta-analysis of 120 years of research authors, Tim Judge and his colleagues synthesised the findings from 92 quantitative studies totalling a combined data set of over 15,000 individuals and 115 correlation coefficients.

What the authors found was that the association between salary and job satisfaction is very weak. In effect, there is less than 2 percent overlap between pay and job satisfaction. A cross-cultural comparison also revealed that this holds true regardless of culture. The relationship between pay and job satisfaction is pretty much the same from the US to UK to India to Taiwan or Australia. And in case you are wondering, it stays the same regardless of how much people earn too. As the authors point out, "Employees earning salaries in the top half of our data range reported similar levels of job satisfaction to those employees earning salaries in the bottom-half of our data range".

These findings are also consistent with Gallup's employee engagement research. Based on 1.4 million employees from 192 organisations across 49 industries and 34 countries – the Gallup research repeatedly shows there is no significant difference in employee engagement by pay level.

What most of us fail to appreciate is that money is a *hygiene* factor, not a motivator. Frederick Herzberg alerted the business community to hygiene factors via a now famous article in the *Harvard Business Review*. Herzberg noted that contrary to popular opinion, job satisfaction could not be positioned on a straight line from poor job satisfaction to high. Satisfaction and dissatisfaction are not opposite sides of the same coin but separate coins and we need to understand

75

hygiene factors and motivation factors to appreciate what determines whether or not someone is satisfied in their job.

Hygiene factors are things in the workplace that, if done poorly, will cause dissatisfaction. Things like status, compensation, incentives, job security, working conditions and company policy. Bad hygiene factors cause dissatisfaction but fixing those factors doesn't create satisfaction – it just removes that particular dissatisfaction. If someone finds out that part of the business is being paid a bonus and they are not – that is likely to feel unfair and create dissatisfaction. If someone doesn't feel that they are paid enough – that can create dissatisfaction but increasing their salary will not create satisfaction – it will just remove the dissatisfaction around pay.

Satisfaction is something very different and it's not really impacted by money. What people really want is to feel valued. They want to know that what they do matters to the progression of the business and understand that they are contributing positively to a shared vision they buy into. Of course, people do want to be financially rewarded but money is not everything.

What we did in our business was have a bonus pool of money that was put aside for all employees and then we would distribute that according to effort, impact and value added. It was not part of employee expectations and everyone could see why it was given to the people who received it – above all it was considered fair and transparent. We rewarded those that did the work and everyone could see that. Not only for rewarding the right people and tangibly demonstrating that we really valued their contribution but also incentivising those that perhaps were not putting in as much effort as they knew they could. If people received less than their peers, then they knew why and this would give them the opportunity to improve next time.

Sir Richard Branson knows the value of looking after his people. One of his core philosophies is, "If you keep your staff happy then your customers will be happy, and if you keep your customers happy then your shareholders will be happy."

The more valued they feel, the more motivated they are and the better results you will achieve. You will also find that there will be fewer HR issues and employee absenteeism because people will enjoy their job rather than hate it which is much too common in some organisations.

Treat Others as You Would Like to be Treated
I still remember when I first realised the importance of this idea. It can seem like a trite comment or parable but it's absolutely spot on.

By trade I'm an electrician and when I was working my way up the career ladder, I got a job in the office training as a quantity surveyor. However, I was still considered as an 'hourly paid' employee meaning I wasn't yet on the staff annual contract. I was young but I was already performing considerably better than many of my peers who were on the more attractive employment contract. Just before Christmas, the company would take the 'staff' employees out for Christmas lunch and drinks. Whereas, the supervisors and operational 'hourly' employees were not invited. Instead, we had to man the phones and take messages while staff and administration personnel, one of whom had only just started in the business, got the opportunity to go to the free lunch. This was totally wrong in my opinion because it created an 'us' and 'them' mentality in the business. I also felt excluded and the very clear message was that we were less important to the business than salaried staff – regardless of performance or length of service. I remember thinking I would never make people feel like when I had my own business. Unsurprisingly, I ended up leaving that company because of the lack of true leadership, collaboration and equality, but I'm thankful I was able to learn from their mistakes!

Many years later, when I did have my own business and we employed over 300 people, everyone was invited to the annual Christmas event and we made sure that everyone was treated as equals no matter what their role was. And people really appreciated it.

There should never be anyone in your business talking about 'them' when referring to other people in the company. It should always be 'WE'. To help facilitate the shared vision and collective spirit we had a social club. Employees signed up when they joined the company and a committee, made up of employees, would organise monthly events that allowed everyone to socialise together. They were a great way for people to get to know each other and connect as human beings beyond the business.

Get to Know Your People

Get to know your employees and lead from the front. Ask about them and their family and pay attention to their answers – take a genuine interest in your people. Make them feel like part of the team. I believe that everybody has a part to play and everyone should be treated equally. Sure, some people will contribute more to the profits of the business and have additional responsibility and ability, but the person at the bottom of the ladder should be treated just as well as the executives at the top.

We also introduced *Personal Touch Visits* where managers would visit sites where their only purpose was to spend time with a particular employee to see how he/she was doing and 'chew the fat' about life. We would take doughnuts out to the team and thank them for their commitment. It was a family.

We even set targets for each manager to carry out these personal touch visits and they would report back to the rest of the management team so that we could deal with feedback proactively. The people in the field are often the best people to provide the most worthwhile suggestions and ideas for improvement or increased efficiency.

Also, in our business there was no special parking space for the executives. If an employee, regardless of level, wanted a space near the door the best way to secure one was to arrive early!

It's also important to give your people suitable time off and decent conditions of employment and they will feel more secure and happy to stay. These are examples of additional hygiene factors – on their own they don't create job satisfaction but get them wrong and they will create dissatisfaction. Provide a pleasant working environment, help people to feel secure in their role and allow them time off to recuperate and enjoy other parts of their life. If you look at the employment conditions in the USA for example, it's little wonder job satisfaction and engagement is so low. There is no legal holiday entitlement in the US. You could work full time and received no paid leave. UK full time employees are legally entitled to a minimum of 28 days paid holiday. Other countries are even higher – Iceland is 36 days a year paid leave and Malta a relaxing 38 days a year! It's probably not necessary to go to those lengths but we all need time off to recharge our batteries and give our best.

Communicating with Your People

How often have you heard about the importance of communication and yet this is still something that is really easy to screw up – especially as the business starts to grow.

One of the weird things that can happen in business is that, as the leader, we can become a little removed from our people in an attempt to give off an air of authority. We are the boss and we want people to remember that. And whilst that may be understandable if that's the way you are wired, if you take it too far it can be counterproductive. While it may not be business savvy to broadcast every blip and headache of your business to everyone, it is important to include people and let everyone know what's going on.

There may be things about the business that you don't want to share or new possibilities that you want to keep close to your chest but seek to share as much as you can. People want to be a part of something and if they feel like they are being kept in the dark they will inevitably fill in the gaps in your communication with their own version of events – creating rumour and unnecessary uncertainty.

In our business, we created an employee newsletter that was sent out every two months providing relevant positive information and communication. It also featured a few employees and their 'likes' etc. We had a kid's corner so that the newsletter was for the family and not just the employee. There were also competitions and other ways for employees and their families to interact with the company.

But remember, communication is not just a top down process. It should flow from the bottom to the top and sideways through the business. Below are some ideas and tips to stimulate communication in your business:

- Ask your people a lot of questions – collectively and individually. Allow them time to really think about the answer and get back to you.
- Rather than just having weekly meetings and seeing what gets raised, ask each attendee to come to the meeting with at least one piece of information or issue that they think everyone needs to know about.
- Encourage meeting attendees to come with a question they would like to know the answer to but currently don't.
- Encourage people to say what's on their mind and speak up about issues that are bothering them.

- Encourage your people to highlight issues or challenges that they have identified. However, if they have found a problem, they also have to come with at least one possible solution to that problem.
- Remove as much of the formal nonsense that can so often creep into business. Business is nothing more than a collection of human beings trying to achieve something. It's OK to be human.
- Encourage people to express their feelings as well as just their thoughts. Again, the idea that we somehow leave our emotions at the door when we come to work is ludicrous. Emotion is human so allow space for that. Too often women in business are dubbed 'emotional' as though emotion is a female issue – it's not, it's a human issue. Emotion, when used properly in business, can be a huge strength.
- Don't allow one or two strong personalities to dominate communication. Ask for the input of those that are naturally less vocal.

Communicate the Shared Vision and Strategy

The vision, values, purpose and mission that you created for your business should not be sitting gathering dust in a folder or stuck on the wall and forgotten about. All your employee communication should reiterate that vision and strategy and seek to demonstrate the businesses commitment to that shared goal.

New employees should be road tested against these guiding principles to ensure they are a good fit with the business and all communication should be disseminated through those lenses.

You don't have to be a great speaker or amazing writer to get these ideas across to people – just be open and honest about what's driving the business and share your passion and goals often.

In our business, I constantly used a boat as a metaphor to explain our vision. Everyone in the business was in the boat. There was no engine and no power other than us. Each of us had an oar and we were heading for a paradise island. When we all knew where we were going, shared the same vision and values and were clear about wanting to reach that paradise island we were all paddling in unison in the same direction. When everyone is working together then the business generates greater energy than the sum of the individual people in the business and success is easier and smoother. But, it gets much harder if even one or two people don't pull their weight or decide to paddle in a different direction.

I'm pretty sure that some of our employees used to think, "Oh no... here comes the boat story again" or they would roll their eyes, but it was a powerful metaphor that helped us to get where we were going and also helped us to quickly identify and address people who were rowing in the wrong direction or not rowing at all!

This was never made into a negative issue where someone was berated for their effort. It was simply about identifying if they were in the wrong boat and helping them to get back in sync, perhaps through training, or simply managed out to a boat that suited them better.

When shared vision and values are demonstrated through action people can see those values in the business and this can create a really powerful culture and boost employee morale. Collectively this can be unstoppable. It is a joy to be part of such a vibrant atmosphere, and miracles really can and do happen.

I used to say, "It's All Good" constantly to my team – whether it was or not. Before long people started to use the phrase too and it brought a lot more positivity and encouraged people to look for solutions rather than problems. No matter what was going on, 'It's All Good', gave the sense that it was all on track. Maybe we needed to re-route a few times or think on our feet but we'd always find a way.

I often think about that boat metaphor and it makes me smile. It was really useful in the business and after I sold I took it one step further and learned how to sail. These days, I spend a good part of each year on various sailing adventures.

Training

It would be unrealistic to assume that you are going to hire all the right people and they are all going to turn out to be superstars. That doesn't happen in real life.

Regardless of who you hire, a great business is always committed to continual improvement, training and development. Training provides the additional tools your people need to succeed.

There is often government funding available for training and development of staff, provided that the training is going to help the company to grow and in turn employ more people and pay more tax due to making more profit.

Consider such funding as a perk if you can find it but remain committed to high quality training regardless. Even without the funding, you should be providing training and developing the skills of your people.

Your people make your business, so developing them will develop your business. Investing in training and development is one of the things that can so easily get missed in a small business or start-up. Don't make that mistake.

We were so dedicated to training and development that our company won a national business award for 'excellence in training'. This was a nice feeling.

Training Needs Analysis

One way to assess training needs is to perform a Training Needs Analysis. It does exactly what it says it does – assesses what training is going to be most useful to each employee based on what they do, their current skill level and what you want them to do or improve upon.

It is the identification of any gap that may exist between the skills, knowledge and experience you have in the business and what you want moving forward. Training needs are usually flagged when the business is going through change or is anticipating change or following employee appraisals. It may be that an employee is struggling in one particular area of their role and training can be a helpful intervention that can help them to raise their performance in that area.

One word of caution regarding training however. For years, business pursued the idea that we should find out what people's weaknesses were and help them to overcome them. A huge Gallup survey into work effectiveness and good management demonstrated that this is not a good use of time. Instead find out what people are naturally good at and help them to develop those skills further, making sure, of course, that you match those skills to a role that requires those skills. Spending time trying to improve innate vulnerabilities is usually a complete waste of time. In other words, if you need a sales person hire someone who naturally exhibits the traits you want in that role rather than trying to make someone else into a sales person.

The only effort you should put into weaknesses is if those weaknesses are actively holding the employee or business back. In which case, it's worth improving that skill just to the point that it stops being a liability and then switch your energies back to a person's strengths.

It's always better to hire the right people in the first place, than to try and put in what was lacking. Of course, if someone is taking on a new role or their role is expanding in some way then finding out how best to support that person through the transition is essential.

Good training not only improves performance for the individual and the business but it often leads to greater self-esteem and engagement. Happy, confident and engaged employees are much more productive and you are much more likely to unlock their discretionary effort – where they will go that extra mile for the business.

Building the Right Team
I was once advised not to employ someone unless you are sure that you can look them in the eye and sack them if it is required. Too many small businesses employ family members or friends that just aren't good enough or up to the task, and then spend months if not

years trying to compensate for that person, moving them around rather than doing what needs to be done and getting rid of them.

Too many businesses promote employees based on how long they've been in the job - "Oh let's give Bob the promotion because he's been here for years." Why should length of service have any bearing on their progression through that business? This is a disastrous promotion strategy because Bob may not have the skills or ability to take on that role. He may not even want the role but takes it anyway because it comes with more money. Length of service is a poor guide to who is best for any role – it should be focused on the value they add, their individual suitability to the role and their ambition.

Everyone has their off days and you should always support people through challenging times and encourage them to upgrade their skills if necessary. But if someone has stopped adding value, or has actually never added value or has become disruptive to the business, then deal with it. And deal with it quickly. It's never easy or pleasant but you should think of the bigger picture and the damage that person is doing to the business and the morale of everyone else.

We had this problem when running our business. Looking back, we probably wasted a year holding onto a team (that we had inherited) who did nothing but cause disruption and hassle. I remember when I realised something had to give. I'd just come back from a winter holiday where I had met a senior executive of a large US firm. We'd been talking about business and one of the pieces of advice he gave me was to "just deal with what you know you need to deal with". As soon as he said it, I knew that for us, it meant getting rid of this non-performing team. I came back, discussed it with my business partners and within a couple of months the team was gone. We couldn't believe how much better things were. It was amazing - no more trivia and hassle. More importantly, we weren't the only ones that had noticed this problem, as other important staff members were aware of the negative effect of this team. The rest of the senior management team and many of the employees who interacted with this team really respected that we had made the bold decision to remove the dysfunctional team. It also demonstrated our commitment to our vision and values of doing the right thing. They were in the wrong boat and they needed to get out.

Build a management team around you. Let employees make decisions, and if they get it wrong, encourage them to learn and improve. Too often employees are too scared to step outside of the lines and try something new for fear of failure. But failure often gets you closer to success faster. The key is to fail forward – use what didn't work to fine tune decision-making and make better decisions next time. Always encourage flexibility so that your employees are ready for change and new opportunities when they present themselves.

It's also really important to ensure there is plenty of opportunity in the business so that your people can see real scope for their own development and career progression. When they see this they are much more likely to be motivated toward that outcome. This is especially important for high-potentials and people in key roles as they will feel motivated to stay and give their all when they can see opportunity above just making a living. When that opportunity isn't obvious or people believe they have hit a ceiling to their growth in your business they may start looking around elsewhere for their next challenge. Wherever possible make sure that next challenge is in your business. Even when your people share your vision and values they will always have their own aspirations. If you can find out what those are and help your people to meet and surpass those aspirations then you can build a fantastic business much faster while also providing a stimulating environment that helps them to achieve their own goals as well.

Giving the right people the right opportunities was something we worked really hard on. For example, we provided secondment opportunities, where employees would be seconded into a new position for three months and the manager of that division along with the employee would then review how it was going. After three months, the position was then offered to that person or not based on their performance and desire to take on the role full time. We found that some people just were not suited for additional responsibility and they could not deal with the extra strain. Some were capable but just didn't want to do the job for other reasons. By seconding the employee rather than outright promoting them to that new role, if it didn't work out the employee was able to save face because it was only ever a temporary position, and the company didn't create an HR issue by then having to remove that person from the position when results were not achieved. It was a perfect solution – both sides could test the water and see if it was a good fit or not. If it worked well, the person was promoted full time to that role and if it didn't work out, the employee simply went back to their own position. Even if they went back to their previous role there were significant benefits because it gave that person a broader and deeper appreciation of a different part of the business which helped to break down the silo-mentality that can sometimes creep into business.

Finally, one of the most destructive things you can do for your business is to hire 'Yes-men' – people that constantly agree with whatever you say and never challenge you on anything. The best leaders in the world know what they are good at and purposely surround themselves with brilliant people who can do the things they can't. Often, they will find people who they believe are smarter or more capable than they are. Far from seeing these people as threats to their own authority or position they recognise that building a great team means strength and diversity, not a bunch of 'Yes-men'.

And remember, keep your end game under wraps. Don't tell your people that you're building the business to sell it. How can you effectively lead your troops if they know that you are planning to desert them? They will get nervous and may not stick around. Only tell them when the time is right and make sure that wherever possible – they are protected. Most of the time their primary concern will be whether or not they still have a job – if you can assure them that they do then a great deal of the anxiety will disappear.

Step Five

Managing and Building the Business

Managing and building the business is a huge part of your success. There are literally thousands of books on management techniques and building your business and I'm assuming that you know how to build your particular business.

Whilst every business is different, there are, however, similarities between successful businesses that are worth noting. Certainly, there were key techniques that we used that make the business building phase faster and more streamlined.

The most obvious one is good management procedures. This means definite policies and processes so that the execution of whatever you actually do in your business is consistently high. Effectively step five is about execution – making sure that what you are delivering is making money, of a high enough standard, day in, day out, to warrant the attention of a would-be buyer. It's about doing what you need to do to stand out as a great business. This means, amongst other things, rigorous and regular reporting and good management controls to make everything in your business easier – from running the business to growing the business and eventually selling it.

In the end, it won't matter how great your idea was or how passionate you are as an entrepreneur, all that really matters is effective tactical execution.

Management Dashboard

The central tool in this process is a thorough management information dashboard. Think of this dashboard as much the same as your car dashboard. Every time you jump in your car you are immediately presented with the key information you need to ensure that your journey is as smooth, safe and efficient as possible. You can see how much fuel is in the tank, how far you've travelled, and can even see how many miles you are getting to the gallon and a vast array of lights will alert you to any potential or current problems.

If there was no dashboard in your car you would not have access to vital information. You would have no idea if the car had enough fuel to get you to your destination, wouldn't know how fast you were going, and you wouldn't know if there were any issues with the engine until smoke starting billowing out of it and you were stuck on the hard shoulder.

Building a business without a management dashboard is like driving your car without your car dashboard – confusing, nerve-wracking and potentially dangerous.

When you run your business, you must spend time gathering the important management information that matters to your business. I completed a leadership course which was really useful in the growth of my business, and it introduced me to Key Performance Indicators (KPIs). I love KPIs. To be honest, I was never one for all the business hype and I never threw around all the latest buzz words. In fact, it used to irritate me when people would talk about "thinking outside the box", or how they were just, "reaching out" or ask, "Where's the synergy in that?" Most of the time the latest business buzz word was used by consultants or people who didn't know what they were talking about but desperately wanted to look like they did! But I do love KPIs – they are the exception to the rule and are incredibly useful in business.

I've always been a bit of a geek for analysing data so having a management dashboard that highlighted our KPIs together with a traffic light system was ideal. It told us immediately if we were tracking toward our objectives (green), hitting a few speed bumps (amber) or stuck in heavy traffic (red). It was a fast and effective way for us to get a working overview of the business so we could assess the strengths and vulnerabilities of the business immediately without being too heavily involved at the ground level.

For us, the KPIs that we considered important ran right across the business including the obvious financial targets such as order book, profit margin and whether we were meeting those targets together and some more unusual ones. For example, we looked at how many tenders we submitted and how many we won. A large part of our income came from larger projects that we needed to tender for so measuring that process and looking for improvements was essential. We also decided to measure staff engagement. At first this seemed to be quite hard to measure – how do you assess if your people are happy and productive? We used a few metrics to gauge this including staff sick days. People who are happy don't tend to take sick days unless they are really sick. But anyone in business either as an employee or an employer knows that a huge proportion of sick days taken are not because someone is sick, it's because they wake up and think, "I can't be bothered today – I'm going to call in sick." People who enjoy their work tend not to make that choice or if they do it's usually triggered by stress in another area of their life.

We used the Bradford Factor as our KPI in this area. The Bradford Factor is a simple formula that allows companies to apply a relative weighting to employee unplanned absences (sickness, Doctors' appointments, emergency childcare, etc.). The Bradford Factor supports the principle that repeat absences have a greater operational impact than long term sickness. In our work, it was these unplanned absences that were having the biggest negative impact on everyone else in the team and also the financial results.

By measuring absenteeism and reporting on that metric everyone knew that we were measuring it. As I mentioned in step four, we had a bonus pot for all staff which was connected to performance and absenteeism also played a part in determining individual bonuses. Everyone knew how much it cost the business, how it impacted profitability and therefore their bonus pot, so this process helped us to connect the dots for people about the actions and choices they made, especially around whether to 'take a sickie' or not and what they would end up receiving as a bonus at the end of the year. Obviously, some sick days are genuine but we were looking to actively reduce the ones that were not.

We also asked staff what we could do to make sure people didn't go off sick. This may sound odd, but often it's the little things that irritate people so if we knew what they were we might be able to fix them and increase engagement. Plus, staff felt as though they were being listened to which was positive for morale.

Give people the freedom to come up with solutions and you will be pleasantly surprised at what they come up with.

Essentially what gets measured gets done or improves – it's as simple as that. If people know that something is being measured or tracked they will pay attention to those metrics too and results will almost certainly improve. The way we saw it, we wanted to make it really easy for people to do well and thrive in their role and be rewarded for their effort and really hard for people to be lazy or get away with not pulling their weight.

A rigorous set of traffic light KPIs presented regularly on a management dashboard allowed us to do that.

Dashboard Information

The top five critical areas of information that you can incorporate into your management dashboard as you manage and build your business are:

1. Current and projected cash flow. Lack of cash flow is one of the most common business challenges and it can be fatal. You need to know what money is in the business and what is projected to come into the business all the time so that you can manage income and expenditure appropriately. Related to cash flow are your accounts payable and accounts receivable – as well as the age of those accounts. Does

anyone owe you money and has that debt become overdue? You need to know this stuff so you can manage it adequately.

2. Financial accounting information (balance sheet and profit & loss statement) and financial ratios. It can also be useful to compare time period – so this quarter against last quarter or this year against last year.

3. Employee satisfaction. Happy employees are going to work harder. Measuring your employee satisfaction and the employee turnover rate is vital to the health of your organisation.

4. Sales information. Track sales as a total and also across all product and service offerings. Where possible break sales down across geography, price points and distribution channels. You should know where your sales are coming from.

5. Customer information. Who are your customers? Ideally you want to know who they are and where they are so you can find more people like them. Customers, now more than ever, will also tell you what they think of you so monitor reviews and be aware of what people are saying about your company online and on social media.

KPIs to Consider

There are literally hundreds of metrics that you could use to explore your business. Initially the variety of KPIs can actually be off-putting. The key is to work out what you are trying to achieve and what is important to you in order to measure whether or not you are achieving your goals. Don't go crazy – just focus on the key issues.

Below are some financial examples for you to consider along with a brief explanation. If you want to understand and improve financial performance, consider the following KPIs:

- **Net Profit** – This is the amount of money left over after paying all the expenses of the business. This KPI therefore answers the question, "To what level are we generating positive bottom-line results?"
- **Net Profit Margin** sheds light on how well your business is run and how adept you are at controlling costs. This KPI answers the question, "How much profit are we generating as a percentage of sales?"
- **EBITDA** (Earnings before interest, tax, depreciation and amortisation) illuminates your businesses operational profitability over time by removing expenses that can easily distort performance such as cost of

capital. This KPI answers the question, "To what extent are we operating our business efficiently to generate profits?"

- **Revenue.** While profit can be inflated by cutting costs, revenue is looking only at sales or the money made by the business. This KPI answers the question, "How much money are we bringing in from sales?"
- **Revenue Growth Rate.** This looks at how revenue is growing and is therefore a useful measure of growth and prosperity. It answers the question, "How much money are we making from sales compared to [last year, last quarter etc]."
- **Cash Conversion Cycle.** Cash flow is the lifeblood of your business and this KPI is one of a number that help you monitor cash flow. This one, also known as the cash cycle, helps to answer the question, "How well are we managing a healthy cash flow?"
- **Working Capital Ratio.** This KPI helps answer the question, "To what extent do we hold enough short-term assets to cover our short-term debt?"
- **Cash Flow Solvency Ratio.** This KPI helps to answer the question, "How easily are we going to meet our debts?" The higher the

ratio the better as it indicates there is more money in the business to cover liabilities.

- **Current Ratio.** This liquidity KPI helps answer the question "Do we have the money to meet our short-term obligations?" You should be aiming for a current ratio of two or more as this means that your assets are twice as high as your liabilities.
- **Return on Investment (ROI).** This KPI helps answers the question, "To what extent are we making efficient investments?"
- **Return on Capital Employed (ROCE).** This helps to answer the question, "How well are we generating earnings from our capital investments?"

If you want to know more about your market, consider:

- **Cost Per Lead.** As the name would suggest this KPI tells you how much it's costing you for each business lead. It seeks to answer the question, "To what extent are the costs for generating new customers justified?"
- **Customer Conversion Rate.** Are you converting leads into customers? This KPI will tell you. It seeks to answer the question, "To what extent are we able to

convert leads (potential customers) into actual customers?"

- **Market Share.** This KPI allows you to see what share of the market you currently enjoy compared to your competitors. It is therefore a measure of relative market strength. It seeks to answer the question, "How well are we growing market share in comparison to our competitors?"
- **Market Growth Rate.** It's important to know whether the market you operate in is growing or contracting. This KPI helps to answer the question, "To what extent are we operating in markets with future potential?"

If you want to understand your customers, consider:

- **Customer Complaints.** This KPI measures how many customer complaints you receive.
- **Customer Engagement Ratio.** This KPI helps to answer the question, "To what extent are our customers engaged with our business?"
- **Customer Retention Rate.** This looks at the loyalty and longevity of your customers. It helps to answer the question, "To what

extent are we keeping the customers we have acquired?"

- **Customer Satisfaction Index**. This KPI seeks to answer, "How well are we satisfying our customers?"
- **Customer Turnover Rate**. Acquiring customers is one thing, keeping them is quite another. This KPI helps to answer the question, "How many customers are we losing?"
- **Customer Life-Time Value.** This KPI explores customer profitability. It's all very well having loads of happy customers but are they profitable? This KPI helps answer the question, "How well do we understand the financial value from our customer relationships?"

If you want to understand and improve employee performance, consider:

- **Employee Churn Rate.** It's costly and time consuming to hire and train staff so you want to be hanging on to them once you get them in the door (assuming they are proficient of course). This KPI helps to answer the question, "How well are we retaining our staff?"

- **Average Employee Tenure.** People who are happy in their work tend to stick around. This KPI therefore seeks to answer the question, "To what extent do our employees stay loyal to our company?"
- **Revenue Per Employee.** This KPI seeks to answer the question, "How productive are our employees?"
- **Employee Engagement Level.** Knowing if your people are happy and engaged is imperative if you want to create a successful business. This KPI seeks to answer the question, "To what extent are our employees committed to playing their part in the delivery of our vision and mission?"
- **Employee Satisfaction Index.** This KPI seeks to answer the question, "To what extent are our employees happy in their jobs?"

There are many other KPIs to consider, including KPIs for social media impact, website heat maps, stickiness, KPIs to measure marketing effort as well as operational performance but the above should give you a flavour of what you might like to consider for your own management dashboard. There are many good books on the topic including Bernard Marr's *Key Performance Indicators for Dummies*. This covers all you will need to know about the topic.

Creating a one or two-page management dashboard that immediately alerts you to the health of various important KPIs allows you, as the founder, to focus on the important aspects of your business without getting bogged down in the minutiae.

Plus, more importantly, it allows you to empower your staff and show that you trust them by giving them the accountability of the role. All you really want to see are the results that let you know how the business is running. How they achieve those results is up to them. Most people respond very positively to this approach because it tells them that you trust them to get the job done, in the best way *they* see fit.

Milestone Accountability

When you are clear on your vision, purpose and the strategy, you can then break your strategic priorities down into milestones along the way. These should be 'bite-sized' manageable chunks. And most importantly, you must assign those chunks to a named person. That person will be accountable for delivering on that milestone or part of a milestone – otherwise it's liable to fall through the cracks.

You should name people, make sure that they know what is required of them and when they need to do it by. Ideally you should never just give out these tasks and impose milestone deadlines. Work with your people to decide who should be responsible for what areas. Human nature is such that we are always more engaged and committed to objectives and timeframes that we have a hand in shaping. Employees and their respective managers should always therefore develop milestones together giving the person tasked with doing the work room to decide when it should be completed (within reason). Most people want to do a good job. Most people also know what is possible in their own area better than those who are not closely involved in the work. By having a discussion and mutually commit to the milestones that work for your employee, you are much more likely to hit that milestone and make progress. There is absolutely no point imposing milestones and deadlines on people without their involvement and buy-in.

This quirk of human nature is called the "Endowment Effect" - we always attribute more value and therefore more importance to things we choose ourselves or have a stake in creating.

One of the first to demonstrate this phenomenon was Harvard psychologist Dr Ellen Langer. In the experiment Langer sold $1 raffle tickets to office workers. The prize was the total amount collected from ticket sales. Of the people that bought tickets half were allowed to choose their own ticket and the other half were simply handed the ticket by the researcher.

Several days later, before the raffle was to be drawn, the people who bought a ticket were approached again on some pretext and asked how much they would need to be paid to give up their ticket. Those that had chosen their own ticket required $8 to sell the ticket, on average. Ten people in the group said they wouldn't give up their ticket at all. Those who were simply handed their ticket agreed to sell their ticket for an average of $2 a ticket and only five people said they wouldn't give up their ticket. Langer suggested these results were down to the illusion of control.

Too often, the senior team start believing their own hype as though they have all the answers and their minions should just get on with that they tell them to get on with. This is a huge mistake because the people who are actually doing the job or dealing with the customers or paying the bills - those on the coalface of the business will usually know far more about certain issues than the senior team. It's just smart business to tap into that insight and use it to your collective advantage.

Once agreed it's also better to get the person who is going to be responsible for the milestone to commit that agreement to paper. This confirms accountability.

Remember, psychologist Professor Richard Wiseman' study from step three... Those who successfully delivered on goals and met their milestones and targets were the ones where their goals were concrete, specific, time-bound and documented in writing.

This accountability is important right across your business from you at the top, down through your management team to your supervisors and other employees. Everyone has to know what is expected of them and what they are expected to deliver.

Pass this responsibility on to your team so that they need to tell you if they are hitting targets or not. By being accountable everyone is far more likely to perform. No one wants to be the bearer of bad news!

Improving Execution

Micro-managing doesn't improve execution. Hiring well and trusting that the people you employ are capable is much more likely to yield execution excellence.

Given the right environment and the right encouragement people will always surprise you. Poor performance is usually down to poor recruitment, poor training or poor fit.

According to Collins and Lazier there are five basic conditions under which people tend to execute well.

1. Clarity - people execute well when they are clear about what they need to do. This means knowing what is expected of them and what deliverables they need to focus on.

2. Skill – people execute well if they have the right skills for the role. This is all about fit – making sure that the talent and temperament someone has is matched to the talent and temperament required for that role. Too often we move people around in a business because we don't want to deal with non-performance honestly, but this is disruptive and can make things worse. Just because you have someone in the business that could do that job doesn't mean that they are best suited to it. Put the right people in the right roles.

3. Autonomy – people execute well when they are given freedom and support. This is the micro-managing issue again – if you treat people like children they tend to behave that way by lowering their capability to meet your poor expectations.

4. Appreciation – people execute well if they're appreciated for their efforts. Recognition and respect for a job well done is a primary motivator, often more than financial reward.

5. Value – people execute well if they can see the importance of their work. When people can appreciate why what they do is valuable and how it fits into the bigger picture or

corporate vision they feel more ownership and pride toward the role. It's your role as the leader of your business to ensure that everyone in your business knows why the work they do is important.

Innovation

Innovation and constant improvement is essential for managing and building your business. It is therefore important that innovation becomes a way you do business and part of your corporate culture. This doesn't mean that you get to add 'innovation' to the values statement or incorporate it into the mission statement and it will miraculously appear. It needs to be woven into the fabric of the company and people need to see you as the leader demonstrating your commitment to innovation.

Below is what it takes to be an innovative company:

1. Receptivity to ideas from everywhere. The technology that started Apple wasn't designed by Apple, it was actually designed by Xerox and used by Apple to create one of the most successful companies in the world. When James Dyson was trying to perfect his cyclone bag-less vacuum cleaner the breakthrough idea

came to him when he was visiting a saw mill! Subscribe to industry journals from outside your industry as well as inside. Attend conferences that don't necessarily have a direct impact on your area.

2. "Be" the customer. Stand in your customers' shoes and experience your own product or service. It is now so much easier to do this because customers are so vocal about products and services online. This can be a blessing and a curse but if you use it as information to improve you will get lots of new ideas that you may not have thought of yourself or have come from inside the business.

3. Experimentation and mistakes. James Dyson spent 15 years and most of his lifesavings developing the Dyson vacuum cleaner. He created 5,127 prototypes before he found one that worked. He's now a billionaire. Encourage your people to experiment and come up with better ways to do things. The only way that this will really take hold is if you allow people to make mistakes. This can be challenging because mistakes can sometimes cost money but innovation is a process of trial and error.

4. People being creative. Encourage your people to be creative. It might sound corny but a suggestion box can be useful. Incentivise good ideas so that the person that puts the idea forward gets some type of reward if the idea ends up saving or making the business more money.

5. Autonomy and decentralisation. Some of the most successful companies in the world allow their people to spend a proportion of their time on whatever project excites them. Trust your people – they actually know a lot more than you might imagine. Make it easy for them to share that knowledge and come up with better suggestions.

6. Rewards. Make heroes of creative contributors, feature them in corporate communications, throw awards ceremonies – wrapped up in a good employee night out. Demonstrate that you as the leader value everyone's input as you all head toward the shared vision.

Look after Yourself

Before leaving this step, it's also worth spelling out that this is the 'grunt' phase. It's hard work and can be stressful as you wrestle with competing priorities, HR issues and just getting enough stuff done. It can be easy to become so focused on the business that you completely lose sight of yourself, important relationships and your own health and well-being. I'd strongly recommend you don't.

You should always seek to lead a healthy lifestyle and look after your body. Take some time off, the world will not stop spinning if you take a break. Don't work all weekend, every weekend. It's not productive or helpful to drive yourself too hard. All that happens is you get stressed and stop your best thinking from emerging. Too much stress can also trigger bad habits as a way to unwind. It will be much more constructive if you go to the gym or get into nature and go for a walk.

Eat healthy food, avoid junk food and too much sugar. Exercise is a fantastic way to expel any excess energy or stress while giving yourself a break from the business. It forces you to get back in your body and out of your head.

You only have one life and you've got to stop and ask yourself why you are doing all this. It's okay to be successful and make a lot of money, but you can't take your greatness to the grave. Consider what is important to you and your family and live by these principles. Treat yourself well first. If you do, your business will most definitely benefit.

Step Six

Pre-Sale Planning: Maximise Profit

If you plan to sell your business to fund your dream lifestyle then your primary business goal will be to maximise profit. This means focusing on the following financial parameters:

- Maximise Tax
- Don't spend more than you make
- Keep your overheads low
- Avoid unnecessary spending
- Try to increase your profit margins

Maximise Tax

This may be the first time you've ever read that advice in a business book but it's very sensible in order to maximise your eventual sale price.

Most business acquisitions are based on a multiple of profit. As a rule of thumb, and a very subjective average, let's say a business is likely to sell for somewhere between three and seven times annual profit after tax. If you are currently making £1 million in profit (after tax) then that would mean a sale price of between £3 and £7 million. That difference of £4 million represents a huge difference in the lifestyle you can expect to enjoy after the sale. If you're thinking of selling your business then it is best to maximise your profit, which also means maximising your tax for at least three years prior to the sale.

Some small business owners would admit, albeit privately, that they accept some 'cash work'. This means they are paid for their product or service with cash which doesn't go 'through the books'. It means that their turnover is lower resulting in a lower profit margin and therefore a lower tax bill. Don't do this. Apart from the fact that this practice is completely illegal and you face stiff penalties if you are caught running your business this way, means that you are effectively shooting yourself in the foot when it comes to a future sale. By reducing the turnover and therefore profit you are reducing the amount you are likely to get for the sale of your business. And considering the impact of that multiplier effect – that could mean losing out on hundreds of thousands of pounds or more.

In addition, your accountant may advise you not to maximise your profit before tax, as you would pay more corporation tax by having higher profits. This is legitimate advice and for those operating a lifestyle business with no plans to sell this approach is smart – perhaps buying a new piece of equipment or conducting maintenance work or repairs would be a strategic and legal way to reinvest in the business therefore reducing the profit and the tax. However, if you are intending to sell the business in the next few years then the same advice applies - you will be in a better position when negotiating the price with a potential buyer if you do all you can to maximise not minimise profit. If the sale of your company is based on a multiplier of profit, then the extra tax that you pay now should be more than recouped when you receive that multi-million-pound cheque when selling your business.

Perks that you and your family or fellow shareholders receive should be reviewed and perhaps removed for the same reason. Again, these are good if you're running the business to provide an enjoyable lifestyle, but if you're serious about selling then you want to maximise that bottom-line figure. If there are costs in the business that actually relate to perks for you, perhaps you get yourself a new car every year, corporate golf days, even family health insurances – rein them in so that the business retains as much profit as possible. Of course, this might not always be possible or wise if the perks relate to your staff. The ill-feeling it may cause could easily back-fire so focus on your own perks and those of your fellow shareholders. Your corporate accountant will make adjustments for these perks when putting their analysis of the business together. So whilst I am suggesting that you minimise these perks where you can, they can always be taken into consideration at the sale stage.

One advantage of owning and running your own business is that you can take most of your remuneration as a dividend and pay less income tax as a result. As a normal employee who receives a wage in the UK, there is a Pay as You Earn (PAYE) tax and the amount increases based on your annual salary. On top of this, an individual is charged a National Insurance Contribution as a percentage of their salary. The business also incurs a hefty charge for National Insurance, which, of course, will affect you as the business owner.

Many business owners take advantage of this policy and choose to receive a small PAYE salary of say £10,000 per annum meaning that they are still contributing to the National Insurance scheme. The remainder of their 'income' is then drawn from the business as a dividend provided the company is making suitable profits. This approach significantly reduces the personal tax liability of the owner(s) because tax on dividends is significantly lower than PAYE tax. This is also good news for the profit multiplier figure because there is less cost in the business because of the reduction in PAYE salary so the profit will increase. Of course, this maximises the corporation tax liability but just get used to the idea that if you are selling your business the more tax you pay the better!

Plus, it's the business that is paying the tax, you as the owner are still better off personally because you pay less personal tax while still maximising the value of your business for improved future sale price.

As you might now expect, with regard to the personal income you take from the business as a dividend, it is advisable to take out as little as possible – certainly in the three years leading up to a sale. This is especially useful if you don't necessarily need the cash. By keeping the profits in the business as retained earnings, you will increase the value of your company and make it more attractive to potential buyers. Having that extra cashflow will also allow you to run the business more effectively and have more of a safety net if finances get tight. You will also be able to self-finance any purchases the business might need to grow which will save money on arrangement fees and interest payments. Leaving profits in the business could also give you a better bargaining position to save on the cost too. For example, you may get a reduced rate if you were to pay for an item in full.

Assuming you have structured the company in the right way as we discussed in step two, when you come to sell and realise the value you have retained in the business you should be entitled to receive Entrepreneurs' Relief on the profit you make on the sale. This is currently only 10 per cent capital gains tax, therefore meaning the taxman gets a lot less than if you had withdrawn profits by way of dividends the preceding few years.

Remember, maximise profit and pay your taxes. By keeping on top of the business finances and paying tax on time, it will provide comfort to a potential buyer that the business has been run well. Not paying taxes or having disputes with the authorities does not look good and could turn a potential buyer off your business. Keep everything is order and above board and your life will be much easier.

Don't Spend More than you Make

This is pretty self-explanatory – your business must be generating a profit and that means you need to be making more than you spend. Apart from maintaining liquidity which is a legal requirement, it's going to be very difficult to sell a loss-making business!

Plan your business spending wisely and don't over capitalise or try to grow too quickly. Take a longer view and do the work. There is no such thing as overnight success.

Keep your Overheads Low

Again, this is straight forward. You don't need to rent fancy office space or buy all your equipment brand new. Business is as much about perception as it is about reality and you can create the illusion of a bigger business without blowing the budget on overheads. There is now a huge array of services available online that can help a business grow without the usual associated costs. A vast network of online freelancers would be willing to help you on a 'per job' basis on everything from website creation to HR advice and support, or virtual assistants, making it possible to grow your business while also staying lean.

Grow as the business grows but be shrewd – remember the goal is to maximise profit above all else. Keep overheads low.

Avoid Unnecessary Spending

Do you really need a new car every year? Probably not. Focus your spending on what will deliver most value in the business. Only spend on purchases or people that will deliver real value to the business and help you to make or save more money.

Again, be smart about spending – especially if your goal is to cash out in a few years. That said, don't scrimp on purchases that are necessary for growth. You do need to speculate to accumulate sometimes.

Try to Increase your Profit Margins

Are you sure about your price points? Do you know the maximum that customers will pay for your product or service or are you just guessing? How did you decide on the price of your product or service in the first place? Business leaders will start a business and look at what it costs to deliver that product or service, adding a reasonable margin to arrive at the price for consumers. Or they will look at the market or their competition and arrive at a price that is comparable.

The other way to consider price is to ask yourself what the market will pay. Looking for ways to differentiate your product or service and add value may allow you to increase your prices without seeing a drop off in sales.

The advent of technology is also a great tool to allow us to test price points in advertising to see if it alters sales. Depending on your business type, you could for example run a short online ad campaign – same offer, different price point, to see if the net gain is worth it. You never know until you test, you may find that raising your prices doesn't impact sales.

Is there anything that you could add to your product or service that costs nothing but has a high perceived value? If so experiment with that offering at a higher price and see what happens.

Know Your Numbers and Improve Where Possible
Make sure your accounts are audited each year and everything is accurate and up-to-date. It is also advisable to maintain monthly management accounts so that you can see how your business is operating on a more regular basis.

Financial knowledge is the key to making financial progress. If it's your business, it's your money; so make it your business to know everything you can about that money. Look at the accounts thoroughly to highlight any potential areas of concerns or potential improvements. Your management dashboard will also help and will allow you to intervene early so as to stop a potential problem from escalating.

If you're not great with numbers, it's perfectly acceptable to delegate the accounting role to a trained professional but you do need to know what you are looking at when that professional gives you the accounts! In other words, you don't need to be able to physically do the accounts but you do need to be able to read them accurately and know what they are telling you. As the boss, you must be aware of what's happening financially. You should know where your money is going and what it's doing.

Monitoring the money also means making your money earn its keep. Never let your money sit idle. It should always be working for you in the same way as your employees are working for you. If you have excess funds in your bank account then consider moving them into an investment account, a mutual fund or an interest-bearing savings account.

Each year you should set financial forecasts and targets, no matter how small your business is. You should have company-wide targets and forecasts that come out of each business unit or division's own targets and forecasts. That way each of your management team has their own targets and knows how they fit into the bigger picture goals. Your business is more likely to meet and pass its targets when each division is accountable and hitting their own targets.

Make sure your asset register is up-to-date and assets are re-valued regularly. This ensures that the value of the assets is accurate. If you do decide to sell then this will certainly be a point of focus. You don't want to be downgrading an asset valuation as this would trigger a large amendment to your accounts at the last minute when you're preparing for a sale. Plus, if the asset devaluation is discovered by the potential buyer via their due diligence process this can cast a question over more of your figures. At the very least, this will slow down the sale process and may even end it as the nervous buyer pulls out.

Do you have any old debts that you have been chasing for years? If so, write them off, especially if you are considering selling in the next year or so. Consider writing off old debts in a financial year that looks a lot healthier than anticipated – this will help ease the pain. Old debts don't look good to a potential buyer – they raise too many questions. Even if you were not at fault and were just unlucky with a bad customer they will act as red flags for the buyer so get rid of them.

During the sale process, the buyer's financial advisors will audit your business and part of that process will be to review the trends over the last few years. They will also create a forecast for, say, the next three years to indicate how well they expect the business to perform under new owners. Therefore, ideally your accounts will show continuous growth and financial improvement year on year, and you should have financial forecasts in the future showing a similar growth trend. This will provide confidence to buyers that their investment is less of a risk because they can see that your business has a track record of strong financial performance. Almost all buyers are confident that they can take your business and make improvements that will leverage their investment – they wouldn't be buying it otherwise! In most cases the improvements they envision being able to make will come by way of cost savings achieved by utilising the resources they already have through economies of scale.

So, if you are writing off any old debts or incurring any one-off costs, ensure that the financial results still show a positive upward trend.

Identify Value Drivers

When you are building your business to sell then it is important to identify the key value drivers that will achieve the highest price possible.

The value of a company is determined by its ability to consistently maximise its risk-adjusted cash flow generation. It follows then, that companies should focus on those factors that help them generate more cash, for longer periods of time and with the least risk possible.

In this sense, there are three broad types of business value drivers: operational, financial and sustainability drivers.

Would-be buyers of your business will be assessing it from a variety of value drivers, specifically looking for evidence that either reduces the risk associated with owning the business or enhances the prospect that the business will grow significantly in the future. The better your performance in these areas, the greater the selling price of your business – potentially increasing the multiple above and beyond your industry standard.

Operational Value Drivers

Operational value drivers might include growth potential, customer diversity, quality of workforce, operating systems and procedures, premises and equipment condition, goodwill and product or service diversity.

When you as the business owner can describe realistic and accessible opportunities for growth that could translate into better cash flow and higher profit then the value of the business will increase. You might also want to consider creating a thoroughly vetted growth plan which documents how these new markets or new customers could be reached. Some areas to consider when developing the growth plan are:

- Does the business operate in a growth industry? If so what additional opportunities might that present in the future?
- Are there additional markets that you are not currently pursuing but could be? How accessible are those markets?
- What additional products could be delivered to existing customers?
- Do you own proprietary technology or processes?
- Will demand for your product or service increase as population grows?
- How could enhanced marketing campaigns and sales efforts affect sales? This could be especially useful if you don't currently engage in a great deal of marketing.
- Are there opportunities to grow through acquisition?

- Can growth be achieved by expanding territory or manufacturing capacity?

Customer diversity is also a sought after operational value driver. A broad and diverse customer base where no single client accounts for more than five or ten percent of total sales is attractive for a buyer. It reduces the risk, should clients decide to leave under the new ownership.

On the other side of the fence the quality of the workforce is also important. The business results have been achieved by the combined efforts of the existing talent in the business, the risk of performance slipping is minimised if the management or key employees are effective and want to stay with the business. You may want to sell your business and many of your key people may want to stay and that will certainly increase the sale price.

Of course, creating a well-oiled saleable business is not just about having the right people in the right roles, it's also about efficient operating systems and documented policies and procedures. If your business has established standard business procedures and they are documented and implemented into the day-to-day operation of the business then this also reduces risk because they provide a 'how to guide' for delivery of the current financial performance, potentially even if key staff move on. Below are some examples of business systems that enhance business value:

- Personnel recruitment, training and retention.
- Human resource management (an employee manual).
- New customer identification, solicitation, and acquisition.
- Product or service development and improvement.
- Inventory and fixed asset control.
- Product or service quality control.
- Customer, vendor and employee communication.
- Selection and maintenance of vendor relationships.
- Business performance reports for management.

Another operational value driver is the condition of the premises and equipment. It stands to reason that you will get more for your business if the premises, facilities and equipment are in good working order and well maintained. A disorganised warehouse or run-down premises will almost certainly cost you money in the eventual sale price. Plus, these types of slip-ups can allow doubt to creep into the mind of the buyer. Another consideration with regard to premises and equipment is whether it is fit for purpose considering the buyer will almost certainly want to increase growth.

Goodwill – name recognition, customer awareness, history, ongoing operation and reputation also demonstrate stability and consistency. Again, goodwill reduces the risk of the purchase. Relationships are key in business success so if your business can demonstrate customer and supplier longevity, it is viewed as an asset. Brand recognition, product or service reliability, customer satisfaction, testimonials and reviews are all distinguishing factors that add value.

The final operational value driver is product or service diversity. The fewer products or services you offer the higher the risk. This is just common sense, not everyone wants the same things or the same service so offering diversity means that you are more likely to deliver to more customers, make more revenue and, hopefully, more profit. Ideally your business should have a healthy product or service mix, perhaps different price points to appeal to different segments of the market.

Financial Value Drivers
For most would-be buyers, revenue and cash flow are the first things to look at. Being able to demonstrate an established pattern of growth and several years of profit growth will add value to your company. Renewable leases, employee policies, staff with transferable contracts, supplier lists and

an established client base will also go a long way in alleviating any cash flow fears, and will also increase the amount a buyer is willing to pay. If your business has recurring revenues, such as long-term maintenance contracts, monthly retainers, support agreements or subscriptions that are contractual and ongoing, they may be valued at a higher level than the non-recurring revenues. Buyers are always willing to pay more for your business if the cash flow is predictable and likely to increase in the future.

Reliable financial information is also a significant value driver for would-be buyers. A buyer wants to see that the business is operating like a well-oiled machine. When the financials are up-to-date and accurate and support the claim that the business is worth what you say it's worth then the sale is much more likely to go ahead. If your financials match what they find in their due diligence process you are more likely to get the price you are asking for. If not, the buyer will use that discrepancy to negotiate you down on price. Lack of financial integrity, where the accounts are either in disarray or don't match the buyer's due diligence, is one of the most common challenges encountered during the sale process.

Sustainability Value Drivers
Sustainability value drivers look at sustainability. But there are two ways to look at sustainability. The first

is through the eye of environmental sustainability – the sustainability of the planet. If your business was in coal mining for example I don't fancy your chances of selling your business anytime soon. Coal is a fossil fuel and most sane and informed people on the planet accept that the use of fossil fuels has been the primary cause of global warming. There is no future for coal and there is no such thing as 'clean coal'.

The other way to look at sustainability is more industry and business specific. Does your business have a future? The value driver here is whether there are suitable barriers to competitive entry. Any features that give your business the advantage over your competitors will strengthen your strategic position which in turn reduces risk for the buyer. Warren Buffett talks about this value driver as a 'Business Moat'. Is your business protected by some type of moat that prevents competitors getting close to you? Below are examples of barriers that widen a business moat and protect it from new entrants or competitors:

- Copyrights
- Trademarks
- Patents
- Trade Secrets
- Developed Processes
- Proprietary Designs
- Proprietary Know-How

- Brand or Trade Names
- Engineering Drawings
- Customised Software Programs
- Step-by-Step Training Systems
- Customised or Proprietary Databases
- Published Articles or Industry Press
- Hard-to-get licenses, zoning, permits, or regulatory approvals
- Contracts with difficult-to-penetrate entities (government, for example)

Remember, buyers are looking for an easy transition into their new business, so evidence that your business is well organised and runs smoothly will always add to your company's value. Presenting your business as an efficient and effective profit generator with neat and organised financial records, together with happy customers and loyal staff will all add to the value of your business.

Step Seven

Letting Go - Make Yourself Redundant

Knowing from the start that your aim is to build a successful business and sell it to fund the lifestyle of your dreams requires a long-range view. Not only do you want to maximise profit and create a streamlined efficient business, but once you've achieved that or even once you are on the right track toward that outcome, it's time to start letting go. Again, this can seem like unusual advice. It's likely that the business feels like your baby so letting go before you have to may not be what you expect to hear. But if you want to be able to walk away from the business easily when you sell, then you need to start planning for that day, today. Essentially you want to 'make yourself redundant' from the business so that a new buyer can be confident that they can take over and run it just as effectively as you did. Plus, you probably won't want to stick around for too long after the sale because it can feel very odd when someone else is calling the shots. Your job is to make the business saleable, make yourself redundant, help during the transition if required and then sail off into the sunset. In my case, I literally did sail off into the sunset.

It is also a nice feeling knowing that the business is so efficient and everyone in the team knows their role so well that the business can run without you – whether you plan to sell soon or not. It also gives you much more freedom. You can focus on the things you want to do and step back from the things you feel you have to do. You can spend more time speaking with your employees and making them feel valued. You can run the business 'from the balcony' instead of being stressed on the shop floor. You can take more time off and enjoy life with your friends and family. You can go on holiday more often or improve your golf swing. The list goes on.

What Got You Here Won't Get You There
Of course, getting to that position isn't easy. But, it is an essential step to maximise the value of your business prior to sale. There is a great book called *What got you Here, Won't get you There* by Marshall Goldsmith that talks about this phenomenon.

To summarise, he states that behavioural problems, not technical skills, are what separate the great from the near great. Incredible results can come from practicing basic behaviours like saying thank you, listening well, thinking before you speak, and apologising for your mistakes. The first step to change is wanting to change.

Here are some of the main points from his book:

- The four delusional drivers of self-interest are money, power, status and popularity. Give them up if you want to be successful.
- Create a To-Stop list rather than a To-Do list.
- When getting feedback of any type, positive or negative, accept it from a neutral place and say "Thank you." If you don't reply with a judgmental comment, you can't get into an argument.
- Create a list of people you should give recognition to and then review that list each week to see if you should send someone praise.
- Give away ALL the credit.
- Just say "Thank You" to more comments rather than making a bigger fuss about things. We often have issues with accepting compliments.
- Gratitude is not a limited resource. Express your thanks more often.
- Your personality is not fixed and improvement does not require you to

become a radically different person. You don't have to change your whole life, just improve one tiny trait.

- Goal obsession is the blindness of goal pursuit at the expense of more important things.
- You can do a lot worse than questioning your flaws. We often get so defensive about these things, but what do we really have to lose? Usually, very little.
- Apologise, apologise, apologise. Just step up and make the apologies you need to make. And then shut up. Don't try to justify it.
- When you listen to someone, make them feel like they are the only person in the room. Devote your attention to them.
- We can't change for the long-run without following up. Follow up shows your colleagues that you care about getting better and that you're taking the process seriously.

As the leader, you should focus on the future strategy and not the day-to-day activities. Your team should be doing that. Seek advice from a mentor to help you focus on the right stuff and let go of some of the reins.

Long before we sold the business, I had set a strategy of how I could detach myself from the business and allow it to run itself. I set this 'goal' as a new separate project and would meet every two weeks with my PA to ensure that the plan was progressing.

I was clear that my main goal was to have the free time and money to travel the world as much as possible, and after only six years of running the company, I decided that it was time to start working out a way in which I could live my dream. Plus, I'd read a lot of the business literature and I knew that if we did decide to sell, demonstrating that it still ran well when I stepped back was going to be crucial to maximise the price.

This was especially true in our case because although I had two business partners they were a lot more operationally focused and didn't want to step into the MD role and run the business, besides they were doing a great job where they were.

As a result, recruiting from within the business was not going to work. Finding someone internal is usually a safer bet as they already know the company culture and can be moulded into the type of leader you want to step into your shoes but this wasn't practical in our situation. We realised that we would need to recruit someone from outside. Looking outside of the business also has its advantages because it brings in new talent who may have new contacts and experiences.

We contracted the services of a recruitment agency. In the meantime, I started to visualise the day

I would be able to walk out of the office for two to three months and not be required in the day to day decision making. By this point we had already implemented KPIs and had a rigorous management dashboard in place that we used to inform us about various aspects of the business.

We interviewed many candidates after setting up a very clear spec of the type of person we wanted - someone who could take the business to the next level. Myself and my two business partners were all involved in the interview and selection process to ensure we found someone we were all committed to.

If you can leave the business for a month and it runs without any issues then you know you are well on your way to success. Also, if you can demonstrate this to a potential buyer then your business becomes much more appealing and more valuable as they realise the business is not dependent on you – often a primary concern for any buyer.

The main considerations that will help you to build and grow a great business *and* facilitate your personal exit strategy beyond those we've already covered are:

1. Effective Delegation
2. Clear Accountability
3. Activating Intrinsic Motivation
4. Succession Planning.

Effective Delegation

If you want your business to grow to a point that it's big enough and successful enough to attract potential buyers then effective delegation is crucial. Considering there are only 24 hours in every day, you're never going to be able to take care of everything. Empowering others allows you to co-opt their time too which allows the business to gain some serious forward momentum. Failing to delegate properly simply creates bottlenecks in the business, prevents high potential employees from really developing, creates frustration for everyone and slows down the growth of the business down.

If you want to exit you need to let go and delegate to other people. This can be notoriously difficult, especially if you have been used to doing everything yourself. This is very common with entrepreneurs who were involved in the business from the start and usually needed to do everything themselves or share the workload with a small trusted team. That is the nature of start-up but the skills that helped you to create the business are not necessarily the ones that will allow you to successfully sell it!

When you consider how you are going to make yourself redundant you need to focus on what you actually do. What parts of the business are you currently responsible for? What do you do from Monday to Friday? Make a list of all the activities and responsibilities you do in your current role and figure out who in your current business could take over each task or responsibility. You may find that you need to split some of your tasks so that they are taken over by people who are skilled, suitable and willing to take on the additional responsibility.

Consider who you have in the team and what their strengths and vulnerabilities are so that you find the best fit. Not only will this delegation free you up to enjoy more freedom, but it also allows your employees to gain more experience and confidence. This increases their individual development and the level of satisfaction and reward they gain from their role.

One word of warning however. Accept from the start that the people you delegate to will make mistakes and embrace it as part of their learning journey. They will also make decisions that you would not have made and are likely to do things slightly differently – as long as you are clear on the outcomes you need, let them find their own way to that destination. Effective and smart delegation allows you to create a better, bigger and stronger company.

Another thing that can easily bog you down as you look for your exit is getting mired in the trivia. This is more about focus than delegation but it's important to deal with the right issues only. Consider whether or not something is important in the grand scheme of things. I rarely got too upset or flustered about the small stuff and just kept my focus on the big picture. Don't hide from tough decisions like getting rid of toxic employees but don't get bogged down in every discussion or query either. Learn to let go of the trivia and release your time and everybody else's.

Clear Accountability

Whatever you decide to delegate – make sure that the person taking over responsibility for that area has full accountability for the deliverables of that role. We've mentioned this before so we don't need to labour the point but tasks without accountability don't get done or they are done poorly so the people in charge need to know they are in charge of that task or decision and will be held accountable for the results.

And for the record, you can't make people accountable by threatening them, badgering them or cajoling them. You need to create the environment where they can embrace accountability.

The people you identify to delegate part of your role to must choose to accept the request and take the accountability for that role or task. You can offer it, but they must decide whether to accept it. And you can't force them to – that won't work. The best you can do is to try to create an environment which encourages them to make that choice.

Some people don't want the extra responsibility or are happy where they are in the business. This can be frustrating for entrepreneurs because they are always on the look-out for the next challenge, the next opportunity or the next high-potential. But you must respect other people's choices – we don't all look at life the same way.

Professor of organisational behaviour at the London Business School, Nigel Nicholson suggests, "You can ask people to think outside the box and engage in entrepreneurial endeavours all you want, but don't expect too much. Both are risky behaviours. Indeed, any kind of change is risky when you are comfortable with the status quo. And evolutionary psychologists are not surprised at all, by the fact that, despite the excellent press that change is given, almost everyone resists it – except when they are dissatisfied."

This is just human nature. So, if the person you had in mind to take on part of your role doesn't want to do it, then respect that choice and find someone else.

Activating Intrinsic Motivation
Motivation is also an important factor. In fact, finding effective ways to motivate your people is key at any stage of the business from start right through to exit.

Financial incentives are an example of extrinsic motivation, i.e. the impetus to change is coming from external sources. Offering financial incentive is one side of the approach known as the carrot and stick. It is part of the reward and punishment school of thought. In other words, the only way we can get people to change their behaviour, meet deadlines or deliver on objectives is to reward them when they do something positive and punish them when they do something negative.

In his insightful book *Drive: The Surprising Truth about What Motivated Us,* author Daniel Pink explores motivation in more depth and provides many compelling examples to the ineffectiveness of reward and punishment. For example, the Federal Reserve Bank in the US commissioned four economists from MIT, Carnegie Mellon and the University of Chicago to investigate the effectiveness of rewards on performance. As you probably know, the banking sector is notorious for paying huge bonuses so they were keen to establish if that was a smart move or not. The research concluded that "In eight of the nine tasks we examined across three experiments, higher incentives led to worse performance." The London School of Economics also confirmed these findings after analysing fifty-one studies of corporate reward schemes. They reported that "We find that financial incentives... can result in negative impact on overall performance."

Actually, the best way to motivate people is to create the environment where they activate their own intrinsic motivation, i.e. they are motivated from within. We've actually known about this since the 1960s when MIT management professor Douglas McGregor wrote a book called *The Human Side of Enterprise* proposing Theory X and Theory Y. The Theory X approach, which is still widely used in business, works on the assumption that people are basically lazy, will show minimal initiative or ambition without incentive or coercion. And, they will avoid responsibility whenever possible. McGregor believed this approach was wrong because it made assumptions about human nature that were wrong.

His alternative was Theory Y – which starts from the position that your people are not stupid (if they are then perhaps that's your fault for hiring them in the first place). When leaders assume their people are capable, want to do a good job, want to be creative and take responsibility for their work then the environment changes and productivity goes up.

For centuries scientists and scholars believed there were two motivational drives. The first is the *biological imperative* or the drive to stay alive. This is an example of intrinsic motivation but most of us don't activate it on a regular basis if at all. We are not fighting for survival very often.

The second motivational drive, reward and punishment, is extrinsic but we already know it's not that effective. It is this motivational drive that is at the heart of McGregor's Theory X.

There is however a third motivational drive, first identified in the 1940s by Harry F Harlow, professor of psychology at the University of Wisconsin. He and his colleagues conducted experiments with rhesus monkeys and discovered that they would solve puzzles without any reward or punishment at all. It appeared that they solved the puzzles just because they enjoyed solving them. At the time Harlow wrote "The behaviour obtained in this investigation poses some interesting questions for motivation theory, since significant learning was attained and efficient performance maintained without resort to special or extrinsic incentives." He suggested that there must be a third motivating drive – that "the performance of the task provided intrinsic reward". In other words, the joy of completing the task was in some cases its own reward.

More recently Edward Deci and Richard Ryan unpacked the characteristics of this third motivational drive through their Self Determination Theory (SDT). They suggest that this type of intrinsic motivation emerges when someone has:

- Autonomy
- Competence
- Relatedness

When our human need for these things is met we are motivated, happy, creative and productive. When they are inhibited our motivation, happiness, creativity and productivity plummet.

Autonomy

Everyone needs to feel as though they have some level of control over what they do. This is why micro-managing is so demoralising for people.

As the leader of the business you need to be clear about what you expect people to deliver but you won't allow this potent motivational force to emerge if you dictate how that person must achieve that outcome. When employees are constantly told what to do and when to do it, or when someone is looking over their shoulder waiting to point out a mistake then the third motivational drive is squashed. These types of dictatorial behaviours actively erode autonomy and reduce self-confidence and self-esteem. They feel defeated before they have even begun so they often feel there is no point being creative or showing initiative because they will just be shot down or cross examined.

Competence

Competence is all about being able to demonstrate capability or being in the state of 'flow'.

Creating a working environment that fosters flow, or allows people to do tasks and take on responsibilities that they are good at or show proficiency in, will help to activate this potent intrinsic drive. Again this is why micro-managing is so debilitating because it sends a message that the manager or leader doesn't think that the employee is competent. If they did they wouldn't feel the need to double check their work.

Relatedness

This characteristic speaks to our need for connection. When we are connected to other people we like, respect or care about we are capable of far more than we could ever do on our own. We can see this in productive teams – the people in the team like each other or at the very least respect each other for the role and capabilities they bring to the team.

Getting this right to enable intrinsic motivation to emerge is not always easy. This needs to be managed but ultimately creating a business where people are pulling for each other is going to be much more successful than a business that is plagued by internal competition and in-fighting.

By far the best way to hit your targets is to genuinely involve your people and encourage them to create productive work groups so that they feel connected to each other and tap into the third motivational drive.

Succession Planning

If your end game is to exit the business for a large payday and sail off into the sunset or even step back and draw an income from the business, it will be much more valuable if you can demonstrate that it runs efficiently and profitably with a strong, effective management team that function well with or without *you*. One of the biggest concerns for any would-be business buyer is whether the business's past success is going to be replicable in the future. The fear, especially when there is a particularly forceful or charismatic founder leading the business, is that it is the individual who is driving that success rather than the business itself.

Being able to demonstrate that you can leave the business and it functions as normal is something that you should be aiming for. Is there someone already in your business that could step into your role? Finding someone internal is usually the best approach because they already know the business, they understand the culture and are probably already following your philosophy.

If there is no one suitable inside the business then you may have to recruit externally. This is always challenging and brings a different set of concerns.

One of the biggest risks when buying an existing business is that the success of that business is somehow down to the charismatic leader or founder and therefore without that figurehead the business will crumble. If you can prove or demonstrate that the business is still making money and has a positive future then that risk is alleviated.

Below are some basic principles of successful succession planning:

- Don't leave it until the last minute. Start planning as soon as you know you want to exit the business. Good planning is about strong personnel practises, not crisis management.
- Focus on policies, procedures and practices, not personalities. Succession planning is about being able to deconstruct your role so that you have very clear policies, procedures and practices around how those tasks and responsibilities are carried out.
- Succession planning should meet the latest HR policies. This will ensure fair, equitable and legally compliant employment practices.

If your business has already established strong practices in governance, leadership and management, then succession planning should be straightforward. The person coming into your role simply needs to use the current practices rather than establishing new ones.

Once you have successfully made yourself (or your role) redundant, you can choose whether you want to enjoy the free time and simply monitor the results of the business, or decide whether you are going to sell. Provided the business is running well in your absence, you could stay in the background and draw an income from the profits. However, if you are clear that you want the lump sum and take your money now, then you can move on to the next step of preparing the business for sale.

At least you will have the luxury of that choice, by effectively 'making yourself redundant'.

Step Eight

Types of Sale/Preparing for Sale

Once you've successfully stepped back from your business and made yourself redundant or at least demonstrated that it works perfectly well without you, then it's time to consider what type of sale you are looking for so you can prepare properly to make that happen.

There are a number of ways to sell your company, each with their own benefits, so before you choose which one is right for you it's wise to really stop and consider exactly why you are selling in the first place. As we discussed earlier, it's really important that you are clear about your objectives and how you want your life to be once you have sold all or part of your company. This will allow you to work out the best route to achieve your objective.

For example, you may want to sell and use the money to relocate abroad, meaning that you won't want to be involved in the business after the sale. My focus was to sell up and have the freedom to travel whenever and wherever I wanted. However, you may have everything you want in your life right at home only you just want more time to enjoy those things. A different sale structure may suit you better so that you receive a cash lump sum and ongoing income in exchange for a smaller role in the business.

Understanding your personal requirements will make sure you choose the right type of sale for your needs. In addition, the size and type of your business will also play a role in your decision.

The main ways to sell a business that we will look at are:

- Trade Sale
- Management Buy Out (MBO)
- Management Buy In (MBI)
- Management Buy In/Buy Out (BIMBO)
- Floating your Company on the Stock Market

Trade Sale
The most common route used to sell a company is a straightforward trade sale. A trade sale is the sale of a business, or part of the business, to another owner, usually another business. It is less risky and costly than floating your company on the stock market and

can usually command a higher asking price than an MBO, MBI or BIMBO.

From my experience, trade sales are the most common form of exit for a company's owner. The potential buyer often makes a strategic decision to purchase the company to acquire their underlying assets such as plant or intellectual property or to gain access to their existing market. Whether integrated into a larger company or maintained as a separate entity the new owner is likely to benefit from economies of scale as well as greater market dominance in their sector.

In terms of buying or selling a company, there are two options: an asset sale, where any assets the company has are purchased by the buyer and are no longer part of the company, or a share sale where the shareholders sell all (or a majority) of their shares and transfer the company as a going concern.

The general rule of thumb is that a buyer will normally prefer to buy the assets of a business and the seller will prefer to sell the shares. This is due to liability and risk as explained below.

Asset Sale

In an asset sale, the buyer may choose which of the assets of the company they wish to buy, such as property and machinery. It is also possible to buy the goodwill of the company - this means the buyer gets exactly what they want from the company without

157

buying the company itself. Hence why a buyer may prefer this route.

In an asset sale, the company itself (a separate legal entity) will be selling the assets. This means that the company still exists and therefore with a few exceptions the seller also keeps all the current liabilities of the business – unless they can negotiate with the buyer to take them over with the business. This is much riskier for the seller and it's why the seller will almost always prefer to sell the shares not the assets.

In practical terms, sale of the assets of a company means that the third party does not acquire the company itself, and without any assets, the company becomes an empty shell, however it is left with the liabilities. This route is more common if the company is having problems in which case it is more of a 'distress' sale.

Share Sale

In a share sale, the company is sold with all assets and liabilities - some of which may be difficult to quantify such as tax, pending court cases or employment law liabilities.

A share sale is clearly a better option for the seller, especially if that seller wants to sell and make a clean break from the business. Once they've sold their shareholding in that business the company as a legal entity remains and all the liabilities of that business remain with the new owner.

This is why due diligence is so important for the buyer – it allows them to establish exactly what they are buying before committing to the sale. The new buyer knows that they are taking on the upside potential and the liabilities of the business so they need to know what those are – they don't want any nasty surprises.

When you are aiming to sell your business, you will probably be looking for a share sale of your business for all the reasons outlined above. Besides, it can be very difficult, regardless of the money involved, to watch a third party deconstruct everything you worked so hard to create. Most people, even those desperate to sell and move on, would prefer to see their business continue on into the future under new ownership *and* exit cleanly without future liability.

Management Buy Out

Commonly known as an MBO, the Management Buy-Out consists of an existing manager or group of managers in your company coming together to buy the business from you. This is why identifying high potentials and creating a strong management team can be such a benefit to the business, not only in the day-to-day running but also in the creation of a possible buyer.

The major hurdle in this type of sale is access to funding – how the management team is going to raise the funds necessary to buy you out. However, they won't have to find all the money right away.

Usually they will only be required to input a relatively small amount of the overall sale price to demonstrate commitment to the deal. This is often known as 'hurt money' for obvious reasons!

The rest of the agreed price will usually be raised through a bank loan or venture capital. The bank loan is, in principle easier and probably cheaper but it will almost certainly come with strings attached where that debt is repaid before any other existing debt.

Venture capital or 'VC' is also used in this type of sale, often alongside bank funding. If the numbers look good, a venture capital company will fund the sale and potentially inject cash into the business in exchange for an equity stake.

That stake is often significant but they are usually only looking to be involved for 3 – 5 years and will be adding value through expertise as well as money to increase the value of their stake, which in turn increases the value of the management stake too. They will usually insist on a member of their team being appointed to the board to assist in decision making and strategic direction. Whether it is a viable option for your management team to buy your business will depend very much on them and the nature of the 'VC' relationship.

Both options will only be available if there is:

- A strong, capable and well-balanced management team in place willing to proceed with the buy-out;
- An existing, commercially viable business; and
- A sound, realistic and proven strategy for the future.

All of which you should have if your exit strategy is to sell via a MBO.

An MBO also offers those already in the business doing a great job the opportunity for their own advancement while also providing job security.

If you feel that you have a management team that is capable of taking the business forward then it might be appropriate to give them first refusal but this will need to be handled sensitively. You don't want too many people in the business knowing that you are planning to sell until you are ready. But, once you are it may be a viable avenue to explore which provides a win/win for everyone.

You should also be aware that this route may not command as high an asking price as a strategic trade buyer would.

Management Buy In

A management buy-in (MBI) occurs when a manager or a management team from outside the company raises the necessary finance to buy-into the business and becomes the new management. A management buy-in team often competes with other purchasers such as venture capitalists, in search of a suitable investment. Usually, the team will be led by a manager with significant experience at managing director level, preferably in your areas of business.

If you have been planning and building your business from the start with a view to selling that business at some point, it is unlikely that this approach is going to be viable for a management buy-in team simply by virtue of the fact that this is only really used when the business has potential but the management team currently in place seems unable to realise that potential. If you have been hiring well, identifying high potentials, investing in training and development while also clearing out dead wood, then this shouldn't be relevant to you. If it is you would be far better to sort the management issue and sell in a different way to increase your purchase price. Remember, having a strong management team in place after you leave will always increase the value of your business – regardless of how it is sold.

Buy-in Management Buy-out
Commonly known as BIMBO, this is a hybrid of both the management buy-in and management buy-out. The team that buys the company is a combination of

existing managers, who retain a stake in the company, and individuals from outside the company who will join the management team following the buy-out.

The term BIMBO was first used in respect of the purchase of Chaucer Foods, a Hull based crouton manufacturer, from Hazlewood Foods plc in 1990.

This method provides the stability of a strong existing management team who know the business and are now invested and focused on building the business as owners with the addition of new management expertise from outside that may help to take the business to the next level. Whether this works comes down to the people – whether they can work together as a coherent management unit rather than 'them and us'. If that can be resolved then this approach can minimise risk.

Floating your Company on the Stock Market

Floating your company on the stock market or 'going public' is probably the most ambitious avenue for selling your company. It is also the least utilised method of sale so we won't go into too much detail about it.

Potentially, floating your company has significant upside if it works but it also comes with greater risk and higher costs. Your company would need to be large enough to qualify to float and it would have to be a limited company. There are a lot of hoops to jump through which will require a great deal of disclosure and transparency into current and past activity.

Although floating your company may be viewed as the epitome of business success it is not for everyone and is often fraught with challenges. It does however offer an opportunity for a large financial gain whilst still maintaining a level of control in the business and maintaining a significant shareholding.

Floating a company involves making a public offering of the shares in a private company and turning it into a public company quoted on a stock market.

In the UK, the main stock markets are the London Stock Exchange (LSE) Main Market, and the Alternative Investment Market (AIM) which is actually a sub market of the LSE. There are stock exchanges all over the world where respective companies will be listed. In the US for example there is the New York Stock Exchange and NASDAQ

There are lengthy and complex rules governing the flotation of your business that will change depending on your location and the market you float in. As a result you will be required to recruit outside consultants to guide you through the process.

This route is not really an exit plan as you will be required to stay in the business for many years, and in most cases you will end up being busier and more stressed than you already were.

Do you Really Want to Sell?

Before pressing the 'go' button on your sale plans it's always worth taking some time to really consider if selling your business is the right thing for you to do at this time.

What is your primary motive? Are you tired of the business and just want a fresh start? Do you want to turn your attention elsewhere? Do you need or want the money?

The point here is that there is always more than one way to achieve any of those goals and the solution is never black or white. Too often the decision to sell is clouded by other issues. Perhaps we receive an offer that seems too good to pass up so we sell before the new owner changes their mind. Perhaps we have been building the business for so long that the joy and challenge has dwindled and you feel that getting out would just be the best option. Maybe you are concerned that your cashflow will not be sustainable, but there are usually other options available to help with this.

Choosing the correct method is important because it will allow you to set the strategy on how you run your company and make decisions.

In the moment, you may think that you can't wait to leave the business, walk out the door and never look back, but have you considered what you will actually do with all that free time? It can be liberating and exciting for a few months but I've lost count of the number of business people I've met that cashed out full of enthusiasm for the adventures or relaxing times they would enjoy only to be pulling their hair out with boredom six months later casting around for a new business to create or buy into.

Perhaps taking a back seat in the business might be a better solution – allowing you to stay connected to the company you started and built without the day to day hands on involvement. This is only really an option is you are still engaged in the business in some form or another. If you really are 'over it' then it's probably going to be better to sell and move on. Just make sure you have a plan – we'll talk about that in more detail in step eleven.

Perhaps as you've explored the possibilities for selling your business you have come to the conclusion that it's not big enough to sell and you would get much more for the company if you built it up for another year or so. Again, this will only be viable if you believe you still have those years left in you and can add value, re-engage with a new vision and put in the hard work to build the business further.

If you find yourself in a position where you have to sell then make sure any prospective buyer doesn't find out otherwise they will use that against you.

If your motivation to sell is mainly about the money and you have a profitable business, then there are other things to consider. If you sell, you will only get a certain amount of money, usually equal to several times your current annual profit. That can be a lot of money but if you don't sell you will have made that money anyway over the next few years and still have the business. Of course, it won't be available to you as a lump sum but the business itself will probably have increased in value over those years making it an even more valuable asset.

Is there an option to sell part of the company to the existing management team, as you step aside, or only get involved at the board meetings? This would give you a cash lump sum albeit smaller, give you more freedom to pursue other things while also providing a healthy on-going income in exchange for a small input of your time and expertise.

If you are unsure what to do, consider talking with a mentor to discuss the options and help clarify your intentions and outcomes. Alternatively, just keep running your business well and a buyer will appear and help to make the decision for you. When you have an efficient, well-run company, not only will life be easier but you are more likely to be noticed by a prospective buyer. That is certainly what happened to us. We knew we wanted to sell at some point and set the business up with that objective from the start. However, it was only when our business landed on the radar of a much larger European organisation who wanted to expand their business into the UK, that our thoughts turned to selling. And because we'd already done most of the hard work the sale itself was very smooth and we achieved an excellent sale price. The effort to create a saleable business from the start may take time to yield fruit but it's always worth it.

Decision Time

So, what's it going to be? Are you ready to sell the company, or do you want to take a back seat, and stay involved and build the business more and wait a while longer?

If you have considered all your options and are sure you want to sell, then it's time to move on to the exciting stage of finding a buyer.

Step Nine

Finding a Buyer

As highlighted before, most business owners sell their business via a trade sale. Step nine therefore focuses on how to find a trade sale buyer.

You're only going to sell your company once, so it really is worth doing a lot of work to find the right buyer.

There are three main scenarios. The first option is that you find the buyer yourself. As an entrepreneur, your natural instinct may be to do what you've always done and find your own solution. Like me, you may not want to pay huge fees to an external agency or consultant for doing something that you could probably do yourself.

The second option is to enlist the help of a selling agent to ensure you find the best buyer and secure the highest price. This can be a useful option, especially if you are already flat out running your business.

However, they can be very expensive and take a sizeable chunk out of your end sale price.

The third option is when a buyer finds you. Fortunately, this is what happened to us.

Although this meant we didn't go looking for a buyer, we had recruited the services of an agency several years earlier to help us prepare the business for sale. Whilst we decided not to sell the company on that particular occasion, the whole process was hugely beneficial and it taught us many new lessons on how the business could be set up better to maximise the sale price. As a result, we will spend a little more time exploring the value in this approach.

Choosing a Selling Agent

Paying someone to help market your business can be a good idea. Whilst you may be understandably hesitant about the fees you must also remember that a reputable selling agent has a very particular skill set and experience selling businesses, not to mention a wide network of contacts which may mean that your business will sell faster and often for a higher price than you could have secured on your own. You can always be involved in the strategy and you will retain control over the selling process without being intimately involved in the search and negotiations. Remember, your business is your most valuable asset, you won't get a second chance to maximise that asset.

Trying to sell yourself and realising too late that you sold for too little is not a mistake you want to make.

Besides, if an experienced selling agent sells your business for even a few percent more than you anticipated the extra should cover their costs and still leave you with more money. Using someone independent to market your business also provides you with extra confidentiality at the early stages. For example, you may not be absolutely sure you want to sell and this exercise may simply be to 'test the water' and gauge potential interest. If you decide to investigate the market yourself it's much more likely that your competitors, suppliers or staff could find out about your intentions. Potentially, this could have a negative impact on your business through a drop in productivity or staff morale for example. The agent can therefore deal directly with interested parties as well as liaising with other professional advisors such as accountants and solicitors without having all these people coming into your business premises raising questions.

Once you market your business the agent will deal with any interest from potential buyers. In the same way recruitment consultants advertise roles without naming the company looking to fill the position, sales agents will often market a business using the business sector and performance but without the name of the business to maintain confidentiality. Only when the agent has established serious interest will more information be divulged about your business. This is also useful because some of the interested parties may be competitors or people who know your business and therefore it prevents you from having to deal with those people directly or from them knowing too much too soon. Using an agent who operates out of their own offices can also help to keep the selling process away from your business for as long as possible.

Finally, and perhaps most importantly, hiring a selling agent allows you to maintain your focus on running and developing your business without distraction. In their haste to find a buyer, some entrepreneurs take their eye off the core business, shifting too much attention to the selling 'prize'. Complacency can creep in as the business deteriorates which will, of course, impact the due diligence findings and, potentially, the final price you are offered.

Set your Expectations Early

Do you know what you are trying to achieve from the sale of your business? Do you know what to expect?

Before you start, set out the essential features that you want from the sale of your company. What is a realistic price for the business based on the current condition of the business and the external market, including the current economy? What price would you be thrilled with and what is your 'red line' in terms of a price below which you are not prepared to sell? Will you accept a part purchase now, with the rest selling at a later date? Or do you want to wrap it all up in one go? Are you willing to stay in the business for a few months or years to help with the transition phase? If so, how long are you willing to stay and on what terms? Knowing what you are aiming for will make the process much easier. If the price offered is too low you know immediately that it's too low because you've already established your 'red line'. If a prospective buyer wants you to stay for two years but you know that six months is your maximum then you don't need to tie yourself in knots trying to make a decision. Being clear about what you want and what you will and will not accept, *before* you start the selling process, will help to make the right decisions when a buyer is found.

Hiring an agent brings a much-needed objective view to the selling process which can help to assess if your 'realistic' expectations are genuinely realistic. Unlike you, your selling agent has no emotional ties to the business. They are however still committed to getting you the best price possible because the more you make the more they make. Many selling agents will work on a percentage fee based on the sale price of your business, or a fixed fee plus percentage. You can expect to pay between two and five percent for their services.

Although you may be a proficient and experienced negotiator, your emotional attachment to the business can cloud your judgement. You could easily get hung up on irrelevant things that may seem important to you, or react to comments from potential buyers – this won't happen with your agent who will be able to stay focused on the price and negotiating the best deal while also providing a calming influence on you as you work through the various stages of the sale toward completion. Assuming that you plan to keep the sale as confidential as possible for as long as possible a great agent will also play the role of confidant, sounding board and therapist!

How to Find the Right Advisor

Like many things in business and life, choosing the right person or team to help you sell your business comes down to a combination of assessing their credentials, past performance and references, to intuition and 'gut feel'. You will be working very closely with your agent, often under a huge amount of pressure so it's essential that you chose someone you can talk to openly, be candid with and someone who listens to you. You want a partner – someone who has your back and is fighting for your best interests at all times.

To find a selling agent you can search online and look for businesses that work in your area. Normally, selling agents are corporate accountants or specialist legal professionals that focus on selling businesses. You could also ask people you know and trust for recommendations but you would need to be sure they would keep your request confidential.

Reputation is important in this area, as with many other professional services, so you should be able to find the professionals that stand out in your area reasonably quickly.

Their expertise in your sector is also critical. Ideally you want someone who has sold your type of business before and therefore has a strong network of connections and potential buyers already looking in your industry. Good agents will know venture capitalists who are looking for certain types of businesses, or they will know owners of large businesses who may be looking to expand and acquire new businesses like yours, or management teams who are looking for the right business to buy in to. You want to be able to tap into those networks and that is why a good advisor is worth their weight in gold.

Throughout the sale process, delicate situations or questions may arise. If handled incorrectly these issues could cause delay or the deal to fall through. Having a good agent who is experienced in the ins-and-outs of the investigative process can help to iron out any glitches as efficiently as possible.

When sourcing your selling agent, it's always advisable to meet with several until you find someone you feel is a good 'fit' – to you personally and also what you are trying to achieve for the business. Ideally, put together criteria of what's important to you and compare the agents you meet.

Your criteria might include:

- Your gut feeling – do you think you could work well with that person or do you get a sense that they may be quite difficult?
- Is the person you've met, the person who will be working for you? If not, make sure you meet your representative or main point of contact – this is the person you will be working with.
- Total expected fees – how much will each agent charge? Is it a mix of percentage and fixed fee or all percentage? Calculate what those fees are likely to be based on your realistic sale price.
- Their physical location and easiness for you to deal with them. Although phone calls can be useful, it's likely that you are going to want to be able to sit down in face to face discussions – based on their location, how likely or easy is that?
- Their apparent knowledge of your industry/ business. Have they sold businesses in your industry or sector before? If so, is it

possible for you to speak to any of their past clients? Check their references and ask detailed questions rather than simply "what were they like?". Find out what the past clients liked and didn't like about the agent. Was there anything they felt could have been improved on? Out of 10 what would they rate their experience with the agent? Did they ever disagree and how was it resolved? Were they happy with the end result? Do they feel the agent delivered value for money?

- Do they have existing contacts of potential buyers? Do they have an up-to-date database of individuals, companies or venture capitalists that are looking for businesses right now?

- Are they happy to answer your questions (however stupid!) and explain the sales process? You want someone that recognises that whilst this is not new for them, it is new for you and they should be willing to support you on that journey and appreciate how much it means to you.

- Are they enthusiastic? You want someone who will be proactive. Obviously, you won't know how enthusiastic they are until you start but you will be able to gauge from the initial meeting how interested they are in you and your business. Do they ask pertinent questions or do you feel like just another client with a business to sell?

Take your time. Finding the right agent may take several months. Doing your homework upfront is essential – remember you are only going to sell your company once so take some time and make sure you choose the right agent.

Other Advisors

If your agent is not from a firm of corporate accountants, then it is likely that you will need to find one. Even if your agent is from a firm of corporate accountants, you will need a team of advisors to ensure the best result. A sales focused agent to source potential buyers and drive through the deal and a corporate accountant and lawyer to ensure that deal is watertight.

A good corporate accountant is critical when selling your business for a number of reasons:

- **It's the accountant that creates the preliminary valuation.** You might think that your business is worth a certain amount but it is your accountant that will objectively assess the business and apply standard techniques to arrive at preliminary valuation. This valuation is therefore verifiable and explainable rather than based on your hunch or hopeful expectation. The valuation is based on your material assets and liabilities, what you own, owe and what's included in the sale. Using their expertise a great accountant can also generate a picture of your income over time and assign a concrete value to the more fluid and variable aspects of your business including past earning, cash flow, balance sheets, equity statements and the company's performance in relation to the economic and market conditions as well as any liabilities that may cause issue down the track.

- **Your corporate accountant will organise and structure the deal.** There are many ways to sell your business as we discussed in the last step. Your business may be bought by another individual who is currently not in business. Another company may buy the business and merge it into their existing operations or they may keep your business separate. You might be selling your assets, majority share ownership or a combination of these. Your accountant's job is to figure out the best deal structure which will allow you to realise the highest asking price with the fewest complications. Their role here is vital because they help you to understand the financial and legal jargon so you can fully appreciate the advantages and disadvantages of each option. You need someone in your corner who is financially fluent and can make sure you appreciate the legalities of the proposed deal.

- **Tax expertise.** Business taxation, what is and isn't allowed, is complicated enough and changes fairly regularly. The complication around tax escalates considerably when you sell your business. Depending on the location or jurisdiction of the potential buyer there may be different taxation issues, sometimes on an international level. Getting this wrong can be bruising both financially and for your stress levels. Getting the right advice is therefore essential. But it's not just the taxation payable on the sale that needs to be accurate, your accountant's auditing experience will organise, document and verify your business's tax position.
- **Risk evaluation.** Aside from helping with the negotiation phase, your accountant will also conduct thorough due diligence – both on your business and the prospective buyer.

As we've said before, it's important that you know exactly what you are selling and can verify your valuation and do everything to prevent nasty surprises that could trigger a downward price negotiation. Your accountant will be instrumental in that due diligence process. They will also conduct due diligence on the prospective buyer as early as possible to ensure they have the capability to close the deal.

- **Planning after the sale**. A great accountant will also help you to plan your life after the sale, making sure you manage the money as efficiently as possible. A financial planner can also help in this regard.

As well as a corporate accountant and potentially a financial advisor (although some accountants are both), you will also require the services of a corporate lawyer. There may be cross over between some of the advisors but a lawyer will ensure the legal documentation around the deal is accurate and you are fully aware of the details and more importantly what those details mean in plain English. Like your accountant, your lawyer can act as a translator between the legal jargon that accompanies such deals and what the various clauses and details actually mean or could mean for you in the future.

The importance of rock solid, reputable advisors can't be overestimated. Getting any of these things wrong – due diligence, taxation, legal issues - can be disastrous. Consider vetting these advisors with the same rigour as you do the sale agent. Create a checklist for each and go through it thoroughly.

The Selling Process

Once you've found your team of advisors, it's good to know what you can and should expect from them and how they will help you to successfully execute a sale.

Your agent is there to drive the sales process along, advise you and act on your behalf in accordance with your instructions. He is not the decision maker – you are. You always have control over the process and whether you accept an offer or not so it's important to discuss with your agent exactly what you want to achieve. If you know what type of buyer you are looking for then be sure to share that insight with your team.

There are several distinct phases of the selling process:

1. Establishing the valuation of the company (corporate accountant).
2. Preparing sales particulars for your company (sales agent).
3. Sending out the sale particulars to potential buyers, following up and generating interest (sales agent).

4. Ensuring that a confidentiality agreement is signed by all parties (sales agent).

5. Preparing a detailed business profile including financial forecasts, and circulating that document to vetted interested parties that have signed the confidentiality agreement (corporate accountant and sales agent).

6. Conducting negotiations with potential buyers (sales agent and/or you).

7. Agreeing 'Heads of Terms' (corporate lawyer and sales agent).

8. Providing assistance to the seller during the potential buyer's due diligence process (corporate accountant and sales agent).

9. Giving detailed advice on the sales documentation and liaising with all other advisors to ensure things are moving forward as required (corporate accountant and lawyer).

10. Advising on warranties and indemnities, and the implication of terms and conditions in the sale documentation (corporate lawyer and/or taxation specialist).

11. The completion meeting to sign the documentation and complete the sale (sales agent, corporate lawyer, you and the buyer).

What Type of Sale Do You Want?

We have already identified your reasons for selling, and you should already know your life plan after the sale has been finalised. Now you need to decide exactly what type of deal you want.

Many purchasers will offer to purchase a controlling stake in your business and a formula to purchase the remainder once they've taken control and understand the business more thoroughly. Usually this 'deferred' approach is a way for the buyer to minimise their risk.

If you want out, my advice would be to get out and sell 100 percent of your business. I certainly wish we had done that.

There are too many unknowns within a staggered exit. You don't know what the new buyer will do to the business and you will not have a huge amount of control over that. They could change things that you feel were instrumental to your success and then not like the results. Your staff may react unfavourably to the new owners which could knock productivity and morale – you have no control over these outcomes and yet are liable for them in some way as the final transfer of the business will usually be dependent on a smooth transition.

How Much is your Business Worth?

Obviously, you will want your business to be valued for as much as possible. This is natural but it also means that you are likely to be a little biased. The value of your business is the price that someone is prepared to pay for it in an open market.

Therefore the sales process itself often comes down to a clash of opinions over what your business is worth. The more detail and evidence that you can provide to back up your valuation the more likely you are to negotiate a price that you are happy with. That final figure will also depend on the type of buyer and their motivation.

A buyer is looking at the potential future profit of the business to decide what they are willing to pay to secure that profit. As a result, they will value your business based on their own strategy. They will look at how they can make changes and savings that will justify paying the asking price or use their findings to seek to alter that price.

You as the seller may look at the valuation differently. One option is to simply choose a price you are willing to sell your business for. This figure may represent a price that you feel compensates you for the years of blood, sweat and tears to build the business, or it may be the amount you have calculated you will need to retire comfortably or pursue your next adventure. You may even be able to justify your price with a simple valuation working back to the figure you want. As an approach, this may work if you are not totally committed to the sale or have time to wait until you find a buyer willing to pay your asking price. However, your asking price may be unrealistic and never achievable.

There needs to be some process and verifiable rigour to the valuation process so that you can back up the figure and also ensure you get the maximum for your business. Besides, a prospective buyer doesn't care how much effort you've put in or what you need to move on to the next stage of your life. All they care about is securing a good business with solid future potential for a good price.

It's also worth bearing in mind that your buyer is going to conduct their own valuation via the due diligence process so if their valuation is significantly different from yours then it just throws up concern and suspicion around what else you've said about the business. It's therefore important that the valuation is realistic and backed up by accurate, objective analysis.

Comparison with a Similar Company
You may be able to see what the market is prepared to pay for a business like yours if you can find a similar recent sale. Of course, what constitutes a 'similar company' is open to a fair amount of debate. Private companies tend to keep their cards close to their chest so the information you may need to establish similarity may not be in the public domain, making the comparison almost impossible. You may be able

to get top line figures such as turnover, net profit and staff numbers but you won't be able to see the details or anomalies that make the real difference.

Although it may be easier to make a comparison to a publicly listed company as there will be more information available, the fact that you are comparing a private company to a public one is also fraught with problems and may give an inaccurate valuation.

Your sales agent or advisors may be able to help with a comparison valuation for similar businesses that they have sold.

There are often two accepted ways to value your business:

1. Net Asset Value (break up)
2. Going Concern (capitalisation of future income)

Net Asset Value
Your balance sheet will provide a crude net asset valuation – the value of the assets in the business minus the liabilities.

However, this approach can be misleading. Plant, machinery or equipment could be over or under valued. Assets such as computers or software may appear as assets but may be almost worthless. Stock and work in progress may be deliberately undervalued to reduce a tax liability etc. (Although if you've done your pre-sale work as suggested you won't have made this error – remember in the few years before you decide to sell you should do everything you can to *increase* profit, not minimise it for tax purposes).

Net asset value will only be useful if all classes of assets and liabilities are corrected to give a realistic picture of the value in the business. Even still, this approach is rarely used for a thriving trading company with steady profit.

Capitalisation of Future income
Due to the limitations of the previous two methods, this is the most common way of valuing a private company. Also known as the 'discounted cash flow model' or 'Return on Investment'.

You will need the trading history of your business going back at least three years. Profits generated over that period are then projected forward to create a forecast of future profits, corrected for inflation, the cost of money and the risk of the investment. A ratio is used to convert annual profit to a value for the business. It is almost impossible to determine a 'typical' ratio for the valuation as there are so many variables and types of businesses. In the construction/utility industry where my business traded, an indicative multiplier could be between four and nine times the annual profit after tax. Obviously, there is a huge difference in value whether the ratio is four or whether it is nine but the ratio used will depend on the industry standard, state of the market, general economic outlook and other variables within the business.

The valuation is always going to be open to discussion. But it's important to arrive at a valuation up-front that you can explain and clearly justify. As mentioned, if a buyer's valuation and a seller's valuation are too far apart it is likely to raise red flags for the buyer.

Preparing Sales Particulars

There are many strategies that you could employ to let the world know that your business is for sale. One obvious way is to advertise the business in the relevant trade publications or online platforms, and then wait for offers of interest to come in. This is probably not advisable because you don't want to tell the world you are selling your business, you only want to tell the right people that your business is for sale. Even if you don't state the name of the business in the advert, you will have to disclose the industry and some vital statistics to tempt a would-be buyer and that may be enough for your competitors, customers, suppliers and staff to figure out that it's your business that's up for sale.

When you use a selling agent, they will advise on the best approach which will almost certainly not include shotgun advertising. They will usually recommend the preparation of 'sales particulars' which gives a high-level description of your company without naming the business or giving away too much information. This 'teaser' document is usually a cut down one to two-page version of the 'Information Memorandum' or 'Offering Memorandum' (more on that in a moment).

The teaser document will detail your business's strengths and unique selling points so as to attract interest but not give away too much information to other potentially interested stakeholders such as competitors. Your sales agent will be adept at creating this document to achieve the twin objectives of attracting interest while maintaining as much anonymity as possible.

The idea is that the initial sales particular should generate interest. Once potential buyers have signed a confidentiality agreement or non-disclosure agreement (NDA) and demonstrated their seriousness and ability to purchase the business they can get access to the more detailed particulars or Information Memorandum.

Identifying Potential Buyers

When it comes to buyers there are strategic buyers and financial buyers. The strategic buyers are those who can see a strategic benefit from acquiring your business, often over and above the business itself. Strategic buyers are therefore often your competitors or even suppliers who are looking to get involved in more of the supply chain. As such, you may already know of potential strategic buyers. The upside of this type of sale is that they will see additional value that a financial buyer will not realise and may pay more for the opportunity. Your business may allow them entry into a new market or they may benefit from economies of scale.

You may also know some financial buyers – those people simply interested in buying a business to make regular future profits. You could therefore use your existing network of contacts to sniff out a financial buyer and invite your contacts to forward the teaser sales particulars to their own contacts. The upside of this approach is that if your efforts to find a buyer yield fruit and you employed a sale agent there will usually be a clause in the contract that reduces the final fee.

The advised method for finding a buyer is to rely on your sales agent. They will create various shortlists using:

- Their own network and their networks network. These people may include accountants, lawyers, bankers, venture capitalists and other brokers.
- Their database of qualified potential buyers.
- Memberships in subscription-based deal groups and websites.

Agents may also advertise online or at industry events, or even use direct mail to identify people who may be suitable to contact with the initial sales documentation. This is where your agent's experience is invaluable as they may know of people who are actively looking for a business just like yours. That said, you should always scrutinise who your agent is sending the particulars to before they are sent to make sure you are happy with the selection and their list doesn't include people you already know.

By creating a few shortlists, you can choose to contact certain potential buyers when you wish and leave the more delicate, strategic contacts until the very last minute, therefore reducing the risk to your business.

Confidentiality Agreement

A Confidentiality Agreement, or 'Non-Disclosure Agreement' (NDA) will be used to protect your confidentiality as you share potentially sensitive information with a potential buyer.

The detailed information about your business will not be sent to just anyone who wants it. Your agent will perform a buyer vetting process which will require the potential buyer to give you more information about them and their suitability and financial capability to buy your business. The NDA therefore protects both parties and ensures that information disclosed goes no further regardless of whether the sale with that buyer progresses or not.

This is a legally binding document that stipulates what the prospective buyer and seller is agreeing to abide by in exchange for more information from both sides. By signing, both parties accept those conditions of confidentiality. Obviously, this includes keeping the information confidential and may also include undertakings that the potential buyers cannot poach your staff etc.

This document is essential because it provides legal protection. Although it is notoriously difficult to enforce an NDA in practice, the act of signing a legal document does tend to separate the serious contenders from the nosey or curious. You should however always be cautious with who you provide information to because whilst an NDA is enforceable, it is not very easy to prove that a certain party has breached the agreement.

Detailed Business Profile or Memorandum

Once signed and returned, your agent will provide more detailed information about your business to the prospective buyers.

This memorandum is the first official document that is drawn up when your business is being sold. You will be required to work with your agent to provide the information they need to create the memorandum and you must also double check the resulting document is accurate. The information or offering memorandum will usually contain:

- A short history of the business for sale – founders and key steps in the growth.
- How it differs from its competitors.
- Ownership structure and why the owner is selling.
- Where the business is located geographically.
- Physical assets – number of bases etc.
- Number of staff and types of employment contracts.
- Organisation chart.
- What product or service you provide and to what market.
- Market share.
- Sales.
- A top line indication of the financial health of the business including turnover, profit, assets, liabilities and profit forecast. This will usually be the most detailed part of the document.
- Future opportunities.
- Customers' information.
- Supply chain details.

It is easy to see why a confidentiality agreement is so important. The amount of detail supplied at this stage would only normally be available to trusted advisors or senior management. It is, however, necessary to share this information so that the potential buyer can better assess the offering and hopefully move the sale forward. It can feel a little uncomfortable but it's a necessary step for selling your business.

Negotiating with and Eliminating Potential Buyers
Once the potential buyer has enough information they will either start eliminating themselves or you will get down to discussions and negotiations.

The basics of good negotiation are simple: know your strengths and play to them while seeking to mitigate your vulnerabilities.

Be polite but firm and don't be afraid to walk away from a deal - although you should never threaten to end talks in an effort to get your way. That's blackmail and also a little childish. Honest dialogue is always the best policy, as you need the other party to trust you.

Never reveal your negotiating position - i.e. what you actually want to achieve at the end of the process. Put simply: be cool. You do not want to appear overly enthusiastic, or even desperate during the negotiation period. It's during the negotiations that the sales agent can really come into their own. You won't even need to be involved for most of it but they will know your position and seek to realise your objective.

The real key to successful deal-making, however, is to understand your buyer's wants and needs. What features of your business do they like? What are their own business's priorities and how will your company help them achieve those? What are their alternatives in the current marketplace? Try to work out their negotiating position and what sort of deal they would like to see. If the sale is a strategic sale, you may be able to guess or anticipate the value your business will bring to their business.

Your mission, in a nutshell, will be to find out (and hopefully inflate) the maximum the buyer is prepared to pay for your company, while deciding whether you are ready to make all the commitments and concessions the sale will be contingent on. If the buyer's terms are too stringent, you should decide what sort of figure you will accept for a more complete break from your company. For example, they may be prepared to offer more if you stay on in the business for two years. Is that something you would consider? Or, would you prefer a smaller amount and a clean, immediate break?

Which areas of your sale terms are open to negotiation, and identify what sort of concessions you might make - without admitting that you will ever make any such move. This is about knowing your own 'red lines' and scenarios or situations you can live with and those you can't. It might also be worth asking your buyer which areas they are particularly concerned about and focusing on those before you discuss price or technicalities.

Be aware, however, of a number of common negotiating tactics that the other party might use - and which you could use yourself.

If you find yourself in a tricky negotiation position, ask for more time to discuss the matter with your adviser, lawyers or partner. On the other hand, if you feel you are close to securing a deal, it is entirely possible to invent a deadline in an attempt to force closure.

Remember your priorities. Don't try to win every battle, focus on what is genuinely important to you and give a little on the other issues so that you both feel as though you have got the deal you want. Always aim for win/win. That said, don't concede on your main points and don't cross your 'red lines' – you will almost certainly regret it later. And perhaps most important of all, don't get trapped into justifying your basic negotiating position. It's your business, you can decide to sell it or not and if the buyer doesn't like the deal they are perfectly within their rights to walk away too. Your flexibility will almost always come down to how committed you are to selling and how fast you want to close the deal. Even if you are desperate to sell as soon as humanly possible – the buyer can never know that!

Agreeing Heads of Terms

The beginning of the actual sale is the finalisation of a 'heads of terms' agreement, also known as a 'letter of intent' or 'heads of agreement'. Although this is not a legally binding document it is best to have this document drawn up professionally by your advisors and lawyer as it sets out the details of the sale, including what will be paid and when, what assets the company has, the contractual obligations already in place, other liabilities, employment contracts, and precisely what the buyer will be purchasing.

Although either party can pull out at any point, there are parts of the heads of terms that are legally binding once the document is signed. For example, you might agree a period of exclusivity where you agree not to negotiate with any other prospective buyer for a period of three to six months and end all existing negotiations with other interested parties. This allows the buyer time to conduct their due diligence and prepare the detailed contract for sale without the risk of being beaten to the prize by another party. The investigations and due diligence process does cost the prospective buyer money so this is a fair enough request.

Some heads of terms force the buyer or seller to pay legal fees if they back out although this is not always the case. It should be viewed as a preliminary document only as it may undergo many changes before it becomes the detailed contract for sale drafted by your lawyer.

Most contracts for sale are large intimidating documents only interpretable by a qualified lawyer, most of which will be technical formalities related to acts of parliament governing tax and company matters. However, you should still read through the document and ask your solicitor to explain every clause you do not understand.

It is possibly the most significant document you will ever sign, and there are a number of areas you should be particularly aware of such as your tax position post sale, any on-going liabilities and when and how the money will be paid to you.

This is an exciting time. It can feel as though the finish line is in sight. All that extra work and stress might start to feel worth it.

I remember this stage in our sale. I was emailed the offer which was based on a multiple of our latest Profit After Tax. For confidentiality reasons I am unable to state the deal numbers but we were offered above the average multiple. When I put that into my calculator, I was trying hard not to get over excited! We had accepted the offer in principle and it all started to feel very real.

Step Ten

Getting the Deal Done

So, the champagne is on ice, you've agreed a 'heads of terms', and you know how much you're getting for your business. That's it, deal done, right? Sadly, no – far from it. This is when the hard work really begins and when the pressure can start to build.

This is when the cavalry arrives to scrutinise you, your business partners and your business. Once you have agreed in principle the deal to sell your business, a team of advisors acting on behalf of the prospective buyer will descend on your business to verify everything you have told them and seek to identify anything that the buyer needs to know, that may not have been disclosed prior to finalising the sale.

At this stage, your corporate lawyers will get more heavily involved. If your deal is big or you have a few hundred employees then be prepared to meet or speak to many other solicitors in the firm who specialise in particular areas of law.

Engaging corporate lawyers is essential as they can save you a huge amount of money and prevent you from getting into legal hot water, but that service doesn't come cheap. If you are not totally committed to selling your company then now is the time to say so. Once this work has started you will need to pay their fees whether the sale is finalised or not. *Only* get the corporate lawyers involved when you are absolutely sure you want to sell your business.

Due Diligence

So far, the prospective buyer only knows what you have wanted to share about your business. Even after signing the confidentiality agreement to access more detail, they are still taking your word that your business is as it is presented. Once the 'heads of terms' agreement is signed, they have a timeframe to conduct their own investigations into your business to thoroughly check all the information on which they have based their offer. Due Diligence is this in-depth process of allowing the buyer to investigate your business before buying.

We looked at due diligence briefly in step two. Knowing this process is going to happen when you sell your business is extremely useful ahead of time because you can essentially set up and manage your business from that perspective. Conducting mini due diligence procedures on your own business each year means you are knowledgeable in all areas of the business and can identify and deal with any risks before they occur. That way, your prospective buyer is much less likely to find anything unexpected because you will already have found it and dealt with it.

From the buyer's perspective, due diligence simply allows them to verify the fundamentals of the business, identify any potential risks that may impact their ability to realise the future profit potential, and assure themselves that the business is indeed run well. As well as scanning the horizon for any future risks they will look back at your past performance, how the business faired in challenging markets or economic conditions.

If you have not done your own due diligence this process can be extremely stressful because you will be expected to provide, 'full and fair disclosure'. If you don't know what the buyer's advisory team will find it can be tense.

Never try to hide something from a buyer. Full disclosure is always the safest option. Besides, if you do try to hide something and your buyer finds it, that omission, whether deliberate or not, will diminish the trust between you and will almost certainly be used to reduce the price. Or worse, they could come after you for compensation after the sale has been finalised.

Documentation of Disclosure

As your prospective buyer conducts their due diligence process they will send all their requests for information, answers and clarifications to your lawyer. This is extremely important because you need to provide that information and your lawyer needs to document those responses so there is a written record of disclosure. Say for example, you told your prospective buyer that your premises are on a flood plain and are therefore at risk of flooding although it's not happened for over twenty years. That must be documented otherwise, if there is a flood on the premises years later, the new owner could sue you for damages because it was not disclosed at the time of sale. It needs to be disclosed in writing, and, once it is, there is no come back should the premise flood in the future.

If things are found during due diligence then it could significantly reduce the value of the deal and the price you will eventually receive from the sale. It may be that you think you've already spent a lot of money on the process so far, so may as well accept the lower price, but it is wise to sit back and re-assess if this is really what you are happy with. You may be better to re-focus on your business, clear up any of the issues that stalled the sale this time, and try again later.

It's worth preparing yourself for the full extent of the due diligence process. The 'due diligence request' from your buyer's legal team is likely to extend to 25 pages and contain questions and request for paperwork and supporting documentation to explain over 150 different aspects of the business – and that's for a modest sized company. Few of these questions can be answered with a straightforward 'yes' or 'no'. Most will require several pages of explanation and evidence. Nothing you've experienced in your business career is likely to prepare you for the barrage of requests and questions you will face – all while you are still trying to run your business.

I remember this stage very clearly – there were more than a few times where I really questioned if it was worth it. I remember speaking to a lawyer to explain our pension situation and another regarding tax. Often, I didn't really fully understand the questions they were asking, never mind their answers. But it all had to be gathered and passed on to the lawyer for documentation.

Also for your own sanity and protection – keep a copy of everything you provide your lawyer and all the documents that go to the buyer's team, together with when they were sent. Originals of the various documents must stay in their normal place in the business so your people are not then looking for documents that you have removed for the selling process. That can be really frustrating for the people who are still busy running the business.

Legal Documents / Process

There are several key legal documents that will be drafted. We've talked about several of these already but for ease they are:

- **Heads of terms:** A skeletal outline which is agreed by the buyer and seller, setting out the main points of the deal, 'subject to contract'. Also known as a letter of intent or heads of agreement.
- **Confidentiality agreement:** Ensures shared documents and information are treated confidentially by both parties.
- **Sales contract:** Comprehensively outlines all of the terms upon which the sale will take place.
- **Disclosure letter:** This can be used to clarify details in the warranties or indemnities that may not be fully accurate so as to seek to limit your liabilities and the time the warranties and indemnities apply.
- **Tax deed:** This requires you, as the seller, to indemnify the buyer for any pre-completion tax liabilities which do not arise in the ordinary course of business or which have not been disclosed in the accounts.
- **Third-party consents:** The seller needs to check whether any specific third-party

consents are required in relation to any material contracts. For example, agreements with key customers or suppliers.

When your accountant prepares your adjusted financial statements, and the buyer's auditors review them, you MUST make sure all the financial elements are correct. This is the whole basis of how your financial reward, known as the Consideration, is based.

Data Room

A Due Diligence Data Room is the place where your agent or professional advisors place copies of the financial, legal and business documents that define the history and future of the company for prospective investors to review prior to submitting a formal offer. It is normally a virtual data room held on a secure folder with online access.

A due diligence data room is accessed by potential buyers after being approved by the seller and after having signed a Non-Disclosure Agreement (NDA). Your advisor is responsible for identifying viable buyers/ investors, securing signed NDAs and scheduling access to the due diligence data room information.

Keep your Focus on the Business

Needless to say, selling your business can be a major distraction and consume huge amounts of time, especially when the due diligence process gets underway.

While it's important to give full access to the buyer and that will mean visiting the premises to see how the business is run, it doesn't mean they can just pop by wherever they fancy. These visits need to be scheduled so that the business is allowed to function without too much interruption. Plus, too many visiting strangers can be off-putting and unnerving for staff as they wonder who they are and what's going on. It is wise to create a plausible cover story to explain the strangers.

You may be tempted to feel that honesty is the best policy and that it would be better to be up-front and honest with your people about your intentions to sell... well I don't think it's advisable. The reason is simple, until the contract is signed, there is no sale. Telling staff that you are going to sell and then finding that the sale falls through is not good for business. As soon as people know about a sale or potential sale human nature kicks in and they immediately worry about their future. This will almost certainly affect morale and performance and may even lead to key people finding new positions. Plus, you can't assure your people about their jobs because you don't know what the new owner will do so it's really best for everyone - including your staff - if you keep it to yourself for as long as possible.

While you may have to involve certain senior staff members of your intention it is always better to keep the circle of people who know as small as possible to limit the possibility of a leak. The last thing you want is rumour and gossip. In the absence of information most of us will fill in the blanks with negative assumptions and fear.

As much as you can, keep the business operating as normal. Don't change your routine or your behaviour. It may also be wise to switch your correspondence to your mobile phone or home email to help prevent leaks. This also allows you to vent your stress around the process away from your employees.

Remember this is your business until the second it's not so keep your focus on the business and make sure that you continue to do everything that made you a success in the first place. Don't take your eye off the ball.

Share Sale and Purchase Agreement

In step eight we looked at the two different types of sale – an asset sale and a share sale. The best option for you, unless you are winding up your business and seeking to sell off the assets rather than selling the business as a going concern, is a share sale.

A share sale is when you sell your shares in your company and the buyer takes on the ownership of that business including all the assets and all the liabilities. In a share sale, you sell and you are out of the business.

You have no claim on future profit and no liabilities for future debt or problems. Of course, in practice it's rarely a clean break, with the buyer insisting on warranties and indemnities to minimise their risk for months and years after you leave.

This is why the buyer's solicitors will normally prepare the share sale and purchase agreement. This agreement will contain the warranties and indemnities intended to benefit and protect the buyer. It is a document that will be created by the buyer's lawyer and then thoroughly checked and argued against by your lawyer!

This is the main document that will be used to cover the deal and the lawyers will work on this and continuously modify it to confirm what has been agreed between the parties. In an ideal world, this agreement would not be drafted until after the due diligence is complete for obvious reasons. There is no point creating the agreement until the buyer is sure they want to buy. But, in reality the complexity of the agreements together with a limited time to conduct the due diligence means that they often run side by side.

A typical share sale and purchase agreement will include the following:

- Definitions and interpretations
- Agreement of sale
- Warranties

- Disclosure letter
- Seller's protection
- Tax indemnities
- Indemnities
- Restrictive covenants
- Completion accounts
- Schedules

Definition and Interpretations

Sets out who the contract is between including statutory details of the business being sold and the amount being paid. This is the headline deal. It will also include a glossary of terms and key words together with a precise definition of their meaning in the context of the agreement.

Agreement of sale

Details how the business will be sold. In your case, as explained, it will almost certainly be a share sale. As a result, it will detail when the shares will pass to the buyer along with ownership.

Warranties

Warranties are statements about the promises you as the seller are making to the buyer as part of the sale agreement. They are actionable and allow the buyer to make a claim for damages if the promises or warrants turn out to be false. They are usually based on information gathered during the due diligence exercise. Warranties are then included in the sales agreement so provide assurances of the accuracy and validity of that information, while also protecting the buyer should the business turn out to be different from the one represented to them by the seller or through the due diligence process. It is a way for the buyer to ensure that they are buying what they think they are buying.

It is not uncommon for warranties to run to tens of pages in the agreement. The seller is seeking to mitigate their risk as broadly and completely as possible and for as long as possible after sale while the seller is seeking to terminate all their obligations as fast as possible after sale.

As a result, there is often a great deal of negotiation and back-and-forth on warranties. Some are reasonable, many are not. And it's your lawyers job to resist giving unreasonable warranties and limit the scope of a warranty statement as much as possible.

I have heard of a situation where the partner of a seller (who he undoubtedly trusted) had hidden things and therefore it caused major problems after the deal was done. Due to warranties that were given by all the partners, all partners were affected by a large counter claim from the buyer due to financial mismanagement by one person. Make sure you know everything about your business before agreeing to the warranties and pay particular attention to the wording – get your lawyer to explain the ramifications of each one.

Warranties are not about guaranteeing future performance they are about guaranteeing past performance and the information that was provided on which the sale was based. This is why knowing your business inside out and conducting your own due diligence regularly is so useful in the sale process. When you know all there is to know about your own business the warranties should not pose an issue for you or your buyer.

Disclosure Letter

You as the seller should prepare a 'disclosure letter' in regard to the warranties. This is where you can set the record straight or provide greater clarification about what is stated in the warranties. Say, for example, a major client has been with you for ten years and you have assured your buyer that they will remain with the business for at least two years. A conversation between you and the client makes you question their long-term plans but you do get them to commit to one year. You would need to prepare a disclosure letter to this effect, especially if the warranty states that this client will stay with the new ownership for two years. If they leave the new owner after one year and you didn't disclose their new position in the disclosure letter you could be sued for lost earnings and/or damages.

Your buyer will be looking to ensure you don't make overly general 'blanket' disclosures that nullify some of the warranties. You will usually be asked to provide specific disclosures to specific warranties.

Seller's Protection

As the seller, you will normally seek to include clauses to limit your liability both in the amount of your potential liability and the time during which you remain exposed to a breach of warranty claim.

The wordings of these clauses are extremely important and your lawyer will be invaluable in protecting you (as will the buyer's) but also in seeking consensus around what is reasonable and fair from both parties.

Tax Indemnity

The tax indemnity is a separate document that states that the tax liabilities of the company have been dealt with correctly and have been properly provided for in the company's statutory accounts.

It will also state that should there be any future tax obligation relating to when the seller owned the company the seller remains liable for those costs.

Indemnities

If the due diligence flushes out a prohibitive problem, the buyer may seek a specific indemnity against that problem arising in the future. An indemnity is much more powerful than a simple warranty because they promise to make good losses to the buyer if a specific event occurs.

As the seller, you would be looking to limit both warranties and indemnities but especially the latter.

Restrictive Covenants

Restrictive covenants are very common in sales contracts and prevent you, as the seller of the business, from competing with the buyer for a limited period.

This is a complex area of law and can be difficult to enforce – especially if they are too broad and too vague. Again, this is required to limit the sellers risk, they don't want you selling your business to them, then setting up in competition weeks later and poaching all your old clients back. Fair enough.

Completion Accounts

When the share sale is finalised, the Completion Accounts will be prepared to ensure that the financial position of the company on completion is the same as that which was agreed at the outset.

If the balance sheet of the Completion Accounts shows the net asset position of the company to be better than that which was agreed, the purchase price will be adjusted upwards and the buyer will pay the additional sum. If, however, the position has worsened then the difference will be refunded to the buyer. Both payments will usually take place shortly after Completion Accounts have been agreed.

Schedules

Depending on the complexity of the transaction, there will be various schedules attached to the main sale agreement covering things like earn-outs and post-completion adjustments. The contract may involve you being kept on in the business for a period of time to smooth the transition. Provisions relating to the transfer of a pension fund will also be included in the schedules.

Final Negotiations

Your negotiation tactics should be the same all the way along. In that you should know what you are seeking to achieve and you should be very clear on where your wiggle room is and what your deal breaker 'red lines' are. This clarity will make negotiation easier. You'll have already set your goal and are clear on your personal vision and what you want in life. Make sure that you have your number in mind. Decide on a figure and as I've said before, be prepared to walk away if you have to. This may sound harsh but social science has proven that we feel mental torment over things we get rid of or lose far more than the joy of accumulation. It's a human quirk known as 'loss aversion'.

Say, I offered you the chance to place a bet on the toss of a coin. The deal is if the coin lands on tails you pay me £100 but if it's heads I pay you £150. Would you take the bet? Most people wouldn't because the fear of losing £100 they already have is far greater and more powerful than the hope of gaining £150 they don't have. Behavioural scientists have concluded that "losses loom larger than gains".

If you don't get the price you wanted for your business – it will haunt you. Make sure that price is realistic and based on solid evidence and then push for that price. If this buyer isn't prepared to pay, maybe the next one will. Of course, you also have to account for the time, effort and financial cost of going through the sales process again and weigh up your options.

Depending on the nature of the seller, and the tenacity of their advisors, some buyers will propose the initial purchase price, but then use the due diligence findings, or legal concessions to drive the price down from there. This is especially relevant if you show that you are desperate to sell. Show them, even if you need to bluff a little, that you don't need this sale and that you will walk away from the deal if you have to.

Completion Meeting
This is the moment you've been waiting for.

It's time to complete the sale and sign the documents. Unlike many of the previous meetings which will have been held on neutral ground, this meeting is usually held at the buyer's lawyer's offices. Everyone is in attendance, you as the seller, the buyers and a small army of lawyers and advisors.

Being in the lawyer's office also means that any last-minute changes can be made on the spot and the deal can be finalised.

This final completion meeting can be confusing. It's likely to be the only completion meeting you will be involved in so knowing what to expect is helpful. It also means that you can help prevent a foul up just as you can almost touch the exit sign.

Get your paperwork ready
Although your lawyer will handle the meeting and guide you to get involved when you need to sign something, it's always better to be prepared yourself too.

Although the buyer's team will be coordinating most of the documents there are some you need to bring too. Ask your lawyer in advance for an itemised list of all the documents and items you need to bring to the meeting.

Examples may include:

- Share transfer forms, completed and signed.
- The certificate of incorporation of the company.

- The statutory book for the company.
- Company seal.
- Title deeds relating to properties owned by the company.
- Chequebooks, paying in books and credit cards owned by the company – it's unlikely the new owner will want you living it up with your company credit card!
- Bank certificates confirming closing balances of accounts.
- A letter from the bank releasing the company from all guarantees and charges.
- A letter of resignation from your company's auditor.
- A deed releasing the company from any claim from the seller.

Before the meeting starts, the buyer will sit down with their team and go through everything one last time. You should do the same.

The night before we signed the documents, we were in our lawyer's office until 3am reviewing everything and then back in the office at 9am to conclude the deal. It can be tempting not to do this because you will already have read this document what feels like a thousand times. Just do it.

As your lawyer guides you though the meeting and the huge pile of paperwork moves steadily from one side of the table to the other after all relevant parties have signed it, everyone in the room will start to grin as they see the finish line.

After months of hard work, stress and pulling your hair out with the tsunami of questions thrown at you during the due diligence it's time to celebrate.

It really is a special feeling knowing that all that effort has paid off and you are about to reap the reward for starting and building a great company. Ironically it can also be quite sad and emotional – shaking hands with the new owner can feel odd. They own your company now, there is no going back. The sadness, I think, comes from a recognition that the sale represents the end of an era, the closing of a very important chapter in your life.

But it's not just about paperwork…

Receiving your Money

As the champagne is flowing and the celebrations get under way it's often easy to miss the crucial matter of money.

Your buyer almost certainly didn't turn up with suitcases of cash and they won't hand over a cheque, these days the money will have been transferred to their lawyer's account prior to the completion meeting. It will sit in the lawyer's account as cleared funds ready to transfer to you once the deal has been completed.

Depending on the time of the completion meeting, it may be possible to transfer the money in the meeting. If not, the buyer's lawyer will hand your lawyer a letter confirming that they have their client's money on deposit and giving an undertaking to transfer the agreed funds to your account as soon as the banks are open for business. Although with online banking there should really be no delay in the money transfer.

Again, once the money arrives it can be quite surreal. I still remember looking at my bank account and seeing the money sitting there. It was more money than I'd ever seen in my life and it was in my account for me to do whatever I wanted with.

Step Eleven

You're Not 'The' Man Anymore

The first day you wake up after selling your business may be a little foggy after all the celebrating! But this is it. You've sold! You're a millionaire! You're Successful? Right?

Today is the first day of the rest of your life. It's time to actually implement those dreams and live the destiny you designed, the purpose you created the business to deliver.

But, hold on… There are still a few things to wrap up before you sail off into the sunset.

Finalising the Completion Accounts
Once the deal is done, the Completion Accounts need to be finalised as the last process of the sale. Essentially you and the buyer will have agreed a price for your business many months earlier. An initial price is usually indicated in the Heads of Terms document

prior to the due diligence process. That figure may change after due diligence but it will be based on an assessment of the current value of the business that you and the buyer agree on.

But things change, markets change and the economy can change which means that there may be a difference in value once the deal is finalised. The Completion Accounts therefore present a final value for the business on the day of sale.

If the Completion Accounts show the value to be higher than the figure agreed then the buyer must make up the difference and pay an additional fee in line with the Completion Accounts. Conversely if the Completion Accounts indicate that the business is worth less than it was when the price was agreed then you will have to refund the buyer with the appropriate amount.

Both payments will usually take place shortly after Completion Accounts have been agreed. As a result, the monies may stay with your buyer's lawyer for a few days after the completion meeting so that this final reckoning of final accounts can be completed.

If you have been running your company tightly the way we discussed earlier in the book, and have been on top of your numbers right through the process as you should be, then you will probably be aware if there is going to be an issue or not. This is also another reason why you should never take your eye off the ball when selling your business – you want the business to be as strong and profitable as it can be on the day of sale so as to maximise your earnings. Although you won't be able to do anything about inflation rates or market trends, you do still have control over your business and how it functions right up until the moment you sign those papers - make it count.

Announcements

Assuming you have managed to keep the sale of the business secret, it's now time to communicate the news to your people. You may not be the owner, but you are now wealthy because of the combined efforts of a lot of employees who have worked for you, perhaps over many years You owe it to them to explain the sale and encourage them to see the opportunities that the change of ownership will bring for them. If you have built your business properly then you value your people and you will care what happens to them after you've left. Therefore, you should have already agreed a suitable communication strategy that you can feel good about when your people hear this news.

How employees and the media will be told of the sale will be included in the purchase agreement. In most cases the new owner will want to control how and when announcements are made. Of course, employees will need to be informed sensitively and it's very likely that the new owner will ask you to be involved in that announcement so that you can introduce the new owner and assure everyone that they are valued and have nothing to fear (assuming that's true).

Unless the new owner plans to consolidate, the more they can share about their plans the better – this will help to reassure people that it is 'business as usual'.

This can be a strange meeting because it will be the first time that you are not 'the' man (or woman) with your employees. They will have been used to you being the boss, maybe for decades, and now someone else is standing in front of them saying that they are the new owners. Remember, that person is the new owner and you are now playing a minor, supporting role in the handover of your business.

Consultancy or Earn-Out Agreements

Depending on the deal you agreed, you may be exiting stage right and leaving the business completely as soon as the announcement to staff has been made or you may need to stick around for a while to help with the transition.

Needless to say, if you are staying on even for an extra three to six months, it is absolutely critical that the announcements go well as you will need to maintain a good working relationship with your people to ensure that the transition is as smooth as possible. If they feel betrayed by your actions then the earn-out period could be really challenging.

However, even if you are staying on, there are going to be big changes. You are not the boss anymore.

The staff have a new person to impress and it's not you! This is totally normal and totally understandable. They are more concerned about their salary and career. Any friendship you thought you had will now be secondary to their necessity to keep their job and impress their new boss. Life goes on.

One moment you are the boss and you are the one people ask when they need decisions, and the next you have to defer to someone else for those decisions. This can be challenging. Be sure to remind those people that you are no longer in charge and they need to ask the new owner. Again, this can be tough because your immediate instinct will be to do what you have always done and jump into answer/decision mode.

What Now?
If the deal you struck means that you sign the papers, make the announcement, check the money is in the bank and disappear this can often feel like a better option but it also has its challenges.

The initial high from achieving such a long-held goal and making a life changing amount of money will last for a while – if you are lucky you might get a few months of euphoria before the internal questions start to creep in. Before long, you won't be able to fill the space created by the sale with long lies, late lunches

227

and lazy holidays abroad, or relaxing time catching up on some good books. The space will gradually turn into 'the void' and you must be ready for this.

People who create, build and sell businesses, even if they only ever do it once, tend to be ambitious and driven. They set goals and they love the game of business. They love the challenges and the creativity of coming up with solutions. They love the interaction with people, even the arguments can seem fun – especially in hindsight. People like you and I don't 'do nothing' very well. We need a goal, we prefer a goal, and we need to know where we are going and why. It's just the way we are wired.

For years, all those needs were delivered by the business to provide this exact outcome and yet once it arrives it can be disconcerting and confusing. The ego inside is a tricky animal and the constant stimulation that you have been used to will need to be replaced by something else. And often we need a challenge and the adrenalin rush.

Then there's the issue of purpose and motivation. Without the constraints of money and responsibilities of your business, what will be your "reason to get up in the morning"? The freedom of being unanchored sounds great, but it comes with the potential of drift and a lack of motivation that can become debilitating, often leading to depression.

There are many famous examples of people being eclipsed by their own accomplishments. Buzz Aldrin was the second man on the moon – an astonishing and rare accomplishment by any standards. And yet he spent the rest of his life in the shadow of that achievement. What followed was 'the void' – in his case, alcoholism, failed marriages, a lost fortune and depression.

Aldrin's experiences, also shared by other astronauts, have meant that NASA now train their people differently, making sure that the goal includes what is to happen *after* the space travel.

But this type of situation doesn't just happen to astronauts. Entrepreneurs are also susceptible to 'the void' once all they have strived for is achieved and they are left on the other side of that achievement looking back. They may be rich and free and that may have been the goal all along, but the reality can feel strangely empty and hollow.

In 2014, 36-year-old Markus Persson sold his company Mojang AB, (the creator of Minecraft) to Microsoft for $2.5 billion. That is an obscene amount of money – the freedom that sort of money provides is almost unimaginable. No doubt there was partying and euphoria. But in a series of tweets only a year later Persson said "The problem with getting everything is you run out of reasons to keep trying, and human interaction becomes impossible due to imbalance". In another he posted "Hanging out in Ibiza with a bunch of friends and partying with famous people, able to do whatever I want, and I've never felt more isolated". Pointing to the 'imbalance' wealth can create, he shared that he'd met a girl who felt afraid of him and his lifestyle, and went with a normal person instead.

Post achievement depression is not rare – it's actually the norm. The joy created by the culmination of a long-held dream can and often does give way to isolation, a lack of purpose, and a sense of drift.

I was 38 when I sold my company and became a millionaire, and I thought that was me made for life. I thought I could retire, and I did for several years. But after the partying and travelling I hit low moods for a time and realised what I missed was the sense of purpose. A goal. Something to spend my life doing. Luckily I found it by getting involved in new businesses and mentoring entrepreneurs, but it took a while to pick myself up.

We all need a sense of purpose, and for some entrepreneurs this need is significant. That purpose was met by the business but without the business, especially if money is no longer a motivator and you have all you need, it can be hard to know what to do with the rest of your life.

Amongst the 'aw poor rich kid' comments in Persson's twitter feed, one person made a very useful observation - "Ibiza was demoralising because it's full of people who have resources but no purpose. You need the opposite".

We all need the opposite.

Too often we can be so focused on building and selling the business that like astronauts obsessed with going to space, we don't consider what we are going to do *after*. This is an easy mistake to make because when we don't have a lot of money or time we can mistakenly believe that more money and more time is the answer to any question we might have, and once we have that extra money and time the opportunities and options will be endless. But, it just doesn't work like that.

Of course, the problem with this advice is that no one believes it. I didn't. I was so focused on building and selling our business so I could have the freedom to travel whenever I wanted that I never considered anything else. I was sure that's what I wanted and couldn't wait to disappear to a new country.

And whilst that freedom has been everything I hoped it would be, on some level it's also been confusing, isolating and sometimes quite lonely and meaningless. That's the contradiction.

It took me years to really reassess what I wanted to do next and begin that reinvention process. I would suggest you take a little time before you exit to consider what that reinvention might look like. Where are you going to go? What are you going to do? Perhaps you

231

set up a charity trust or move into politics or buy into something that you are passionate about.

Whatever it is, you need to find something that captures your imagination again. Or at least start thinking about what that might be so that you can move in that direction once the holiday is over and it's time to get back into life.

Ideally create a game plan. The first three to six months – just do what you want, whenever you want and try all the things that you've always wanted to do.

That game plan might include:

- Getting your personal finances in order. Ideally, you want the money you make from the sale of your business to provide a comfortable income for the rest of your life. That requires planning otherwise you may spend it at an alarming rate. I did at first!
- Figure out some rules for how you are going to handle tricky situations. There may come a time when a friend or family member asks for money. Have you thought about how you might manage that? Will the knowledge that you are now wealthy create the imbalance that Persson talked about and create problems for you down the track? This is a common complaint for lottery winners who end up having to move

out of their community and away from their friends and family – just for some peace and quiet. Ironic, seeing as they had that peace and quiet before the lottery win!

- Is there anything you've always wanted to do - go back to university, do your PhD, learn a new language, do charity work or live in a different country for a while? This could be your time... make some plans that will keep you busy and engaged as you work out what you want to focus on next.

- Get curious. In life, we don't always have the time or energy to explore different things. We get set in our ways based on our upbringing and culture and we just do what we need to in order to earn a living, and try to squeeze life in between the gaps. When the gaps are our life we have time to stop and become curious about the world – enjoy that.

- Hiring a coach or mentor to help you figure out your next steps.

Embrace the changes. Don't shy away from the sale for fear that you will fall off some cliff of depression somewhere. Just be aware that the journey is not over – far from it.

You have a new, exciting life to discover.

Conclusion

Since selling my own business I have worked with people at various stages of the business building and selling process. By far the biggest challenge and often the most frequently left out step is beginning with the end in mind.

The vast majority of businesses are created by chance or opportunity and develop organically without any real sense of where the business owners are heading and, perhaps most importantly, why they are doing it.

Looking back, I think I was incredibly fortunate to find something I was passionate about – travelling. That passion and my innate drive for freedom came together into a perfect storm of purpose and drive that fuelled the business. But more than that, I honestly believe that by being clear on my end game created the opportunity to even start that business. Time and time again I've witnessed in my own life and other people's that clarity triggers the law of attraction and it's almost as if our dreams are so infused with energy, emotion and determination that they send a message to the universe which conspires to bring it about. Without that 'why', it can be extremely easy to drift.

Please don't skip the first step in your rush to get to the nuts and bolts of building and selling your business. Stop for a day or two and really contemplate your life. Who are you? What are your values? What do you want? Not what you think you want or what other people want you to want – what inspires *You*?

Trust me the middle bit is easy compared to the start and finish! Figuring out what really matters to you isn't something we are often told about in business books. Sure, there is plenty about vision and strategy and even the tactics of the execution but very little about the person.

I can't stress how crucial this is.

Thinking about what your life might be like after you sell is also worth some special consideration – especially as you get closer to the realisation of your goal. You may have the money and freedom you were always so sure you wanted, but the reality may be quite different. Be prepared for that. The key is to understand yourself and be true to yourself.

Making a huge amount of money and having the time to enjoy it is not success unless it is giving you what you truly and deeply want. Truly understanding your purpose in life and what will make you happy and content could be considered as 'success'. Getting to that position, or being that way, is part of life's journey. It will be a huge part of your business journey. It is a challenge. There are ups. There are downs. It could take many years but it will be worth it. And it will be fun. Setting your vision and goal and then finally achieving that goal is the objective, your end result. Building that company and successfully exiting is the accomplishment.

So, go out there and make things happen. Be positive. Be confident. Be compassionate. Be grateful. Grab the bull by the horns and start to make your dreams come true. It's your life and no-one else can live it for you. Don't take your greatness to the grave. Live your life so that when you are taking your last breath on this planet, you can look back and say to yourself *"I did it, I **Designed my Destiny**"*.

Acknowledgements

Dedicated to my parents, Margaret & Davie. I am proud that I made you proud.

To my Turkish rose.

Thank you to all friends and family (there are too many to mention) for your encouragement and confidence in me to get this project finished. Andy, you showed me the ropes at an early stage in my career and are still doing so now! Cheers.

My dream would never have been realised without the hard work, determination, support and commitment from all the staff and team at IQA. You were a joy to lead.

And the business would never have got to the level it did without my two business partners. Davie Mac – you are the best business partner that I could have ever hoped for. I miss Angela's sandwiches! Chris – instrumental to the growth and success. Whatever happened?

It took a wee while to get this book written and finalised, and I'd probably still be writing it now had I not had the assistance of a few people who I would like to acknowledge.

To Karen, the Word Architect, for taking my jumbled up stories and helping to put them into a coherent and readable format. You have been a joy to work with and I'll see you for the next book!

Captain Jon for offering his expert knowledge on business, and for some fantastic sailing, and of course the life changing chats on board.

And a special word to a lady who not only helped me to exit my business and always be on hand to keep me right, but who also was extremely helpful in getting this book finally out of my laptop and onto paper. Yolanda – you are a star!

There are so many people who have influenced my journey on a positive, and a not-so-positive but helpful way. Thank you to you all, I am very grateful that our paths met and lessons were learnt.

Peace and Good Vibes.

Printed in Great Britain
by Amazon

79914878R10139

The Sports Afield Book of Hunting and Shooting Records and Facts

The Sports Afield Book of Hunting and Shooting Records and Facts

Astonishing Accomplishments and Fascinating Facts from the World of Hunting and Shooting

by

Jens Erik Perto

with contributions by

Jens Ulrik Høgh

SAFARI PRESS INC.

Perto, Jens Erik

First edition

Safari Press

2015, Long Beach, California

ISBN 978-1-57157-421-3

Library of Congress Catalog Card Number: 2014945729

10 9 8 7 6 5 4 3 2 1

Printed in China

Readers wishing to see Safari Press's many fine books on big-game hunting, wingshooting, and sporting firearms should visit our Web site at www.safaripress.com.

Note from the authors: The illustrations in this book have been gathered from a large number of sources. Many of the pictures have been bought at auctions, from private collections, or from similar sources where it has not been possible to detect the name of the photographer or trace the source of the picture and, hereby, the holder of the copyright. We apologize if we have inadvertently failed to credit someone.

To Anne Mette, Sigrid, and Asger
for all your patience

Table of Contents

Denotes contribution by Jens U. Høgh.

Part 3—Big-Game Hunts and Hunters

Part 4—Rifles, Cartridges, and Shooting

Part 5—Birds and Small Game

Preface

The intent behind this work has not been to produce a systematic or complete list of certain events. The ambition has solely been to select and present some of the many facts and stories from the world of hunting and shooting which we found most interesting, surprising, grotesque, horrible, or amusing.

The primary goal of entertaining interested readers has also led us not to complicate the text with references to the hundreds of sources behind the facts. Likewise the list of literature used is by no means complete but contains only the most relevant, important, and more or less readily available sources.

One of the criteria for including facts and stories has been that you should be able to identify the person or persons behind the feats mentioned. During our research a few hunters known to the authors have not wanted any publicity around their hunting activities. As a consequence hereof an occasional feat has been omitted from the book although the bag actually surpasses the "record" mentioned.

Accordingly, it is important to keep in mind that we have not tried to make a "record book." All entries in this book are based upon written information or documented firsthand reports, but nevertheless some of these "records" may have been surpassed by another feat without our noticing.

For the sake of good order we must also emphasize that today many of the accomplishments mentioned will be considered unacceptable and condemned by any decent person, regardless of whether you are sympathetic to the concept of hunting or not. Just as it is impossible to undo past deeds, it is meaningless to conceal or judge the deeds of the past by the standards of today. Critics are asked to remember that we have only endeavored to describe the facts as they were reported, without necessarily having any sympathy with the deed or the person behind it.

Finally, we realize that the sensational aspects of some of the following stories have hardly been diminished by being retold over the years. However, all entries in this book originate from firsthand interviews or written sources and, apart from any of our own mistakes or misunderstandings during our research, all the information is, as far as we know, factual. Incredible but true!

Introduction

Compiling material for this book has been a long and time-consuming process, but it has also been very enjoyable, interesting, and instructive. It all began with the acquisition of a collection of old hunting photographs at an auction. Originally we intended to use a few of these photographs to illustrate historical articles on hunting we published in Scandinavia. However, we soon found we had collected so many interesting historical facts and incidents that we realized that we would have to publish them in a book in order to share them with a wider audience.

The vast majority of the accessible information on these highly specialized subjects originates from the British sphere of influence and this has inevitably had a great impact on the availability of entries. The American reader will probably wonder why there are comparatively few entries about North American game species. This is solely due to the lack of available information. The reasons for this originate in the differences between European and American hunting traditions.

History

In Europe, from the Middle Ages until the early decades of the nineteenth century, hunting was generally a pastime reserved for the royals, the nobility, and other members of the elite. Nearly all the arable and forested land of most European countries was divided into estates, and the game belonged to the landowners. This meant the introduction of severe legislation against poaching—often under the penalty of death for even minor offenses. By controlling almost all the land it was possible for the landowners to introduce game management in order to ensure huntable populations of animals.

Even today wildlife is a resource which the landowner can use as he sees fit, provided it is in accordance with the current hunting legislation. Generally speaking, there are few democratic aspects of hunting in Europe. For the sake of proper management, however, most countries have systems of allocating licenses to kill the larger species such as moose, red deer, or the large carnivores. For the smaller species, there are no bag limits, not even for migratory bird species, and the numbers killed are entirely left to the owner's discretion. The game the landowner does not use for his own consumption is still sold on the market, as it has been for centuries.

Throughout European history hunting has been a status symbol and as most hunters belonged to the elite and accordingly were literate, many of them kept records of their bags and displayed their trophies. When hunting became accessible to ordinary people, the tradition of keeping records and trophies was continued by them, and the result is that far more data from European—especially British—sources exists than from any other part of the world.

In North America the history of hunting is very different. The early settlers enjoyed unlimited hunting but also cleared the land to grow crops. This meant excessive harvest of game and in conjunction with the loss of habitat and the increased competition for food from domestic animals, the inevitable result was a declining population of most of the larger game species. This led to the first American law regulating deer hunting being passed in Rhode Island as early as 1646. However, the general assumption that America's resources were limitless meant that unregulated hunting and trapping for commercial purposes led to a severe decline of wildlife, with many species being eradicated from large parts of the country. At the initiative of President Theodore Roosevelt, this development was turned completely around in the early decades of the twentieth century. The result was the North American Wildlife Conservation Model, which is unique. Unlike the European system of game management, it is very democratic and does not leave game management to the individual landowners but endeavors to manage the national and local game populations on a scientific basis. In North America everyone has the opportunity to hunt and kill a share of the game. With commercial trade in wildlife prohibited and scientific game management in place, most American game species made an impressive comeback. As examples, the 1907 herd of 41,000 elk or wapiti had rebounded to 740,000 by 1992; the 13,000 pronghorns of 1910 increased to more than 1 million; and 0.5 million whitetails of 1900 increased to 22 million.

As a consequence of this historical development, the size of the game bags taken by the individual North American hunter has for the last century been very limited compared to what early European hunters achieved. In addition, there was no widespread tradition in America of keeping accurate records. Before the introduction of game management in the United States, most of the successful hunters did not keep records, and trophies were not revered and measured like they are today. All in all, this means that only a few historical records of North American game bags can be found.

Big Game

The tradition of keeping parts of animals as trophies stems from prehistoric times and trophies have traditionally been seen as symbols of the hunter's skills, strength, and power. Probably for the same reasons, hunting large game species has been a status symbol in Europe since the Middle Ages and huge collections of trophies have been kept here since at least the fifteenth century. Many of these are open to the public in different castles in Central Europe. Careful records of the game killed and larger trophies have survived until today, and are invaluable sources for hunting historians.

To understand how the enormous bags of European big game were taken, it is necessary to know how the game was hunted. The methods used were a far cry from the modern concept of hunting in North America, and today we would call it a slaughter, not a hunt. Many hunting techniques were used but the largest bags came about when driven hunting was introduced. Hunters were posted at strategic places and the game was driven toward them by sometimes hundreds of beaters. Often large nets were used to lead the game in the direction wanted. Sometimes the game was even driven into a body of water in order to make them less difficult targets.

Although these methods were gradually "civilized" over the centuries, driven hunting is still very common throughout the European continent, whether the game is moose in Sweden, red deer in Spain, or wild boar in Romania.

In Asia and especially in India, driven hunting was practiced long before the arrival of the British colonists and continued until hunting was banned in India. This explains the astonishing bags of big game made by some of the rulers and members of the British Raj. Due to the sheer amount of game available in Africa, driven hunting was not necessary, and killing numerous animals for no other purpose but the sport was considered bad taste. Accordingly, the largest bags recorded here were made by professional hunters killing for meat supply, eradicating vermin, or shooting game in order to make room for farming and settlement.

The tradition of recording the size of trophies was founded by the British taxidermist Rowland Ward, who published his first book on the subject in 1892 called *Records of Big Game*. The idea has since spread and today there are many different systems of recording trophies, with the Boone and Crockett Club and Safari Club International's systems being some of the best known. As mentioned in the preface, this book is not a record book. We have highlighted particularly impressive trophies not according to the number of points scored in accordance with any measuring system, but due to being extreme in absolute terms, whether this is number of points, antler length, spread, weight, or other characteristics of the given species.

Small Game

There are virtually no bag limits for shooting small game in any European country, and management is left to the landowners' discretion within the prescribed seasons. In many European countries hunting is a social activity involving scores of hunters and beaters. Driven hunting is still a tradition in many European countries and obviously this kind of hunting or shooting has resulted in far more large bags than any other type of small-game hunting.

Rearing birds in order to enable a party of eight or ten guns to shoot hundreds and sometimes over a thousand birds a day is still practiced in a number of European countries, especially on the British Isles, in Denmark, in Spain, and to a lesser degree in Eastern Europe. Historically, most of the surviving records of these activities have been found in Britain and in the archives of a number of European estates.

Fortunately the massive bags of small game made in Britain and Central Europe around the turn of the nineteenth century are a thing of the past. Personally, I still participate in bird shooting each season in several European countries but I am not without reservations about this activity. During my more than forty years as an active hunter I have always been ambivalent regarding large bags from a day's shooting. On one hand I'm fascinated by them and on the other hand I'm instinctively against them as excessive shooting in the long run indirectly poses a political threat to my possibilities of experiencing the joys of hunting in the future.

I shall not claim that I wouldn't like to shoot a large amount of game in one day, provided it is done in an ethical way. But I also realize that we must always be able to justify our conduct as hunters to the non-hunting majority. Today hunting has much narrower limits in terms of what is acceptable, and our right to hunt in the future depends upon hunters keeping within these limits.

Proper Focus

Focusing on the tangible results of a hunt—be it trophy or bag size—makes hunters vulnerable to criticism. If we are not careful and do not take into consideration the views of the non-hunting majority, we might be deprived of our right to enjoy hunting.

Some of the socially negative aspects of too much focus on the tangible results of hunting were excellently recorded by the British politician George Wyndham (1863-1913). In a letter to his father, the first Baron of Leconfield, Wyndham described how he experienced his contact with the elite of British shooting fraternity at the turn of the nineteenth century:

"They live for shooting and 'record bags' on their several estates. And, in order to secure these bags, they have abandoned most of the old precepts, shooting at everything near and far, taking the best places on their own shooting, being rude to their guests who shoot badly and generally destroying the amenities of what was a pretty sport by turning it into a vulgar and arduous competition."

In the years following World War I, bags fortunately became more moderate and even the privileged hunter's focus was to a much higher extent directed toward quality rather than quantity. In spite of this, reports of great shooting records have retained their fascination for me and for many other hunters, judging from the publicity many of these somewhat dubious achievements have garnered over time.

When shooting reared birds, the numbers can be regulated according to the owner's willingness to pay for them and accordingly the size of the bags have always been closely related to the degree of the hunter's wealth and enthusiasm for shooting. To a certain extent this is also true for international trophy hunting of larger game species.

But when it comes to large bags of wild (migratory) birds, I know from personal experience that it normally takes scores or more days in the field with little or no tangible results to experience just a moderately "great" day when wind, weather, and the flight of birds will yield a large bag. The true reason for creating this book is my respect for the enormous effort, perseverance, and dedication to hunting that is the hallmark of the most successful hunters of these species.

One of the most important lessons I have learned from many days spent hunting around the globe is that hunting success cannot be measured by the number of heads, inches of horn, or any number of points a trophy can qualify for. The true, but sadly immeasurable, rewards of hunting are the great experiences, the friendships, and the enjoyment that we get from our excursions in the hunting fields.

Part 1
Dangerous Game

Chapter 1

Elephants, Rhinos, and Hippos

Largest Elephant

The largest known specimen of an African savanna elephant was killed in 1955 in Angola by the Spanish-Hungarian hunter José Fenykövi. It had a shoulder height of 13 feet, 1 inch, and is estimated to have weighed around 24,000 pounds—twice the weight of an average male elephant—giving the phrase "big-game hunting" an entirely new dimension. The elephant is mounted and displayed in the hall of The Smithsonian Institution in Washington.

Hunter José Fenykövi sitting on the largest-bodied elephant ever recorded.

Mike LaGrange is probably the hunter who has killed the most African elephants.

Most Elephants

Mike LaGrange (b. 1949) was for a number of years in the 1970s and 1980s employed as a control officer for Zimbabwe's Parks and Wildlife Management Authority. One of his tasks was to reduce the elephant population in areas where their numbers exceeded the biological carrying capacity. During his career, LaGrange probably killed more elephants than anyone else—more than 6,000 in total. He operated with a team of assistants who used radios and automatic rifles in order to eradicate entire family groups of elephants, as experience has shown that this is the best way of reducing their numbers without upsetting the herd's important social structures.

Elephant Control

In colonial times, game-control officers in most of Africa operated more or less on their own in the vast areas they were responsible for managing. This way of culling crop-raiding elephants resembled traditional elephant hunting for sport and accordingly these officers' total bags must be put in perspective when compared with elephant culling in modern times.

The most successful of the early control officers was Roy John Dugdale Salmon (1888–1952), better known as "Samaki" Salmon, who operated in Uganda in the years between the two world wars and culled more than 4,000 elephants. His armament consisted of two bolt-action rifles from John Rigby in .416 Nitro Express and a .470 Nitro Express double rifle from William Evans. (The latter was used when tracking wounded animals in dense bush.) Like most of his colleagues, Samaki Salmon was an excellent shot. Among his many extraordinary feats were shooting 40 elephants in one day, 70 elephants in three days, and 400 elephants in one week. On one occasion he killed 12 elephants with 14 shots in less than 2 minutes. Too bad for Salmon that he wasn't paid for piece-work.

"Samaki" Salmon (far right) during a safari with the Prince of Wales.

White Gold

Historically no hunting "trophy" ever had the same importance as ivory. Since the earliest civilizations, this material has been precious and sought-after.

As Europeans gradually gained access to the interior of Africa, and especially when modern firearms became available at the end of the nineteenth century, the commercial trade in ivory increased exponentially. However, as the ivory hunters primarily went for large tusks, they did not damage the elephant population to nearly the same extent as today's poaching epidemic does, where animals are killed without regard to age, sex, and tusk size.

There are no records of the total amount of ivory that was exported from the Dark Continent in the heyday of the ivory trade, but in 1898

A pile of tusks from a successful elephant hunt like this represented a market value of thousands of pounds sterling in the early twentieth century.

alone it was 550 tons, of which almost half came from the Congo. During the years between 1880 and 1900, the import to London alone was 3,700 tons of ivory, an average of almost 400 tons per year. That means some 60,000 elephants were killed just to supply

The consumption of ivory was enormous in the last century. This photo shows the inside of a London ivory warehouse shortly before World War I.

Incredible but True!

The heaviest set of elephant tusks in the world together weighed 440 pounds!

the London market. In addition there were other ivory markets, with the most important situated in Antwerp, Hamburg, and Marseille.

At the time, the "conversion rate" of ivory was generally considered to be "a pound for a pound" meaning one pound sterling for each pound of ivory. The actual price, however, very much depended upon the size and quality of the tusk in question. Regardless, this meant that there was big money to be made by hunting elephants, provided you were able to find the elephants and survive the hardships of safari life in those days, which included tropical diseases and hostile natives.

Only a very few professional ivory hunters managed to do better than break even by this way of living. Many were killed by elephants or natives and many more died penniless. Also, there is a vast difference between this occupation and elephant control or culling, where the object is to reduce the population by killing off entire herds of animals. Ivory hunters had to seek and find the largest bulls and follow their tracks over vast distances, often in vain.

Heaviest and Longest Tusks

An elephant's tusks continue to grow throughout the animal's life, which rarely exceeds 60 years. The average annual growth is 3.5 to 4 inches, but day-to-day use and damage limits the length so the tusk will never achieve its full potential of 20 feet.

The weight of the tusk is not only related to the length but also to the circumference and size of the nerve cavity. After the age of 35, this cavity is gradually filled up with dentine and from that point on, the weight of the tusk increases more rapidly.

The heaviest set of tusks ever recorded came from an elephant killed in 1898 by a slave called Senoussi at the slopes of

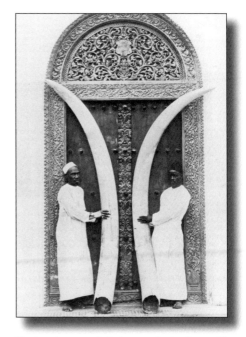

The heaviest set of elephant tusks in the world. Together these tusks weigh 440 pounds.

Kilimanjaro in present-day Tanzania. The tusks weighed 235 and 226 pounds respectively, totaling 461 pounds. The heavier tusk was slightly over 10 feet long while the lighter one measured 10 feet, 3.5 inches. The circumference at the root was 23.6 and 22.8 inches respectively. The longest set of tusks ever recorded are 11 feet, 4 inches and 10 feet, 9 inches in length, but they "only" total slightly over 290 pounds in weight.

Powell-Cotton's record trophy tusks weighed 198 and 174 pounds respectively.

P. H. G. Powell-Cotton was an internationally known trophy hunter before the turn of the last century. He was also among the first hunters to make use of a telescopic sight.

Largest Hunting Trophy

The largest elephant tusks discussed above are not considered the largest *hunting trophy* in the record books because they were not killed after a dedicated and selective hunt for an animal with the largest possible tusks—although some would say this distinction is just a typical example of ethnocentrism. Regardless, "officially" the largest trophy elephant was killed in 1905 in the Eastern Congo by P. H. G. Powell-Cotton (1866–1940), a major in the British army.

The biggest trophy elephant was killed in Congo in 1905.

9

The tusks of Powell-Cotton's record elephant were not especially long for their weight—9 feet and 8 feet, 9 inches respectively—but they had a circumference at the bases of 25 and 23.8 inches. Furthermore, they retained this thickness for most of their length, which gave them an impressive weight of 198 and 174 pounds respectively.

Powell-Cotton was a very dedicated hunter who collected Asian as well as African trophies. His friend, the famous taxidermist Rowland Ward, insisted that the record elephant should be full-mounted. As this meant that his trophy room had to undergo structural changes, Rowland Ward offered to do the taxidermy for free. Today both the tusks, the replicas of the tusks, and the full mount can still be seen at Powell-Cotton's private museum at his former home in Quex Park, Kent, which is open to the public and is always worth a visit.

Walther Dalrymple Maitland Bell is the most successful ivory hunter measured by financial gain.

Profits from White Gold

The most successful ivory hunter measured in terms of financial profit was W. D. M. "Karamojo" Bell (1880–1951). In total he killed 1,011 elephants during his many safaris in East, Central, and West Africa in the years 1902–1914. His safaris often lasted several years. "Karamojo" Bell was an extraordinary shot and a well-known advocate of small-caliber rifles with solid bullets for big-game hunting. Accordingly he shot most of his many elephants with bolt-action rifles in caliber .318 Westley Richards and .275 Rigby (7x57). He even killed a good many tuskers with the diminutive .256 Mannlicher (6.5x54) in a lightweight rifle from Daniel Fraser of Bell's native Scotland. A number of hunters tried to do what Bell did but were killed as they did not have Bell's extraordinary ability to place the small bullet in the elephant's brain from any angle whether the animal was moving or not.

Of Bell's total of 1,011 elephants, 983 were bulls. The remaining 28 were cows he had to kill in self-defense or in order to provide meat for his many hundred bearers on his safaris.

Bell estimated his net profits from ivory hunting exceeded £70,000, or $350,000, at a time when a well-paid skilled worker earned £2 ($10) a week. It is not possible to convert this amount directly to today's money but as James

Purdey & Sons have built their side-by-side shotguns to the same specifications since 1880, it might illustrate the size of Bell's profit that at the time he could have bought 775 Purdey guns for it. Today a Purdey gun costs almost £68,000 or $110,000, and accordingly 775 Purdeys cost more than $85 million.

Bell's outstanding results must also be related to the fact that just a decade and a half later—in 1927 and 1928—the average annual harvest for a successful ivory hunter was 1,000 to 1,100 pounds a year. By comparison Bell's best safaris yielded between 5 and 7 tons of ivory.

Best and Worst Day

Bell writes that one of his best memories of a hunt was when he was accompanied by a friend who was known never to be impressed and rarely praised anything or anyone. While his friend watched the proceedings from a treetop, Bell ran down and shot, one by one, no less than six elephant bulls in as many minutes. The reward came when he returned to his friend, who commented, "I'll be damned, Bell!"

Bell also had a full month of hunting without ever seeing a single elephant. According to his memoirs, however, his worst day went like this:

> During the rains I once marched 6 miles an hour for 8½ hours tracking an elephant bull with enormous feet—only to find out it was tuskless. Shot it immediately to avoid repetition!

Profitable Safaris

As stated above, Bell was the most successful ivory hunter, at least measured

The heavy tusks obtained by the ivory hunters had to be carried out of the bush the hard way.

in profits. His most profitable safari took place at the beginning of the twentieth century and lasted fourteen months. The costs amounted to £3,000 ($15,000 at the time) but he earned £9,000 ($45,000) from the sale of the ivory. On this trip Bell killed 210 elephants—only mature bulls with large tusks.

Bell's record for one day was nineteen bulls. (On a later safari he killed forty-four bulls in three consecutive days.) Financially, Bell's best day yielded eleven bulls with twenty-one tusks weighing a total of 1,643 pounds, or an average of 77 pounds. These tusks gave him an income of 863 pounds sterling, almost $5,000 at the time or roughly $13,000 in today's money.

However, Bell had bad years too. The worst cost him a loss of $32,000 at

James Sutherland was one of the most famous ivory hunters. Like many of his colleagues, he died in the wilderness.

a time when a well-paid skilled worker earned $10 a week.

Expensive Trophy

The price of ivory rises with the size of the tusk; the larger the tusk, the higher the price per pound. In December 2005, an extraordinary set of elephant tusks were sold at an auction in London.

The tusks weighed 192 and 189 pounds respectively and were the third largest set ever recorded. The auction house would not reveal the identity of either the seller or buyer. The seller claimed that the tusks were from an elephant killed in Tanzania by a poacher in 1970 and that the poacher was killed by game officers.

The tusks were then allegedly sold to a piano maker in the Borders region of Great Britain. As ivory is the best material for making piano keys, one must presume that the tusks were bought for this purpose. Supposedly the tusks were kept in the company's basement only to

The third-largest set of tusks from an African elephant is also the most expensive hunting trophy of modern times to change hands. The tusks were sold on an auction in London in 2005 for nearly $1 million.

reappear more than thirty years later when a new proprietor went through the company's stock.

He put the tusks up for sale in 2005 and the hammer fell on a bid of £380,000. Including premium, this is the equivalent of £440,000 or $730,000. The explanation of the tusks' provenance is dubious, however, as no piano maker has existed in the Borders since before World War II.

Most 100-Pounders

The elephant hunter's equivalent of finding the Holy Grail is a set of tusks that pass the magic mark of 100 pounds a side. Even in the heyday of big-game hunting, the years between the two world wars, 100-pounders were few and far between. Today they are extremely rare and it is big news when one is occasionally shot. Most of the known 100-pounders live in national parks and reserves, primarily Kruger Park in South Africa. When a hunter today is fortunate enough to kill a 100-pounder, it is usually—but not always—an animal that for some reason has left the comparative safety of a reserve.

While very few hunters have ever killed more than one 100-pounder,

PH Eric Rundgren took more 100-pound elephants than anyone else.

some of the professional guides have led their clients to a handful of elephants with tusks over the magic threshold. No one has been as good at finding 100-pounders as the Swedish/Kenyan professional hunters Anders "Andrew" Holmberg and Eric Rundgren.

Best—or luckiest—is Holmberg (b. 1918), as close to a third of all the elephants he led clients to or killed for himself were 100-pounders. He began as a professional hunter at the tender age of twenty-one and during the next five decades he either led clients to or personally killed 200 elephants. In itself this was an extraordinary feat, but not entirely unusual among his colleagues. The special thing about Holmberg's career is that out of the 200 elephants, 63 had tusks of 100 pounds or more. In 1950 he killed his best elephant, with tusks weighing 141 and 138 pounds respectively.

Holmberg's colleague Eric Rundgren (1918–1992) began his career as an officer for Kenya's Game Department and then continued as a professional hunter in the safari industry, which grew immensely in East Africa after World War II. In total he shot around 1,200 elephants. Between 40 and 50 of these had tusks weighing more than 100 pounds each and on top of this he led clients to an additional 30 to 50. In total, he took part in the killing of between 70 and 100 elephant bulls having tusks over 100 pounds each, a feat that has not been surpassed by any other hunter. Rundgren's biggest elephant had tusks with the impressive weights of 174 and 172 pounds respectively.

Indian Elephants

As the Indian elephant, *Elephas maximus*, has been domesticated for centuries and because the wild specimens of this animal very early were confined to the most inaccessible parts of Southeast Asia, it has never been hunted in anywhere near the scale of its African counterpart. Since the nineteenth century, the hunt has primarily been concentrated around rogue bulls.

The record bag of Indian elephants was made by a British major named Rogers, who in the late nineteenth century shot more than 1,500 specimens as a control officer in Ceylon. There other officers, Gailwey, Skinner, and Layard, killed around 1,300, 1,200, and 1,000 respectively. These figures say a lot about the population at that time compared to the tiny population of wild Indian elephants today, which probably does

The number of Asiatic elephants has not been large enough to support sport hunting in modern times. Individual hunters managed to take a few hundred on the island of Ceylon in the nineteenth century.

Incredible but True!

The record bag of Indian elephants was 1,500 made by a British major named Rogers.

not amount to as many as one of the aforementioned gentlemen shot in a lifetime. The main cause of the demise of the species is, however, not hunting but the explosive growth of the human population all over East Asia which has deprived the elephant of its habitat. Elephant hunting was banned in India as early as 1871.

Indian Tusks

The Indian elephant does not normally grow tusks anywhere near the size of its African counterparts and the females usually do not grow tusks at all.

Only a very few tusks have ever reached a weight of 100 pounds and the average for an adult male is only around 40 pounds. The all-time record for Indian tusks is a set from the Western Terai in Nepal, which in 1921 was presented to the British King George V. The tusks weigh an astounding 160 and 161 pounds and measure 105 and 102 inches respectively.

Throughout history only seven Indian tusks have ever weighed over 100 pounds. The remaining five weighed 2x112, 2x106 and 102 pounds, which really makes the record set exceptional.

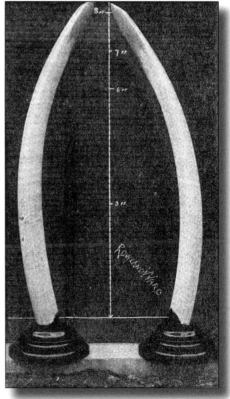

The king's record tusks from an Asiatic elephant.

today the export of mammoth ivory to China alone is more than 60 tons annually. Every summer thousands of skeletons and tusks appear when the snow melts and the upper layers of the permanent frozen ground in northern Siberia are washed away. Some sources claim that there still are millions of deep-frozen bodies of mammoths in the tundra of Siberia. To a certain degree this may also be the case in some of the northernmost parts of Canada and Alaska.

Prehistoric Trophies

The woolly mammoth, *Mammuthus primigenius*, would have been an impressive trophy for a hunter. A museum in Brno, Czech Republic, has a mammoth

A Tough Ending

While elephants have always been pursued for their ivory, in nature it is actually their molars that ultimately decide the animals' fate. As there is no predator capable of killing an adult elephant, an elephant will die of starvation when the last of its six sets of molars has been worn down—unless it meets a more merciful end in the form of a well-aimed bullet from a safari hunter.

Ancient Ivory

Several thousand years after the woolly mammoth, *Mammuthus primigenius*, became extinct, large quantities of ivory from this species are still picked up annually in Siberia. One expedition to Siberia in 1882–1884 led by Dr. Bunge found over 2,500 prime tusks on the three small islands of Lyakhov, Kotelnyi, and Fadeyev. Even

Mammoth tusks on a market in Siberia in 1912.

16

The largest known set of mammoth tusks measures more than 13 feet in length and weighs just under 500 pounds.

tusk that is 16½ feet long. The heaviest set of tusks found so far is in the State Museum in Lincoln, Nebraska. Their lengths are 13 feet, 10 inches and 13, feet 8 inches, respectively, but their combined weight is surprisingly "only" 498 pounds, just 37 pounds heavier than the largest set of tusks from an African elephant.

Most Black Rhinos

One of the most famous professional hunters ever was a Scot named John A. Hunter (1887–1963). He was sent to Kenya by his father after an unfortunate incident with an older woman. After a few years he became a control officer for the game department and in the 1940s he was ordered to cull all the rhinos in a vast area that had been allocated to the natives as farmland. Hunter did not keep personal

17

John Alexander Hunter shot more than 1,600 rhinos in total. That's a record.

the Central African Republic starting in 1924, and killed between 300 and 400 rhinos. Hunter's friend and colleague, Eric Rundgren, shot just 250, and there are hardly any other hunters who killed as many as 150 rhinos during their careers.

White Rhinos

All the figures listed above are for the black rhino, *Diceros bicornis*. The white rhino, *Ceratotherium simum*, has historically been so rare that there was never any substantial hunting for this species before South African hunters started breeding it in fenced farms. However, there is little doubt that some hunters killed substantial numbers of white rhinos as the Boers almost exterminated the species in

records of his hunting results, but based upon documentation of his services for the game department in Kenya, he is considered to be the most successful rhino hunter in the world, with a bag totaling more than 1,600 animals. He killed no fewer than 996 rhinos in the Makueni District alone between 26 August 1944 and 31 October 1946, an average bag of almost one rhino per day.

Today this number may seem absurd considering the small number of rhinos left worldwide, but in those days it was common practice to remove the game from areas with good soil for farming. In total, Hunter killed 1,078 rhinos in Makueni, which made it possible to turn the bush into farmland that in 1962 fed 2,187 families.

No other hunters came even close to Hunter's rhino totals. The second in line is probably the Frenchman Etienne Cannone who operated in what is today

Etienne Cannone.

18

its area of distribution between the Limpopo and Zambezi Rivers during the years 1870–1890.

The highest recorded number of white rhinos killed by one man is probably the twenty-three specimens which the famous hunter and naturalist F. C. Selous (1851–1917) killed for various museums and collections.

Asiatic Rhinos

Asia is home to three species of rhinos, the Indian, the Sumatran, and the Javan. None is even close to its African cousin when it comes to body size, length of horns, or number of specimens. The weight of an Indian rhino, *Rhinoceros unicornis*, is around

Today it is difficult to imagine how plentiful rhinos were in many parts of Africa before World War II.

4,400 pounds while the Sumatran rhino, *Dicerorhinus sumatrensis*, the smallest rhino, weighs around half of

Indian rhinos have never been as common as their African counterparts.

that. The Indian subspecies has only one horn, with a record length of 24 inches. The small species from Sumatra has two horns and also holds the record in length for Asian rhinos with a measurement of 31 inches.

Rhinos have never been as numerous in Asia as they once were in Africa. The largest recorded bag of Asiatic rhinos I have been able to find is from the records of the Maharaja of Cooch Behar; he notes five rhinos were killed during shikars in both 1886 and 1899. From his thirty-seven years of records, we also know that a total of 311 rhinos were bagged on his enormous hunting grounds.

In Nepal, the King George V of England (1865–1936) participated in a shikar from 18–28 December 1911, where no fewer than eighteen Indian rhinos were killed, in addition to forty-four other big-game animals.

Hippopotamus

It is not known exactly who the most successful hippopotamus hunter was as this species does not offer much in terms of sport, unless you surprise one on land at daybreak as it is returning to the water after feeding during the night. The most likely holder of the record bag is the French professional hunter Etienne Cannone (1902–1976), who shot thousands of hippos in the Aouk River of Central Africa and sent the dried meat to Fort Archambault where it was used to feed the native laborers building the Congo-Ocean Railway from 1924 to 1932. That the protein

was needed badly is emphasized by the fact that the construction of the railway cost the lives of 17,000 laborers—mostly due to malnutrition and diseases.

When the Congo-Ocean railroad was being built during the years 1924 to 1932, thousands of hippos were shot to feed the huge workforce.

Walrus

The largest animal hunted with a rifle in the northern hemisphere is the walrus, which can weigh around 3,300 pounds. The largest trophy walrus is from the collection of Le Duc de Orleans. The animal was killed in Greenland in 1921 and its longest tusk measures 37¼ inches.

In the Arctic, occasionally both beluga whales and narwhals are killed with rifles, but this is not considered hunting by the definition of the authors of this book. It is also an open question whether the largest walrus isn't actually heavier than the largest specimens of the two whale species.

Incredible but True!

Which animal species is most dangerous to humans?

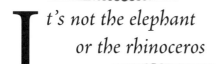

It's not the elephant or the rhinoceros

Nor is it the lion, king of the jungle!

But the lowly mosquito!

Elephants, Rhinos, and Hippos

Most Lethal

Among hunters there is an eternal debate regarding which species is the most dangerous. The hippopotamus has a reputation of being the big-game species that kills the most people in Africa. But as the species has a limited area of distribution and never ranges far from the water, the actual conflicts with this animal are comparatively limited. Crocodiles are probably much worse in this respect, but there are no records of the number of incidents as the animals often make their kills in remote areas and rarely leave any "evidence." The poisonous snakes feared by so many people kill some 50,000 people worldwide every year. When in the tropics, many Westerners are very worried about being bitten by a poisonous snake, but during my research for this book I could not find a single record of a visiting European or American hunter who died as the result of a snakebite.

Among the trophy-hunted species, it is not surprising that the Big Five get all the attention. In its heyday, the black rhino was renowned for unprovoked attacks and killed several well-known hunters. Today, however, the black rhino has been almost eradicated by poachers and accordingly there are very few conflicts with this species. The white rhino is much less aggressive than its cousin and rarely causes any grave risk to humans.

The great cats—tigers, lions, leopards, and jaguars—were formerly among the most common man-killers among the Big Five, but their reduction in numbers have sent them down the list, although lions still kill hundreds of people in Africa annually. In Tanzania alone it is estimated that seventy persons are victims of lion attacks annually.

Buffalo are usually only dangerous to people if the animals are wounded by bullets or snares. Topping the list of the most dangerous of the Big Five, then, is probably the elephant, which kills around 500 persons annually. The reason for this is the elephant's widespread distribution combined with its constant conflicts with farmers. But man's most lethal opponent in the animal kingdom is actually very small. It is the malaria mosquito, which indirectly causes the deaths of millions of humans every year.

In terms of how many deaths it causes every year, the most dangerous animal in the world is the malaria mosquito.

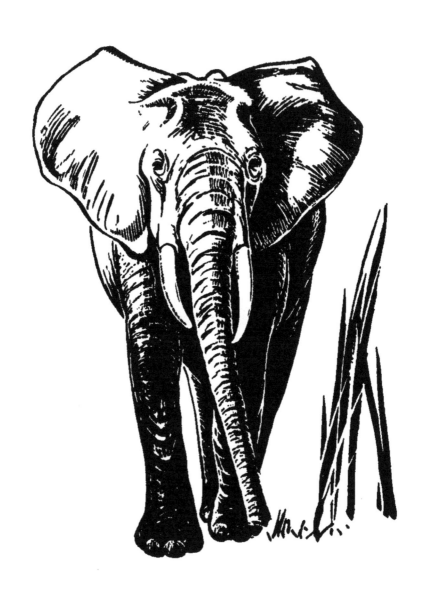

Chapter 2

Wild Cattle

Largest Wild Ox

With a shoulder height exceeding six feet, the Asiatic gaur, *Bos gaurus*, is the largest wild ox in the world. The biggest bulls allegedly weigh more than 2,900 pounds. Formerly the great bovine was distributed over large areas of India and Southeast Asia, but the growth in human populations has driven it off most of its former range. Hunting for this species came to an end in the late 1960s. In terms of its horns, it carries the second-largest headgear of the Asiatic bovines (after water buffalo): The greatest span recorded is 56 inches and the longest horn is 37½ inches.

The largest recorded number of gaur killed in one day was 11, on one of the

The gaur is the largest of the wild bovines.

Maharaja of Cooch Behar's hunts in March 1902. For comparison, a total of only 48 gaur were killed on the Maharaja's hunting grounds during the 37-year period from 1871 to 1907.

High-Altitude Game

Of all the big-game species, the one that lives at the highest altitude is the yak, *Bos mutus*, which still can be found in its wild state, primarily in the Tibetan part of the Himalayas. Unfortunately, they no longer exist in huntable numbers.

South of Horpu Cho in 1899, the Englishman Edgar Phelps shot a yak at an altitude of 5,600 meters, or 18,372 feet. The species has been observed grazing even higher—at 6,100 meters (20,000 feet) of altitude. Of the smaller ungulates, the highest living is the bharal or blue sheep, *Pseudois nayaur*. It has been found in the same height as the yak but normally only lives up to an altitude of 5,000 meters (16,400 feet).

More unusual, the English zoologist W. L. Abbott in the 1890s found an elephant track on Mount Kilimanjaro at an altitude of 4,575 meters (15,000 feet). On the same mountain in East Africa, the frozen body of a leopard was found

No species of big game is found at higher altitudes than the yak.

at an altitude of 16,400 feet—a fact with which a wondering Ernest Hemingway began his famous short story *The Snows of Kilimanjaro*.

Rarest Trophy

Among the rarest hunting trophies in the world are the frayed-tipped horns of the kouprey, *Bos sauveli*. In spite of the fact that the kouprey is the second-largest of all the world's wild bovines—with a shoulder height of six feet—this rare species has been known to science only since the 1930s, when the French hunter Francois Edmond-Blanc participated in the Seventh Indochinese Expedition. In 1937, in what is now Kampuchea, he killed an exceptional bull, confirming decades-old rumors of a large, unknown species of wild oxen living deep in the remote savanna areas of northeastern Cambodia where the country joins Laos and Vietnam. When the kouprey was discovered, the population was likely a few thousand animals. Due to the many decades of war in the area, it is unlikely the kouprey still exists, and if so the population most

Francois Edmond-Blanc photographed in 1939 with a kouprey, one of the rarest big-game trophies in the world.

26

The small Vu Quang ox from the jungles of Vietnam is the most recently discovered large mammal.

likely constitutes a maximum of a few hundred animals, which is probably too small a number for the species to survive. The kouprey was the last major mammal to be described scientifically until the small saola, or Vu Quang oxen, *Pseudoryx nghetinhensis*, was discovered in Vietnam in 1992. To this date only a total of eleven Vu Quang oxen have been seen. For obvious reasons this species was never hunted.

Cape Buffalo

In hunting literature, the thrills and dangers of hunting Cape buffalo are often described to the point where you are led to believe that a hunter will survive only if he carries a large-caliber double capable of hitting a charging buffalo in the eye. That this is not really true is proven by the results of the world's most successful Cape buffalo hunter.

In the northern part of Portuguese East Africa (today's Mozambique), Sena Sugar Estates was constructed during the 1920s and thousands of workers were to be fed by game meat. As there were lots of buffalo in the area,

the company employed a number of hunters to provide the needed amount of meat per week.

One of these was an accountant in the company by the name of Joseph Gustav Guex. He was of Swiss origin and eager to hunt, but had no prior experience before taking the job as a buffalo hunter. His short stature and small frame prevented him from getting used to heavy-caliber rifles, and after some experimenting he chose a .318 Westley Richards bolt-action rifle for the task.

The cartridge is equivalent to a moderately loaded .30-06 with a 250-grain bullet. With this he killed some 7,000 Cape buffaloes. In total he had six accidents with this species of game and only one time was he injured to a degree that he chose to return to Switzerland for surgery on his back. Two of his colleagues—the Italian Salzone and the Portuguese Araújo—killed around 4,000 buffalo each, also in Mozambique.

In Kenya Eric Rundgren killed between 3,500 and 4,000 buffalo on control, in addition to a few hundred more killed while guiding clients.

A fine Cape buffalo taken in Uganda in the early 1900s.

Despite their reputation, Cape buffaloes rarely attack humans.

The lifetime record bag of Cape buffaloes belongs to Gustav Guex. His weapon of choice was a bolt-action in caliber .318 WR, which is more or less in the same category as a .30-06.

His colleague John Hunter killed around 2,000.

The most successful Scandinavian buffalo hunter is probably the Danish professional hunter Karl Larsen, who for a number of years made a living from selling buffalo hides and allegedly killed them "by the thousands."

Longest Horns

Of all the hunted game species of the world, the water buffalo, *Bubalus bubalis*, grows the longest horns, closely followed by the Cape buffalo, *Syncerus caffer*. Just as with the Cape buffalo, it is often female water buffalo that grow the longest (though not the heaviest) horns.

The British Museum is in possession of a female water buffalo head with one horn measuring 77 inches; the longest known horn from a bull water buffalo is "only" 70½ inches. When it comes to greatest width, the record belongs to a buffalo killed by the British hunter A. K. Macomber in 1933; it has a spread of 93¾ inches.

The horns of Cape buffalo have a different configuration, which means that the trophies of the two species cannot be compared directly. The record Cape buffalo horns total 141 inches, but in order to get the horn length you must deduct the distance between the bases of the horns, which varies greatly. The result is that the horns of the largest Cape buffalo are a few inches shorter than the equivalent horns from the largest water buffalo.

This buffalo with a 58-inch spread was taken by Andrew Holmberg in 1951 and was, at the time, a new world record.

Water Buffalo

The population of the wild water buffalo, *Bubalus arnee*, never achieved the same density as that of the African buffalo. This is reflected in the records of the Maharaja of Cooch Behar, whose hunting grounds were considered to encompass some of the best water buffalo terrain outside Ceylon. During thirty-seven years, a total of 438 water buffalo were killed here.

In April 1895 the largest bag of water buffalo on one hunt was achieved: eight bulls in addition to a single tiger. The same Samuel Baker who later discovered the source of the Nile allegedly shot at least 200 and probably more water buffalo during his eight

Sir Samuel Baker is considered the most successful water buffalo hunter of all time.

years in Ceylon and has the largest recorded lifetime bag of this species. This was not a small feat considering that this was in the days of blackpowder rifles, and the hunting took place in the most humid parts of the island; misfires and dangerous follow-ups on wounded animals were common.

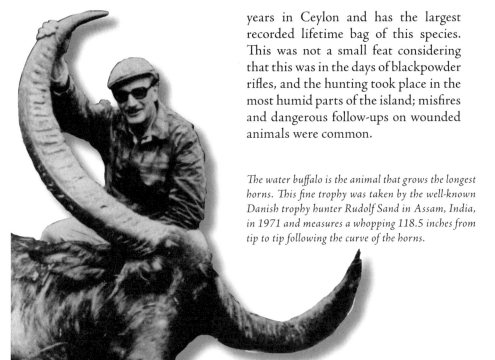

The water buffalo is the animal that grows the longest horns. This fine trophy was taken by the well-known Danish trophy hunter Rudolf Sand in Assam, India, in 1971 and measures a whopping 118.5 inches from tip to tip following the curve of the horns.

A huge water buffalo taken in northern India shortly before the outbreak of World War I.

Bison

The European bison (*Bison bonasus*) and the American bison (*bison bison*) are the biggest land mammals on their respective continents. The shoulder height can exceed 6.5 feet (2 meters) on both species, but as the European species has longer legs, the American variety normally is somewhat larger and heavier. The largest American bison bulls weigh more than 2,400 pounds whereas the European bulls rarely weigh over 2,000 pounds.

Both species of bison have been very close to extinction. In Europe this was primarily due to loss of habitat through centuries; it originally ranged from the British Isles in the west to the Pacific in the east. In North America the decline of this species was caused by the slaughtering of the enormous population of bison for a mix of political and commercial reasons.

In spite of several hundred years of trying to protect the species, the last free-roaming European bison, also called wisent, in Central Europe was killed in 1919 by a Polish poacher by the name of Nikolaj Szpakowicz. Immediately before World War I there were around 785 wisents left in the Bialowieza area of today's Poland, but by the end of the war German troops had killed all but nine.

The last free-roaming wisent in the world was shot in western Caucasus in 1925, allegedly because the Russian revolutionary leaders considered the species a symbol of oppression as it had only been protected in order to enable the aristocracy to hunt it.

A rare photo of a wild European bison taken before World War I.

Anonymous American bison hunter in Montana around 1875.

Fortunately the remaining 54 animals left in zoos enabled a sustainable reintroduction of the species in the Bialowieza area in 1929. Fortunately the Russian leaders changed their minds about the wisent and after having occupied eastern Poland in 1939 they introduced a death penalty for killing one—and actually executed three soldiers for the offense.

When the Germans re-conquered the area in 1941, they continued to protect the wisent and at the end of the war there were 24 in Poland and 12 in Germany. A dedicated breeding effort resulted in the reintroduction of the species into unfenced areas in 1952. Today there are populations of free-roaming wisent in no less than ten eastern and central European countries and the total population is over 3,000 animals.

As the wisent had been extirpated from most of Western Europe since medieval times, only a few hunting records have survived. The largest recorded bag of wisent was made in 1752 on a hunt arranged by

Augustus III of Poland where 60 were killed. The largest recorded bag by one man is from one of the annual hunts that the Russian Tsar Alexander II held in the Bialowieza forest. On a

European bison killed in Caucasus by the famous British big-game hunter St. George Littledale in 1908.

hunt from 31 August to 12 September 1900, an unknown number of hunters killed a total of 685 head of game, including 42 wisent. The most successful wisent hunter during this hunt was Prince Albert of Saxony-Altenburg (1841–1902) who killed 12—in addition to 37 red stags, 39 roebucks, 16 other deer, 24 wild boars, 10 foxes, and 1 woodcock.

Tsar Nicholas II and a European bison bull taken in the Bialowieza Forest, which is now a part of Poland.

Worst Slaughter

During the first decades of the nineteenth century there were between 30 and 200 million bison roaming on the American prairies, depending on the source of information you choose. Most experts agree that there were around

This mountain of buffalo skulls represent only a few of the millions of buffaloes that were killed in just a few years. The fact that it was possible to gather such a number of skulls in a single location illustrates the incredible numbers of buffaloes that roamed the plains when the hunters arrived.

60 million bison in North America before the commercial killing of this species began in the latter half of the century. There are credible reports of herds numbering 4 million animals. The sheer size of bison herds often delayed transport considerably, as when a train in 1869 was forced to stop for nine hours until a herd of bison had passed the railroad track.

Although the Native American population had increased their bag of bison considerably after the introduction of the horse to the continent, the herds still seemed endless and numberless in 1840.

The rumor of limitless hunting opportunities spread around the world and began attracting hunters who in the beginning just came for adventure.

As early as 1843 the Scotsman Sir William Drummond Stewart (1795-1871) crossed the Atlantic just to hunt bison. His party found a herd of more than a million animals and when the "hunt" ended a few days later the prairie was "dotted with dead bison as far as one could see." The party did not take any part of the animals but left them where they fell and did not even bother to count the number killed. In the wake of this "gentleman" came a number of adventurous hunters and the railroads made good money on "hunting trips" where for the cost of $10 a day you could shoot as many bison as you wanted from the windows of a moving train.

At the beginning of the 1870s the slaughter of bison increased dramatically as tanneries in Europe increased

This bison hunter is chasing the herd on horseback, but most hunters used long-range rifles.

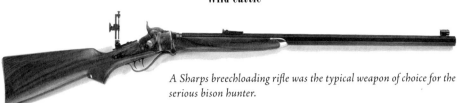

A Sharps breechloading rifle was the typical weapon of choice for the serious bison hunter.

their demand for buffalo hides for producing leather. Up to this point, the commercial hunting had been for local meat markets and therefore of limited consequence for the future of the species, but suddenly a hunter could get $3 for a hide and up to $50 for a perfect hide in the best winter condition—at a time when an unskilled laborer would be happy with a dollar a day.

This was the beginning of the largest and most grotesque slaughter of wild animals the world has seen. The American politicians did not intervene as the killing of the bison was considered an important part of solving the problems with the Indians. In just two years—1872 and 1873—the railroad transported 1,250,000 bison hides out of Kansas. On top of this the Indians are believed to have killed 350,000 bison in the same period.

In the following decade, depending on the time of year, between 2,000 and 100,000 bison were killed each day! In a single place, 6,500 rotting carcasses were found and the Santa Fe railroad conductor told a local newspaper that

Only the hides of the bison, and to a certain extent the tongues, were utilized. Millions of tons of prime venison was left to rot on the prairie.

along a 100-mile-long stretch you could jump from carcass to carcass without ever having to touch the ground.

The bison "hunters" worked in teams with a few good shooters and a large number of skinners. A single hunter could typically boast of having killed 1,500 bison in a week. As the bullets of the time were made of pure lead the hunters normally used large bores, often in .50-caliber. Many used two rifles so one could cool while the other was used. So many shots were fired that some hunters had assistants whose only job was to cut out the bullets of the dead bison in order to reuse the lead for casting new bullets.

In front of numerous witnesses the hunter Tom Nixon (1837–1884) shot 120 bison in just 40 minutes in 1873— and killed more than 3,200 bison in 35 days. In only 60 days during 1875, O. A. "Brick" Bond (185?–1927) killed 5,855 bison, including more than 300 on the most successful day. James Hamilton Cator (1852–1927) shot approximately 16,000 bison from 1872 to 1875 while his colleague J. Wright Mooar (1851–1940) claimed a figure of

20,500 bison in his six-year-long career and thereby has the dubious honor of being the most successful bison killer of all time.

As the hunters ran out of bison in one area they went on to other killing fields. During the winter of 1877–78, more than 1,500 bison hunters were active on the prairies of northwest Texas. When spring came, the stacks of hides to be shipped out covered an area of more than four acres. By the beginning of the 1880s the American bison was completely eradicated apart from a few hundred animals. It only took a decade to kill off some 30 million bison.

Fortunately there were a few far-sighted hunters like Charles "Buffalo" Jones (1844–1918) who caught a number of animals and kept them on ranches. In this manner a few groups of animals formed the basis of the present population of bison in America, which today consists of more than 500,000 animals.

The extent of the bison slaughter during the 1870s is hard to comprehend.

Chapter 3

Big Cats

Largest Lion

Which lion is the largest depends on the measurements applied. The size of the skin is not useful in this respect as all animal skins are very elastic. One commonly used measurement is the length of the dead animal when taken between pegs driven in the ground at the tip of the tail and at the animal's snout. However, this measurement only gives you the length of

the animal and does not necessarily say everything about its size.

The weight of an animal is probably the best measure, but as lions are capable of devouring large quantities of food in a very short span of time, this can have a significant influence on the animal's weight at any given moment. Another problem with using weight as a measurement is that it is difficult to bring a scale into the field and most weights given in hunting literature are in reality "guesstimates." For these reasons, the size of predators' skulls are now used to rank the animals as trophies.

The largest, or at least heaviest, precisely recorded lion living in the wild was a man-eater which was killed in 1936 by Lennox Anderson near the South African city Hectorspruit in Eastern Transvaal. The animal was placed on the local railroad's truck scale and it weighed 689 pounds; a normal-size lion weighs between 330 and 525 pounds. Length from tip of tail to the snout was 10 feet 6 inches.

Most Lions

In the beginning of the twentieth century, lions were considered vermin

Until the 1970s, hunting in Africa was mainly a sport for local residents and very wealthy hunters. In 1958, a traditional big-game safari cost around $3,500, twice as much as an average annual salary for a skilled worker. This is the Danish opera singer Lauritz Melchior (1890–1973) on his safari to East Africa just after World War II.

everywhere in Africa and therefore there were no hunting restrictions for this species. Killing the big cats was considered a good deed; many successful hunters never recorded the number of animals killed and accordingly there are no precise records of who shot the most.

However, from East Africa where the lion populations were the densest, a number of famous hunters' results have been recorded. One of the most successful lion hunters was undoubtedly the American-born mining engineer Leslie Simpson, who claimed to have killed 365 lions in Kenya in one year, an average of one every day.

During their careers the brothers Clifford and Harold Hill killed 160 and 135 lions respectively—most in an attempt to protect the two-legged livestock on their farm: ostriches.

The first game ranger of Kruger Park in South Africa, Colonel Stevenson-Hamilton, wrote in 1931 that he had killed around 200 lions in total.

The famous professional hunter John Hunter is considered to be the most successful of all. He started hunting lions as early as 1908 and sold the skins in Nairobi for a pound apiece. In the beginning of the 1920s Hunter allegedly guided two female American safari clients who in the same year killed over 100 lions.

In 1924, the game department of Kenya ordered Hunter to kill cattle-eating lions in a number of areas in the country. Unfortunately Hunter did not keep exact records of his bags of the large felines, but his total exceeded 600. During just three months he killed 88 lions and in a single night's baiting he killed 18 lions with his .416 Rigby rifle. Incredibly, this is not the largest

In many parts of Africa, lions were so numerous that farmers were forced to hire professional hunters in order to limit the loss of livestock.

In accordance with the spirit of the time, many hunters regarded any animal with fangs and claws as a pest. This is Prince Wilhelm of Sweden after a successful lion hunt.

bag in one night, however. In 1921 the Maharaja of Datia had also killed 18 lions in one night, and his three accompanying friends—among them the professional hunter Jim Fey—shot lions over nearby baits, making the total bag 34 lions and 2 leopards.

A year later four donkeys were killed at a farm near Naivasha. The owner was the same James Fey mentioned above and with a friend he made a *boma* (a blind made of thorn branches) and sat down to wait by the dead donkeys. During an hour and a half, the two men killed 14 lions.

During the construction of the Uganda Railroad through Kenya, the railroad company was plagued by lions that killed not only the beasts of burden but also a large number of the Indian coolies who were building the railroad. A former Indian soldier (whose name quite typically for the reports of those colonial times was not recorded) was, along with his son, given the task of killing the man-eating men-

ace. His technique was to imitate the call of a goat and when the lions appeared, the son shot them. In this rather risky way, the two men managed to kill 90 lions in nine months.

The second most successful lion hunter on record was Eric Rundgren, a professional hunter of Swedish origin who was an apprentice of J. A. Hunter's. After World War II he served as a game warden and, like Hunter, was commissioned to kill lions that presented a danger to humans and livestock. In the line of duty he killed 434 lions, and if you add the lions he killed as a professional hunting guide, his total bag exceeds 500.

The sheer size of the many bags mentioned above says a lot about the density of the lion population before the explosion of the human population in East Africa, which really accelerated in the 1960s. Today a male lion is one of the most difficult and expensive African trophies to hunt.

Incredible but True!

The largest big-cat bag in one night was 34 lions and 2 leopards; these were shot by the Maharaja of Datia. Three friends accompanied him.

George Rushby frequently came upon horrifying scenes like this during his work as a professional hunter.

Man-Killers

George Rushby (1900–1969) was a colorful character who moved to Africa after having been a fighter pilot

It took George Rushby fourteen years to eradicate a pride of man-eating lions that caused the deaths of more than 1,500 people in present-day Tanzania.

Incredible but True!

A *pride of lions in the Njombe district of Tanganyika (present-day Tanzania) killed at least 1,500 people during a twenty-three-year reign.*

during World War I. He began a career as an elephant hunter in what are now Mozambique, Tanzania, Zambia, and Congo, often as a poacher. From 1937 to 1953 he was game warden for the Tanganyika Game Department, specializing in controlling harmful lions and elephants. In 1941 he was given the task of killing a pride of lions that had been terrorizing the Njombe district since 1932, a mission his predecessor had failed to accomplish.

Because he had a lot of other things to do, such as killing 1,400 crop-raiding elephants, it took Rushby many years to accomplish his task. In 1946 he managed to kill fifteen members of the notorious pride. Only after fourteen years was the job done, and during their reign the pride had managed to kill and eat at least 1,500 people in the vast and remote area. This fact certainly gives the expression "the lion's share" a new dimension.

Big Cats

This lion was mounted in 1732, making it the oldest full mount of an African animal still in existence. (It hasn't aged well!)

Oldest Mount

The oldest full-mounted trophy of a dangerous animal that still exists appears to be a lion located in Gripsholm Castle in Sweden. It dates back to 1732 and was reputedly a present from the Bey of Algiers to King Frederick I of Sweden (1676–1751). If so, it is an example of the now-extinct North African Barbary lion. The standard of taxidermy, however, doesn't exactly pay homage to the great trophy.

Many Tigers

Many British officers and civil servants in India were avid hunters.

Tiger hunting was a popular sport among Indian rulers. This is the Nizam of Hyderabad with a large tiger he shot in 1889.

When it came to tigers, the most successful civil servant was George Yule (1829–1892), who killed more than 500 of the great striped cats in a span of only 28 years. But the hunting done by the colonial masters did not come near the exploits of the local princes. During his 37 years of reign the Maharaja of Cooch Behar and his guests killed 365 tigers, 311 leopards, 438 buffalo, and 207 Indian rhinoceroses.

The princes' *shikars* were often conducted from the backs of elephants and the hunting arrangements were often of a huge scale as when the Maharaja of Rewa in 1899 invited Viceroy Lord Curzon on a hunt with 5,000 beaters. The result of the joint efforts of the hunters and beaters was a bag of 16 adult tigers.

Largest Tiger Bag

The man who killed the most tigers in history was the maharaja of the former Indian state of Surguja, Ramanuj Saran Singh Deo (1917–1965). He hunted extensively in India, but also in Nepal and Africa. For many years of his hunting career the maharaja kept careful records of everything he bagged, and we know

With a total bag of 1,710 tigers, the Maharaja of Surguja is the most successful hunter of this species. Nearly 500 of these were killed with the rifle shown.

from these that he killed 1,157 tigers. His lifetime grand total was 1,710 tigers, including a white one. He was so obsessed with hunting that in 1947 the trigger-happy maharaja killed no fewer than three rare Asiatic cheetahs. Only five years later this species was declared extinct in India. Some 60 years later, attempts were made to reintroduce this species to India from the only remaining population, fewer than one hundred animals living in Iran.

David Hasinger killed the biggest known wild tiger in 1967.

Largest Tiger

In November 1967, the American hunter David J. Hasinger killed the largest known tiger with a single shot during a hunt in Uttar Pradesh, about 50 miles south of the Chinese border. The tiger weighed 855 pounds. The normal weight of a male tiger is around 550 to 660 pounds. The length of the animal, between pegs, was 10 feet, 6 inches. Measured along the back of the animal, the length was slightly over 11 feet.

Royal Tigers

The House of Windsor has had many hunting traditions, including tiger hunting in India. The most successful tiger-hunting member of the royal family was probably King George V who, during his visit in India in 1911, found time for a week-long shikar. It was a driven

---

Incredible but True!

The largest known tiger was killed by David J. Hasinger, in Uttar Pradesh, 50 miles south of the Chinese border, with a single shot. The tiger weighed 855 pounds.

From the end of the nineteenth century throughout most of the twentieth, all British kings and heirs to the throne went on at least one tiger hunt in India.

From the end of the nineteenth century throughout most of the twentieth, all British kings and heirs to the throne went on at least one tiger hunt in India.

hunt of enormous proportions with each hunter transported around in howdahs tied to the backs of elephants trained for the purpose. From this elevated position he killed 17 tigers.

His granddaughter, the present Queen Elizabeth, also participated in a tiger hunt. The event took place during her visit to Nepal in 1961, where one of the last truly great shikars was arranged near Ranthambore. The hunt involved scores of elephants accompanied by more than 2,000 beaters and servants. The Queen, probably very wisely, declined the invitation to shoot and left this to her husband and entourage. The result was more modest than on earlier hunts—two tigers in all.

Incredible but True!

Eric Rundgren, a professional hunter, holds the record for the most African leopards shot. He killed more than 500 spotted cats and once had to strangle a leopard with his bare hands to defend himself from attack.

Professional hunter Eric Rundgren shot the most leopards in Africa. Here he is with the one he had to strangle with his bare hands when it attacked him.

Leopards in Africa

Like the lion, the leopard was historically shot as vermin; the numbers killed by trophy hunters are comparatively small.

The hunter who killed the most African leopards is Eric Rundgren, who, as a control officer, killed more than 500 spotted cats during his career. On one occasion during a trophy hunt he was charged by a leopard wounded by a client. Rundgren had to strangle the animal with his bare hands and try to hold it down with the weight of his own body until the animal was finished off by an assistant. Just another hard day at the office for Rundgren.

The result of King George V's shikar in Nepal in 1911 was a bag of seventeen tigers.

The Maharaja of Cooch Behar possessed some of the best hunting grounds in India.

raja of Cooch Behar. During the years 1871–1907, he arranged a vast number of large driven hunts in great parts of Assam, The Duars, and Cooch Behar, where he and his guests killed a total of 311 leopards and 365 tigers, or roughly ten of each species annually.

Most Man-Eaters

Very few records of leopard hunting in Asia have survived. Best known are the hunts for the man-eating leopards, which were much more common in Asia than in Africa. The English colonel Jim Corbett (1875–1955) is probably the most famous hunter in

Asiatic Leopards

Leopards in Asia were primarily killed in conjunction with the large driven hunts for tigers. One of the very few who kept records of sport hunting for Asiatic leopards was the Maha-

Two anonymous British hunters in India with a man-eater they dispatched.

Jim Corbett and the hide of the Rudraprayag leopard, which allegedly killed more than 250 people.

46

Jim Corbett killed more man-eating leopards and tigers than anyone else.

has been estimated that these cats killed at least 1,200 humans. The record belongs to the Panar leopard, which allegedly killed more than 400 people. It was surpassed only by the Champawat tiger, with 436 documented kills.

Most Jaguars

Alexander "Sasha" Siemel (1890-1970) was born in Latvia and baptized Aleksander Ziemelis. He was an adventurer, hunter, guide, author, and actor who spoke seven languages. In 1923 he was hired by cattle ranchers in Brazil to kill cattle-eating jaguars in the Mato Grosso area. He was taught this "trade" by natives who used nothing but

this field due to his many books about the subject. He operated in the years 1907–1938 in northern India and Nepal and killed a total of 33 man-eaters—14 leopards and 19 tigers. It

A sight we will never see again: typical trophies from a shikar in India.

Aleksander Siemel killed more jaguars in South America than any other hunter.

a spear as a weapon. In the beginning Siemel used a rifle, but due to the density of the jungle he switched to a spear and in 1925 killed his first jaguar that way after it had been bayed by his dogs. During the rest of his career he killed more than 300 jaguars, most of them with a spear.

Incredible but True!

A leksander Siemel killed more than 300 jaguars—more than any other hunter in South America—while most of the time using a spear!

Largest Cougar

The Latin name of the cougar, puma, or mountain lion is *Profelis concolor* and it lives only in North and South America, ranging from high up in British Columbia to the southernmost parts of Argentina and Chile.

On average a female cougar weighs around 100 pounds and a male around 120 pounds. The heaviest recorded cougar was a male killed in Arizona that weighed 274½ pounds.

Although cougars often grow slightly larger than leopards, they are normally a lot less aggressive and attacks on humans are rare. Accordingly it is not unusual to kill cougars with bow and arrow or a revolver when they have climbed a tree or have been cornered on a mountain shelf by a pack of dogs.

Most Cougars

For many years cougar populations in the United States were managed

Although cougars typically are a little larger than leopards, they tend to be less aggressive toward humans and that makes them a lot less dangerous to hunt.

In spite of a crippled left hand and a blind eye, Jay C. Bruce worked as official cougar hunter for the state of California for thirty years.

by hunters employed by the government. These hunters were paid per kill, which resulted in some enormous bags. In 1918, wildlife officials in the state of California advertised for a cougar hunter and one particular application caught their attention. The applicant was Jay C. Bruce, who had lost the use of his left hand but who had still managed to kill no less than 31 cougars during four winters using a revolver.

After an interview that primarily consisted of Bruce telling hair-raising hunting stories, he was hired as the United States' first official cougar hunter. His salary was $25 a week plus a bonus of $20 for each cougar killed.

Bruce was industrious and started out with an average of 30 cougars a year; in 1927, he killed 42. In 1928 he lost the sight in his right eye but, undaunted, he continued as a cougar hunter for another 19 years. When he retired in 1947 his carefully kept records showed a total of 668 cougars killed.

Giles Goswick hunted for the state of Arizona during approximately the same span of time as Bruce and killed more than 700 cougars; he also guided trophy hunters.

The most successful cougar hunters, however, were probably the brothers Clell and Dale Lee who, with the aid of their highly trained dogs, killed more than a thousand cougars in Arizona and New Mexico, in addition to a number of jaguars in Mexico and in parts of South America.

C.E.Beebe and dog "Hoover" with a catch of mt. lions
J.W.Meiers

With the right dog, in this case a mongrel named Hoover, a day's bag of cougars can be quite impressive.

Chapter 4

Bears and Wolves

Largest Polar Bear

The largest recorded polar bear was killed by the American Arthur Dubs in 1960 in Kotzebue Sound, Alaska. The bear had a length of 11 feet, 1 inch from the snout to the tip of the tail and weighed 2,207 pounds. Only by weighing an entire bear can you get a precise measurement of its size; measurements of the skull and skin are only indicators of the actual size.

Henry Rudi and friends in front of the cabin.

Arthur Dubs and his record polar bear.

There are lots of accurate body weights of polar bears on record. This is because many of these bears were hunted from ships where they could easily be weighed before skinning.

Rudi's best season yielded 115 polar bears.

Most Polar Bears

The most successful polar bear hunter ever was the Norwegian Henry Rudi (1889–1970). During his total of 40 arctic trips in the years up to 1947—including 25 winters—Rudi killed a total of 713 polar bears on the islands of Svalbard, Jan Mayen, and Greenland. In 1953, in the very different spirit of the time, Henry Rudi was awarded the Norwegian King's Medal of Merit for his efforts. In the Arctic Museum at Tromsø, Norway, there is a permanent exhibition about Rudi next to other famous Arctic explorers like Roald Amundsen and Fridtjof Nansen.

Largest Brown Bear

It is difficult to determine which brown bear (*Ursus arctos*) is the largest ever recorded, as few hunters have had access to a scale in the wilderness of Alaska and there are few precisely recorded weights of the brown giants. The heaviest brown bear in captivity weighed 2,130 pounds, but much of this was due to a nine-inch-thick layer of fat.

As bearskins are very elastic, there are also many less-than-correct records of an animal's size based upon measurements of the skin. A good example is a Kodiak bear killed in 1894. Strapped to a wooden frame, with stones to pull it down, the skin measured 13½ feet from the tip of the snout to the end of tail—a measurement that undoubtedly does not reflect the true length of the live animal.

The most widely recognized method of measuring body size is "squaring"—a skin measurement based upon half of the sum of the distance from snout to tip of the tail and the distance between the front paws measured over the animal's back. One of the largest brown bears we have been able to find precise records of is a Kodiak bear killed in 1946 that measured 11 feet 4 inches by the squaring method.

Squaring a bear hide—adding the length and the width and dividing in two—is a common way to measure the size of a bear. The body weight is also interesting to know but typically difficult to obtain in the field due to obvious practical problems.

Size isn't everything when it comes to brown bears, however. I was charged by a 9-footer during a hunt in Alaska in 2002 and believe me, at close range, this is plenty big!

Most Alaskan Bears

It is not known who killed the most brown bears in Alaska. A likely candidate is the eccentric American judge George W. Folta (1893–1955), who killed more than 200 during his lifetime. On one single occasion he shot three 10-foot bears with his

The hide of a real monster taken 14 March 1949, on Kodiak Island, Alaska, squared 11 feet, 4 inches.

Bears and Wolves

Alaska brown bear taken by Capt. C. R. E. Radclyffe in 1903.

.35 Remington. On average, the judge shot four to six bears annually until he died—presumably happy—during a hunt in 1955.

Largest Bear Hunt

From the 25th to the 27th of June 1869, the largest bear hunt in history—as measured by the number of participants—took place in an area north of Lake Siljan in Sweden. Some 4,000 beaters arrived from four different parishes in order to participate in the hunt. The beaters surrounded a vast area and during the three days of hunting they managed to kill 23 bears, 9 moose, 3 wolves, and a single lynx. Apparently the participants were very happy with the result, which tell us something about how much the peasants of the time feared and loathed large carnivores.

There were many other places in Europe where large driven hunts for bears were conducted. At the end of the nineteenth century two parties of hunters consisting of 10 and 12 rifles killed 28 and 22 bears respectively during a three-week-long hunt in Transylvania. These results were overshadowed by the later Romanian president Ceausescu's dubious exploits in the same area.

Most Brown Bears

The Romanian dictator Nicolae Ceausescu (1918–1989), who was never inhibited by modesty, called himself "the greatest hunter ever." If one measures greatness by the sheer number of bears killed, he might have been right. In just two mornings in 1969 he killed 31 brown bears on one of the countless

The infamous Romanian dictator Nicolae Ceausescu was obsessed with the idea of becoming "the greatest hunter of all time" and he spent fortunes fulfilling his dream.

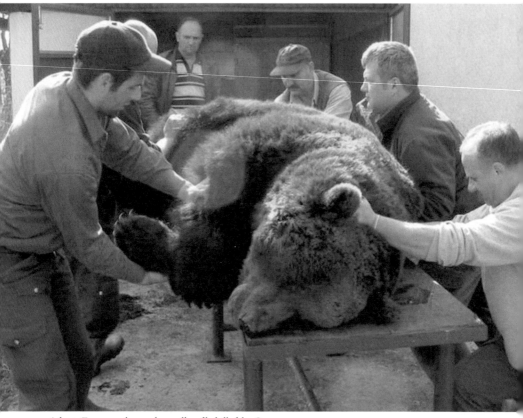

A huge European brown bear allegedly killed by Ceausescu.

driven hunts he arranged with himself as the only rifle at his personal hunting reserve, which encompassed practically all of Romania. In 1974, he killed 22 bears in one day, and this record stood until 15 October 1983, when the dictator killed 24 bears during the day's hunt at the Cusma Estate.

At the 1986 Hunting Exhibition, Romania presented the skins of 28 huge bears to the world—all killed by Nicolae himself. His bear skins make up a large number of the trophies listed in the different record systems. Some

critics, however, note that the hairs of the skins were quite wide apart due to a lot of stretching. This makes sense if you consider that the dictator's bear skulls, which are obviously a lot harder to stretch, never occupied nearly the same number of records in the trophy lists.

When it comes to the largest number of bears killed, no hunter has ever come even close to the trigger-happy Romanian dictator, which is unfortunate as he killed bears regardless of sex and age of the animals. According to the Romanian hunting journal *Diana's,*

European brown bears don't grow nearly as large as their North American and Russian relatives. This boar from Sweden is an extraordinary specimen weighing around 650 pounds.

issue 1/1990, Nicolae Ceausescu was credited with over 3,900 bear kills during his 24 years of reign, making his annual average more than 160 bears a year. Even the most hunting-crazy Russian Tsars and princes never came close to Ceausescu's bag.

Largest European Bears

The average weight of an adult European brown bear is between 450 and 550 pounds, but considerably larger specimens have been recorded. A bear shot in the Ural Mountains weighed 1,057 pounds, and the Romanian dictator Nicolae Ceausescu allegedly shot a Romanian bear weighing 1,430 pounds. However, according to our source—a Romanian civil servant in Ceausescu's hunting administration—the bear was very fat, as it had been fed fruit and cakes.

Largest Black Bear

The North American black bear (*Ursus americanus*) varies a lot in size throughout the species' geographical range. The average weight of the bears is higher in the eastern parts of the continent than in the western parts. Male bears typically weigh between 135 and

This photo of a married couple with a bag of seven bears was taken in Alaska in 1907.

The heaviest known black bears have all been extraordinarily fat.

Holt Collier was born a slave on a Texas plantation and became the greatest black bear hunter in history.

DRAWING THE LINE IN MISSISSIPPI

Holt Collier caught the bear that President Theodore Roosevelt refused to kill in 1902. The incident coined the phrase "Teddy Bear." In the contemporary cartoon, Collier is portrayed as white—probably because the artist was not able to imagine that the great hunter was, in fact, black.

600 pounds. Females generally weigh 25 percent less. The heaviest recorded specimen was a 10-year-old male killed in North Carolina in 1998. This animal weighed 878 pounds. In November 2010 an American bow hunter killed a 17-year-old bear in Pennsylvania weighing 877 pounds, but this animal had most likely been fed by humans.

Black Bear Hunters

It is claimed that the two great American heroes Daniel Boone (1734–1820) and Davy Crockett (1786–1836) killed hordes of bears, but the stories about them were evidently written with a good deal of artistic license, and the numbers are neither precise nor trustworthy. But even if you choose to believe these guesstimates, there is no doubt that a later American hunter killed considerably more bears than both of these celebrities combined.

Holt Collier (1846–1936) was born a slave on a plantation in Texas. As a ten-year-old boy he was equipped with a muzzleloader, shot, and bullets, and told to keep the slaves supplied with game meat. That same year, Collier killed his first black bear.

When he died eighty years later, Collier had killed more than 3,000 black bears, more than anyone else in history. Holt served in the Confederate army as a cavalryman and sharpshooter before working as one of the most sought-after bear guides in North America.

President Theodore "Teddy" Roosevelt (1858–1919) hired Collier as his personal guide on a bear hunt in Mis-

Wolves vary a lot in body size. This specimen, taken in Austria at the beginning of the 1900s, is typical for a European wolf, with a body weight of approximately 80 pounds.

sissippi. The hunt was followed closely by the press but it did not go as Roosevelt hoped, as he did not get a chance to shoot. But Collier was a man of action and a few days later he caught a large male bear with his lasso and tied it to a tree so Roosevelt could shoot it.

Roosevelt, however, refused to shoot the bear under these circumstances. A cartoonist quickly made a drawing of the animal-friendly president and a cute bear. This was the birth of the "Teddy" bear, and the toy manufacturers quickly made the most of it—all of it due to a fearless ex-slave and a prominent client

This wolf taken in Alberta, Canada, in 2009 is thought to be the heaviest specimen killed by a hunter. The weight is around 200 pounds. The name of the hunter was never disclosed.

The average weight of wolves increases as you go north. This beautiful male wolf was taken in northern Norway in the late 1940s.

who did not want to shoot under unsporting conditions.

Big, Bad Wolf

Male wolves (*Canis lupus*) grow considerably larger than females, and normally a large male wolf weighs around 135 pounds. But from North America, Europe, and Russia there are frequent reports of male wolves weighing more than 175 pounds.

The official record has for many years been a male wolf from Alaska weighing slightly over 174 pounds, but in 2009 a wolf of the same size was killed in Bulgaria. Later the same year the wolf shown in the photograph was killed by an anonymous hunter in Alberta, Canada. There are some disagreements over the exact weight, but all sources agree that it

was at least 198 pounds. Whether Little Red Riding Hood's grandmother fell out of the carcass when it was skinned remains uncertain.

Eager Wolf Hunter

John George I of Saxony (1585–1656) managed to kill 3,782 wolves during the first half of the seventeenth century on driven hunts using wheel-lock rifles. This number constituted the all-time record until the reign of the last Russian Tsar—at least as far as we have been able to establish. No one in the history of recorded wolf hunting has surpassed Tsar Nicholas II, the last Russian Tsar. His total bag exceeded 10,000 wolves, including more than 100 pure white wolves.

Nicholas II (1868–1918) is most likely the hunter who has bagged the most wolves in a lifetime.

Wolves were numerous in the Russian Empire and as peasants were not allowed to possess firearms, the animals were quite intrepid and intrusive. On moonlit nights you could entice hungry wolf packs to chase horse-driven sleighs filled with hunters, using a squealing piglet as a "call." As the wolves tried to reach the piglet or the horses, the hunters killed them with guns and even pistols and axes. In this way more than a hundred wolves were sometimes bagged during a single night. One report describes the remains of almost 300 wolves in the snow at daybreak after such a hunt.

Nicholas was not intimidated by wolves. At one time he and a companion were surprised by a pack of wolves that attacked his companion's horse. The wolves managed to kill both the horse and its rider before the Tsar managed to kill a couple of them with his revolver and drive the rest of the pack off.

The Emperor, however, was not the only Russian with a firm hand regarding wolves. In 1877 a correspondent for *The New York Times* reported on a Russian peasant he met who had saved himself from an attack by a pack of wolves by killing seven with as many blows from his hatchet. Who needs a gun, anyway?

Wolf pelts used to be in great demand.

There are still large wolf populations in North America and Russia.

Four Hundred Wolves a Year

In the United States there were a number of pioneers who made a living from wolf hunting, but few of them recorded their experiences. Peter A. Watson was an exception; he survived a spectacular wolf attack and his story was published in September 1899. At the time, Watson was fifty-five years of age and had worked for a decade as a wolf hunter for The Nebraska Cattle Rancher's Association. He hunted from horseback with the aid of a pack of specially trained wolf dogs.

His method was simple. When he had spotted a wolf with his telescope, he made a detour and cut off the animal's route. When the right moment came, he galloped toward the surprised wolf and sent the dogs after it. After a mile or two, the pack would bay the wolf and the dogs would kill it within minutes. It was quite rare that Watson had to help the dogs, so he carried only a revolver on these hunts. In this manner he dispatched more than 4,000 wolves during the first ten years of his career.

But in 1899, while his dogs were chasing one wolf, Watson was attacked by a big female wolf that locked its jaws into his thigh while his horse galloped off in panic. Unfortunately the wolf was hanging over his revolver and as he tried to get hold of it, the animal grabbed his arm instead of his thigh. With great difficulty, Watson managed to grab the revolver with his left hand and put some shots into the frenzied animal. When only a single shot was left, the wolf still had a firm grip in his hand, which "it energetically chewed." Taking a grave risk of shooting himself in the hand, he put the barrel of the revolver into the mouth of the wolf and, with his last bullet, sent the animal on to the eternal hunting grounds.

Killer Wolves

Wolves attacks on people are not as rare as some biologists claim. There are numerous examples of wolves learning to hunt people and killing several before a bullet put an end to their practice. Normally the wolf is a very shy animal that presents no danger to humans, but when the animal's inbred fear of man is lost, the intelligent canine becomes very dangerous, especially to children, who constitute the majority of wolves' human victims throughout history.

One of the most famous examples is from the years 1763–1767 when a pack of wolves is thought to have killed 99 people around the city of Gévaudan in southern France. From 1804–1853 there were 111 wolf-related deaths in

Estonia, and 108 of these were children. In Sweden the "Gysinge Wolf" killed 11 children and a young woman in the years 1820–1821. Another lone wolf in Karelia killed eight children and a woman in 1831–1832. This part of Finland was again the scene of no less than 21 wolf-related human fatalities from 1839–1850. In the European part of Russia the authorities recorded 376 victims to wolf attacks just during the years 1849–1851. In 1870–1887 no fewer than 1,445 people were killed by wolves in the same region. The wolf scourge in this part of Russia seems to have reached its peak when 203 wolf-related deaths were recorded in 1899.

India too, has been hard hit by wolf attacks during history. In 1875 the North Western Frontier district was hit by a wave of wolf attacks that killed 721 people. Three years later, wolves killed 624 people in all of India. Contemporary records are no less sensational and there is hard evidence of their accuracy. From February to August 1981, a pack of wolves in Bihar killed 13 children. In 1986 another pack killed 17 children in Ashta. Sixty children were killed by wolves in 1993–1995 in Bihar, and in 1996–1997, 74 people were attacked by wolves in Uttar Pradesh.

The wolf has always been the enemy of man due to the danger it poses to livestock. The fact that the wolf also poses danger to humans has been denied by many in recent years and old stories of wolves killing humans have been ridiculed. Today we know for a fact that wolves can be dangerous to people if the animals lose their inherent fear of man.

Part 2
Other Big Game

Chapter 5

American Deer

Deer Hunters

Few records have been kept of the harvest of white-tailed deer (*Odocoileus virginianus*) and even fewer of mule deer (*Odocoileus hemionus*). The simple reason is that those who hunted them in large numbers rarely put pen to paper or even counted their bags of game. After the introduction of game management in the early twentieth century and the resulting limitation of the individual hunter's bag, there was even less reason to do so. It seems unlikely, however, that any American market hunter ever approached anything like the enormous game bags made by some members of the European aristocracy, with the possible exception of the famous buffalo hunters in the late nineteenth century.

One successful American hunter who did keep meticulous records was Thomas Meacham of New York, who died in 1850. He shot a total of 2,550 deer, 219 bears, 214 wolves, and 72 mountain lions during his lifetime.

John Q. Dyce (1830–1904) of Pennsylvania was also a successful hunter, but unfortunately his grand total is unknown. However, it is recorded that he frequently shot nine deer in a single day. His most successful hunting exploit was when he (accidentally?) shot three white-tailed deer with a single shot, the bullet piercing the brain of a buck, then going through the throat of the doe before finally lodging itself in the heart of a fawn.

The most successful American deer hunter I have been able to find reports of is Seth Iredell Nelson (1809–1905) of Potter County, Pennsylvania. He kept a

Incredible but True!

I*t is reported that John Q. Dyce of Pennsylvania once shot three white-tailed deer with a single shot, with the shot going through a buck, a doe, and a fawn.*

game book and recorded a bag of more than 3,500 white-tailed deer, over 500 elk or wapiti, and a similar number of bears. In addition, Nelson killed hundreds of cougars, wolves, and bobcats. His grand total thus exceeded 5,000 animals, most of them taken in Clinton County, Pennsylvania. After his death, Nelson was buried on the top of Karthaus Mountain, overlooking the one-time hunting paradise he had once roamed.

Recent Deer Hunters

Due to the lack of precise records, it is hard to determine the most successful hunter of white-tailed deer. Since the early twentieth century, each state has greatly limited the number of bucks a hunter can take annually. Accordingly, in order to shoot a large number of

bucks, you need to have either plenty of time to hunt in different states or have a very long hunting career—preferably both. One likely candidate for the most successful whitetail hunter in recent years, however, is Larry Benoit (1924–2013) of Maine. For more than seventy years he tracked white-tailed deer through the woods of northern New England and southern Canada, shooting at least 200 white-tailed bucks in spite of the relatively low density of animals in these states. A small number of other American hunters have shot nearly the same number of deer, although no exact records are available. But considering the difficulties of this type of hunting, it represents a much larger effort and far more hunting skill than most of the large bags made in Europe from far denser populations of game.

A successful deer hunt in northern Wisconsin.

Seth Iredell Nelson was one of the greatest deer hunters of America's pioneer era.

A deer hunter with the classic American rifle—a Winchester.

Oldest Deer

The oldest white-tailed deer I have been able to find records of was a doe called Elizabeth living on a deer ranch in Michigan. She was 24 years and 7 months old when she passed away of old age. Another very old deer was a blacktail doe living on Gambier Island in British Columbia. She became tame in 1918 when she had her first fawn and died in the winter of 1938–1939 at the age of more than 22 years.

Heaviest Deer

It is always tricky to get exact records of the live weight of larger game species. Few hunters have access to a scale in the bush and accordingly most weights recorded are taken from animals that have been field-dressed. The heaviest white-

tailed deer on record was a buck taken near Tofte, Minnesota, in 1926 by Carl J. Lenander Jr. In field-dressed condition the animal weighed 402 pounds and accordingly the live weight was calculated by the Conservation Department to have been around 510 pounds. The weight of the Tofte buck was matched by another Minnesota buck killed in November 1981 by George Himango on the Fond du Lac Indian Reservation.

The heaviest mule deer I have found records of was a buck killed by Laurence Rowe near Allenspark, Col-

Incredible but True!

History repeats itself. The heaviest white-tailed deer on record was a buck taken near Tofte, Minnesota, in 1926 by Carl J. Lenander Jr., weighing 402 pounds field-dressed. It was matched in 1981 by another Minnesota buck killed by George Himango on the Fond du Lac Indian Reservation.

orado, in 1938. It weighed 410 pounds dressed and must have weighed around 520 pounds alive.

Longest Beams

It makes little sense to try to determine the "best" whitetail trophy as this varies according to the rules of the measuring system used. What can be measured objectively are the length of the antler beams, the spread between them, and the number of tines.

For almost 100 years the longest beam on record belonged to a white-tailed buck that was killed in Michigan in 1913. This buck was a nontypical with 32 points, an inside spread of 20¼ inches, and the longest beam measuring 32¼ inches. Eighty years later, this record was broken by a typical buck with beams measuring 32 and 32½ inches.

However, in 2010 Brian Stephens of Ohio killed a nontypical white-tailed buck with his muzzleloader on the opening day of the season; the buck's left beam was 35⅛ inches long. For comparison, the current Boone and Crockett world-record buck (typical), killed in Saskatchewan by Milo N. Hanson in 1993, had a total of 14 tines, an inside spread of 27¼ inches, and a beam length of 28½ inches.

Antler Spread

The narrowest inside spread of the whitetail trophies entered in the Boone and Crockett record book is only 13½ inches and comes from a buck killed in Texas in 2000. The widest inside spread is 32 inches and comes from a

head picked up in Comanche County, Kansas, in 1991.

The largest outside spread I have seen recorded is 34½ inches found on a white-tailed buck which was killed in 1964 in Todd County, Kentucky. A head of same size was picked up in Hancock, Maine, in 1975.

A farmed nontypical buck called Big Louie grew a set of antlers with an outside spread of 38 inches, but it makes little sense to compare farmed animals with their free-roaming counterparts as they are intentionally fed hormones in order to grow enormous antlers.

Antler Points

There are different definitions of what constitutes a tine, depending on species and scoring system. (In Europe many hunters claim that a projection of an antler is only a proper tine if you can hang a hunting bag on it.) However, the major measuring systems agree that in order to be a proper tine, the antler projection must be at least one inch long and longer than it is wide. Obviously the largest number of points is found on nontypical heads.

With the development of deer farming for huge trophies by the aid of hormones and steroids, it is hard to tell what the largest number of tines is at present, as the record is broken very frequently. If we stick to unfarmed animals, a contender for the greatest number of tines is found on the famous "Hole in the Horn Buck" from Ohio. It was found dead in 1940, killed by a train. This head had 45 tines and an inside spread of 24⅜ inches. Another

Incredible but True!

I n 1940 a buck was found killed by a train in Ohio and became the famous "Hole in the Horn Buck," with 45 tines and an inside spread of 24⅜ inches.

Stats by State

If you want to maximize your chances of taking a white-tailed buck in the United States, it is a good idea to go hunting in Texas, which leads the nation both in availability of bucks and the population density in general. In 2010 the five states with the most bucks harvested were:

- Texas (357,378)
- Michigan (212,341)
- Georgia (155,255)
- Wisconsin (148,378)
- Alabama (129,000)

45-pointer was shot in 1995 by Tony Fulton of Mississippi.

In 1892 a remarkable nontypical white-tailed buck was killed by an unknown hunter in Texas. The buck's rack had 47 points. It scored 284⅜ inches and was the world-record rack until 1940.

However, the total number of bucks harvested annually is obviously related to the available hunting areas. Instead of the total harvest it makes sense to see how many bucks were harvested per square mile, and this alters the five leading states to the following:

- Texas (5.8)
- South Carolina (4.8)
- Wisconsin (4.4)
- Indiana (4.3)
- Georgia (4.1)

The longest known antlers of modern deer belong to the Alaskan caribou.

Obviously bucks must be older than average in order to grow nice racks. In 2010 the five states with the highest percentage of bucks 3½ years old or older taken by hunters were:

+ Arkansas (68 percent)
+ Louisiana (65 percent in Deer Management Assistance Program Areas)
+ Texas (59 percent)
+ Kansas (56 percent)
+ Oklahoma (51 percent)

Record Head Density

The likeliness of getting a top-class whitetail trophy depends on factors that include quantity and the quality of available food, deer density, climatic conditions, and genetics. This becomes evident if you look at the entries of white-tailed bucks in the Boone and Crockett record book.

For comparison purposes, the number of entries from each state has been converted to the number per 1,000 square miles of land. During the period from 1999 to 2009, the ten highest-ranking states had, on average, an annual entry of the following numbers of bucks in B&C's book of records:

+ Illinois: 1.07
+ Kentucky: 0.85
+ Iowa: 0.80
+ Ohio: 0.79
+ Wisconsin: 0.79
+ Indiana: 0.74
+ Rhode Island: 0.65
+ Delaware: 0.60
+ Missouri: 0.57
+ Kansas: 0.39

Late Recordings

Some world records take a long time to be recognized as such. One example is a mule deer killed in Alberta in 1926 by Edmond Broder. Realizing it was an outstanding trophy, he had it mounted. But it was another thirty-six years—1962—before Broder was persuaded to have it officially measured by Boone and Crockett. It was declared the world-record nontypical mule deer, a title it has held ever since.

It took an even longer time for the former world-record elk to be recorded. It was taken in late 1899 in Colorado by a miner named John Plute. He was out hunting for meat with his .30-40 Krag rifle. He shot a giant bull elk and left the antlers in the woods, as they had no

Incredible but True!

A mule deer that was killed by Edmond Broder in 1926 in Alberta, Canada, was officially recorded in 1962 by Boone and Crockett and still holds the world record for nontypical mule deer.

This incredible mule deer was killed in Alberta in 1926 by Edmond Broder. Thirty-six years later it was officially measured and declared the world record.

value. But when stories about the size of the rack began to circulate, he went back and fetched them to prove his integrity. He then gave the rack to a friend, John Rozich, and after being passed down in the Rozich family they were measured and declared a world record by Boone and Crockett in March 1961.

The former world-record typical whitetail rack has an even stranger history. In November 1914, James Jordan (1892–1971) killed a buck in Wisconsin. Although virtually no one thought of measuring trophies in those days, Jordan realized he had shot a monster buck and sent it to the local taxidermist, George Van Castle, for mounting.

Van Castle, however, moved to Minnesota and later to Florida before Jordan could try to get his trophy back. Not able to trace the taxidermist, Jordan gave up hope of ever seeing his great trophy again. He later moved to Hinckley, Minnesota, where the taxidermist had lived before moving to Florida.

In 1964 a distant cousin of Jordan's, Robert Ludwig, bought a whitetail mount at a garage sale in Sandstone, Minnesota, for $3. Ludwig had the rack measured, and it was declared a new world record, although no one knew anything of its origin. The news got around and eventually reached Jordan, who went to see it.

Jim Jordan finally got his name next to his buck in the record book in December 1978, some sixty-four years after he killed it and, unfortunately, two months after he died. Jordan's trophy held the world record until the arrival of Milo N. Hanson's buck in 1993.

Longstanding Record

The longest standing Boone and Crockett world record is a woodland caribou head from an animal taken in Newfoundland in 1910. The antlers were donated to the B&C Club's National Collection by H. Casimir de Rham and are now on display at the Buffalo Bill Historical Center in Cody, Wyoming. The second-oldest world record is a bison taken in Yellowstone Park in 1925.

Incredible but True!

The longest-standing Boone and Crockett world record is a woodland caribou head from an animal taken in Newfoundland in 1910. The antlers are on display at the Buffalo Bill Historical Center in Cody, Wyoming.

Longest Antlers

Among all the living deer species, there are two almost even results among the contestants for the title of the longest antlers, and both species are from North America. The winner is a caribou (*Rangifer tarandus*), from Alaska, which had an antler length of 71⅞ inches. The bull was taken near Mulchatna River by John R. McCarl around the end of the nineteenth century, but there is no record of what year he took it. Close behind comes W. F. Sheard's elk rack, which has an antler length of 71¼ inches. For comparison, the longest recorded antler of a red deer, *Cervus elaphus*, is 68 inches.

Chapter 6

European Deer

Roe Deer

In Europe most hunters are as dedicated to hunting roebucks as American hunters are to hunting whitetails. However, the hunting conditions are very different as even today most hunting areas in Europe are on private properties where it is left to the owner to manage the game population as he sees fit within the hunting season. This means that some privileged hunters have amassed large bags of game that would be impossible under the much more democratic way that hunting opportunities are allocated in the United States.

Elector Johann Georg II of Saxony was the most successful roe deer hunter of all time.

Largest Roe Deer Bag

There is no doubt that the Elector of Saxony (Germany), Johann Georg II (1613–1680), was the most successful roe deer hunter in history. His hunting diaries disclose that his total bag of roe deer consisted of 16,864 animals. And he was a chip off the old block when it came to hunting. His father, Johann Georg I (1586–1656), who ruled from 1611–1656, killed a total of 11,489 roe deer. These vast numbers stem from two factors. First and foremost, the two princes did little other than hunt and wage war.

Second, you would scarcely consider the "hunting" technique they used as anything other than slaughter. With the aid of fences and dogs, the animals were driven into large nets. These nets allowed the "hunters," with a large number of guns and loaders, to kill hundreds of animals.

Killing a roebuck in Europe at the end of the 1800s was such an unusual feat that the lucky hunter brought the freshly killed animal to a photographer's studio to document the event.

Large Bags

Hungary has some of the densest populations of roe deer, especially on some of the islands of the Danube. On one of these an anonymous Hungarian hunter killed 113 trophy bucks during nine days of stalking (the European term for traditional hunting on foot) in 1909.

However, the Austro-Hungarian Archduke Franz Ferdinand (1863–1914) probably still holds the record for the most roebucks killed by traditional methods. In the spring of 1899 he participated in a three-day hunt at Count Tassilo Festetic's estate and killed "66 carefully selected old bucks."

His colleague, the Russian Tsar Nicholas II (1868–1918), also had a taste for hunting roebucks. During his annual hunt at the Bialowieza Forest in Poland in 1900 he and his eleven guests

The Russian Tsar Nicholas II and his guests killed no less than 325 roebucks during a single hunt in the fall of 1900.

Archduke Franz Ferdinand of the Austro-Hungarian Empire probably still holds the record for most roebucks killed during a few days of stalking.

killed 623 hoofed animals. A total of 325 of these were roebucks. Three were does, which probably were not meant to be shot during the drives.

During a single morning in the 1880s, the Austro-Hungarian Crown Prince Rudolf killed 18 roebucks at the Hungarian estate Keszthely, supposedly from a horse-drawn cart.

The day before the outbreak of World War I in 1914, a party of five hunters killed 52 roebucks in the morning and evening at the Polish Count Tarowski's estate.

The "Baillie Monster" scored 238.6 CIC points.

Largest Roebuck Head

While most American hunters are familiar with the trophy measuring systems of Safari Club International and Boone and Crockett, the predominant measuring system in Europe is run by the International Hunting Council, often referred to by the acronym of the organization's French name, *Conseil International de la Chasse*: CIC.

The CIC system of measuring is much more complex and often includes subjective qualities like beauty and symmetry, which can add to the score or cause penalty points. When it comes to roebuck heads, the weight of the antlers is included in the score, which makes it even harder to create a "just" ranking of trophies. Gener-

Since medieval times, big-game shooting in Europe has been a privilege of the fortunate few. This is Countess Fritze Frijs in front of the large Danish estate Frijsenborg.

Carl Georg Stjernswärd's roebuck. The height is a bit shy of 11 inches and the weight is a little bit above 2 pounds. With a score of 246.9 CIC points, it is the official world record.

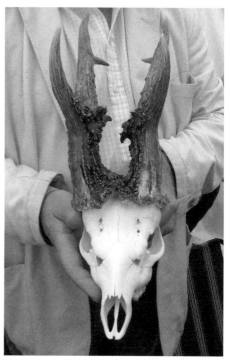

Tom Troubridge's roebuck antlers. The height is nearly 12 inches and the weight is close to 3 pounds. It measures 275 CIC points, but is not considered the world record.

ally, however, the best trophies are divided into three groups according to the number of points they qualify for: bronze medal (105 points), silver medal (115 points), and gold medal (130 points).

Measured according to the CIC rules, Tom Troubridge's buck (shown in the above photo) scores 275 points. It weighed 44¾ ounces and had a length of 11¾ inches. However, due to the enlarged pedicels, the trophy is considered abnormal and not a valid record. The record goes to head number two from the left in the photo—the impressive, but pointwise much smaller, trophy from Sweden taken in 1982 by Carl Georg Stjernswärd. It scores 246.9 CIC points, weighs 33⅜ ounces, and has an average antler length of "only" 10½ inches.

Abnormality of pedicels first became an issue when Peter Baillie, who was at the time chairman of the British Deer Society, killed a roebuck in England in 1974. The head was quickly nicknamed "The Baillie Monster." It weighed 40¼ ounces and measured 238.6 CIC points, but it is evident that the weight of the abnormally thick pedicels is out of proportion with the rest of the trophy.

This Hungarian roebuck killed in 1965 held the world-record title until 1982, with a total score of 240 CIC points.

They also weigh more, normally between 90 to 135 pounds, with record animals weighing up to 180 pounds. The antlers are generally also one and a half times the size of European heads. The record length is 18⅝₆ inches and belongs to a head taken in the Altai Mountains in 1898.

Roebuck Success

When it comes to large roebuck trophies, Denmark's, and most likely the world's, most successful hunter is Erik Hahn Pedersen (b. 1959). As of this writing, he has taken 64 heads scoring

The longest antler length of a European roebuck is 14⅜ inches. The head belonged to a buck killed in 1967 by Christian Muff during a hunt in the Caucasian Mountains. Its spread was 10⅜ inches. The second-longest antler was from a buck killed in Romania in 1959 by Mr. J. Bucsa. The longest antler was 14¼ inches and the head measured 166.85 CIC points.

Siberian Roe Deer

Even the largest European roe deer cannot possibly compete with the much larger subspecies of roe deer, the Siberian roe (*Capreolus pygargus*), which lives in Central Asia. Siberian roebucks are 6 inches taller than their European cousins—around 36 inches.

Siberian roe deer are far bigger than their European cousins.

European Deer

Erik Hahn Pedersen is one of very few hunters in the world who has managed to kill more than one roebuck scoring over 200 CIC points.

over the "magic" 100 points according to the CIC system. Of these 64 heads, 15 have qualified for a bronze medal (105–124 points), 12 for a silver medal (125–129 points), and 24 for a gold medal (130 points or more). The 40 largest heads he has taken have an average measurement of 135 points. He is one of only a handful of hunters worldwide who has taken more than one roebuck head measuring over 200 CIC points. Erik's goal is to take more than 100 heads measuring more than 100 points.

Heaviest Roebuck

The average weight of a live roe deer is 55 to 70 pounds, with bucks normally weighing half a dozen pounds more than does. However, there are great variations behind these figures.

A Swedish study of 500 adult roe deer revealed a variation in weight of field-dressed animals of no less than 29 pounds from the heaviest (59.7 pounds) to the lightest animal (30.8 pounds).

The record for European roe deer probably belongs to a buck killed in Västerbotten, Sweden. Without intestines, head, lower legs, and skin, the animal still weighed 63.2 pounds. On the hoof the animal probably weighed close to 110 pounds.

Oldest Roe Deer

A Polish study showed an average life span for roe deer of only 3.5 years. In Denmark, scientists found that the average life span of roe deer that survive their first year is only 3.1 years. Only 14 percent of roe deer will live longer than three or four years. These studies put the longest recorded life span of a roe deer into perspective: A free-roaming doe that was ear-tagged as a fawn in Brunswick, England, in 1943 was shot less than 50 yards from where it had

European rulers have always coveted big antlers from red deer stags.

Duke Ernest II of Saxony-Coburg-Gotha was a terrific shot and a very successful red deer hunter.

been tagged—more than 20 years later during the autumn of 1963!

Largest Red Deer Bag

Red stags have historically been the most highly regarded of all big game in Europe. Elector Johann Georg I of Saxony (1585–1656) declined to become king of Bohemia partly because of the state of the country, but allegedly mostly because the Bohemian stags were "inferior in both numbers and size." Today it is hard to determine whether this story is true, but it is definitely a fact that Johann Georg I was a very keen hunter. His total lifetime bag of red deer was 35,421 animals.

As war and conflicts were rampant during his time, Johann Georg I could not devote as much time to hunting as he would have liked. That was not as much of a problem for his son and successor, Johann Georg II (1613–1680), who killed the most red deer in history: 43,649 red deer.

The names of these two nobles appear numerous times in this book. As previously described in the roe deer section, however, you have to remember that their enormous bags were achieved by methods no one today would consider as resembling true hunting.

Modern Red Deer Record

When it comes to hunting methods acceptable today, it is actually one of the descendants of the two Johann Georges who holds the record. In the years between 1837 and 1886, Duke Hugo Ernst II of Saxony-Coburg and Gotha (1818–1893) killed a total of 3,283 red deer, of which 2,316 were stags. Seven of these had between 20 and 24 points while more than 200 had more than 14 points.

Oldest Trophy

The oldest known full mount in the world is a red deer stag that was added to the Royal Danish Art Chamber in 1691. The stag has been restored several times and is now displayed at the Danish Hunting and Forest Museum in Hoersholm north of Copenhagen.

The oldest mounted trophy in the world is this Danish red deer, which left the taxidermist sometime before 1691.

Another view of the red deer, one of the oldest mounted trophies in existence.

Trophies of red deer can be found in huge collections of former European rulers. Many of these collections are hundreds of years old.

Red Stag Trophies

In Europe there are several very old collections of stag heads, although wars and fires have reduced some of them during the centuries. The most comprehensive collection is found at the castle of Moritzburg in Saxony (Germany), which is open to the public.

Among the many trophies, you can find the rack with the largest known spread. It has 22 points and a spread of 75½ inches. Unfortunately nothing is known of the origins of this trophy other than that it was included in the collection before 1586.

The longest known beam length for a red stag antler is 68 inches and belonged to an animal killed during 1862 in the Carpathian Mountains (between Poland and Romania). It now resides in The Powerscourt Collection in Ireland. The head has 44 points and a spread of 65 inches.

The record number of tines belongs to an uneven 66-pointer. This head was taken by the Elector Frederic III of Brandenburg (1659–1713) in the year 1696. It is claimed that his successor accepted "a company of tall grenadiers" in exchange for the trophy.

Dubious Records

There is little point in trying to determine which red deer trophy is the largest, even within the recognized measuring systems. Intensive breeding on highly sophisticated deer farms around the world makes it impossible to conduct an objective comparison of the heads of free-roaming stags and those which are bred and released, or hunted inside a fence. The problem is illustrated by the fact that the International Hunting Council, CIC, in 2006 revoked the world-record title from a Bulgarian red stag head. It turned out that the stag had been transported from is breeding ground in the Alps to Bulgaria where an unsuspecting hunter shot it as a new world record scoring 278 points.

When it comes body weights there are also great variations. A good-size

This is the red deer trophy with the largest known spread: over 75 inches. The mean length of the antlers (47 inches) is 22 inches short of the record antler length.

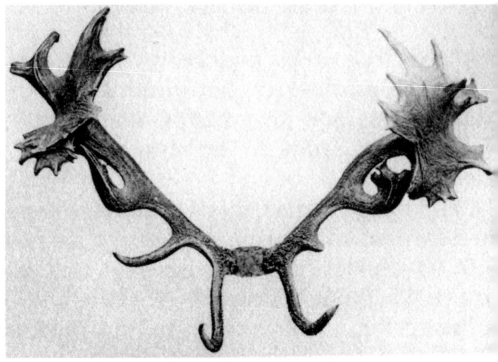

This 66-pointer taken in 1696 holds the record for most tines on a red-deer trophy.

field-dressed red stag in Scandinavia or Scotland weighs around 220 pounds, but in the Carpathians there are examples of stags weighing over 650 pounds even after field-dressing.

Busy Days

At the end of the nineteenth century, a number of deer species were introduced to New Zealand as there were no large native mammals on the islands when the Europeans arrived. Like many other species introduced to areas where there are no natural predators, the red deer population in New Zealand quickly grew to a size where it caused massive crop damage. In 1923, a farmer named J. G. Sutherland was permitted to shoot red deer off his fields and later reported to the authorities that he had killed 667 red deer in five days, including 194 in a single day.

Chapter 7

Other Hoofed Game

Biggest Moose

Among the world's eight scientifically recognized subspecies of moose, the Alaskan variety, *Alces alces gigas*, is the largest, with a live weight of a big bull around 1,500 to 1,600 pounds. Moose living on the other side of the Bering Strait will normally reach around 90 percent of this weight.

The largest recorded Alaska moose was a bull with a weight of 1,797 pounds. The stated weight of wild animals should be taken with a pinch of salt as they nor-

Capt. C. R. E. Radclyffe with an Alaska moose taken in 1908.

Swedish hunter Leif Jacobsson with the largest known trophy of European moose, taken in 1982.

moose recorded weighed 1,310 pounds. The butchered weight—e.g., the body without intestines, head, skin, and lower legs—normally constitutes around 55 percent of the weight of a live animal. Although the Swedish moose normally is somewhat smaller than its American cousins, the record for a Swedish moose is more than 900 pounds, so this animal must have weighed around 1,600 pounds live according to the rule of thumb described above.

The smallest subspecies of the long-nosed deer are the Asiatic Amur-moose, *Alces alces cameloides*, which normally only have a live weight around 450 pounds, somewhat less than a large red deer.

mally cannot be weighed in the field and accordingly the number is often a "guesstimate" rather than a fact. After field-dressing, the heaviest Alaska

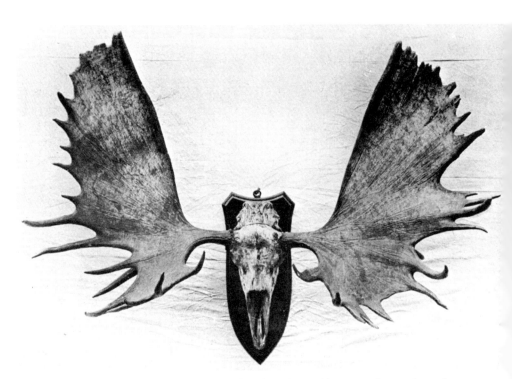

The largest known moose trophy in the world is from the Yukon and has a spread just under six feet.

Incredible but True!

Scientists estimate the total number of moose in Newfoundland to be 150,000. These 150,000 moose are spread out over only 42,800 square miles!

Many Moose

The densest population of moose in the world is in Newfoundland, where scientists estimate the total number to be 150,000 spread over an area of 42,800 square miles. The Gros-Morne National Park covers 695 square miles and is home to around 5,000 moose, the greatest density recorded. In spite of a population of only 500,000 people, Newfoundland had 741 traffic accidents involving moose in 2010.

No country has a larger harvest of moose per square kilometer than Sweden. The most successful season was 1982 when 174,709 moose were killed. This figure makes up half of all the moose killed in the world that year.

This figure also proves the importance of proper management, as the total kill for the 1939 season was less than 10,000 moose. As of 2012, some 80,000 moose are culled annu-

ally out of a total spring population of approximately 200,000 animals.

In all of North America around 90,000 moose are killed annually, a number that is estimated to be less than 10 percent of the total population.

Most Moose Bagged

In Sweden five hunters killed more than 1,000 moose in a lifetime. They are Jan Åkerman, Arne Bromée, Knut Edén, Johnny Rülcker, and the most successful, Karl-Henry Lundin (1921-2004). Lundin killed 1,038 moose with his own rifle, but in addition to this number we must add a large but unrecorded number of wounded animals he put out of their misery after tracking them with his widely famed moose dogs.

Swedish hunter Karl-Henry Lundin probably holds the world record for the largest number of moose taken in a lifetime.

Largest Moose Bag

One of Sweden's best moose hunting areas is the royal hunting fields in the mountains of Halle- and Hunneberg in Västergötland. In 1885, when the moose population was almost extinct in most other parts of Sweden, thirty hunters (including the then-Prince of Wales) killed 73 moose in just one day of driven hunting at Halle- and Hunneberg.

Most Moose in a Day

The Swedish Baron Stig Ramel (1927–2006) is probably the person who had the most successful moose-hunting day in history. On 12 October 1972, he was attending a driven moose hunt at Hasselfors Bruk estate near Närke,

On the Halle- and Hunneberg hunting ground belonging to the king of Sweden, 73 moose were shot on a single day's driven hunt in 1885.

Sweden. Sixty moose were killed—29 bulls, 11 cows/heifers, and 20 calves. Ramel's share included 12 animals—6 bulls, 4 cows/heifers, and 2 calves.

Ten years later, hunters participating in a driven hunt around Kukkola in Tornedalen, near the Finnish border, probably set the speed record for moose hunting. In a single drive, 26 moose were shot in a span of just 30 seconds. Unfortunately, we do not know the size of the entire day's bag.

Moose Heads

In 1982 Leif Jacobsson shot a bull moose near Jokkmokk in northern Sweden; with an antler span of 54⅓ inches, it is the largest known head of a European moose. The highest number of points is 42, found on the head of

Baron Stig Ramel is probably the hunter who has shot the most moose in a single day.

Incredible but True!

Near the Finnish border at a driven hunt around Kukkola in Tornedalen, 26 moose were shot in a span of just 30 seconds!

In some areas of North America the density of the moose population approaches that of Scandinavia.

a bull killed by Ulf Eskildsen in 1986 near Kraddsele (a lake in Västerbotten, Sweden). Another, somewhat malformed, head also with 42 points was later taken in Sweden.

Outside Europe the largest recorded spread is 81½ inches, which was measured on a rack of an Alaskan moose (*Alces alces*) taken in 1972 by Peter Zipperle. Although it has the largest recorded spread, it ranks number 258 in the latest Boone and Crockett record book. The

points on each antler are not traditionally counted by hunters in North America and accordingly the largest number is not recorded.

Top Moose Trophies

Early in the twentieth century, Mr. A. S. Reed went on a hunting trip to Cook's Inlet in Alaska. He killed six moose that probably constitute the best bag of moose trophies ever taken. Five of the heads were exceptional by any standard, with spreads of 65, 66, 67, 72,

A huge moose taken in the Yukon in 1912.

and 76 inches respectively. As if this were not enough, Reed claimed on an earlier hunting trip to have taken an even bigger moose with a spread over 80 inches.

Unfortunately this head was lost, as it was placed leaning on a hunting cabin that burned to the ground. Too bad, as this head would have constituted a world record if the measurement was correct. On the same trip that Reed killed the five huge moose above, he shot nine brown bears, the largest over ten feet. In addition, he took "five caribous, some white sheep (*Ovis dalli*), and walrus." The numbers of the last animals taken were apparently not significant enough to be put down in writing. Imagine living in those days and being able to have hunting experiences of this nature!

Antlers and skeleton of one of the largest known Irish giant deer.

Largest Head

Of all deer species today the moose carries the heaviest set of antlers. But our ancestors hunted deer with even larger headgear—the Irish elk or giant deer, *Megaloceros giganteus*. It got its name from numerous finds of preserved skeletons in Irish bogs. It was widely distributed in Europe and Western Asia until it disappeared around 7,000 years ago.

Bodywise, the Irish elk was about the same size as a European moose with a shoulder height around 82⅔ inches and a weight around 900 pounds. The largest known head of an Irish elk has a spread of 14 feet and a weight around 90 pounds. It is supposed that the mere size of their antlers prohibited the species from living in forested areas.

In order to produce a set of antlers of this size in 150 days, the animal needed to consume more than two ounces of calcium and one ounce of phosphorus per day for 60 consecutive days when the antler growth was at its peak.

Chamois

For European hunters with access to mountain estates, there is no hunting more challenging than stalking chamois (*Rupicapra rupicapra*). In the years leading up to World War I, however, most chamois were killed during grandiose driven hunts, "a sport for men among kings." The remainder were shot by stalking, "a sport for kings among men."

The Austro-Hungarian Emperor Franz Josef (1830–1916) was a keen hunter in general and a hunter of

Stalking chamois: "A sport for kings among men."

chamois in particular. He took pride in stalking the animals and invited like-minded princely hunters to his low-key hunts in some of the best areas of the Alps. The duke of Vendôme, Prince Emmanuel (1872–1931), was

Incredible but True!

The largest known head of an Irish elk has a spread of 14 feet and a weight around 90 pounds. The Irish elk was a species from Europe and western Asia and disappeared around 7,000 years ago.

known as a keen hunter and a good shot. In 1908 he was invited by the emperor to the Tyrolean mountains for "a simple chamois hunt." The result of his three days of stalking was a total of 35 chamois, the largest bag ever recorded for this kind of hunting.

Not surprisingly, the bag was greater on driven hunts. Eleven hunters killed 81 chamois during a royal Spanish hunt in September 1912. King Umberto I of Italy (1844–1900) accounted for no less than 49 out of a total of 69 chamois during one day of driven hunting in 1897, and according to some of his closest hunting friends, this was not at all unusual for the straight-shooting monarch.

Ernst II, duke of Saxe-Coburg and Gotha (1818–1893), managed to kill 2,000 chamois during his hunting career, while the bag of the Austro-Hungarian

The Archduke of the Austro-Hungarian Empire, Franz Ferdinand, pictured during a driven hunt for chamois. He is probably the most successful hunter of this species.

Archduke Franz Ferdinand (1863–1914) exceeded 1,000 by the beginning of the century. His grand total is not recorded, but it was likely well over 2,000, which would make him holder of the record of most chamois killed during a lifetime.

Up and Down

Throughout the world's many mountain ranges there are quite a number of larger mammals living between the summits. But only a single larger game species can be hunted both in the heights and the depths: the Nubian ibex, *Capra nubiana*. It is found along the mountainous southwestern part of the Arabian Peninsula, Syria, Jordan, Israel, and in Egypt and Sudan along the Red Sea. In some areas around the Dead Sea (between Jordan and Israel) the Nubian ibex inhabits areas as low as 1,312 feet (400 meters) below sea level.

The Nubian ibex is the only big-game animal found 1,300 feet below sea level, in the vicinity of the Dead Sea between Israel and Jordan.

The world-record Marco Polo sheep was a ram with horns measuring 75 inches.

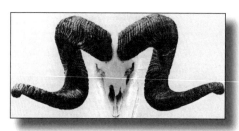

The horns of a High Altai argali can weigh as much as 50 pounds.

Longest Horns

Apart from the wild bovines, the three species of animals with the longest horns are the Marco Polo sheep, greater kudu, and giant sable. Measured by the length alone, the winner is a Marco Polo ram, *Ovis ammon poli*. The record horn measures 75 inches and belonged to a ram found dead in the Pamirs in 1895. However, in the same year the English colonel H. C. B. Tanner killed

the second-largest ram recorded, with horns only two inches shorter.

Massive Horns

If you think that the mass of a set of horns also ought to be included when rating a trophy, the record goes to a cousin of the Marco Polo ram, the Altai argali, *Ovis ammon ammon*. The biggest horns of this species belonged to a ram killed by D. Maydar in Mongolia in 1973. The longest horn is 71¾ inches, but the base has a circumference of 21 inches. For comparison, the base circumference of the Marco Polo mentioned above is "only" 15 inches. An Altai argali is the largest of all wild sheep and can reach a body weight of more than 450 pounds; its horns alone can weigh up to 50 pounds.

More Long Horns

While the Marco Polo sheep may hold the record for the longest horn, the

---

Incredible but True!

The Altai argali, a cousin to the Marco Polo ram, is the largest of all wild sheep. It can reach a body weight of more than 450 pounds and its horns alone can weigh up to 50 pounds!

The largest known set of kudu horns belongs to the animal that Carlo Caldesi found dead in the bush in Mozambique in 1963.

greater kudu, *Tragelaphus strepsiceros*, is in hot pursuit. The record belongs to an animal that the Italian big-game hunter Carlo Caldesi found dead during a safari in Mozambique in 1963. The longest horn measured 73⅞ inches.

The genus *Hippotragus*, or sable antelope, is considered by many hunters the most beautiful antelope in Africa. While the common sable does not compete in the longest-horn department, a rare subspecies of sable, *Hippotragus niger vardoni*, or giant sable, does. The largest known example of giant sable horns comes from a male killed by the Spanish Count de Yebes in 1949 in Angola. The horns measured 66½ inches.

The horns of a giant sable dwarf those of the common sable.

Most Expensive Game

Conservation groups occasionally auction off hunting rights to species such as wild sheep and black rhinoceros, with the profits going to habitat conservation for the species in question. On these

The Spanish Count de Yebes and the world record giant sable.

occasions enormous amounts have been paid by multi-millionaires with a special interest in the cause. However, apart from these special auctions, the hunt for a markhor, *Capra falconeri*, is the most expensive hunt money can buy. The markhors live in Central Asia, mainly in Pakistan. The species have been saved from extinction by dedicated hunters who are paying for the costs of conservation in their range.

In 2008 the Norwegian hunter Øjvind Christensen paid $81,200 for a license to hunt a Chitral markhor in Pakistan. In 2011 the same license had risen to $150,000 and will likely continue to increase in price.

The result of 125 days of hard hunting in the mountains: Rudolf Sand and his splendid markhor taken in 1984.

Hunting markhor used to be a sport exclusively for British army officers on leave. One of them was Maj. C. Rose, seen here with his fine 56-inch trophy.

Largest Herds

We have all seen pictures of enormous herds of wildebeest migrating through Africa's Great Rift Valley and have heard of the vast herds of bison that used to cover the American prairie. But the biggest herds of ungulates ever recorded were actually formed by millions of springboks in South Africa.

In the western part of South Africa, explorers and settlers observed so-called *bokkentreks*—huge migrations of springboks caused by an overpopulation and an ensuing shortage of food. The herds were so densely packed that all other game was pulled along or trampled, and vast areas were completely cleared of vegetation. Hardly any of the animals survived the trek; most died of hunger or drowned while attempting to cross the Orange River or plunged into the sea when they reached it. As late as 1915, thirty miles of the coastline of present-day Namibia was choked with drowned springboks. There are no records of the numbers of animals in these herds but they must have numbered in the millions.

In 1849 the hunter John Fraser watched a herd that took three days to pass the village of Beaufort West in Cape Province. In July 1896 an enormous herd covered an area 135 miles long and 14 miles wide as it approached the Karoo Kloof near the Orange River. This is equivalent of an area of almost 2,000 square miles covered with springboks. These treks dwindled as the Boers decimated the game populations in order to protect their crops in the nineteenth century and even more so after rinderpest ravaged South Africa in the years around 1900.

In the 1915 bokkentrek, dead springboks lay scattered along thirty miles of the coastline.

The largest herds the world has ever seen consisted of springboks.

Long Gone

The bluebuck of South Africa, *Hippotragus leucophaeus*, holds the dubious honor of being the first species to be eradicated by humans with firearms. The bluebuck was closely related to the roan and sable antelopes, but was smaller in body, approximately the size of a common reedbuck. The species was first described scientifically in 1719 and already at that time its area of distribution was limited to the southernmost parts of South Africa's Cape Province.

In 1774 the Swedish zoologist Carl Peter Thunberg wrote that the species was becoming rare; the last recorded one was killed in 1799. There

The South African bluebuck was probably the very first big-game species to be exterminated due to shooting.

Incredible but True!

*T*he largest hunt, with a bag of around 6,000 animals, took place in South Africa in 1860 and was given for Prince Alfred, the future duke of Edinburgh. More than 1,000 natives drove more than 25,000 head of game. Several natives were trampled to death.

are indications that a small population survived farther north for another fifty years. Today the only remains of this species are a small number of skulls and horns in addition to four mounted animals at museums in Leiden, Vienna, Paris, and Stockholm.

Largest Hunt

In view of the enormous populations of game in nineteenth-century South Africa, it is not surprising that this was where the largest hunt ever recorded took place. In 1860 Prince Alfred, later the duke of Edinburgh, visited the Orange Free State where a driven hunt was arranged for the

The number of quaggas killed in the biggest driven hunt of all times (1860) was not recorded exactly, but was certainly enormous. By 1880 this South African species of zebra was extinct.

noble guest. More than 1,000 natives drove game in from a vast area, and it has been calculated that at least 25,000 head of game passed the hunters: wildebeest, zebras, quaggas, blesboks, ostriches, hartebeest, and springboks. The bag was around 6,000 animals, but the hunt was not without costs. Several natives were trampled to death by panic-stricken herds of animals while many more had limbs broken.

Largest Wild Boar

Wild boars (*Sus scrofa*) vary a lot in size within their geographical range of distribution. In most of Europe a boar weighing more than 330 pounds on the hoof is considered a really large animal, but in places like Sweden, Turkey, and Russia, boars weighing more than 600 pounds are sometimes killed. The upper limit presumably lies around 900 pounds, but no one knows as very few hunters have had their prey weighed.

Emperor Maximilian I (1459–1519) was a very ardent hunter, and according to his records he killed more than one boar over 800 pounds with his so-called *saufeder*, a seven-foot hunting spear especially made for boar hunting.

In many places in the world, feral pigs are hunted and these animals can sometimes outgrow their wild ancestors. Some of the largest examples published have turned out to be released directly from pens, so we have refrained from reporting on records of "monster" feral pigs.

Largest Pig Tusk

The largest wild boar trophies are typically found in mountainous areas in a belt stretching from Turkey over Eastern Russia and Iran. Tusks exceeding twelve inches are not unheard-of here.

In Rowland Ward's records, the longest tusk from a wild boar came from an animal killed by A. W. Lanz. It measures no less than 15 inches. This tusk, however, is not the biggest from a wild pig. The all-time record in

It remains uncertain exactly how heavy a wild boar can become, but it's possible they can exceed a live weight of 900 pounds.

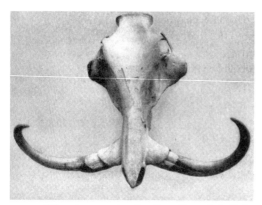

Although a warthog hardly will reach half the body weight of a Eurasian wild boar, this African species definitely grows the largest tusks. The world record is close to 25 inches.

enormous areas was driven toward the posts of the blue-blooded hunters. The game, of which the wild boars normally were only a small part, was killed with muzzleloaders, crossbows, javelins, and hunting swords. On one such hunt, the Landgrave [Count] Johann Georg of Brandenburg in the year of 1581 accounted for 501 wild boars, 677 stags, and 968 hinds.

In more modern times the records were held by the Central European monarchs, and most of the crowned heads who were interested in hunting killed more than 1,000 wild boars. The German Emperor Wilhelm II (1859–1941) killed more than 4,000 wild boars during his lifetime.

Another prominent German hunter was Prince Luitpold of Bavaria (1821–1911), who had a 12,000-acre fenced

this respect comes for the collection of Edmund G. Loder and is from a warthog. Its longest tusk reaches the incredible length of 24 inches, the same length as a standard rifle barrel.

Largest Wild Boar Bag

Elector Johann Georg I of Saxony (1585–1656) managed to kill 31,902 European wild boars during the many extravagant driven hunts he participated in during his lifetime. His son and heir to the throne, Johann Georg II (1613–1680), was one of the most avid hunters in history, but when it comes to wild boars he did not even come close to his father's record. Nevertheless, he killed 22,298 wild boars and therefore claimed an unrivaled second place on the list of great boar hunters.

Many princes of the time killed thousands of boars on grandiose hunts where practically all game from

Johann Georg I of Saxony is the hunter who killed the most wild boars during a lifetime.

Prince Luitpold of Bavaria portrayed after a successful driven hunt. Huge daily bags like this one have always been the result of hunting in fenced or extremely large areas.

area for boar hunting. Here the aging prince and his two sons often killed 600 wild boars on their annual hunt, which normally took place during a single week in November. During Prince Luitpold's last season (1911), the ninety-year-old hunter managed to kill 133 wild boars in a week. In all fairness, however, it must be added that this "feat" was only possible due to an ingenious system of fences and runways in the hunting area that ensured the monarch an extraordinarily large number of chances.

Latest Discovery

The last (or maybe latest?) major mammal in Africa to be "discovered" was first described by a European in 1905. The animal in question was a giant forest hog, which was killed in Ethiopia by the English Captain Richard Meinertzhagen (1878–1967). This "new" species of pig was named *Hylochoerus meinertzhageni*. After the discovery it was determined that the giant forest hog is quite widely distributed in a belt north of the equator, but due to the animal's preferred habitats and nocturnal habits there still is little scientific information available about this species. However, the population is sufficiently dense in a number of African countries that hunting is permitted.

The giant forest hog wasn't discovered or scientifically described by a European until 1905. Of all the big-game species that can be legally hunted, this is the one discovered most recently.

Part 3
Big-Game Hunts and Hunters

Chapter 8

Unusual Hunts

Hands-On Leopard

One of the few men to fight off a leopard with his bare hands is Carl Akeley (1864–1926). Considered the founder of modern taxidermy, Akeley accompanied Theodore Roosevelt on his famous East African safari in 1909. Akeley's encounter with the leopard took place on an earlier expedition, in 1905, when he was heading for camp in the growing darkness and passed a carcass on which a leopard was feeding.

After missing the animal with a shot from his double rifle, Akeley managed to hit the cat with the second shot, but only in its hind leg. The ninety-pound leopard came at him like a fur-clad chainsaw, but Akeley managed to protect his throat with his right arm. Grabbing the cat's throat with his left hand, Akeley managed to clench his right fist and press it down the animal's throat. He also managed to topple the cat to the ground and began hammering his knees violently into the animal's chest.

Akeley was far from a large man with great strength—he was only 5 feet 2 inches tall and weighed 135 pounds.

After a while, though, the cat started to lose its grip and Akeley was able to get his hand free. During the entire incident Akeley's sixteen-year-old native companion had stood paralyzed, but finally he got around to giving Akeley

Carl Akeley and the leopard he killed with his bare hands.

his knife, at which point Akeley finished off the leopard. After returning to camp Akeley managed to clean his wounds and get himself patched up to a degree where he did not suffer any permanent injury from the attack. Some years later, Akeley had another close shave when he barely avoided being killed in an elephant charge. Destiny finally caught up with him in 1926, when the famous taxidermist died from fever in the Congo during his fifth African expedition.

Unperturbed

Around 1912 a Texas hunter by the name of "Yank" Allen was employed by the Liebig's cattle ranch in Southern Rhodesia (now Zimbabwe) to shoot lions. During his employment, Allen killed more than 200 of the big cats

with his old double rifle in .577 blackpowder express. One day Allen stumbled while being charged by a lion, and while trying to regain his balance he accidentally hammered his rifle so hard in the ground that the stock broke off. Nevertheless, Allen managed to hit the lion so hard on the head with the barrels of the rifle that it was killed on the spot. Apparently Mr. Allen was not a man who was easily rattled.

Cool Kid

On 7 May 1888, the *New York Times* published the story of fourteen-year-old Willie Altemese (1874–?) from the Poconos in Pennsylvania. A few days earlier he had walked from his home into the forest carrying an ax in order to get firewood. Soon he returned and

"Yank" Allen was a professional hunter who saved himself from an attacking lion by killing it with a blow to the head with the barrels of his broken rifle.

110

In this situation most of us would probably choose to chop firewood another day, but not Willie Altemese.

quietly asked his father if he would help him handle three bears he had just killed. Naturally the father was a bit skeptical, not least because the boy seemed perfectly calm and composed. Nevertheless there were three dead black bears, all killed with an axe, lying in the forest. It turned out that a sow bear with yearlings had been lying under the tree and had attacked the boy as he began to chop. Resolutely he killed the animal with a blow to the head and then gave the two large cubs the same treatment. I imagine Willie was not a kid who got bullied much at school.

Bad Timing

The Scottish-born hunter Kenneth Andersson (1910–1974) worked in southern India in the years around World War II, where he killed eight man-eating leopards and seven tigers in addition to a number of rogue elephants. Many hunters have experienced a firearm malfunction during a hunt, but few have had the bad timing in this respect that Andersson experienced.

He was stalking a man-eating leopard and inadvertently surprised a sloth bear with a cub that was lying in a hole near the jungle path Andersson was following. The bear was so close that Andersson had no option but to shove the muzzle of his .405 Winchester into the mouth of the enraged and roaring animal and press the trigger.

What he heard was a *click!* The enraged bear tore the rifle out of Andersson's hands and reared up to attack. Andersson's heroic native tracker threw himself between Andersson and the bear, and this enabled Andersson to get hold of the rifle again.

The rifle could not be reloaded, so Andersson had to use it to club the bear to dissuade it from further mauling the

Kenneth Andersson survived a misfire at a crucial moment during a close encounter with a Malayan bear.

tracker. This he managed, but the bear caught the stock of the rifle between its teeth and tore it away from Andersson. Fortunately the bear cub began to whimper, whereupon the bear left the hunters and disappeared. The tracker survived, albeit with a large number of scars and a slight limp to serve as lifelong memories of the incident.

Lucky Coins

It is a common superstition that bad luck will result from having money on you while hunting. But this is not always the case, as shown by the experience of Sir Samuel Baker (1821–1893). Early in his career as a water buffalo hunter in Ceylon during the 1840s, Baker had a buffalo at bay in a swamp and shot a lead bullet into the animal without any effect apart from enraging the animal. Baker reloaded his muzzleloader with his last remain-

Sir Samuel Baker was one of the most successful water buffalo hunters in the world.

Samuel Baker and his brother in a tricky situation involving a wounded water buffalo. Baker was saved by the change he happened to have in his pocket.

ing bullet and shot again, with the only result that the wounded bull came a few steps closer.

Baker tried to seem threatening and stared the enraged animal straight in the eyes while it stomped its front legs in the mud of the swamp. Without taking his eyes off the animal, he put a double charge of gunpowder in the barrel and cut a piece of his shirt and wrapped it around a small roll of coins from his purse before ramming the load down the barrel. At this moment the bull jumped forward and Baker had to throw away the ramrod in order to cock the hammer. However, the bull stopped seven paces from Baker, who realized that with his unusual load he would only be able to kill the bull at point-blank range. The bull finally decided to charge, and Baker pressed the trigger when the bull's horns almost encircled him on both sides and the rifle's muzzle was almost touching the animal's forehead. The result was that "three shillings in change was driven into his hard head." The bull dropped on the spot. Who says money can't buy happiness?

Most Meat with One Shot

We've all heard stories where two animals are killed with one shot. Normally this happens when a bullet hits another animal after having passed through the first animal. But the record of "most" game in one shot—as measured in pounds of meat—belongs to Frederick "Deaf" Banks (1875–1954). During an expedition where Banks, a culling officer, had to shoot elephants that were causing crop damage, Banks found himself far up a steep mountainside in the Toro district of Uganda.

Banks shot an elephant in the brain with his diminutive .256 Mannlicher (6.5x54) and as the dead animal tumbled down the hillside, it swept the legs out from under another elephant, which in turn took a third animal with it. The fall killed all three. That made Banks the first man to kill three elephants with one shot—and with a rifle that is normally only used for hunting deer and smaller species! The story only became public via his porters long after the safari was over, and when Banks was asked why he had not told the story to anyone, he answered that he felt certain that no one would have believed him.

American Elephant Shooting

The first elephant to walk on American soil since the woolly mammoth was

Both the first and the second elephant in North America sadly died from being shot with small-caliber rifles. Unfortunately there are no illustrations from these events; the drawing illustrates a similar situation in Paris.

the Asiatic circus elephant Old Bett (Betty Big Bett), who arrived in New York in 1796. In the following years the elephant was displayed at markets up and down the East Coast. However, the animal's career came to an abrupt halt when a deeply religious farmer in Maine became so disgusted with the fact that the animal was displayed on a Sunday that he shot and killed it with his muzzleloader as it was passing his property. The unhappy owner immediately ordered another elephant, and Little Bett arrived in 1817.

One might think that the beleaguered elephant owner had been taught a lesson. Nevertheless, when displaying the animal, he claimed that its skin was so thick that it could not be wounded by rifle bullets. Not surprisingly, this claim inspired weak souls to make a practical test. On the 25 May 1826, a group of young men fired a series of shots at the poor animal when it passed a bridge in the village of Chepachet, Rhode Island. The elephant dropped on the spot as a bullet hit its eye and entered the brain. Q.E.D.: Elephants are NOT bulletproof.

Single-Shot Tigers

On 30 April 1903, the Englishman W. H. Collins was involved in an extraordinary incident near Naduvattam in India. A local worker told him that one of the plantation's horses had been killed by a cheetah, so Collins took his Jeffery single-shot rifle in .400 NE and went out to dispatch it.

When he threw a rock into the nearby bush, and much to his surprise four tigers emerged just forty yards away. In the next forty seconds, Collins managed to kill three of the tigers with one shot each while the fourth disappeared into a ravine, wounded. Collins sent for his four terriers and they managed to put the tiger at bay so Collins could finish it with one last shot.

Mixed Weapons

Gilbert Colvile (1888–1966) was an eccentric of English origin who moved to Kenya in 1907. Shortly afterward he "went native," living with the Masai, sleeping in a hut, and wearing skins just like his native friends. Nevertheless, he became the richest man in Kenya with

Gilbert Colvile was a wealthy eccentric who hunted lions with a spear. The photo shows him with a more conventional choice of weapon.

more than 20,000 head of cattle and five farms covering more than 250,000 acres of land.

Colvile was also a great lion hunter and killed 275 lions, which may not be very surprising considering his occupation and living situation. Interestingly, he killed twenty-eight of these lions with a spear in the true Masai tradition.

Thirty-Two for Thirty-Two

Duke Ernst II of Saxony-Coburg-Gotha (1818–1893) was the most successful red deer hunter in modern times. He was also one of the best rifle shots of his time. During a driven hunt in the 1880s, in the presence of the author W. A. Baillie-Grohman, the duke used his double rifle in .450 BPE to kill two running red deer crossing a valley. The distance was later carefully measured at 440 yards.

This was far from the only example of Duke Ernst's remarkable shooting skills. On an Imperial driven hunt at the game-rich estate of Letzlingen, the duke was given the best post in the absence of the aging German Emperor. The drive took about three hours and afterward there were thirty-two dead stags scattered around the duke's post. Even more remarkable than the sheer number was that the stags, most of which had been shot while running, had been killed with exactly thirty-two shots, all of them placed through the shoulder and right over the heart.

Bragging Rights

Charlie Goss (d. 1963) was a legendary character who operated in the most remote areas of East Africa for forty years. During the years 1926–1941 Goss was a professional hunter. He was an exceptional shot and killed more than 1,000 elephants with his .600 NE double during his lifetime. However, Goss was not above showing off his skills. During a safari between the two world wars he announced to his two accompanying friends that

Charlie Goss and most of the result of a spectacular morning hunt. Three huge elephant bulls, and he also got a leopard.

"Buffalo" Jones was a colorful character who not only was instrumental in saving the American buffalo from extinction but also went on to catch rhinos and lions in Kenya using a lasso.

he would now kill two buffaloes with one shot, and seconds later, two dead buffalo were on the ground, killed with the same bullet. When visiting a saloon Goss would often perform a William Tell act, shooting fruit off the head of his partner. This act came to a halt one day, however, when Goss missed the fruit and shot off his partner's left ear.

Throwing a Loop

Charles Jesse "Buffalo" Jones (1844–1918) was a colorful character who originally made a living from shooting bison in the 1870s. As the buffalo herds dwindled, Jones had the brilliant idea of catching some buffalo alive to help save the species. Between 1880 and 1886 he caught over fifty calves and had them raised by domestic cows.

The plan was to crossbreed the two species in order to get the best of both worlds. Unfortunately his attempts only produced animals with the bad characteristics of both species. But Jones became one of the most important conservationists of the American bison. By the end of the 1890s he had a herd of more than 100 bison that became part of the foundation of today's population of free-roaming bison in North America.

In 1910 Jones went to Kenya with a few partners and a journalist in order to prove that African game could be caught with a lasso without being harmed in any way. Understandably, the settlers in Kenya were somewhat skeptical of the visiting cowboy's claims, but Jones proved his point by catching and releasing a number of different animals: rhino, zebra, cheetah, hartebeest, eland,

Incredible but True!

*C*harles Jesse "Buffalo" Jones went to Kenya in 1910 and successfully lassoed a rhino, a zebra, a cheetah, a hartebeest, an eland, and a warthog, each of which he let go. He did lasso a lioness which he sent to the Bronx Zoo in New York.

and warthog. On the 25 March, Jones ended his trip by catching a lioness with his lasso and sending it to the Bronx Zoo in New York.

Changing Luck

Bill Judd (1870–1927) was a highly respected professional hunter who came to East Africa in 1899 after having fought in the Boer War. He became an ivory hunter in the Lado Enclave and served as a professional hunter with President Theodore Roosevelt's safari in 1909.

Judd's famous friend F. C. Selous (1851–1917) described an incident that happened when he and Judd were riding mules through a rough area of the Mau Plateau in Kenya. Without any warning a lioness suddenly jumped out of the bush and attacked, throwing Judd out of the saddle. While in midair, Judd managed to fire a shot from his rifle and the moment he landed he got up, ready for another attack. But the lioness lay dead on the ground—the bullet had entered the right eye and penetrated the brain!

Judd's extraordinary luck ran out on 20 December 1927. He was elephant hunting with his son, Jack, but in spite of four shots from Judd's Westley Richards double in .577 NE, a charging elephant drove a tusk through his body and trampled him. Only after the father had died did the son manage to kill the elephant with a brain shot from his .350 Rigby.

Revolver Hunting

One of the longest verified shots with a standard revolver was made by the well-known American gunwriter Elmer Merrifield Keith (1899–1984). Having often practiced shooting at long distances with his Smith & Wesson .44 Magnum, Keith in 1954 tried to finish off a mule deer that had been wounded with a rifle by another hunter.

His friend followed the proceedings through his binocular and could tell that Keith's first shot went high and the second shot hit the ground below the deer. The third shot was a hit, but his friend was not sure exactly where. The fourth shot killed the deer. When the hunters got up to the deer it turned out that the third shot had grazed the jaw while the last one was perfectly placed in the lung region. The distance was 550 yards.

On another occasion, with a single shot from the same revolver, Keith shot a running hare at 96 paces.

Bears with a Knife

Benjamin Lilly (1856–1936) was known as "The Last Mountain Man." He was an eccentric in the classical sense and spent his life in the wilderness accompanied only by his beloved dogs. In accordance with the spirit of the time, he considered all predators as vermin and hunted them zealously and very successfully. Lilly made long, formidable knives for self-defense dur-

Elmer Keith and his .44 Smith & Wesson six-shooter.

Benjamin Lilly consumed many of the cougars he killed, believing the meat gave him supernatural powers. This photo shows him hunting during the 1920s with his pack of hounds.

or a hunting sword. Hunting chamois was the Emperor's greatest passion and he hunted them on foot armed with a hunting spear or a crossbow. Maximilian despised firearms, although they were already in widespread use as hunting weapons by the elite. According to the written sources of the Emperor's shooting skills, he did not need the "fire tubes." On one occasion Maximilian killed 100 rising ducks with 104 shots from his crossbow. On another occasion he killed 26 hares in a row with a single crossbow bolt.

ing bear hunts and killed a total of six bears with them "in fights." The bears in question were not specified by Lilly, but were most likely grizzlies as they are much more aggressive during a confrontation than the black bears. It is not known precisely how many bears and cougars Lilly killed during his life but there is no doubt that the number was significant, as documented by a plate on the lid of a box where he buried a dog in 1925. Lilly engraved: "Here rests Crook, a bear and lion dog which helped me kill 210 bears and 426 lions since 1914—owned by B. V. Lilly."

Crossbow Hunts

The last German-Roman Emperor, Maximilian I (1459–1519), was a great sportsman who valued personal challenges. He often traveled to the most remote corners of his realm in order to take on a large bear or an especially aggressive wild boar using only a spear

Emperor Maximilian I was known as a keen hunter and outdoor writer. His abilities as a marksman were remarkable.

Rocked

During his expedition to Central Asia in 1926, William J. Morden (1886–1958) spotted a Mongolian gazelle close to camp. In spite of the lack of cover in the open terrain, Morden managed to stalk within a couple of hundred yards by moving only when the animal was feeding. Morden had a Springfield rifle in .30-06 with open sights.

When he shot, he realized he had underestimated the distance when he saw the bullet hit the ground close to the animal. But the gazelle ran after

William Morden's guide and the gazelle Morden killed under very unusual circumstances.

Frederick Courteney Selous was the most famous hunter of his day and one of the most important contributors to the collection of the British Museum.

the shot and then stopped and lay down as if wounded. When Morden reached it, the animal was dead. An examination did not detect any bullet hole. During skinning, Morden discovered that a piece of a rock had hit the gazelle in the neck.

Six with Five

One of the most famous hunters of the Victorian era was Frederick Courteney Selous (1851–1917). Selous killed 106 elephants but was somewhat hindered by his cumbersome 4-bore blackpowder rifle, which

Selous at age twenty-three with the rifle that killed six elephants with five bullets.

Sashino Siemel and the jaguar he killed on his fourteenth birthday with a spear.

used hardened lead bullets weighing 1,750 grains and produced almost unbearable recoil. He writes how he one day shot five elephants before running out of bullets. One of the bullets, however, was visible under the skin of one of the dead elephants after having passed through the animal's body. Selous resolutely cut the bullet free, loaded his rifle with it, and managed to kill a sixth elephant that day.

Birthday Spearing

Latvian Sasha Siemel became one of the leading jaguar hunting guides of South America after World War II. During a hunt in 1960 he was accompanied by his son, Sasha Jr., better known as Sashino (b. 1946).

On the son's fourteenth birthday they were tracking a jaguar and the dogs managed to put the animal at bay in the densest bush imaginable. Regardless of the circumstances, Sashino managed to kill the jaguar by thrusting his spear into the neck of the animal just as it was starting to spring at him. He thus became the youngest hunter ever to kill a jaguar with a spear.

Small Load, Big Bear

In 1953 a young girl named Bella Twin was grouse hunting with her friend Dave Auger near Lesser Slave Lake in Alberta, Canada, when they saw a big grizzly bear coming toward them. Instead of running, the two children hid themselves, hoping the bear would pass them. The only weapon the two youngsters had was Bella's single-shot .22 LR. Unfortunately the bear spotted them and approached.

Incredible but True!

Bella Twin was a child when she took down a grizzly with one shot from her .22 long rifle. She was with a friend near Lesser Slave Lake in Alberta, Canada when they were charged by the grizzly. The grizzly was a new Boone and Crockett record.

This huge grizzly went straight to the top of the record book when it was killed by a frightened native girl named Bella Twin with one bullet from her single-shot .22 long rifle.

When it was very close, Bella fired at the side of the bear's massive head. Much to the girl's surprise, the huge animal instantly dropped to the ground and lay jerking for a while. Just to make sure, Bella shot her remaining seven cartridges into the head of the bear. It turned out that the male bear was the new Boone and Crockett record and stood as such for many years.

The Lancers

When British officers stationed in India had time off, one of their favorite pastimes was "pig-sticking"—hunting wild boars from the back of a horse using a lance as weapon. The hunt

The outcome of a day of "pig-sticking" in northern India in the 1880s. The hunt was done from horseback. The camel was used as a pack animal.

demanded great horsemanship, a skill considered a cardinal virtue among the British upper classes.

During the hunt a large number of natives would act as beaters and drive the wild boars out into open terrain, where the mounted hunters would wait with their lances. When the boars were pressed out into the open, they would run at top speed and the hunters would pursue the animals and kill them at full gallop. Often the boars would turn around and attack the horses when pressed sufficiently, which only added spice to the sport.

The largest bag from one of these hunts we have been able to find was from a two-day hunt at Moescoondie in India in January 1906, where a total of seventeen hunters participated and killed 149 wild boars in this spectacular way. Several of the participating hunters and their horses were injured during the many daredevilish maneuvers of the hunt. The best pig-stickers killed hundreds of wild boars and sometimes even leopards from horseback.

Chapter 9
Remarkable Hunters

Amenhotep III was presumably the first hunter to kill more than 100 lions.

Ancient Roman perception of moose hunting in northern Europe.

First Trophy Hunter?

The earliest known record of a specific big-game hunting bag was found in Egypt. From scripts in small seals shaped like scarab beetles, we know that pharaoh Amenhotep III, during the first ten years of his reign (1400–1390 B.C.), killed "102 ferocious lions to his own arrows." Just a hundred years later, lions were extinct in Egypt.

Hunting Queen

One of the earliest known huntresses was Anne (1574–1619), daughter of the Danish King Frederick II. In 1589 she was married to James I of England. An eager hunter of both deer and foxes, Queen Anne hunted on horseback, which was quite demanding and not without risks. She was dedicated and eccentric when it came to hunting—she was even accompanied by female archers dressed like Amazons when foreign heads of states were visiting England.

Her marriage was quite stormy and matters did not exactly improve in this respect when in 1613 she accidentally killed her husband's beloved hunting dog, Jewel. "Harsh words were exchanged," but the king made up for it by presenting her another jewel, a diamond costing the princely sum of £2,000.

In her later years the queen was so overweight that she could no longer hunt

England's Queen Anne in her prime.

of Bell's colleagues, Aurelio Rossi (1898–1942), who operated in Central Africa 1926–1928, toward the end of the era of professional ivory hunting. On average he walked around 120 miles per elephant killed or a daily distance of more than 12 miles for 210 days in a row, which was the standard for this profession.

The walking skills of professional ivory hunters James Sutherland (1872–1932) and G. H. "Andy" Anderson (1878–1946) stood them in good stead. In spite of the latter having a stiff leg due to a lion attack seven years earlier, the two hunters walked 500 miles in just twenty-three days in order to avoid being captured by the Germans after the outbreak of World War I in 1914.

from horseback, but that did not keep her from the joys of the sport. She had a hunting cart made, which was drawn by two horses, and from this she hunted deer around Windsor Castle until her untimely death at forty-five years of age.

Footwork

Being a professional elephant hunter was far from an easy living. The most successful ivory hunter of all, W. D. M. Bell (1880–1951), wrote in his memoirs that, on average, he walked seventy-three miles for every elephant he killed and during his entire career as an ivory hunter covered almost 80,000 miles on foot. He also wore out no less than twenty-four pairs of boots per year.

The amount of walking needed for elephant hunting was confirmed by one

As a professional ivory hunter, W. D. M. "Karamojo" Bell walked more than 62,000 miles.

Maj. Andy Anderson walked 500 miles in 23 days with a stiff leg.

"Deaf" Banks

Frederick Grant "Deaf" Banks (1875–1954) was a professional elephant ivory hunter in Uganda who killed some 3,000 elephants. He began his career in 1904 at the famed Lado Enclave in east-

Incredible but True!

*P*rofessional ivory hunters James Sutherland and G. H. "Andy" Anderson put their skills to good use when they walked 500 miles in just 23 days to avoid being captured by the Germans after the outbreak of World War I in 1914 . . . and Anderson had a stiff knee from a lion attack seven years earlier!

The Italian ivory hunter Aurelio Rossi had to walk in excess of 120 miles for each elephant he shot.

ern Congo. His nickname was caused by the fact that he was so hard of hearing that his gunbearer had to touch his left or right shoulder to direct his attention to an animal in the bush if Banks had not noticed it himself. When asked how he could risk being an ivory hunter with this handicap, he claimed that the absence of sound enabled him to concentrate better.

It certainly took quite a lot to scare Banks. On different occasions he was tossed in the air by a buffalo, trampled by an elephant, and severely wounded when a rifle exploded in his hands. During one expedition, his hut was hit by lightning and all his possessions destroyed in the ensuing fire. None of these events, however, made the hardened hunter think twice about his way of making a living. While Banks originally was a poacher, he was later employed by the game department as a control officer to reduce the elephant population in Uganda. In dense bush Banks used a .577 NE double but elsewhere he preferred the diminutive

Frederick "Deaf" Banks killed three elephants with a single bullet from this diminutive .256 Mannlicher cartridge. The ruler is measuring it in centimeters; the total length is just over 3 inches.

Frederick "Deaf" Banks pictured in the beginning of the last century following a successful ivory hunt.

.256 Mannlicher (6.5x54) with a solid bullet weighing only 156 grains. Banks was a very good shot and during just one day in the Lado Enclave he killed thirteen elephants with as many shots from his .577 NE.

Predators Galore

Large carnivores were a major problem on the American frontier, and settlers quickly hit upon the idea of organizing large driven hunts to eradicate predators and protect their livestock. One of the most spectacular of these took place in Bradford County, Pennsylvania, in the summer of 1805. Some 5,000 people lived on small farms in the region and their livestock was constantly harassed by wolves, cougars, bears, and smaller predators. At a meeting, the residents agreed that all men

able to bear arms should participate in a destruction campaign in June when the predators had cubs.

The hunters were divided into teams of ten led by an experienced hunter who knew the forest well. Most participants were equipped with a flintlock (only a handful had rifled firearms), an ax, a hunting knife, and food for two days. The hunters encircled a vast area and, after horns sounded to signal the start, all headed for the center of the circle, shooting any and all predators encountered on the way.

Some 600 men and boys participated, and the initial circle was designed to leave 300 yards between each hunter. The diameter of the circle was almost 37 miles and the plan was to divide the hunt into two days of walking so that the hunters would cover about 18 miles per day. The hunt

Licenses and bag limits for large predators in North America are a relatively new phenomenon. In the old days it was up to the hunter how many he wanted to kill.

In the North American wilderness it was possible to obtain large bags of predators. This hunter is showing his harvest of skunks during a winter around 1900.

commenced at 6:30 AM, and the hunters walked toward the center in a disciplined way. By the time it got dark, the diameter of the circle had been halved. There were now only 150 yards between the hunters, who lit fires in order to keep the game within the circle during the night.

The take on the first day was 92 bears, 58 wolves, 40 lynx, 13 cougars, and 20 foxes. The next day the hunt ended in a small circle where the remaining game desperately tried to get away but was shot on sight. The grand total for the two days was 145 bears, 90 wolves, 72 lynx, 28 cougars, and 37 foxes. These figures include both adult and young animals. The furs generated a princely sum of $2,500 and every hunter got 35 pounds of bear meat to take home for the pot.

The Booysen Brothers

In 1920 the well-known South African big-game hunter John Burger hunted elephants in the Lualaba district of the Belgian Congo accompanied by two brothers named Booysen. Every day the three men left camp to hunt on their own. One day one of the Booysen brothers returned early and found a baby elephant. He tried to catch it, which turned out to be a big mistake. When Burger returned a few hours later, he found all that was left of Booysen was "a pulp of molested meat." Naturally, the mother elephant had been nearby and immediately came to rescue its offspring.

One might think that an incident would make the other Booysen brother think twice about hunting in the area again, but evidently not. Shortly after the incident he returned to hunt with Burger. This time they stayed in two different camps situated a few miles apart. The surviving Booysen brother wounded a lion and was mauled when he tried to track it in dense bush. He survived the attack, but lost both a leg and an arm.

Anticlimax

William Buckley (1873–1948) was one of the first Europeans to hunt elephants in the legendary Lado Enclave, a politically contentious corner of the eastern part of the former Belgian Congo. Unlike his colleague W. D. M. Bell, William Buckley preferred large-caliber rifles for elephant hunting—the larger, the better. As Buckley was unhappy with his .450 NE double, he ordered an equivalent rifle in .600 NE from London. While Buckley impatiently awaited the arrival of his new rifle, he entertained the other elephant hunters with stories of the incredible numbers of elephants he would shoot when he got it.

William Buckley got a surprise when he mail-ordered a new .600 N. E. double rifle.

latter more dangerous. The number of dramatic confrontations with wild boars is so large that we can only mention a few of the most spectacular. On 10 December 1906, the Portuguese King Carlos (1863–1908) got a personal lesson in the dangers of wild boar hunting. A large boar attacked and killed the horse he was riding before turning to attack and wound several other hunters in the king's party.

In January 1908 it was the Spanish King Alfonso XIII (1886–1941) who experienced the dangers of wild boar

When a large wooden box finally arrived from England he eagerly opened it, only to find a consignment of Bibles in the local language. It turned out that the bishop of Uganda, whose name also was Buckley, had ordered the good books and the two shipments were interchanged. What the missionary did when he got the rifle is, sadly, not recorded.

Charging Boars

The wild boar has always been respected by hunters for its courage and fighting spirit when cornered. European hunters with experience of hunting both bears and boars often consider the

King Alfonso XIII of Spain was nearly killed when a wild boar presumed to be dead suddenly woke up and attacked him.

Incredible but True!

O n 1 August 1921 near Grenoble in southern France, a large boar overturned an open car, dumping it into a ditch and continuing the attack until one of the passengers was able to kill it with a shot from his revolver.

hunting. Unarmed, he was moving toward an apparently dead boar when it suddenly got up and attacked him. He was saved by a quick-witted hunter who killed the charging boar with a well-aimed shot through the forehead, dropping it a few feet from the king's boots.

A no less dramatic incident took place on the evening of 1 August 1921, near Grenoble in southern France. A car with three passengers had to stop as a large boar was standing on the road. The boar charged and had its snout scalded as it punctured the car's radiator. Enraged, the boar again attacked the car and managed to get its shoulder under the bumper, eventually overturning the open vehicle into the ditch where it continued attacking the wreck. The affair finally ended when one of the passengers killed the boar with a shot from his revolver.

The Red Vampire

Nicolae Ceausescu (1918–1989) has often been compared to a former ruler of Transylvania —Count Dracula—for his tyrannical rule and uncontrollable blood lust. Although Ceausescu was one of the most successful hunters of big game in modern times, the exact figures vary a lot depending on the source of this information.

For instance, the number of brown bears that Ceausescu allegedly killed varies from "over 400" to "almost 4,000." However, it is a fact that Ceausescu maintained an extensive game management program, which helped game populations thrive. During his rule Romania's brown bear population exceeded 7,000 animals, a figure only surpassed by Russia.

Hundreds of Romania's best hunting areas were reserved for Ceausescu and his guests, and the dictator was obsessed with killing large trophy animals. Allegedly he killed a total of 34 animals that qualified for a bronze medal under the CIC scoring system,

Nicolae Ceausescu hunting bears with one of his Holland & Holland .375 H&H double rifles.

117 qualifying for a silver medal, and 270 qualifying for a gold medal. The odd distribution of medals is due to the fact that Ceausescu only had a trophy officially measured if it looked like it would qualify for a gold medal.

At his death more than thirty-three red deer trophies measuring over 220 points were found in Ceausescu's collection. No one knows how much game Ceausescu killed. That the figure contains thousands of animals is beyond doubt, however. Some sources claim that the grand total approaches 100,000 head of game, including 40,000 roe deer, 30,000 red deer, and 20,000 wild boars.

These figures seem unlikely as they imply that Ceausescu killed more than 4,000 head of game every year during his twenty-four years in power. Then again, when the dictator hunted, it was often with hundreds of beaters driving the game from a huge area and toward Ceausescu's post. As the only armed hunter, he would be placed in a high seat with one or two assistants to reload his Holland & Holland double rifles. Therefore, his bags of game were enormous by any standard.

First Safari Client

The word *safari* is of Arab and later Swahili origin and means "long journey." In a more modern context, safari clients are hunters who go to Africa to hunt under the guidance of a professional hunter. According to this definition, the first known safari client was Lord Randolph Churchill (1849–1895), father of the famous Winston Churchill.

Randolph Churchill was probably the first safari client in the modern sense of the word.

In 1891 Lord Randolph went with the experienced professional hunter Hans Lee on a six-month-long safari in Mashonaland, the northern part of present-day Zimbabwe. The safari was the first truly luxurious travel into the Dark Continent and it was trailblazing for adventurous millionaires, as Churchill reported on the safari in the British newspaper *Daily Graphic*.

The safari consisted of four heavy Cape wagons, three lesser wagons, and a light Scottish hunting wagon. The staff consisted of fourteen coachmen and assistants, two cattle herders, four syces, four cooks, a surgeon, an officer of the Bechuanaland Police, a safari manager from the army, numerous native servants, three white servants, and Lord Churchill's butler. The vehicles carried enormous amounts of impractical luxury articles in addition to twenty-four rifles and shotguns and other necessities. There were 20 tons of goods including canned food and dried fruit, and a piano to provide music during the dinners. The hunting was not especially successful, but this had never been Lord Churchill's ambition.

Churchill didn't kill a lot of animals on his safari, but he received a huge amount of money to write about the trip for the Daily Graphic. *He could have bought a new shotgun from James Purdey & Sons for the fee he was paid for each article.*

He accounted for his share of the many quail, ducks, and pigeons the party killed, but did not shoot much larger game. Only occasionally did Churchill shoot a hartebeest or a roan. During the lion hunts, he left the shooting to Hans Lee. After one of these Churchill wrote: "The idea of galloping at full speed on a second-rate horse through thick bush, chased by a lion, was singularly unpleasant to me."

Custer and the Grand Duke

As the most colorful officer in the American cavalry, George Armstrong Custer (1839–1876) was a natural choice to host the Russian Grand Duke Alexei Alexandrovich (1850–1908) on a buffalo hunt as part of the Grand Duke's lengthy visit to the United States in 1872.

The hunt took place on the prairie west of Omaha and the arrangement was most extravagant. The twenty-one-year-old Grand Duke arrived in a caravan of wagons loaded with caviar and champagne, escorted by cavalry and a group of friendly Sioux Indians just to add an exotic touch to the arrangement.

The purpose of the hunt was to fulfill the Grand Duke's burning wish to shoot a bison from the back of his horse. This he accomplished on the very first day with assistance from the famous scout and hunter William Cody, better known as Buffalo Bill, who lent the Grand Duke his best horse and rifle. The young prince was so enthralled by his accomplishment that he jumped off the horse, cut off the bison's tail, and held the blood-dripping trophy high while howling like a wolf.

Custer was an excellent host for Grand Duke Alexei during his visit to the United States in 1872. Alexei had the time of his life in the company of colorful buffalo hunters, cavalry men, and Indians. He remained Custer's close friend until the general's demise at Little Big Horn.

Later, when the Grand Duke expressed doubt that an Indian could kill a bison with a bow and arrow, Custer arranged a demonstration. Mounted on a pony, one of the Indians of his entourage chased a buffalo into the camp and in front of the gawking guest, put an arrow completely through it.

A week later in Colorado the next hunt in honor of the Grand Duke was arranged, and a large mounted entourage of both civilian and military personnel, including Custer's superior officer, General Phil Sheridan, was led by Alexei and Custer. As the entourage approached a herd of bison, Custer suddenly felt like demonstrating to his Russian guest how the cavalry fought the Indians. Accordingly he ordered his men to charge the herd "like it was a flock of redskins!" Shooting wildly, Custer and Alexei led the charge and when the herd of bison panicked most of the entourage opened fire in every direction. Sheridan threw himself to the ground to avoid the hissing bullets filling the air and, according to two eyewitnesses, cursed the two immature gentlemen's "grandiose demonstration of impropriety."

When the shooting finally stopped, Alexei had killed a dozen bison, which were butchered and put on ice to be shipped to the court in St. Petersburg. Overwhelmed by enthusiasm, the young prince embraced Custer and kissed him. Custer had won a friend for life and the two corresponded diligently until Custer's death five years later.

Duke Ernst II was one of the most active hunters in Europe during the nineteenth century. During the last years of his life he hunted from his wheelchair.

Incredible but True!

The brother-in-law of Queen Victoria, Duke Ernst II of Saxony-Coburg-Gotha, loved the hunt so much that he even went out in his wheelchair and literally hunted until the day he died.

Hunter to the End

Queen Victoria's brother-in-law, Duke Ernst II of Saxony-Coburg-Gotha (1818–1893), was known as a passionate hunter and a brilliant rifle shot. The duke's hunting season began in the Tyrol where he hunted chamois in mid-July. Then he returned to Thuringia and hunted red deer starting in mid-August when the stags were out of velvet.

The duke managed to kill around 3,500 head of red deer in his lifetime; over 2,300 of these were stags. During his mountain hunts he killed a total of 2,000 chamois, mostly by stalking. His overwhelming passion, however, was stalking red stags during the rut and always on his own. During his last season (1892), he was driven out to the rutting area in a wheelchair while it was still dark, and he would then stalk as far as his weakened legs could carry him. On 22 August 1893, the duke was again hunting from his wheelchair. He had killed two 12-pointers during the first drive of the day and the second was about to begin when the duke had a massive stroke. His last words before expiring were, "Let the drive commence!"

Grumpy Heir

The Austro-Hungarian Arch-duke Franz Ferdinand (1863–1914) was obsessed with the number of kills and meticulously had every head of game recorded as a documen-tation of his accomplishments as a hunter. When the fifty-one-year-old Archduke was assassinated in 1914, exactly 272,511 head of game were listed in his hunting records. At his preferred residence, Konopiště Cas-tle, you can still see his collection of around 30,000 trophies.

The Archduke was infamous for his hot temper. On the hunting estates of Austria and Hungary, every game manager feared the trigger-happy heir to the throne, who was a good shot and killed all game coming past him, regardless of sex and age. Neither did he mind whether the game was free-ranging or in a small enclosure, something that was frowned upon by many of his contemporary hunters with higher ethical standards. (One of these was his uncle, Emperor Franz Josef

Archduke Franz Ferdinand and family and the Archduke's stag number 5,000, photographed on 30 September 1910.

(1830–1916), who personally killed over 55,000 head of game.) It has been speculated whether the heir's excessive shooting was in fact a much-needed outlet for Franz Ferdinand's rage.

Curse of the White Chamois

A traditional belief in the Alps is that if you kill a white chamois, you yourself will die within a year. Naturally, modern hunters do not believe in this kind of superstition; they just see a white chamois as an attractive trophy. But perhaps history provides a warning.

The only son of the Austro-Hun-garian Emperor, Crown Prince Rudolf, shot his mistress and himself in 1889 in a fit of depression because they could not marry—and he did it less than a year af-ter he had shot a white chamois.

Franz Ferdinand then became heir to the throne. Franz Ferdinand killed a white chamois on 27 August 1913. Almost a year later, on 28 June 1914, as he and his wife drove in an open car through the streets of Sarajevo, a young Serbian nationalist, Gavrilo Princip, fired seven shots at the royal couple, killing them both and starting World War I.

In the late summer of 1989, in the presence of his wife, Romanian president Nicolae Ceausescu shot 66 chamois from a cable car. Two of these chamois

Hunters Beware!

The old saying that the hunter will die within a year after killing a white chamois was ignored by at least three prominent Central European rulers—all of whom died within a year.

Cecily Herbert was only in her mid-twenties in 1906, when she and her cousin Agnes embarked on a safari in Somaliland accompanied only by native porters.

were white. Ceausescu and his wife were executed in front of TV cameras on Christmas Day, 1989.

Hunting Ladies

Two of the earliest female international big-game hunters were the cousins Cecily and Agnes Herbert (ca. 1880–1963). In 1906 they went on a hunting trip to Somaliland, where they hunted without the assistance of a professional hunter.

The safari was not without drama as one of the camel handlers died from thirst when the party was unable to find water, and Agnes's gunbearer was killed

by a charging rhino. In addition to this, Cecily was wounded by a lion, although Agnes managed to finish off the animal before serious damage was inflicted. In spite of the dramatic aspects of this trip, the safari whetted the two ladies' appetites

Agnes Herbert photographed shortly before her departure on an expedition to Alaska in 1908. The rifle is a 6.5x53R Mannlicher.

Legendary archer Howard Hill was the first hunter to kill an elephant using bow and a non-poisoned arrow.

for adventure. The following years the two young cousins went to Alaska to hunt bear, moose, and walrus, and then took a trip to the Caucasus for tur, a species of wild goat. At the time both these destinations were extremely wild and inaccessible.

King of Bow Hunters

It is unlikely any bow hunter ever surpassed the feats of American Howard Hill (1899–1975). His skills with a bow are legendary. He won 196 bow-shooting field tournaments in a row and in 1941 he attracted 35,000 spectators for a shooting show where he did stunts such as hitting a coin flipped into the air and shooting a prune off the head of a friend from a distance of twenty yards.

Hill was a tall and strong man, 6 feet, 2 inches tall, who always shot a longbow. During a hunt filmed in 1950, he became the first white man ever to kill an elephant with a bow and arrow. In total, Hill killed more than 2,000 head of game with his bows and arrows,

including three elephants, a Cape buffalo, bison, moose, and many other species of North American game that are very difficult to approach, such as the mountain sheep.

Howard Hill was also the archer behind the arrows that hit the stuntmen when the motion picture *Robin Hood* was filmed with Errol Flynn in the leading role. Under their shirts the stuntmen wore steel plates covered with balsa wood, and Hill shot them with blunt arrows. During an interview, Hill was asked what would happen if he missed the protecting plate, and he answered, "I don't understand what you mean."

Hill's self-confidence was not unfounded. Eleven men were "shot" in the film—often when they were running or

Incredible but True!

H oward Hill was the first white man ever to kill an elephant with a bow and arrow, all caught on film during a 1950 filmed hunt. In total he killed more than 2,000 head of game with bows and arrows.

Incredible but True!

W*ho holds the title for the most bags of the Big Five?*

It's not clear who killed the most of the Big Five species. It could have been Eric Rundgren . . .

. . . or it could have been John Hunter.

galloping on horseback—but to satisfy the director, Hill had to fire a total of forty-five arrows at the stuntmen. None of them were hurt during the filming.

Most of the Big Five

If you add up combined bags of the Big Five species (leopard, lion, buffalo, rhino, and elephant) there are two professional hunters, Eric Rundgren and John Hunter, who are in a class of their own. Unfortunately neither kept meticulous records and accordingly their respective bags have been calculated on the basis

This is, as far as we know, the only existing photograph of Lady Minna Jenkins and the trophies from her Tibetan expedition.

After hunting in Africa and shooting five tigers in India, Lady Jenkins in 1906 decided to make an expedition to Tibet, which was then an inaccessible and inhospitable area that only a handful of Europeans had visited, as the country had been closed to foreigners since 1850. In 1904, however, Great Britain made a treaty with Tibet and a few Europeans outside the diplomatic corps were allowed access, including Lady Jenkins.

As the only European member of the many-months-long shikar from Leh in India and through "both Tibets" as it was then called, Lady Jenkins completed one of the very few major hunting expeditions ever attempted here. In spite of severe frostbite and an almost fatal fall, she killed

of their reports to game departments, their clients' payments of license fees, their own and colleagues' records, and a number of other indicators and sources. In all, Eric Rundgren killed around 1,200 elephants, 3,500 to 4,000 buffalo, 250 rhinos, 500 to 600 lions, and 500 leopards. His total exceeded 6,000 head of big game. John Hunter killed around 1,500 elephants, more than 1,500 rhinos, more than 2,000 buffalo, over 600 lions, and 400 to 500 leopards. Because of the uncertainty surrounding the numbers, it seems fair to call the two famous hunters' accomplishments even.

Female Solo Hunter

The Welsh Lady Catherine Minna Jenkins was, like the Herbert cousins, a female trophy hunter who traveled to remote and almost unknown areas in order to hunt exotic game species.

With more than 19,000 foxes on his conscience, Johann Georg I earned the title of greatest fox hunter of all time.

Tibetan gazelle, blue sheep, Tibetan argali, chiru, urial, ibex, and markhor, something no other hunter has ever managed, male or female. One of the few species she did not get in spite of many attempts was a wild yak from the Tibetan mountains.

Thickest Hunting Ledgers

The two Saxon Electors Johann Georg I (1585–1656) and his son Johann Georg II (1613–1680) left the most comprehensive hunting records known. According to the meticulously kept records, the father killed a total of 116,443 mammals. This included 35,421 red deer, 31,902 wild boars, 19,015 foxes, and 11,489 roe deer. He also shot 872 wolves and 238 bears as well as hares, fallow deer, otters, beavers, and other small game.

His father shot the foxes, the wolves, and the wild boars. Maybe that is the reason there were more red deer and roe left to be hunted by the son, Johann Georg II. He managed to kill more than 109,000 head of game in his lifetime.

The principle of "German hunting" is to drive the game from a huge and temporarily fenced area into a small area in front of a shooting area from which the ruler can comfortably kill the scores of game with a little help from his loaders.

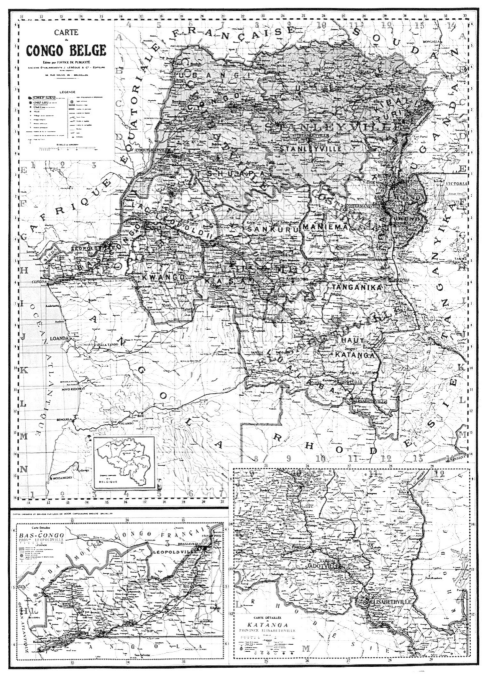

The Congo Free State, later known as Belgian Congo, was the private property of King Leopold and his very own 900,000-square-mile hunting ground.

The son was not quite as successful as his father. However, his grand total ended with 109,318 head of game, including 43,649 red deer, 22,298 wild boars, 2,740 foxes, and 16,864 roe deer. In addition came 2,195 wolves, 239 bears, and small game.

Most of the hunting was for red deer, as the figures indicate, and trophy size was measured by the number of points on the "best" antler. When studying the records it is obvious that the trophy quality suffered from the lack of proper selection of animals to be culled. Johann Georg I killed one 30-pointer, one 28-pointer, one 26-pointer, three 24-pointers, nine 22-pointers, 25 20-pointers, 133 18-pointers, 374 16-pointers, 1,202 14-pointers, and 3,147 12-pointers. A generation later, the son killed six 22-pointers as his largest trophies, and markedly fewer overall trophies than his father did, in spite of a significantly larger number of stags killed.

The enormous bags were due to the special type of "hunting" conducted at the time. The majority of the game was killed in "German hunts," an especially costly form of driven hunting where the game was killed from a grandstand placed over a moat or a fenced court. Over several days the game was driven from the surrounding areas toward the grandstand by the aid of meticulously made walls of fabric and by hundreds of beaters.

The "hunter" would stand at the end of a funnel into which all the game was driven. Although the firearms were primitive wheel-lock guns, which were time-consuming to

Incredible but True!

B elgian King Leopold II was the sole owner of the Congo Free State, making him the owner of the largest hunting ground and landowner in the world. Although he was a hunter, he never visited the Free State.

load, there were plenty of assistants and it was hardly a challenge to kill most of the exhausted game once it was swimming around in the water beneath the royal grandstand.

Largest Hunting Ground

At the Berlin Conference in 1885, the Belgian King Leopold II (1835–1909) was acknowledged sole owner of the so-called Congo Free State, later called the Belgian Congo. That made the king the largest landowner in the world as well as the owner of the largest hunting ground. Although King Leopold was a hunter, like most other royalty of the time, he never visited the Free State.

Incredible but True!

Two professional ivory hunters survived separate elephant attacks. James MacQueen had his right arm torn off and Captain Palmer-Kerrison survived a tusk through his abdomen. Both men continued hunting elephants.

William J. Morden and a Marco Polo ram shot on the Central Asian expedition he conducted on behalf of the American Museum of Natural History.

Some fifty-eight years after Leopold's death, the Romanian president Nicolae Ceausescu (1918–1989) became history's second-largest holder of hunting lands when he seized large parts of the country to use as his personal hunting grounds. Unlike King Leopold, he used his hunting grounds extensively.

Tough Cookies

Most professional ivory hunters were made from tough stuff. James MacQueen was a Scotsman who hunted elephants in the early twentieth century. During one hunt, a "dead" elephant suddenly got back up on its feet, charged MacQueen, and tore off his right arm. Miraculously, the Scot survived and the incident was not enough to deprive him of his desire to hunt elephants. He continued his career, shooting with the aid of a tripod.

Another tough hunter was Captain Palmer-Kerrison, a control officer for the Ugandan Game Department whose primary task was to kill elephants damaging native crops. One day Palmer-Kerrison had brained two elephants when a third bull suddenly came out of the bush and charged.

Palmer-Kerrison managed to put a bullet in its chest but the bull pierced the hunter's abdomen with one of its tusks. Then the animal carried the hunter for a short distance—like a butterfly on a needle—before the elephant started to waver and then dropped dead. Incredibly, Palmer-Kerrison recovered completely and continued to hunt elephants.

Tortured for Trophies

In 1926, Americans William J. Morden (1886–1958) and James L. Clark (1883–1969) went to Central Asia in order to collect specimens of

James L. Clark and Morden were tortured by Mongols for trespassing on their land and poaching their argali rams.

the world's largest sheep, the argali, including the Marco Polo argali, for the American Museum of Natural History. On horseback and later on domestic yaks and on foot, the two hunters covered more than 7,500 miles through Central Asia.

The expedition had many hardships, including a variation in temperature from minus 44 to plus 135 degrees. The altitude differed from 17,000 feet in the Pamirs to 500 feet below sea level in the Turpan Depression. The expedition was a great success and the two scientists brought home horns from Marco Polo rams and other exotic species.

Things got a bit out of hand when Morden decided that the expedition should cross Mongolia in order to collect more species. This country had

Trophies obtained on Morden's and Clark's expedition.

two years earlier become a Soviet vassal state, and the two Americans believed that their Russian visas were also valid for Mongolia. Deep in the wilderness of the country, however, the members of the expedition were caught by Mongolian soldiers who accused them of being spies. The two Americans were tortured and almost executed before managing to convince their Mongolian captors they were just hunting.

Sleep and Success

The Vikings had a saying: "Sleeping men are not victorious." But there are exceptions to every rule. During an elephant hunt along the Tana River in Kenya in 1945, Eric Rundgren visited the camp of a fellow hunter, Martinus Nel. His friend showed him a number of large tusks from the elephants he had shot, the biggest weighing an impressive 163 and 164 pounds.

While the two hunters were admiring the trophies, the famous South African hunter Van Rensburg arrived from his own camp, situated on a small island in the river. Van Rensburg explained that he had had a malaria attack and had to stay in bed while his two friends hunted elephants.

While sleeping in the middle of the day, Van Rensburg was awakened by a large elephant bull entering the camp. In spite of his febrile condition, Van Rensburg managed to shoot the bull in the heart and now he needed some assistance. Rundgren and the other hunters immediately set off for the island and soon found the animal dead. The tusks weighed 174 pounds each!

Poaching Success

If you measure a poacher's success by the economic outcome of his activities, there is little doubt that the most successful were found among the professional ivory hunters. A few of these operated within the law, but most did not. The most successful of the lawbreakers probably was Maurice "Mickey" John Norton (1873–1949). Norton rarely occupied himself with trivial matters like buying a hunting license and he evaded the law by moving on to a new country when the situation got too hot to handle or when an order for his arrest was issued.

Norton killed elephants in present-day Zambia, Congo, Tanzania, Kenya,

William Cotton Oswell was one of the earliest Victorian hunters in Africa.

This is the record buffalo when it was still alive. The Rowland Ward record is solely due to the enormous spread of the horns.

Malawi, and Uganda. In total he killed more than 2,000 elephants as a poacher. After World War I, Norton turned to dealing in ivory and made a little extra on the side by poaching the occasional elephant when he could. Eventually he was employed as a game ranger in then-Tanganyika where he killed an additional two thousand elephants, this time perfectly legal and as a part of his job.

Floaters

One of the earliest British big-game hunters in Africa was William Cotton Oswell (1818–1893). After ten years in India where he hunted tigers and wild boars, he went to the Cape Colony of South Africa. During an expedition to the interior of the country, Oswell met the famine-plagued Baka tribe and wanted to help by shooting some game for them.

After shooting a hippopotamus, Oswell and his partner Mungo Murray were disappointed when they realized that the animal immediately sank to the bottom of the river. Frustrated, the men shot an additional thirteen hippos, all with the same result. The two hunters did not know that a dead hippo will surface after a while from the buildup of digestive gases in its intestines. A short time later, the Bakas had more food than ever before.

Equality Debate

Clay Palmer-Wilson (1907–1985) was born and raised in Uganda but operated as a professional hunter in Tanganyika (present-day Tanzania). In 1946 he was guiding a film photographer by the name of Manuel Cabrera and one day they bumped into a herd of buffalo. Palmer-Wilson spotted a cow with an enormous spread and said, "Stop the camera—that buffalo is a world record!," whereupon Cabrera killed the buffalo with his .375 H&H.

The experienced hunter was right: The buffalo's horns had a spread of 64 inches, which made it number one according to Rowland Ward. The affair caused a still-ongoing debate whether the thinner but longer horns from a buffalo cow should be accepted as the world record, regardless of their size. Oddly enough, other trophies from species where the females grow the longer horns, such as oryx and rhino, have not been nearly as controversial.

Powell-Cotton shipped back more than 6,000 mammals for scientific research. These are a few of the trophies gathered during an expedition to eastern Africa.

Phlegmatic Hunter

Percy Horace Gordon Powell-Cotton (1866–1940) was an English big-game hunter who conducted numerous hunting expeditions to both Africa and Asia. He was considered one of the greatest big-game hunters ever; his collection contains over 6,000 large mammals. Half of the collection consists of hoofed species, including 180 bushbucks and more than 500 duikers.

Powell-Cotton personally killed 30 bongos—all by stalking. His collection of primates contains an almost unfathomable 187 chimpanzees and 204 gorillas. Because he spent so many days in the field, Powell-Cotton quite naturally had many unusual experiences. For instance, he killed the largest trophy elephant on record. During his honeymoon (a safari to East Africa) he survived a lion charge thanks to a brave porter. The porter was armed only with a stick and while the lion still had its

P. H. G. Powell-Cotton was one of the keenest hunters and naturalists that the world has ever seen. Here he is portrayed during an expedition collecting primate specimens for various museums.

claws in Powell-Cotton's back he kept it from killing its victim by beating it until one of the gunbearers could finish the animal off with a shot.

He also had an unflappable disposition. On one safari in West Africa Powell-Cotton was hunting with the famous gorilla hunter Fred Merfield. During a rest day in camp Merfield went out with his .22 rimfire to shoot a couple of francolins or guinea fowl for the pot. While Merfield was crawling through some dense brush, he came face-to-face with a large male lion and considered himself lucky to be able to back out of the situation and escape unscathed. When Merfield returned to camp and told about the incident, Powell-Cotton asked him why he hadn't shot the beast. Merfield showed him his .22 rimfire and mumbled something about a peashooter.

Count Gregers Ahlefeldt with the world-record impala that was killed under strange circumstances.

"I would have thought that a man of your ability could have shot it through the eye," Powell-Cotton said. "Even a .22 rimfire would have been lethal at that distance provided it was placed correctly." Old P. C. then went back to reading his book.

Record Coincidences

The Danish Count Gregers Ahlefeldt-Bille (1905–1985) went on his first safari in Africa in 1937 and visited the Masai Reserve in Kenya. Before Ahlefeldt left he mentioned his trip to his friend Dr. Bøje Benzon, who had hunted the same area three years earlier with the same professional hunter, Syd Downey. Benzon jokingly said that among the many thousand impalas in the area, Ahlefeldt ought to try to find an extremely good one Benzon had seen when he was there. He described the impala, which was easy to recognize from its very long horns and because the left horn was twisted much farther out to the side and back than the right one.

Ahlefeldt told Syd Downey the story; Downey remembered the animal well but had not seen it since. The very first morning of the hunt, Ahlefeldt and Downey saw a herd of impala only a few hundred yards from camp. They carefully stalked within shooting range of a good male, but just as Ahlefeldt was about to shoot, another male stepped forward—a huge male with a left horn that was twisted more to the side and back than the other. Ahlefeldt's first shot resulted in a "click" because in his excitement he had not fed a cartridge

In 1926 Kermit and Theodore Roosevelt Jr. managed to shoot this panda together.

into the chamber, but the result of the second attempt was a new world-record East African impala; the longest horn measured 36⅛ inches.

The Panda Club

In 1926 the giant panda was an animal science knew only from

The panda was one of several Asian species brought back to the Field Museum in Chicago.

descriptions and a few skins. There were no skeletons or parts in any scientific collection, and the animal had never been seen alive by any Western scientist. Many zoologists had doubts that it still existed.

A few years earlier, the brothers Theodore Jr. (1887–1944) and Kermit Roosevelt (1889–1943), sons of the naturalist, hunter, and former U.S. President Theodore "Teddy" Roosevelt (1858–1919), had made a large scientific expedition into Asia where they had collected more than 2,000 species of small and larger animals. As a result, the brothers were chosen to go into the largely unknown part of Indochina where the Himalayas gradually transform to open steppe. They planned to collect examples of any species they encountered and chart the terrain they went through. But the most important task was to collect one or several giant pandas for the Field Museum in Chicago.

The expedition was a great success. The Roosevelt brothers collected 2,000 smaller mammals and more than 6,000 birds and reptiles. In addition

Professional hunter Eric Rundgren photographed a few years after winning his ill-conceived bet.

to this they shot 40 big-game animals, including a giant panda. As the brothers were certain that they both had shot at and hit the old male, they had to share the honor (which it was at that time) of being the first Westerners to shoot a giant panda and therefore prove its existence to science. Only a small handful of hunters followed the Roosevelt brothers' example, and it is unlikely that the "Panda Club" has ever had even a dozen members.

Strange Wager

The famous professional hunter Eric Rundgren (1918–1992) had many clients during his career, but one of the most extraordinary was a gentleman with whom he would play cards in camp. After being systematically beaten over several days, Rundgren owed his client $500. As he asked himself how he was going to pay, the client challenged him to put a mark on a live buffalo for $500.

They were at Mto wa Mbu in what was then Tanganyika and the place was crawling with buffalo. It was not long before they found a bull lying close to a bush. Rundgren got out of the car and picked up a twig he planned to use to make an "X" on the bull's skin. He approached the bull within a few yards when it suddenly got up and disappeared around the bush.

Rundgren ran after it until he realized that it had turned and was coming straight for him. He swerved, but too late. A second later he was on its horns and then was sent flying through the air into a thornbush. When Rundgren finally managed to return to the car, with torn clothes and a lot of bruises, he was met by the wide smile of the client, who said, "You still owe me $500!"

Rundgren responded, "Double or nothing if I put a mark on an elephant!"

The client accepted this immediately. Rundgren knew this task would be much easier, although extremely dangerous if anything went wrong. Rundgren chose a single-tusked elephant bull that was walking along the riverbed, pulling off branches from the trees along it. The wind was good as Rundgren stalked closer. The elephant was pulling the foliage off a high branch when Rundgren jumped forward and swiftly made an "X" on its wrinkled flank before sprinting off. Completely shocked, the bull tried to get away so fast that it rolled over into the riverbank before getting to its feet and fleeing.

Incredible but True!

Tony Sanchez-Ariño has had a sixty-three-year career as a professional hunter where he killed or was involved in killing a total of 4,024 of the Big Five. Neither he, his clients, nor any member of his staff has ever had a hunting accident during his career.

In spite of having guided or personally killed more than 4,000 members of the Big Five in a career spanning more than six decades (as of 2014), PH Tony Sanchez-Ariño has never had an accident.

Best PH

In literature big-game hunting is often described as being more dangerous than it really is. Although you can get hurt or even killed hunting the Big Five, the risk is actually not that great if you are careful. This claim is put into perspective by the Spanish professional hunter Tony Sanchez-Ariño (b. 1930).

If measured by the number of hunting days without accidents, Sanchez-Ariño is in the same league as J. A. Hunter, who is considered one of the best professional hunters ever. After 59 consecutive hunting seasons, Sanchez-Ariño had in March 2010 killed or been involved in the killing of a to-

tal of 4,024 members of the Big Five: 165 leopards, 338 lions, 2,085 buffaloes, 127 rhinos, and 1,309 elephants. As of 2014, neither he, his clients, nor any member of his staff has ever had a hunting accident during his 63 years as a professional hunter.

Longest PH Career

Harry Selby (b. 1925) was born in South Africa but arrived in Kenya, where his parents had bought a farm, at the age of three. He shot his first antelope with a .22 rifle at the tender age of eight years. Only twelve years later he was hired as a professional hunter by the famous safari company Ker & Downey. For the

Harry Selby at the beginning of his career.

Harry Selby after sixty-five seasons as a professional hunter.

After almost losing her scalp to an attacking rhino, Kathleen Seth-Smith did not hesitate to continue her safari.

following fifty-five seasons he was active as a professional hunter, an accomplishment which has not been surpassed by anyone else. If one adds Harry Selby's active years as a "private" hunter to his years as a professional, he has had a total of sixty-five seasons.

After having hip surgery, Selby is no longer as active as he once was and refuses to include his later years of hunting in the calculation above as, he says, "I nowadays only kill a handful of warthogs and antelopes annually."

Teenage Elephant Huntress

Harry Selby was often accompanied by his daughter, Gail, on elephant hunts, and at the tender age of sixteen she expressed her wish for an unusual birthday present: a valid elephant license, as she wanted to shoot one herself.

Selby had been given a distinguished present by a client, the famous author Robert Ruark. This was one of Walter "Karamojo" Bell's rifles in .275 Rigby (7x57). As Gail was a slender girl, she chose this already thoroughly tested "elephant rifle," loaded with solids, for the task. She met the challenge in fine style, killing her elephant bull with one shot to the brain.

Tough Huntress

Kathleen Seth-Smith was from Devon and born into a family of hunters. Shortly after her arrival in Kenya in 1918 she began big-game hunting. She used two rifles from John Rigby & Co., a .275 High Velocity and a .350 Rigby Express. During a hunt on the slopes of Mount Suswa in Kenya in April 1926, Seth-Smith was charged by two rhinos from very close range. She was carrying

Gail Selby and her elephant, shot with Bell's .275 Rigby rifle.

the .275 and the tiny rifle could not possibly stop a rhino, let alone two, so the slender woman got hit by both animals. Fortunately the rhinos disappeared but left her nearly scalped and with several broken ribs. It took her two days to reach a hospital, but only three weeks later she was hunting again. Six weeks after the accident she undertook a 280-mile-long safari through northern Kenya on foot, with her head still bandaged.

Incredible but True!

B ert Schultz killed an elephant bull, went back the next day to collect the kill, and was met by another bull that he promptly killed. When their tusks were weighed, they were an exact match. Both bulls had tusks weighing 105 and 98 pounds respectively.

Symmetry

Shooting an elephant with one or both tusks weighing over 100 pounds has always been a rare thing, even during the golden years of big-game hunting between the two world wars. Bert Schultz (1900–1971), who was a control officer in Zambia's Luangwa Valley from 1922 to 1960, shot more than 1,000 elephants. During a private sport hunt, Schultz had an extraordinary lucky spell. Shortly before sunset he killed a large elephant bull, but due to the dwindling light he had to wait until the next morning to remove the meat and tusks from the dead animal.

When Schultz arrived at dawn the next morning, he found another large bull elephant standing next to the dead

Bert Schultz killed an elephant bull with tusks weighing 105 and 98 pounds. Twelve hours later he killed an identical bull in the very same spot.

one, and he quickly filled his annual license of two elephants with a well-aimed shot.

When the tusks were removed from the two dead elephants, it turned out that they were identical in weight: Both animals had tusks weighing 105 and 98 pounds respectively.

Seasoned Huntress

Patricia Strutt (1911–2000) married into the cotton empire of the Strutt family and was thus introduced to the Scottish Highland at the age of nineteen. She stalked stags there for seventy consecutive seasons. For many years she only used open sights on her .275 Rigby, but for her eightieth birthday she presented herself with a new, scoped .25-06 rifle from the famous gunmaker David Lloyd of Nottingham. Mrs. Strutt claimed she probably was the only woman in Great Britain to have sold her "Granny Bonds" in order to buy a hunting rifle.

The eccentric lady was a multimillionaire, but infamous for her tightness with money. The employees at her estate knew that the greatest tip they could hope for after a long day's hunt was a dram or two of the cheapest local whiskey. On the other hand, Mrs. Strutt was in excellent shape even in her later years.

She could not wait for "The Day of Roaring"—September 20th—the opening day of the stag-hunting season. In order to keep in shape for stalking, she went skiing in Switzerland every winter until she was an octogenarian and every day during the rest of the year she walked four miles in the hills around her estate. In total Patricia Strutt killed some 2,000 red stags.

First Female PH

Margarete Trappe (1884–1957) was the wife of a German farmer in what was then German East Africa (now Tanzania). During World War I she served as a voluntary scout for General Von Lettow-Vorbeck, using her considerable skills as a hunter

Patricia Strutt in the highlands shortly before her death.

Margarete Trappe (center) was the first female PH in Africa.

and rider to slip through the English lines and report on troop movements. Margarete Trappe had such a talent for surviving in the bush that her native staff believed she had supernatural gifts such as being able to milk elephants and talk to hippos. Soon after the end of hostilities she became Africa's first female professional hunter and operated all over East Africa.

From the Grave

In 1899 the English doctor Vinston Waters decided to help some natives near Nairobi, Kenya, by shooting some marauding elephants that were destroying crops. When Waters saw a large elephant bull, he shot it with his .577 BPE double rifle. As the shot did not have the desired effect, he fired the other barrel, which only made the elephant charge him. With an empty rifle Waters had no other choice than to run for his life—with the elephant hard on his heels.

At the moment when the animal reached out for him with its trunk, however, Waters disappeared! He happened to fall into a hole in the ground covered with branches—a native Kikuyu trap. Fortunately there were no poisoned sticks in the bottom, as there often were in these traps.

The elephant, confused, wandered around for a while before moving off. Apart from some minor bruises Waters was unharmed, and, true to the colonial spirit of the time, he immediately started tracking the elephant and finished it off a short time later.

Incredible but True!

While chased by a bull elephant near Nairobi, Kenya, (which he had just put two shots into), Vinston Waters fell into a trap built by the Kikuyu people. The trap stopped the elephant and Waters was able to track and kill the elephant a little later.

Most Gorillas

Most names of gorilla hunters have not been recorded. However, a handful of famous names are connected to specimens killed for scientific reasons. In November 1920 Prince Wilhelm of Sweden (1884–1965) went out on an expedition to Central Africa to collect specimens of gorillas for scientific research. The expedition was licensed by the Belgian authorities in Congo to "kill one gorilla off each volcano." The result was a total of fourteen gorillas killed, in conjunction with a large selection of other game.

Prince Wilhelm of Sweden shot fourteen gorillas on his expedition to Central Africa in 1920. It was all for scientific purposes, but even then the feat created a public outcry.

The expedition was later documented with both a book and a film about the hunting adventure. Although the purpose was purely scientific, the prince's exploits caused a lot of debate and criticism, although the mountain gorillas were far from being threatened at the time.

Wilhelm, however, was far from the most successful gorilla hunter. For many good reasons it has never been considered appropriate to kill the large primates—man's closest relatives. However, many museums in Europe and the United States wanted specimens for their collections, and the only way of getting them was hunting. The most successful gorilla hunter was Fred G. Merfield, who operated in southern Cameroon in the years between the two world wars. In total he killed 115 gorillas, a number of

them with his mentor, the famous big-game hunter Powell-Cotton.

The One-Arm Hunter

The last German Emperor, Wilhelm II (1859–1941), was almost as ardent a hunter as his close friend Archduke Franz Ferdinand of Austria. Wilhelm hunted all over Germany and was a frequent guest in Austria-Hungary, Great Britain, and Russia. Everywhere he hunted, he dressed in the Imperial Court's hunting uniform of shiny riding boots, jodhpurs, jacket, and a hanger.

The German ruler primarily stalked red stags and roebucks in addition to driven hunts for wild boars and deer. Wilhelm was very hard on the game population at the hunting grounds he visited as he shot at anything that passed him. He preferred to kill many young bucks instead of one old and clever one. In total the emperor killed 78,330 head of game, including around 10,000 hoofed animals, a few bears, and a gray whale (shot in Norway).

In spite of these impressive numbers the emperor often got a bad case of buck fever. His faithful companion on all hunts, the head gamekeeper Schmidt, said that he often had to put his hand over the sights of the emperor's rifle when he used the gamekeeper's shoulder as a rest. Schmidt would only remove his hand when the emperor's shakes were over.

Wilhelm had a paralyzed left arm all his life, so he shot using one arm only and for this reason the emperor preferred light firearms.

Kaiser Wilhelm II killed fifty stags on a single day of hunting at Rominten in May 1895.

Wilhelm's life as an emperor ended with his abdication from the throne at the conclusion of World War I in 1918. His good friend Franz Ferdinand had been assassinated four years earlier, and the Austro-Hungarian Empire fell apart. Wilhelm had declared war on his cousin Tsar Nikolai II who was later murdered by the Bolsheviks. Accordingly the British nobility did not have any warm feelings for the dethroned monarch after the war, and Wilhelm's hunting days were over.

He was exiled to Holland, where he died in 1941.

Bold Bow Hunter

In the 1920s the American hunter Art Young (1883–1935) became convinced that a modern bow hunter did not need a professional hunter with a rifle behind him in order to hunt dangerous game. To prove his theory he went to Alaska to hunt brown bears, armed only with a bow and arrow. These hunts were all filmed close up, which says a lot about the cameraman's trust in Young's shooting skills.

In 1925 he joined his friends Saxton Pope (1875–1926) and the author Stuart Edward White (1873–1946) on a trip to Kenya where they went on a seven-month-long safari into the Serengeti. The three bow hunters killed a total of 52 lions. The following year, Young went to Greenland where he killed both a polar bear and a walrus with his bow.

Art Young and Saxton Pope posing during one of their many trips together.

Part 4
Rifles, Cartridges, & Shooting

Chapter 10

Rifles and Cartridges

Most Popular Rifle

Determining which type of hunting rifle has been used the most over history is difficult. If rebuilt military rifles are included, the Mauser 98 probably is most widespread. More than 100 million Mauser 98 rifles were made throughout its history.

The "original" Mauser factory in Oberndorf, Germany, produced only 24,000 rifles for the civilian market. But many of the military Mauser 98 actions were later converted for use in hunting—exactly how many is not known, but it is counted in millions.

On the other hand, there is little doubt that by far the most popular civilian rifle ever made was Winchester's classic lever-action rifle, the Model 1894. This rifle was designed by John Moses Browning, and Winchester made a total of more than 7,500,000 of them during a span of 112 years (1894–2006).

Although the Mauser 98 was a military product, it became immensely popular among hunters. Millions of these rifles have been converted from military to civilian use over more than a century.

British gunmaker John Rigby & Co. used to be the sole importers of Mauser actions. This anonymous lady used a Rigby Mauser in .350 Rigby to bag a fine lion.

Not Very Efficient

The early European big-game hunters in Africa were brave men. In addition to diseases and other dangers, they had to use heavy, cumbersome firearms that were capable of killing big game but not particularly efficient. This is well illustrated by the Hungar-

In North America the Winchester 94 became the standard choice for everything from small game to moose and bears. The rifle is handy, well suited for saddle scabbards, simple, and reliable. No wonder it's still popular.

Incredible but True!

Winchester produced the classic lever-action rifle Model 1894, designed by John Moses Browning, for 112 years, totaling 7,500,000 rifles from 1894 to 2006.

ian Count Samuel Teleki von Szék (1845–1916). During his 1887 expedition to East Africa he used double rifles in .500 and .577 Black Powder Express. In the course of supplying fresh biltong to feed the safari's porters, Teleki killed 10 elephants, 61 buffalo, 21 rhinos, 9 zebras, 6 hartebeest, and 2 waterbuck. There is little doubt that the Hungarian count was a capable hunter—nevertheless, he was charged by no less than 11 of the 61 buffalo he killed.

Largest Hunting Rifle

The largest rifle in ordinary production is a .700 Holland & Holland Nitro Express. In the early 1970s, Holland & Holland received an order for a bespoke rifle in .600 NE.

Everyone at the time was convinced that this would be the last .600 NE ever made, and the company used this heavily in their marketing efforts. Little did they know that most of the English big-game cartridges would make an astounding comeback just a decade and a half later as ammunition availability improved. In the wake of this development the American hunter Bill Feldstein walked into Holland & Holland's shop in London in 1987 and ordered a double rifle Model Royal in .600 NE.

Holland & Holland had to refuse as by contract they had already made "The Last .600," and sold it as such. To an American, the logical solution was naturally to order a rifle in .700 Nitro Express. Although the cartridge did not exist at the time, it was soon designed by Feldstein and American cartridge maker Jim Bell.

The cartridges for a .700 NE are quite impressive.

The bullet weight is 1,000 grains and the muzzle velocity 2,000 fps. This results in a muzzle energy of 8,925 ft./lbs. Even in a double rifle weighing 18 pounds, the recoil energy from firing a .700 NE is 162 ft./lbs., or more than ten times the recoil of an ordinary hunting rifle in .30-06. The cartridges cost more than $100 each, but if you are able to afford a Holland & Holland double rifle in .700 NE, this is hardly a decisive factor.

Smallest Gun

The smallest firearm ever made was a semiautomatic pistol in the diminutive caliber 2.7mm Kolibri. The bullet only weighs 3 grains and the muzzle velocity is 650 to 700 fps, resulting in a muzzle energy of around 3 ft./lbs. A total of 1,000 of these minute pistols were produced, half of them in a slightly larger caliber called 3mm Kolibri. As a hunting firearm it is of little use, but as suggested by the author

A .700 H&H NE, the more traditional big-game round .470 NE, and a .30-06 for comparison.

of *Cartridges of the World*, Frank C. Barnes, it might do to dispatch an overly aggressive cockroach!

The world's smallest firearm in serial production is this little semiautomatic pistol.

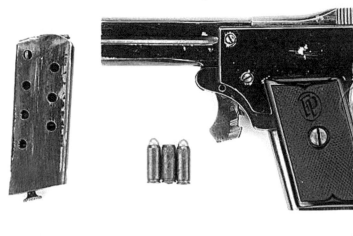

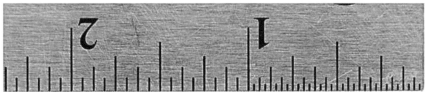

The length of the Kolibri pistol is only about 2.5 inches.

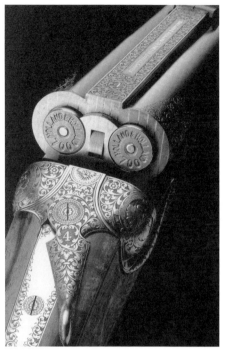

The most expensive hunting firearm in current serial production on the market is a Holland & Holland Royal de Luxe double rifle in .700 Nitro Express.

Most Expensive Rifle

We will exclude extraordinary firearms with extreme embellishments such as elaborate engraving and with gold and gems from this category. These rifles can be interesting but in order to make a valid comparison, the rifle must be a "standard" product made to "ordinary" specifications included in the maker's normal price list.

With these presuppositions, the most expensive firearm on today's market is a double rifle from Holland & Holland in caliber .700 Nitro Express. The price for a model Royal de Luxe in

2011 was roughly $250,000. For comparison, the same maker charges less than $165,000 for a double rifle in a more common big-game cartridge.

Most Species with One Rifle

The single rifle that has most likely killed the most different game species is a Schultz & Larsen M60 in caliber 7x61 Sharpe & Hart that belonged to the Danish big-game hunter Rudolf Sand (1923–2002). He got the rifle as a present from his cousin and used it for the rest of his hunting career to kill 271 different game species.

There are only a handful of big-game hunters in the world who have killed anywhere near as many different species,

Rudolf Sand posing with the rifle that killed the largest number of species in the world.

This is probably the rifle that killed the most big game ever: J. A. Hunter's .500 double.

and as far as I know none of them used the same rifle throughout. The game species Sand took with the rifle varied in size from a fox to much larger species including lion, tiger, polar bear, bison, water buffalo, banteng, Cape buffalo, gaur, and giant eland. Sand shot a total of 762 head of game with this rifle in addition to a large number of practice shots. Beware of the man with one gun!

Sand kept his targets from zeroing the rifle at 220 yards during the 1960s and when it was tested again at the same distance with 150-grain Nosler bullets in 1997 the groups still had almost the same spread as when the rifle was new in 1960—very close to two inches, or one minute of angle.

Well-Used Double

The most experienced professional hunter in Africa was John Alexander Hunter (1887–1963). Early in his career he became an advocate of large-caliber rifles for big-game hunting. His

The John Rigby & Co. double rifle the Maharaja of Surguja used to kill almost 500 tigers.

philosophy was: "You can't give a man's job to a boy!"

Hunter was once charged by a herd of aggressive elephants, but he survived the episode by killing twelve animals with his .505 Gibbs bolt-action rifle. His preferred rifle, however, was a double rifle in .500 NE with which he killed more than 600 elephants and more than 900 rhinos, in addition to other game. This .500 NE is very likely the rifle that killed the most big game in the world.

Tiger Rifle

The Maharaja of Surguja holds the record for killing the most tigers, so it is hardly surprising that he also was the owner of the rifle that killed the most tigers. Like many other Indian princes, he was very interested in hunting arms and had several bespoke guns made in England.

In 1936 he went to John Rigby & Co. in London and ordered a special double rifle. On top of being built to the Maharaja's measurements, it was made in .416 Rigby, a caliber the company had introduced for use in bolt-action rifles in 1911. The maharaja's double rifle was delivered in 1939 and was the only one of its kind ever made by Rigby. The cartridge had the same ballistic performance as the classic .416 Rigby but was based upon the rimmed case from a .470 NE so it could be used in a double rifle.

As there were extra development costs, the rifle became quite expensive—allegedly $3,000. (For perspective, in 1940 a best grade sidelock shotgun from James Purdey cost $750.)

With his specially built rifle, the Maharaja of Surguja killed almost 500 tigers in addition to leopards and a large number of other big-game species.

One Cartridge for All Big Game

The well-known big-game hunter and author of *African Rifles & Cartridges*, John Taylor (1904–1969), used a wide range of rifles and calibers during his many years in Africa and was a diligent advocate of large-bore rifles for elephant hunting. During his career he killed over 1,000 elephants, mostly as a poacher.

In spite of the fact that he preferred and recommended the larger bores for big game, he nevertheless personally fired more than 5,000 cartridges at game with his five rifles in .375 H&H—two doubles and three bolt-action rifles. With just one of the latter he killed more than 100 elephants and 411 buffalo, in addition to rhinos, lions, and lesser species.

If you count a single caliber used on just one big-game species, the record-holder is probably the .318 Westley Richards, as the Swiss hunter Gustav Guex used an unknown number of rifles in this caliber to take 7,000 Cape buffalo, as described in Chapter 2.

Dog Gone

In the late nineteenth century, the bicycle became a common means of transportation in northern Europe.

Many versions of the Velo Dog revolvers were manufactured. Most of them had a hinged trigger to make it easier to fit the firearm in a pocket.

A Velo Dog cartridge resembles a .22 magnum. Here shown next to a .22LR.

The problem for cyclists was that they were often attacked by the many dogs that ran loose everywhere at the time. The French gunmaker Charles-François Galand (1832–1900) realized that there was a market here. He accordingly introduced a short-barreled pocket revolver named Velo Dog; the first half of the name was an abbreviation of the French word for bicycle, *Velocipede*.

The revolver was especially developed for cyclists so they could avoid the annoyance of being bitten by the aggressive dogs simply by shooting the critters. The problem was so widespread that a large number of different dog revolvers were soon offered by many different makers, and you could even get a model that was built into the handlebar of the bicycle. The caliber of the first dog gun, officially called 5mm Velo Dog, was also of Galand's design and resembles a centerfire .22 Magnum.

Charles Cottar was a sworn follower of the small-caliber school and it nearly cost him his life. The photo shows him being treated after a close encounter with the leopard in the foreground.

Harry Caldwell and a man-eating tiger killed with a .22 Savage Hi-Power. Don't try this at home.

Small but Sufficient

Some small-caliber enthusiasts have gone to great lengths to prove that the placement of the bullet is of greater importance than the size of its diameter. It is well known that Walter "Karamojo" Bell shot hundreds of elephants with his .275 Rigby (7x57) by carefully placing his round-nosed 173-grain solid bullets in the brain. Bell was an extraordinary marksman, and he may not have paid sufficient attention to this fact when drawing his conclusions. He described how he successfully killed twenty-three Cape buffalo with his .22 Savage Hi-Power. Bell wrote that he used the diminutive cartridge in order to see how

Incredible but True!

Charles Cottar once decided to shoot a rhino with a diminutive cartridge, the .250 Savage and its 80-grain bullets, during a safari filming in 1916. He killed the rhino with four shots. Two of the bullets were found flattened on the animal's skull.

efficient the small 70-grain bullet was for the purpose.

Harry Caldwell, an American missionary in China in the early years of the twentieth century, apparently agreed with Bell. He used his .22 Savage for all kinds of game, including tigers. Other hunters, however, had second thoughts about the use of such diminutive cartridges for larger species.

After the introduction of the .250 Savage in 1915, the famous professional hunter Charles Cottar used this cartridge and its 80-grain bullets with great success for antelopes. But one day during a filming safari in 1916, Cottar decided to shoot a rhino with the diminutive cartridge. The animal charged, and against all odds Cottar managed to kill it with four shots

fired from a distance ranging from twenty-five down to eight paces. Two of the bullets were found flattened on the animal's skull. Years after the incident, Cottar was interviewed by *Outdoor Life* and said, "I shall never make an experiment like that again, and never forget this. Behind me was the continuous clicking of the camera and toward me came 4,000 pounds of fury with a large horn while I only had an 80-grain missile to stop it." Not a comfortable thought—not even today.

The Hard Way

In 1903 the famous English gunmaker John Rigby & Co. introduced the .275 Rigby cartridge in a rifle built on a Mauser Model 98 action. This rifle was to become world famous, although, in reality, the only changes from the Mauser 7x57 were a new name, English-style stock and sights, and a 140-grain pointed bullet instead of a 175-grain roundnose projectile. Rigby's objective was to increase the velocity and make the trajectory flatter in accordance with the new trend in military cartridges.

Critics rightfully claimed, however, that pointed bullets were less stable and more likely to alter course when penetrating

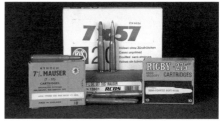

Many hunters used .275 Rigby cartridges, loaded with full-metal-jacketed bullets, for big game.

Soon after the advent of small-caliber light rifles, they became very popular for big-game hunting using full-metal jacketed bullets. Shown above is Lord Ronaldshay with his .275 Rigby bolt-action at the turn of the last century.

their target, especially when using solids. In spite of this criticism, Rigby continued to have its .275 ammunition loaded with pointed bullets until World War I, when the production of ammunition for civilian purposes all but ceased for the duration of the war. When Rigby could once again supply fresh ammunition to its customer base, the .275 Rigby cartridges were loaded with a much less pointed projectile.

The reason for this was a very practical demonstration of the ballistic differences between the two types of bullets. During the war, Rigby's managing director served as an officer and was hit in the head by a spitzer, or pointed bullet, from a German 8x57 rifle. The bullet did not kill the man but went through his steel helmet, followed its internal surface, and exited again without injuring anything but the man's pride. I think it is fair to say this is "learning the hard way."

Accuracy vs. Energy

Among firearm enthusiasts there is a never-ending discussion of which cartridges and calibers are best for different types of hunting, especially when it comes to big-game cartridges. A widespread myth (probably initiated by John Taylor in his book *African Rifles and Cartridges*) is that an elephant can be knocked unconscious by a large-bore rifle if the bullet hits somewhere near the animal's brain. This is not the case, as proven by the following incident.

As mentioned earlier, in 1988 Holland & Holland made the largest and most powerful double rifle ever, a .700 Nitro Express (18.3x89R). With a bullet weight of 1,000 grains, the rifle delivers a muzzle energy of 8,925 ft./lbs. When the owner tested the rifle in the field for the first time, he used it for a head shot on an elephant. Although close, the hunter did not hit the animal's brain, and the elephant was not knocked out—it did not even stumble after the first shot, but was killed by a second one.

Although even the largest and most powerful calibers are not capable of stunning an elephant with a bad hit, there is no doubt that a powerful rifle with a large caliber is better than a smaller one for stopping a charge in thick bush. In present-day Zimbabwe, the game department has recorded fatal accidents in connection with hunting since 1951. The records show that most of the human deaths were inflicted by elephants in dense bush. The records show that not a single hunter under these circumstances saved himself from death or mutilation when using a rifle in .375 H&H caliber. But more than 50 percent of the hunters who were using a rifle with a caliber over .40 managed to stop or alter the course of the animal's charge and walk away unharmed. For even the most recoil-shy hunters, these statistics lend a lot of appeal to a heavy .40-caliber rifle.

A heavy bullet of large diameter is always the best choice when hunting dangerous game.

Chapter 11

Hunters and Their Rifles

Gunmaker John Rigby became famous as the finest supplier of British made bolt-action repeaters. He was also an extraordinarily good rifle shot.

Early Modern Marksmanship

In a letter to *The Field* in January 1870, the London gunmaker John Rigby (d. 1916) discussed the practical use of blackpowder rifles for hunting with the then-new "Express Cartridges." In two days at a Scottish estate, Rigby killed 28 red deer and 3 feral goats with two breechloading double rifles in .450 and .500 BPE.

The shooting distances varied between 60 and almost 300 yards. Most of the animals were killed while running, and many were hit in the head. Only a single deer shot at was lost. Rigby had personally built both rifles and made the ammunition for them; bead and half-round notch sights were used. John Rigby was well qualified to prove how well his rifles could shoot; he had won the prestigious Wimbledon Club in 1864 and been head of the National Irish Rifle Team at twenty-eight international competitions.

Longest Hunting Shot?

At dawn on 21 May 2000, Kreg Slack and his wife, Nadine Perry, sat at a shooting bench preparing to fire at metal silhouette targets. Kreg was using a specially built rifle in .338 Lapua Magnum, and Nadine's task was to observe the impact so Kreg could adjust his scope.

As Kreg was about to fire his first shot, he noticed a prairie dog sitting on the top of its mound not far from the targets, and as the little varmints were in season, he decided to try to shoot it. A prairie dog is a target about the same size as a pack of cigarettes. The first shot hit some distance from the animal, and after a quick adjustment, Kreg shot again and his second shot hit about a foot from the animal. Kreg adjusted his sights again and hit his target straight through its center. The prairie dog never knew what hit it. The distance from the muzzle of Kreg's rifle to the prairie dog was 3,125 yards, and that makes it the longest successful hunting shot officially recorded.

Worst Shots Ever?

Naturally it is hard to pinpoint the worst shot ever, but here is a good candidate for this dubious honor. The Englishman Ewart Grogan (1873–1966) took part in an extraordinary expedition during three years from 1898 to 1900 when he walked from the Cape to Cairo, a feat which earned him fame throughout the British Empire. In 1899, he explored the Ruwenzori Mountains and their volcanoes, situated in the border country between Uganda and Belgian Congo.

He also hunted elephants on the forested slopes of the mountains. Grogan used a 4-bore double rifle with bullets that weighed 1,750 grains. In an area with extraordinarily thick jungle, Grogan managed to find an elephant bull and fire a shot from a distance of two yards without hitting the animal. After the shot, the elephant ran off at full speed and during Grogan's pursuit no signs of blood were found, and the animal never showed any signs of resting or stopping. A year later Grogan wrote in his book *From Cape to Cairo*, "I think it is still running!"

But maybe an even worse shot was fired in 1913 by the professional hunter Rudolph Naude. He was guiding Maud and Kenyon Painter on their safari

Incredible but True!

The longest successful hunting shot officially recorded was made by Kreg Slack with a specially built rifle in .338 Lapua Magnum. He shot a prairie dog straight through its center at 3,125 yards.

Ewart Grogan and some of the trophies he obtained on his walk from the Cape to Cairo. During his journey Grogan possibly made the worst shot of all time.

in Kenya. During the hunt, Kenyon wounded a lion, which disappeared into some dense bush. Naude's assistant hunter, Thompson, went after it and was charged. During the ensuing attack, Thompson was badly mauled with wounds in his body, arms, and legs. Despite this, Thompson managed to get his rifle back and shoot the lion, breaking off its attack.

Although in excruciating pain, Thompson shouted to his boss and asked whether the lion was dead. Naude lost no time in shooting at the lion to make sure, with the only result that the animal regained its feet and bit Thompson again! In the end the lion was killed, but whether Thompson survived the incident is unfortunately not recorded.

The Kick of a Lifetime

In the days of blackpowder, the only way to increase a rifle's striking energy was to increase the caliber and thereby the bullet weight. Accordingly, rifles of 4 and 8 bore were popular for hunting pachyderms in the tropics. The German explorer and big-game hunter Hermann von Wissmann (1853–1905) literally got a kick from unintentionally firing both barrels of his heavy 4-bore double rifle. During the search for a wounded elephant he grabbed the rifle from a gunbearer and cocked both hammers.

He wrote: "I threw the heavy rifle to my shoulder and pressed the trigger. A deafening roar thundered in my ears. I was pushed back several meters and fell flat on my back. My rifle flew up and away in a tall arch. As I shortly after regained all my senses I heard my invisible opponent run off through the bush. Fortunately I was unharmed and only bled profusely from my nose. When my men arrived I had picked up the rifle twenty yards behind me where it had landed with both barrels halfway into the ground."

Without tiring the readers with boring calculations, I will add that you are not only exposed to twice the recoil when both barrels are fired simultaneously—the recoil actually increases by a factor of four. Wissmann experienced recoil equivalent to firing forty rifles in .30-06 simultaneously.

Wissmann did not have much luck with his double rifles. During a driven hunt in 1905 he fell asleep at his post and suddenly awoke. As he did, he knocked over his rifle, which went off and killed him instantly.

Sir Samuel Baker photographed in a studio with rifle and trophies.

Rare Recoil

One rifle that must have been a challenge to use is the percussion rifle that Henry Holland built for Sir Samuel Baker (1821–1893). It is recorded in Holland & Holland's archives as a 2-bore, or 1⅓ inches, which makes it closer to a 3-bore, which is 1⅙ inches. Regardless of the actual caliber, the bullets weighed half a pound and were propelled by a blackpowder load of 220 grains. This load propelled the bullet to a muzzle velocity of 1,500 fps. Due to the enormous bullet weight, the resulting energy was no less than 17,700 ft./lbs., with a recoil equivalent to firing four .375 H&Hs simultaneously.

Samuel Baker nicknamed the rifle "Baby," which says a lot about both his stature and sense of humor. His native assistants' name for it—*Jenab al Mootfah*—says a lot more as it translates to "Child of a cannon."

Baker describes in a picturesque way what it was like to fire the rifle: "Bang went the Baby; round I spun like a weathercock, with the blood pouring from my nose as the recoil had driven the sharp top of the hammer deep into the bridge. My Baby not only screamed but kicked viciously." He added, "Actually, it was hard to tell who suffered the worst shock from the rifle—the elephant or me!"

Baker also admits that he quite understandably dreaded firing the rifle. "I rarely fired it and remarkably it never fired a shot without felling what was fired at."

Baker's rifle "Baby" is a part of Holland & Holland's collection in London. For obvious reasons, nobody has fired it for decades.

John Moses Browning is arguably the most successful firearms designer in history.

Elsewhere Baker describes how the recoil once threw the rifle out of his hands and it landed twelve yards away. During a period of several years Baker—for some reason—only fired a total of twenty shots with the rifle.

Diligent Designer

Throughout history, many ingenious firearms designers have emerged but none in the same class as John Moses Browning (1855–1926). This quiet Mormon who avoided the limelight all his life left a heritage of 128 patents and more than 70 firearm designs. Several of these are still produced, and many enthusiasts claim that his designs have never been surpassed. This truly unique feat has no equal in industrial history. Some of the best known designs from John Moses Browning's hand are:

Browning .22 Automatic. A neat little semiautomatic rimfire launched in 1914 and still in production.

- Winchester 1893: Pump-action shotgun; progenitor to the American's beloved pump gun.
- Winchester 1894: Lever-action rifle; the world's most popular hunting rifle.
- Browning Auto-5: Semiautomatic shotgun of which more than 5 million were produced over eighty years.
- Browning .22 Automatic: Semiautomatic rifle.
- FN B-25 Superposed. Over-and-under shotgun/double rifle; the archetype of a modern over/under and still made.

In addition to these, Browning designed a number of semiautomatic pistols, military rifles, and machine guns. Most famous are the BAR (an automatic rifle successfully used in both world wars), and the Browning BMG (Big Machine Gun). Its .50-caliber cartridge is still a standard NATO caliber. Browning also designed the Model 1911 semiautomatic pistol in .45 ACP caliber, which was the standard sidearm of the United States Army for more than eighty years and which is still used by some elite units.

Best Rifle Shot Ever?

William Frank "Doc" Carver (1851–1927) called himself "Champion Rifle Shot of the World." That's quite a statement, but there is little doubt that he actually was the best and most versatile rifle shot in history. His colorful career was nothing short of fantastic.

Dr. Carver fully realized the importance of marketing. He called himself "Champion Rifle Shot of the World." It might have been true.

Incredible but True!

*J*ohn Moses Browning left a heritage of 128 patents and more than 70 firearm designs, several of which are still produced. This truly unique feat has no equal in industrial history.

Champion shot Bogardus became the first of the great American show shooters. His abilities with a shotgun were phenomenal. Carver, however, boldly claimed that he could do exactly the same—with a rifle!

Carver was in his early twenties when he got into shooting. He had settled as a dentist in Nebraska but it is doubtful he ever practiced. Instead he taught himself the art of shooting almost to perfection during a very few years, and his skills quickly earned him a local reputation. He is said to have killed more than 30,000 bison for the railroad, but this cannot be substantiated. A wager between Carver and another colorful bison hunter known as "Buffalo Curly" made local headlines. The wager was quite simple: See who could kill the most bison on a single trip on horseback along Frenchman Creek. The two hunters were each accompanied by an entourage to mark the animals killed. When the day was over, Carver had won hands-down with 160 bison, whereas his opponent's much lower result is long forgotten.

In December 1877, the famous champion shot Capt. A. H. Bogardus announced he would shoot, with a shotgun, 5,000 glass balls thrown into the air during a span of 500 minutes.

A few days before the event, a letter appeared in several East Coast newspapers. It was written by a totally unknown dentist from Nebraska, Dr. W. F. Carver, and he claimed he would accept a wager between $250 and $500 that he could beat any shot in the world in all the competition disciplines.

Carver also claimed that he could hit more glass balls with a rifle than anyone else could with a shotgun, and that he could hit more flying targets from a horseback than anyone else could standing on the ground. The letter ended with an open wager of $1,000

One of Doc Carver's greatest admirers was the Prince of Wales.

that Carver could kill more bison than anyone else during a single riding trip (if no bison were available, he added, elk could be substituted).

The letter was seen as a funny example of megalomania. Bogardus accepted the challenge without hesitation, convinced that the letter was from a madman. Before Carver arrived on the East Coast, however, Bogardus had left for a European tour and there was no one to compete with.

This, however, did not stop Carver. He arranged a show at Winchester's shooting range and, in front of 5,000 people, started out by breaking a vast number of glass balls thrown in all directions and angles. Then he hit 26 out of 45 flying silver dollars, broke 1,000 glass balls in 80 minutes, and finally killed a flying swallow with one well-aimed shot. All this with a rifle! Overnight, "The Spirit Gun of the West" became famous from coast to coast.

In a few months he had defeated all American challengers before leaving for Europe on a tour. He performed for the higher bourgeoisie, the aristocracy, and many crowned heads. His greatest admirer was the Prince of Wales, who decorated him with a medal after his show. Carver had destroyed 14 out of 15 glass balls thrown within 15 seconds and then fired 16 shots in the air from his lever-action rifle in only four seconds. Carver continued the show by breaking 100 thrown glass balls without a miss, followed by breaking 28 out of 30 glass balls, many of these being doubles, from the back of a galloping horse.

The prince was so excited that he made a wager with other spectators that Carver could hit 150 glass balls in a row. Carver won the prince's wager by hitting 153 in a row in 11 minutes, a new record. Carver's shooting accomplishments were never surpassed.

Dick Cooper downed planes like these with his double rifle.

Richard "Dick" Cooper was a good wingshooter, a useful skill in the trenches of World War I.

Dangerous Birds

Richard "Dick" Cooper was a wealthy Englishman who enjoyed shooting driven pheasants before World War I. He later became a well-known figure in Kenya's hunting circles. In 1929 he was invited to dinner with his friend Bror Blixen who was the professional hunter for the famous German Flying Ace of World War I, Ernst Udet. During the dinner the two former soldiers shared memories of the war they had fought on opposite sides.

Cooper said that when he was an officer in the trenches in 1917, he and his men had repeatedly been attacked by low-flying German airplanes that killed many of his men with machine-gun fire.

Fed up with this, Cooper brought his double-barrel .450 Holland & Holland rifle back to France with him the next time he returned from leave. The next time Cooper's unit was attacked by German planes flying in formations of three he coolly waited until he could clearly see the pilot sitting crouched behind his machine gun in the plane.

"I gave him a good lead and was almost flabbergasted when the plane went directly into the ground after my shot, like a dead pheasant," Cooper continued. "The situation was repeated with the next plane. I could barely believe my eyes, but the boys were cheering, so I quickly reloaded the rifle and fired a last shot when the third plane passed over us. He too had to bite the dust!"

Ernst Udet then asked Cooper about the planes' markings. Cooper said, "I

Incredible but True!

Richard "Dick" Cooper (English officer in World War I), shot down three German planes in France during World War I with his own double-barrel .450 H&H rifle!

don't recall their markings, but they were small and uncannily efficient one-seated planes with canvas-clad hulls."

"Those planes," Udet answered softly and without any reproach, "were from my Fourth Division, and until today we always wondered what happened to them!"

Who Needs a Shotgun?

The so-called "rook rifle" was very popular in the late 1800s. Later, rimfire rifles took over the scene due to using far cheaper ammunition than the centerfire rook rifles.

Talented rifle shots emerge from time to time without making any fuss of it. This does not make their feats less impressive. In 1877 *The Field* reported that a Mr. H. W. L. Haigh had, in a single afternoon, killed 123 running rabbits with his .250-caliber Rook rifle from Holland & Holland. He shot the animals as they came jumping out of their holes at an average distance of 50 yards.

A few years later, in 1883, an English colonel by the name of Howard in India killed a deer, a buzzard, two peacocks, a sand grouse, and a duck, all with a rifle during a single day.

A Mr. P. R. Chalmers reported, also in *The Field*, that he had witnessed an unnamed Frenchman perform quite a shooting feat with his rifle. First the Frenchman killed three Highland stags. Then he secured his first dinner course by standing on a tall riverbank and killing a jumping salmon with a shot

New Model "Ross" Hammerless Ejector Rook and Rabbit Rifle

Initially a large part of Holland & Holland's production constituted rook and rabbit rifles. This is the second best model, not fully engraved.

Art Jackson is one of the most successful competition shooters in U.S. history. He was twenty-two years old when he stepped into the limelight, setting a new world record.

through its head. Maybe shotguns (and fishing rods) are overrated?

Bull's-Eyes until Dark

In the summer of 1940 there was a major rifle shooting event in New York. One of the disciplines was a "Swiss Match," which consisted of scoring as many bull's-eyes in a row as possible. The shots were fired from a prone position without a rest and the distance was 200 yards. The bull's-eye measured 7.2 inches in diameter with an inner circle of 4 inches. The world record, set in 1936, was 196 bull's-eyes in a row.

Around 4 PM, the twenty-two-year-old and then completely unknown Art Jackson (b. 1918) decided to try his luck and lay down at his post with half a box of match ammo. Hours later, when the setting sun behind the targets made it impossible to see the cross wire of his scope, Art Jackson had to stop shooting. He had still not missed a bull's-eye, although the cheering audience had sponsored one box of ammo after another as his own supply had run out after twenty-five perfect hits. The official record was 324 bull's-eyes in a row—although the audience had counted 325—and 238 of them were hits in the inner circle.

Little Sure Shot

Annie Oakley (1860–1926), or Phoebe Ann Mosey as she was baptized, was the youngest child of six when her father died of pneumonia in 1866. The family was hard-hit by poverty and Annie had a terrible childhood at the workhouse and in foster care. However, she had been taught to hunt and shoot, and the young girl's extraordinary talent for shooting soon supported the entire family.

By the time Annie was fifteen she had killed so much game in the forests around her home that the income from the sale of meat enabled her to buy the farm for her mother. Annie was excluded from all local shooting contests because she always won everything she competed in. In 1876 she was "discovered" by the exhibition shooter Frank Butler when he visited her hometown and offered a large monetary reward to anyone who could outshoot him.

He laughed scornfully when he realized that he was about to compete

Annie Oakley—or Phoebe Ann Mosey as her r
name was—photographed shortly after her de
as a show shooter.

A slightly older Annie at the peak of her career.

The king of Senegal offered Buffalo Bill the incredible sum of 100,000 francs for Annie Oakley so she could kill the lions that were plaguing his country. Here the young Oakley is shown with a shotgun and a few of the many medals she won on both sides of the Atlantic Ocean.

With a .22 rifle, Annie could hit a flying dime at thirty yards. With the same rifle she would cut a playing card in half and make four or five holes in the top half before it hit the ground. She shot apples off the heads of both her husband and her dog. But it was not only in the circus ring that she impressed. She won many serious shooting competitions and set several records during her career. She was one of the greatest superstars of her time.

The Prince of Wales—later King Edward VII—presented Annie with a silver cup with the inscription: "To the best shot I have ever seen." That she was pretty, too, hardly lessened his admiration. German Crown Prince Wilhelm was also captivated by the beautiful sharpshooter and followed her tour around Europe. He begged her to shoot the coal of a cigarette in his mouth, as she did in her show, and in the end she gave in and promised to do it provided he would hold the cigarette in his hand.

When World War I broke out many years later, Annie wrote a personal letter to her admirer—who in the meantime had become emperor—and asked for "another shot." Wilhelm never answered, and Annie was later jokingly blamed for not having prevented the war when she had the chance.

In her old age, Annie Oakley entertained friends and visitors by lying on her back with three double-barrel shotguns at her side while her husband threw six clay targets in the air over her. They never hit the ground in spite of the fact that she was suffering from permanent damage to her back and a

with a skinny sixteen-year-old girl, but his grin was quickly wiped off as he was emphatically beaten. He married her the same year and never departed from her side again.

Annie was "adopted" by the famous Indian chief Sitting Bull when he saw her shoot in 1882. He gave her the name *Little Sure Shot.* Annie became a part of Buffalo Bill's legendary Wild West Show in 1884 and was on tour with it for the next seventeen years. During this period she performed for many of the world's crowned heads and received numerous awards.

crippled leg after a car accident. In spite of her deteriorating health, she still broke 97 clay pigeons out of 100 late in life. During her lifetime she managed to teach some 15,000 young women to handle a gun, and she herself fired over a million rounds.

Straight-Shooting Gentleman

Horatio Ross (1801–1886) was known as the best shot in Great Britain with rifle and shotgun as well as pistol. As the son of a wealthy Scottish landowner, he could indulge in his passions throughout his life and was gifted with both the skills and the desire to be the best.

Young Horatio's introduction to firearms, however, was not a happy one. When Napoleon began to rattle his sword, Horatio's father gathered a regiment of local volunteers with himself as commander. When the regiment was to be presented its banner,

The aging Ross as he will be remembered—with a gun in his hands.

Horatio Ross (sitting with a telescope) assisting one of his sons. Ross himself was a natural talent in many different fields. He was a marksman, hunter, athlete, and photographer.

the commander insisted that his six-year-old son, Horatio, carry it. All went well until the soldiers fired a volley as a salute and young Horatio got so scared that he ran into the castle and hid, to the father's intense displeasure.

In order to accustom the boy to the sound of gunfire, the father ordered a servant to fire a gun over the boy's head several times a day. But this did not cure the son's fear of shooting. Only when the servant got the brilliant idea to let young Master Ross himself fire the weapon at an inoffensive sparrow did Horatio learn to accept guns and soon to love them. As an adult, Ross showed off his shooting skills at the Wimbledon Cup and other tournaments. But it was in hunting and at improvised competitions that Horatio Ross really had a unique talent.

Once Ross was visiting the famous gunmaker James Purdey, who had just finished a double rifle for another customer. Purdey asked Ross to test-fire the rifle at some chalk circles at a distance of 100 yards. The bull's-eye had a diameter of 1.5 inches. Ross fired without a rest and hit the bull's-eye with eleven out of twelve shots.

On another occasion Ross was competing against Lord Vernon, also an excellent shot. The distance was 100 yards and Ross won hands down in spite of the fact that Lord Vernon used a rifle and Ross a pistol. Later the same day Ross won a bet of £100 by sending a bullet through a flying hat thrown in the air 100 yards away.

An even more remarkable bet for £100 was whether Ross could kill twenty swifts on the wing with his pistol in one day. Around the tower of his castle there were many swifts, and Ross won his bet before breakfast.

The Miracle Man

Adolph Toepperwein (1869–1962) was practically born into shooting as he was the son of a German gunmaker who built special rifles for the bison hunters in Texas. In his youth he became locally famous for his skill with firearms. When Adolph was in his teens, he saw Buffalo Bill's Wild West show and was enthralled by the many good shooters. From that day he swore that he would beat them all.

In the meantime, he had to make a living with a more mundane job as

a cartoonist at a local newspaper. The salary made it possible to buy enough ammunition for practice, and soon he was invited by a local theater to join them as a permanent part of their variety show.

Shortly afterward, the director of the show decided to pay Toepperwein's expenses for a trip to New York, hoping to bring his talent to a greater audience. However, the talent scouts on Broadway were skeptical as there were many exhibition shooters at the time.

Incredible but True!

A beggar sitting outside an arena in a small Mexican city looked to the sky and prayed for help from the Lord when two bent silver coins fell next to her. They were the result of an exhibition shoot by Adolph Toepperwein who shot three silver pesos in the air. Two of them flew out of the arena and right to the beggar.

Adolph and Elizabeth "Plinky" Toepperwein. For decades they performed together for Winchester.

some silver coins the policeman threw in the air and wanted to keep as souvenirs after the show. Three silver pesos were thrown in the air but only one fell down in the arena. The remaining two flew over the walls. No one in the audience knew that outside the arena was a beggar sitting with her gaze toward the sky and asking the Lord for help when two bent silver coins fell next to her.

The other "miracle" also happened in Mexico when the circus was passing an abandoned church at a distance of approximately 100 yards. In the tower of the church a barely visible bell was hanging, and Toepperwein's colleagues

In a last desperate attempt, Toepperwein's agent invited one of the most famous talent scouts to join Toepperwein on a trip to Coney Island where the shooter proceeded to go from one shooting gallery to the next and hit every target in each one with uncanny certainty while a growing crowd gathered around him. The talent scout was now convinced that Toepperwein was more interesting than a "good banjo player or a trained sea lion." For the next ten years Toepperwein worked for a large traveling circus.

Toepperwein's talent for shooting was not only legendary; twice, it was miraculous. On one occasion, Adolph was performing in a bullfighting arena in a small Mexican city. A local police officer asked Toepperwein to shoot at

Plinky was a remarkable shot with pistol, revolver, rifle, and shotgun. She was also one of the very best female trap shooters ever.

Incredible but True!

Annie Oakley publicly declared that Elizabeth "Plinky" Toepperwein was the best female shot the world had ever seen. Plinky could shoot the buttons off her husband's shirt as well as the cigarette out of his mouth!

asked if he could hit it. Adolph aimed and shot, compensating for the wind, and delivered four rapid hits which made the bell ring merrily. No one in the circus caravan knew that there was neither a rope nor a clapper in the old bell and that the villagers on the other side of the church, hearing the bell ring, were convinced that they had witnessed nothing less than a sign from God. The rumor spread and believers began to make pilgrimages to the place. Soon the church was restored and the village flourished due to the "miracle." It was many years before the truth emerged.

In 1901 Toepperwein got a contract with Winchester as their exhibition shooter. During a visit to an ammunition factory a year later he met eighteen-year-old Elizabeth, with whom he fell in love and married a few weeks later. Elizabeth Toepperwein (1884–1945) had no experience with shooting, but she was a fast learner and turned out to have such a talent for handling handguns that she too was hired as an exhibition shooter and traveled with Adolph. Her show-business name became "Plinky" and her skills were equal to her husband's. A popular part of the couple's show was when Adolph turned his profile to Plinky who then proceeded to shoot off the buttons of his vest and end by shooting a cigarette out of his mouth!

At the clay target range Plinky hit 100 out of 100 targets 193 times and 200 out of 200 targets 14 times. Her personal record was 393 clay targets in a row. Annie Oakley publicly declared that Plinky Toepperwein was the best female shot the world had ever seen.

In 1907 Adolph decided to attempt setting a new record. An assistant standing 10 yards away threw wooden blocks with a side length of 2½ inches into the air and Toepperwein would try to hit them with a single shot from a semiautomatic Winchester .22 LR. The record attempt was over on the 22 December 1907, after ten consecutive days of shooting. All the wooden blocks were used and Toepperwein's arms were so stiff he could barely lower them. Toepperwein had fired at 72,500 targets. Apart from nine blocks, he had hit them all.

In 1959 Remington's exhibition shooter, Tom Frye, tried to beat Toepperwein's record. The attempt took thirteen days and nine hours. Frye hit 100,004 blocks out of 100,010 thrown. He missed only six blocks, which is a fantastic feat, but Toepperwein's is still considered greater as Frye had his assistant throw the blocks away from him and up in the air, while Toepperwein's were thrown vertically and so were much more difficult to hit.

The Laconic Marksman

Herb Parsons (1908–1959) grew up on a farm in Tennessee where he was presented at the tender age of seven with a single-shot rifle in caliber .22 LR. As a teenager he saw the famous exhibition shooter Adolph Toepperwein's show and decided to pursue a similar career. He came closer to realizing his dream

Herb Parsons became the last of Winchester's great show shooters. Like his predecessors, he mastered both the rifle and the shotgun to a degree that thrilled millions of spectators throughout North America.

when Winchester hired him as a salesman. He quickly improved sales by putting on improvised shows for the customers. In the early 1930s, Parsons's idol, the aging Toepperwein, took Herb under his wing and taught him the subtleties of exhibition shooting.

In the following years he gave many hundreds of shows for Winchester and after World War II his career really took off. Parsons mastered all types of Winchester firearms to an uncanny degree of perfection and he repeated the same feats in show after show.

He would throw seven clay pigeons into the air and pulverize them with his pump gun before they hit the ground. He would throw a stream of nuts, marbles, and washers into the air and hit them all with his .22 LR.

Suddenly, though, a washer would fall untouched to the ground and the crowd would roar with laughter. Parsons would then say, "Oh, I must have hit the hole," and the crowd would laugh even louder. Herb would then take a stamp out of his wallet, lick it, and stick it to the washer so it covered the hole. Then he would toss the washer toward the sky and fire a single shot at it. Nothing apparently happened and the washer would fall to the ground. Then Herb would ask a member of the audience to go and pick up the washer— only to find that in the center of the stamp was the hole from the bullet. This was repeated in show after show.

Once, during a show at a racecourse in Maine, an unexpected situation arose. A flock of crows flew over the crowd and approached the forest at the end of the racecourse several hundred yards away.

Tom Frye sitting on top of the small mountain of wooden blocks he "killed" with a .22 rimfire. It was a remarkable record, but not as outstanding as the record set by Toepperwein.

Herb, who was still an avid hunter, shouted to the crowd: "What's behind those trees?"

"Nothing," was the answer. "The forest continues far into Canada!"

Herb then picked up his .30-06 from the table and squeezed off a shot. A few seconds later one of the crows exploded in a cloud of feathers before the eyes of the jubilant crowd.

Herb Parsons's laconic comment was, "That bullet had to hit something!"

Wood Blocks

In 1987 John "Chief A. J." Huffer (b. 1937) attempted to set a new record for hitting 2.5-inch wooden blocks thrown in the air, just as the famous Toepperwein and Frye had done before

him. But Huffer threw the blocks himself for a period of fourteen hours a day, eight days in a row. He stopped when he missed the first time, after having hit 40,060 blocks. In 2008 Huffer, at the age of seventy, made the *Guinness Book of World Records* by hitting 1,500 flying targets with the preferred arm of his childhood—a slingshot.

Dangerous Hobby

Today fatal hunting accidents are fortunately rare, but this was not always the case. *The New York Times* reported in September 1907 that the numbers of people killed during hunting was astonishing. Annually approximately 10,000 hunters went whitetail hunting in the popular Adirondack Mountains, and some 500 were killed by other hunters . . . and

City slickers from the East Coast flocked to the Adirondack Mountains to hunt whitetails at the beginning of the last century. Both the adventure and the meat appealed to the young men from the city. Unfortunately, most had no hunting experience and a poor safety record.

Erskine Childers was calm enough at his own execution to lend advice on the art of shooting a rifle.

around 3,000 bucks. In other words, one hunter was killed or wounded for every three bucks killed!

These figures naturally made hunters and legislators reflect on the situation. A doctor from Utica who hosted a party of hunters in the Adirondacks in 1906 had a marvelous idea. He issued all the members of the party a red cap, and his hunting party was likely the first in history to use a signal color as a safety measure.

Unfortunately, one guide in the party decided to walk through a thicket in an attempt to drive a deer out to his client. The guide had to go down on all fours to penetrate the dense thicket, and in order not to ruin his fine red cap, he took it off. When the client saw something crawling through the brush, he made a well-aimed shot and killed the guide, convinced it was a black bear since it wasn't wearing a red cap.

the same number were wounded. That made for a fatality rate of 5 percent during a season of just a few weeks.

For comparison, the United States sent a total of 4 million soldiers across the Atlantic in 1917–1918 to fight in the trenches of Europe, but even in that terrible war, the casualty rate was only 3 percent. The 10,000 hunters in the Adirondacks typically killed

It Is Difficult!

Notwithstanding the feats of great shooting described in this chapter, rifle shooting actually is a difficult discipline. Let us therefore end with a rather mundane comment. When the Irish nationalist Erskine Childers (1870–1922) stood in front of a firing squad on 24 November 1922, his last words revealed a profound understanding of the best way to increase accuracy in the noble art of rifle shooting: "One step closer, boys—it gets easier that way!"

Part 5
Birds and Small Game

Chapter 12

The Game

Snipe

One of the smallest and most challenging of all game birds is the snipe. Apart from the fact that the jack snipe (*Lymnocryptes minimus*) is far less common and somewhat smaller than the common snipe (*Capella gallinago*), there

Lord John Alexander Elphinstone was a very successful snipe hunter.

is no significant difference in how hard they are to hit. The following report has not been verified (and is probably not entirely true) but it illustrates the difficulties surrounding the noble art of snipe shooting.

In the late nineteenth century, a quartermaster in the British 64th regiment by the name of Malloy was stationed in Ireland, where he took every opportunity to hunt a certain jack snipe. In one day he fired no less than eighteen shots after the bird without killing it. This particular jack snipe served him faithfully for almost an entire season until one day when Malloy was crossing the meadow where it lived and flushed the bird once again. He spontaneously exclaimed, "Well, here's my old friend again!" before throwing his walking stick at it and killing the bird on the spot.

The most successful snipe hunt I have been able to find recorded took place on the island of Tiree, which is one of the Inner Hebrides. Lord Elphinstone (1869–1955) and his friend Mr. J. D. Cobbold hunted snipe from 25 October 1906, for the following eight days. In total the two hunters killed 1,108 snipe. Due to bad weather the two hunters only had half a day of shooting during two of the nine days and accordingly "only" killed 56 snipe in total while the remaining seven days gave a total of 1,052 birds.

Two years later the two gentlemen shot a total of 1,292 snipe with a single day yielding a bag of 217 birds. In order to reach this absurd number, however, the hunters spent a total of eleven days in this remarkable snipe terrain and accordingly the average bag per day was not as large as in 1906.

Most Snipe in a Season

The largest recorded bag of snipe during one shooting season was made at Lord Sligo's estate in County Mayo, Ireland. In the season of 1846–1847 his gamekeeper killed 3,330 snipe, thirty more than the season before. These figures tell a lot about the effect that the practice of drainage agriculture later had on the population of snipe in Europe.

In the latter half of the nineteenth century there were still professional wildfowlers who made a living from

SNIPE SHOOTING.

The swamps of Louisiana in the late nineteenth century were some of the world's best snipe habitat.

shooting ducks and other wildfowl for the market. One of these was Patrick Halloran (1862–1927), from Kilkee in County Clare, Ireland. During several of his fifty active seasons he killed more than 1,000 snipe with a record of more than 2,000 killed in the season of 1879–1880. In his fiftieth and last season in 1924–1925, Halloran was sixty-nine years old but still managed to kill 768 of the long-beaked birds. During his entire career Halloran killed more than 40,000 snipe.

Halloran, however, was not the most successful snipe hunter the world has seen. In the swamps of the southern United States there is another subspecies called Wilson's snipe with the very descriptive scientific name *Capella gallinago delicata*. Near Oaklawn in Bayou Teche, Louisiana, Mr. J. J. Pringle killed no fewer than 366 snipe on one September day in 1887. Pringle's best season ever was 1874–1875 where he recorded a total bag of 6,115 snipe. During his twenty seasons as a professional wildfowler from 1867–1887, Pringle spent

The woodcock is, in many places in Europe, considered the most prestigious prey among the winged game.

a total of 711 days shooting snipe and made a total bag of 69,087 birds, an average of almost 100 snipe per hunting day.

Woodcock

The woodcock (*Scolopax rusticola*) is very popular among bird hunters in Europe due to its sprightly and irregular flight and unpredictable presence in the field: here one day, gone the next.

The most successful woodcock hunt I have found records of resulted in 228 birds shot on 3 January 1910, at Ashford Estate in County Galway, Ireland. The year 1910 was a good year for shooting these forest-dwelling birds at Ashford as five consecutive days of hunting yielded 587 woodcocks.

Woodcock on Time

Ireland has often been described as the woodcock hunters' mecca. During the Christmas holiday in 1802, Lord Claremont (1764–1829) made a wager of £300 that he could shoot more than 100 woodcocks in a forest at Lord Farnham's estate in

Ashford Estate in Ireland holds the record for most woodcock bagged in a single day.

Lord Claremont bet that he could shoot 100 woodcocks in a single day.

County Cavan. In spite of the fact that Lord Claremont used muzzleloading flintlock guns, he managed to win his wager by a wide margin as he killed 102 woodcocks before 2 PM the following day.

On Fair Isle, situated between the Orkney and Shetland islands in northern Scotland, Mr. George Stout was hunting woodcock on 28 October, 1908, and killed 109 woodcocks with his .410 shotgun. He saw more than 300 and could have shot more had he not run out of cartridges.

Best Season

The largest bag of woodcocks in a single season was made by Mr. Jes Jessen (1908?–1977) on the island of Fanø, who in 1952 killed 243 woodcocks. His legendary English setter, King, was probably the world's most successful woodcock dog, retrieving 1,205 of the nimble birds. Jessen's other dogs, Bella and Cora, retrieved some 800 and 600 woodcocks respectively. (A Herta

pointer belonging to Col. Vilhelm Wedell-Wedellsborg (1873–1946), also retrieved around 600 woodcocks.)

For many years Jes Jessen was the most successful Danish woodcock hunter with credible records. From 1926 to 1975 he shot a total of 3,489 woodcocks. Jessen had a rival on his native island, the seaman Børge Fischer Jensen (1920–1999). During a span of thirty-five years the quiet sailor and seal hunter killed a total of 3,996 woodcocks, an average of 114 a year during his career as a hunter.

However, as Fischer did not keep a proper record and never kept a single trophy in shape of a pin feather or

Jes Jessen was one of the world's most successful woodcock hunters. Here he is photographed with his legendary English setter, King.

Incredible but True!

The Dane Mr. Dimitri Buchtrup has bagged a total of 4,404 woodcocks from 1946 to 2013. Mr. Buchtrup was born in 1929 and he is still hunting.

tion of predators. In those early days, few people distinguished between the different species of crows and birds of prey, and accordingly it is difficult to establish the accomplished bags of each species. According to the records I have been able to find, the most successful hunter of winged predators was the gamekeeper Carl Brehm (1883–1950) from the Danish estate Rosenfeldt. Brehm opposed the use of poison and traps and stuck to the shotgun. By 1943 he had shot 25,212 corvids and birds of prey.

If we stick to crows, however, there is hardly anyone who has killed more than the Danish hunter Bjarne Frost (b.

ever had a bird mounted, but only had a notepad with a line for each bird, his total is disputed. The question of who was really the most successful woodcock hunter was finally settled some years later when both gentlemen's records were surpassed by a third Dane, who is the country's (and maybe the world's) top woodcock hunter of all time, Mr. Dimitri Buchtrup (b. 1929). From 1946 through 2013, Buchtrup has bagged a total of 4,404 woodcocks, and he is still hunting.

Corvids

One of the most difficult birds to get within shooting range of in Europe is the hooded crow (*Corvus cornix*). At one time it was one of a gamekeeper's primary tasks to reduce the popula-

As a gamekeeper at Rosenfeldt Estate in Denmark, it was Carl Brehm's primary task to reduce the numbers of winged predators. Unlike many of his colleagues, Brehm was not in favor of using poison and traps.

1945). It is interesting to see the development of Frost's annual bag with a modest beginning of one crow in 1961, one in 1962, and none at all in 1963. Beginning in 1969, Frost taught himself to imitate the bird's different calls and cries, and began using a single mounted bird as a decoy. His annual bag rose quickly to more than a hundred in 1972 and to several hundred by the end of the 1970s. The annual numbers rose until his record year of 1987, when Frost killed 2,486 hooded crows.

Frost's biggest problem was not access to good terrain—crow hunters are always welcomed by farmers. Hunting regulations were changed in Denmark, and the crow shooting season shortened so much that Frost was unable to hunt as much, so he began traveling to Sweden, where he has killed many of his crows over the past twenty years. Frost is also one of the few hunters who makes overseas expeditions for the sole purpose of hunting crows. He has even gone to Africa, sharing camps with big-game hunters, some of whom clearly consider him quite mad. Bjarne Frost has been in Africa twenty-six times to hunt crows as well as other bird species.

From 1961 to the end of the 2012 season, Bjarne Frost bagged 40,060 crows, mainly in Denmark and Sweden, making an annual average bag of 785. This record will undoubtedly increase as Frost has now retired and has more time for his passion than ever before.

Bjarne Frost is most likely the world's most successful crow hunter.

Jays

On 27 September 1977, the game-keeper at Holckenhavn Estate in Denmark told his employer, Eiler Holck (1913–1999), that there was a continuous flight of jays (*Garrulus glandarius*) along the coastline. This was so unusual that Holck the next morning decided to find a place behind a hedgerow along the coast in order to shoot jays during their flight. He soon ran out of cartridges and sent his game-keeper home for fresh supplies so he could continue shooting until noon when the flight died out. The result was 179 jays—the biggest number ever recorded for a single man on a single hunt. The record will probably never be broken as the jay is now protected in most European countries.

The Passenger Pigeon

The most numerous bird in the world, until the end of the nineteenth century, was the American passenger pigeon (*Ectopistes migratorius*). The pigeon looked a bit like a mourning dove but was much larger and was widespread throughout eastern North America. The population was estimated to be somewhere between 3 and 5 billion birds.

The first Europeans who settled in North America often described enormous flocks darkening the sky for days when passing an area. In 1866 a flock of passenger pigeons was observed in southern Ontario, Canada, that was a mile wide and 150 miles long. It took the flock fourteen hours to pass the place

The passenger pigeon was once the most numerous bird species in the world. The bird illustrated is Martha, who dropped dead from her perch in Cincinnati Zoo in 1914. She was the last specimen alive.

of observation. It has been calculated that the flock contained around 3.5 billion birds, the majority of the total population. The noise from the many wings was said to be deafening.

In the autumn the pigeons mainly ate beechnuts, acorns, and chestnuts, which were found in enormous quantities in the American forests. The passenger pigeon bred in enormous colonies with sometimes hundreds of nests in every tree in the area. Observers described how trees broke down under the weight of the birds. The largest breeding colony recorded was found in central Wisconsin in 1871; it covered an area of

The flocks of passenger pigeons were so enormous that people thought there couldn't possibly be any end to them.

850 square miles and had a population of approximately 136 million pigeons.

This enormous population of pigeons was exploited in all sorts of ways by entrepreneurial people. The fact that the pigeons bred in colonies made it easier to catch them, and all sorts of methods were used to kill them. Large bonfires were lit in order to drive the birds off their nests and catch them in large nets. The birds were also fed with grain marinated in alcohol to make them easier to catch. For many years passenger pigeons were the only source of meat for the poor. The birds were even used as fertilizer in the fields.

When the railroads were built, it became easier to transport large numbers of dead birds to the larger cities. The scale of slaughter was enormous. During five months in 1878, around 50,000 pigeons were killed daily at Petosky, Michigan, in a breeding colony that turned out to be the last really large one. One trapper claimed to have killed more than a million pigeons and hereby earned $60,000—the equivalent of $1 million in today's money. Another source tells us about a trapper who sent more than 3 million pigeons to the cities on the East Coast.

In the latter part of the nineteenth century the combination of deforestation and commercial trapping of pigeons in the breeding colonies began to have an effect and the population dwindled at a shocking rate. The last verified observation of a passenger pigeon in the wild was made near Sargents Pike in Ohio on 22 March 1902, when a boy killed it with his rifle. The last living specimen dropped dead from its perch on 1 September 1914 in the Cincinnati Zoo.

Wood Pigeons

Unlike the passenger pigeon, populations of wood pigeons (*Columba palumbus*) in Europe have been increasing. In Great Britain alone, a survey showed that the population of wood pigeons grew by almost 350 percent between 1967 and 1997. Unlike most other species mentioned in this book, the increase in the population of wood pigeons has

For many years, Archie Coats held the record for a bag of wood pigeons in a day.

resulted in ever-increasing record bags for pigeon shooting over decoys.

Wood pigeons are considered vermin in Great Britain and can as such be shot all year-round, which obviously provides favorable conditions for setting new records.

For many years the record bag of one day's wood pigeon shooting belonged to Archie Coats of Britain who on 10 January 1962 shot 550 birds in Hampshire, England, and who would have shot many more if he hadn't run out of cartridges. Since this feat, however, the record has been broken several times in increasingly shorter intervals. Mr. John Ransford didn't expect much when in the early 1970s he went into a local farmer's wheat field in order to do him a favor by shooting pigeons. Ransford killed 560 pigeons in one afternoon. Since then the record has grown constantly, and several hunters

The population of wood pigeons in Europe has tripled during the last three decades.

The record bag of wood pigeons in a day is coming closer and closer to one thousand.

have reported days of shooting more than 700 wood pigeons.

A good candidate for the twentieth-century record is the late Mr. Malcolm Unitt. For a number of days in the late 1970s he had kept a harvested field near Leatherhead, Surrey, under observation and noticed how the pigeons were swarming there. As his car was getting serviced, Unitt asked his wife to drive him out to the field and asked her to pick him up again after the car was done.

He was dropped off at 8:30 AM and put up his blind under an oak tree that can still be seen from the M25 highway encircling London. At 11:40 AM Unitt had still not fired a shot and if he had had a car he would have gone home and considered the day one of the mysterious ones where the pigeons wouldn't fly.

However, shortly afterward, he shot his first pigeon and from then until he was picked up at 6:30 PM, the action was constant. Unitt had brought four cases of cartridges plus 100 more in a plastic bag, and when he stopped shooting there were only a few

left. He estimated that he fired 1,075 shots. He and his Labrador retriever picked up 820 pigeons, but as both the hunter and the dog were exhausted, there were undoubtedly some that were left behind.

There is no doubt that with the increasing number of pigeons and the improved decoys, these records will be broken, if it hasn't happened already. Many British pigeon hunters are not inclined to record their bags in writing. There are persistent rumors that a Cheshire hunter has broken the 900-pigeon barrier in one day's shooting, but I haven't been able to have this report verified.

Apart from knowledge of the pigeon's habits and correct placement of blind and decoys, it takes luck, perseverance, and shooting skills to make these enormous bags in a single day. Some of the famous British professional pigeon hunters such as Archie Coats have undoubtedly made enormous total bags, but unfortunately they haven't kept records. One of the most successful pigeon hunters I have

The largest bags of wood pigeons have all been made during the last decade, but because of antihunting sentiment, there are few pictures available.

found records of is Frans Marcher of Denmark (b. 1934), who shot a total of 23,520 pigeons in the years 1946–2012. Another Dane, Bjarne Frost, who was mentioned earlier in this chapter, started pigeon shooting in 1961 and through 2012 he had killed 22,896 wood pigeons and 692 Eurasian collared doves (*Streptopelia decaocto*).

Dove Days

On 4 February 2005, Steve Marsden of Britain (b. 1958) shot 7,314 eared doves (*Zenaida auriculata*) in the Cordoba province of Argentina. The population of this species is estimated to be somewhere between 50 and 60 million birds. The doves cause tremendous damage to crops in the ever-expanding agricultural areas of Cordoba, which is also the cause of the recent explosion of the dove population.

Marsden is a well-known competition shooter. During his record day he used two semiautomatic 8-shot Benelli shotguns to fire 9,500 cartridges—a hit rate of around 77 percent. During three-quarters of an hour in the afternoon he killed 744 doves, or 17 doves per minute. On the next day, Marsden killed an additional 350 doves in 500 shots—all fired from his left shoulder. For some reason his right shoulder had become a little sore.

Two years later, Marsden beat his own record. On 3 October 2007, he went to the same area and killed 10,335 doves in ten hours—this time with over/under guns in 20-gauge. Almost half the doves—precisely 4,516—were killed in doubles. In total Marsden used 12,100 cartridges during this day.

In South America there are pigeons and doves in incredible numbers. This photo is from the Cordoba area in Argentina.

207

Steve Marsden photographed during his first attempt at a record bag.

shotguns in 20-gauge, or approximately one shot every four seconds for over fourteen hours. His total bag was 11,301 doves.

Teal

Few species of game will challenge a hunter's shooting skills as much as the nimble little teal (*Anas crecca*). The most successful teal hunter I have been able to find reports of is the Scot Martyn Thomas Kennard (1859–1920). He was a wealthy hunter who early in the twentieth century killed enormous numbers of waterfowl in Kashmir, Northern India. In the seasons from 1907 to 1919 Kennard bagged a total of 58,613 waterfowl, of which 26,075 were teal—almost 2,200 a year.

In Europe it is probably the British Lord Lewisham (1851–1936) who

These figures are somewhat justified by the fact that between 20 and 25 percent of the annual crop of maize, sorghum, rice, and wheat is eaten by the doves. In addition, hosting dove shoots gives the local farmers an extra source of income. All of the birds killed are consumed, and they constitute an important source of protein for the less privileged members of the area's human population.

Marsden's record was beaten—also in the Cordoba province of Argentina— a little more than two years later by the Texas dentist Todd White. From 6:10 AM to 8:31 PM on 30 January 2010, Dr. White fired 14,250 cartridges from a total of seven semiautomatic Beretta

To date, Lord Lewisham has bagged the most teal during one shoot.

The teal is the most agile and acrobatic flyer of all the duck species.

killed the most teal in a morning's flight. On 6 October 1913, he was at a water hole near the village Laughton in Lincolnshire, England, and between 7 AM and 11 AM he shot 186 teal in addition to 53 mallards and 8 widgeons—a little over one duck per minute.

On both sides of the English Channel there were formerly a number of professional waterfowlers killing birds for the market. With huge shotguns mounted in punts, these hunters stalked close to flocks of birds resting on shallow water, hoping to kill as many as possible in one shot.

Near the coast of Holland, Capt. G. J. Gould on 29 November 1898, killed the largest recorded number of teal with one shot from his punt gun—132 in total.

In terms of the number of teal killed in one season by the same man, the record comes from Ireland. During the season 1908–1909, an unfortunately anonymous hunter experienced some great shooting in the swamps south of Downpatrick in County Down. The total bag was 782 teal in addition to 566 mallards, 52 snipe, 1 woodcock, and 32 "various."

Danish hunters are favored by the country's key position on the teal's migration route from northern Scandinavia and Russia to the British Isles. For this reason some of the most successful teal hunters are Danish, with a significant number of them having killed more than 1,000 of the nimble little ducks. The most successful teal hunter alive is probably Bjarne Frost (b. 1945) who from 1961–2012 has made a total bag of 11,207 *Anas crecca*, mainly shot at the estates of Borreby and Gavnø.

Ducks Galore

Before the draining of vast wetland areas for agriculture in the latter part of the nineteenth century, large bags of ducks could be taken in some places. Unfortunately, most reports do not mention the different species of ducks but only the total bagged.

The largest number of (unspecified) ducks killed by one man in one day's sport with a shotgun is from Kashmir in India. On 24 February 1912, Martyn

Most of the earlier records did not specify the different species of ducks bagged, which makes it impossible to determine who the most successful hunter of each species is.

Thomas Kennard (1859–1920) killed 509 ducks. During the years 1907–1919, this avid hunter killed 58,613 waterfowl, of which 13,894 were mallards.

Another enthusiastic duck hunter was Maharaja Ganga Singh of Bikaner (1880–1943) who, on 31 October 1910, killed 401 ducks in three hours. Fully 212 of these ducks were killed during the first hour of hunting. The hunt took place in his home state of Bikaner in India but the exact location is not reported. Maybe for a good reason—most hunters would be reluctant to share the exact whereabouts of such a fantastic duck-hunting spot.

Professional Duck Hunting

In the United States in the late nineteenth and early twentieth centuries, there were many places where hunters shot ducks for a living from special rafts with large shotguns resembling punt guns. One of these professional

Professional market hunters in America formerly shot ducks on the water during the night. For this purpose, special boats were equipped with lights and a battery of shotguns that could be fired simultaneously.

Incredible but True!

Martyn Thomas Kennard of Kashmir, India, holds the record for the largest number of (unspecified) ducks killed in one day with a shotgun. He shot 509 ducks in one day and 58,613 waterfowl in twelve years.

hunters by the name of Davies killed between 600 and 700 ducks a day on several occasions in the swamps around Salt Lake City in Utah. In 1904 a bag limit of 50 ducks was introduced, for obvious reasons.

Shortly before the new legislation became effective, on 1 September 1903, John W. Young had a marvelous day of duck shooting on Bear River Bay in the Great Salt Lake. From 5:00 until 9:30 AM, he killed 205 ducks and from 4 PM until dark he got an additional 60. On an earlier occasion, during the Christmas holidays in 1902, Young killed no fewer than 251 ducks from 1:45 to 4:30 PM He wasn't a bad shot, either. The 251 ducks were killed with 348 shots from his double-barreled 10-gauge—a hit rate of more than 72 percent.

Large European Bags

One of the largest bags of wild ducks shot by one man in one day in Europe happened on 2 December 1983. Sir Joseph Nickerson (1914–1990) experienced a marvelous duck flight on his property, Reads Island, in the River Humber in England. Nickerson was one of the best game shots of his time and had hunted ducks on the island every year since 1934. He had experienced flights resulting in bags of 10, 20, 30, and very rarely, 50 ducks.

Normally the ducks flew only in the morning and evening, but on 2 December 1983, the ducks kept coming all day and Nickerson spent almost ten hours in the blind with his gun and loader. Unfortunately he would not report the exact size of the bag, but a picture of him in front of it clearly shows more than 300 ducks, and many of them are not in the picture.

The current record holder of the record for shooting wild ducks, however, is most likely Bjarne Frost of Denmark (b. 1945), who is as passionate about shooting ducks as he is about shooting crows. His total bag including the 2012 season was 55,196 ducks and consisted of no less than 14 different species: 31,405 mallards, 11,207 teal, 4,204 tufted ducks, 3,543 widgeons, 1,686 eider ducks, 747 pintails, 642 goldeneyes, 550 pochards, 395 shovelers, 390 gadwalls, 140 scaups, 127 long-tailed-ducks, and 40 velvet scoters. Depending on your definition of ducks, you

Among European hunters, Sir Joseph Nickerson is probably the one who has achieved the largest bag of wild ducks.

might add his bag of 997 red-breasted mergansers.

Diving Ducks

The most successful hunter of ocean-dwelling diving ducks is Henning Loft (b. 1923). In Denmark it is legal to hunt sea ducks from small, slow motor boats and Loft was a true master of approaching the birds. The ducks have to fly upwind in order to become airborne, and a skilled and patient hunter can slowly and carefully approach the birds in a small boat until the ducks are within range when they take off from the water. Loft began this kind of hunting in 1947 and continued his career in the Bay of Aarhus in East Jutland for almost forty years. In the winter there are enormous numbers of migrating sea ducks here, especially eiders, common scoters, velvet scoters, and long-tailed ducks.

Henning Loft is the world's most successful hunter of sea ducks.

central workshop and slept during the evenings before going to work.

While the husband was working, his wife reloaded shotgun shells and met Loft by his boat at 4 or 5 AM, handing over fresh shells and a lunchbox. (True love!)

Henning Loft also managed to hunt on land quite often. Until 1967 the Danish hunting season was from 1 August to 28 February, and from his journals you can see that Loft often hunted more than twenty days in each of the peak months of September, October, and November—pretty impressive for a working man.

Geese

No game has increased as much over the last century in Europe as the geese, especially the greylag goose (*Anser anser*). The population of breeding greylags in Denmark was only 20 pairs around the turn of the nineteenth century; it is now around 10,000 birds. The number of migrating birds has increased and the flyway population is estimated to

Henning Loft managed to kill more than 50,000 diving ducks, mainly eiders and common scoters. Unfortunately one of his hunting diaries was lost and accordingly the exact total and number of each species is no longer available. However, Loft's most successful day yielded a bag of 236 eider ducks and his best week 826, while his best season produced more than 3,000 ducks.

Loft worked at night as a mechanic in the National Danish Railroad's

The majority of Henning Loft's impressive bag was eider ducks.

The Game

The population of geese in Europe has multiplied many times during the last decades.

be somewhere between 500,000 and 1 million birds, and growing.

Accordingly the national bag of greylags is now five times as big as in the 1960s, in spite of a considerable reduction in the hunting season since 1967.

Unlike other great goose nations like the United States and Canada, there are no bag limits for Scandinavian hunters and accordingly the largest bags are achieved in Sweden and Denmark.

The largest bag of one morning's goose hunting I have been able to find was made at the Trolle Ljungby Estate as recently as 1 December 2010. The flight began at dawn (8:30 AM) and the law requires hunting to stop no later than 11 AM.

During these two and a half hours, twelve hunters killed an astonishing 660 geese over decoys. All the geese were bean geese (*Anser fabalis*), except for 10 or 15 Canada geese (*Branta canadensis*), 5 or 10 greylag geese (*Anser anser*), and a few greater white-fronted geese (*Anser albifrons*).

As the populations of geese increased, so did the daily bags.

An African pygmy goose is smaller than a teal, with an average weight of a male just 10.1 ounces.

Top Goose Hunter

The most successful goose hunter in Denmark, and probably the entire world, is Bjarne Frost (b. 1945). He began on a small scale with one greylag goose in 1969. It took two more years before the next entry of geese was made in Bjarne's records; this time it was three bean geese.

From that year the annual goose bag increased gradually but it wasn't until the end of the 1980s that Frost had the opportunity to hunt geese on a larger scale. This partly took place at the Borreby Estate in Denmark and partly on a number of estates in southern Sweden. At famous goose localities like the estates of Råbelöv, Trolle Ljungby, and Karsholm he got access not only to ordinary goose hunting but was later asked to protect crops by shooting geese in the spring during the extended season established locally for this purpose.

Frost's preferred technique is to create a landing zone between his decoys with almost 100 yards of distance between a maximum of two hunters. Frost explains that his preparations include scouting for the preferred feeding places, placing and erecting hides, putting out decoys, and making the correct calls, but it is only successful if the first flock of geese actually lands between the decoys. If not, he must make corrections to the setup.

In 1985 he bagged more than 200 greylag geese in a season for the first time and some years later an almost equal bag of Canada geese was added to his records. In the following years his total bag rose almost constantly. In 2003, he shot a four-digit bag of geese in one season with a total of 788 greylags, 309 Canadas, 16 bean, 20 greater white-fronted geese, and a single pink-footed goose. In 2009, Frost killed more than

Bjarne Frost is not only Denmark's but probably the world's most successful goose hunter.

1,000 geese of one species and a total of 1,500 geese in one season as he shot 1,158 greylags, 685 Canadas, 54 bean, 24 greater white-fronted, and 9 pink-footed geese, an astonishing total of 1,880 geese.

The record year so far was 2011: 2,268 greylags, 930 Canadas, 231 bean, 69 greater white-fronted geese, and a single pink-footed goose, a total of 2,599 geese during one (extended) season.

In all, from 1969 up to and including the 2012 season, Bjarne Frost has shot an incredible 27,678 geese—17,988 greylags, 6,690 Canadas, 2,072 bean,

Quail are the smallest of the gallinaceous birds.

866 greater white-fronted, and 62 pink-footed geese.

On top of this total are a few other goose species from overseas countries shot in Frost's attempt to shoot all the goose species of the world that can be hunted legally. One of the gems of his collection is an African pygmy goose (*Nettapus auritus*), which Frost went to Zimbabwe to hunt. This tiny goose is about 80 percent the size of a teal.

Incredible but True!

*T**he largest bag of quail ever recorded was at least 9 million in 36 hours. This is recorded in the Book of Numbers in the Bible. In that same region as late as the 1920s more than 3 million were caught annually in nets and exported to England.***

Quail

The quail is a treasured game bird everywhere it occurs, including around the Mediterranean Sea and in the Middle East. But it may come as a surprise that the largest bag of quail ever recorded comes from a highly respected source: the Bible.

In the Book of Numbers we learn how the Israelites, when in the Sinai desert, complained that they only had manna to eat and no meat. The Lord became angry and ordered Moses to tell the people: "You will eat meat because you cried before the Lord: 'Who will feed us meat? We really had it good in

The first (and largest) bag of quail ever recorded in history is described in the Bible at great detail. The engraving is from a nineteenth-century edition.

Egypt.' The Lord will give you meat and you will eat. You will eat, not for one day, or two days, or five days, or 10 days, or 20 days, but for a whole month—until it comes out of your nostrils and becomes nauseating to you."

On an April day calculated to have been around 1580 B.C., a wind sent by the Lord came up "and blew quail in from the sea; it dropped them at the camp all around, three feet off the ground, about a day's journey in every direction. The people were up all that day and night and all the next day gathering the quail—the one who took

the least gathered 10 homers—and they spread them out all around the camp."

Different scientists have estimated the volume of a homer to be the equivalent of anything from 48 to 80 gallons. A gallon container can hold about 32 quail. Provided we presume that women and children did not take part in the hunt this probably means that the 600 or so men in the group collected at least 9 million quail during the 36 hours.

Whether you think the above is true or not, the number is brought into perspective by the fact that as late as in the 1920s, more than 3 million quail were caught annually in nets in that region and exported to Europe.

Modern Quail Hunting

When it comes to quail hunting in a more modern sense, the largest recorded bag of quail killed in one day by one hunter was made by the Italian M. E. Peretti on 24 April 1924, when he killed 207 of the nimble little birds

The quail is the only migrating gallinaceous bird species and a highly treasured quarry in southern Europe, the Middle East, and in the United States, although the species here are different from those of the Old World.

216

with his shotgun. The bag was made on a lengthy hunting trip from 19 April to 17 May 1924, on the Italian island of Zannone. During this period, six guns killed 3,806 quail with the largest bag in one day being 675 birds.

The largest recorded bag in one day is from Siguenza in Spain where a bag of 980 quail was made by five hunters on an unrecorded date before World War II.

Partridges

Before it became common practice to rear pheasants in the late nineteenth century, the different species of partridges were the predominant game birds of Europe. Farming methods in those days were much more compatible with the partridge's needs and, just by

The red-legged partridge originates from the Iberian Peninsula where it is reared on a very large scale.

controlling predators, enormous numbers of partridges could be shot without ever rearing or releasing a single bird.

During the nineteenth century, driven shooting in most of Europe was for partridges.

The German Baron Maurice von Hirsch was a very generous host at grand-scale shoots.

guest at Schloss St. Johann and other estates, he killed a total of 4,191 partridges. Not a bad invitation to get for a passionate partridge hunter like Ashburton.

One of the most famous hunters of all time was Lord Ripon (1852–1923). He too, naturally, was a frequent guest of Baron Hirsch. During a five-week visit in 1889, Lord Ripon shot more than 7,000 partridges. During his 56 seasons Lord Ripon killed the astonishing number of 124,195 partridges.

Another part of the Austrian Empire, the later Czechoslovakia, also held large numbers of partridges. As a guest in a party on a shoot that took place on 12 September 1904, a Mr. Theodor Dreher shot 1,434 partridges.

The most successful partridge shoot I have found records of took place on the Hungarian estate Cábuzi in September 1904. During eight days of shooting, ten guns killed a total of 17,026 partridges. The largest bag in one day was 4,213 partridges.

It is hard to imagine the number of partridges in those days. Baron Maurice von Hirsch (1831–1896) owned a number of large estates and often invited guests to his grand shoots. The British Lord Ashburton (1866–1938) was hunting partridges as a guest of the hospitable baron in 1893, and on 11 October he was in a party of seven hunters who shot 2,983 of the driven birds. During the fortnight Ashburton was the baron's

The largest bag of driven partridges made by one man in a single day stems from Elveden Estate in Suffolk, England.

218

Solo Record

As the owner of the famous British estate Elveden, Maharaja Duleep Singh (1838–1893) decided to go partridge hunting on 8 September 1876. The maharaja had not invited any guests but was the only gun on the shoot and shot the largest bag of partridges ever recorded for a single person hunting for one day. He brought exactly 1,000 cartridges and killed 780 partridges, which were all driven toward and over him.

British Record Day

Although the partridge was still the predominant British game bird at the end of the nineteenth century and gradually declined thereafter, the record bag in a day was made as late as 1952. On 3 October 1952, "Mr.

Grey partridges were formerly numerous all over Europe but the populations have diminished.

Sir Joseph Nickerson was the host at the most successful partridge shoot in England.

Partridge," Sir Joseph Nickerson (1914–1990), invited five friends to shoot at Rothwell Estate in England, which Nickerson had leased. The six hunters, all shooting with three guns and two loaders, killed 2,119 partridges in addition to 56 pheasants, 151 hares, 11 rabbits, 2 pigeons, and 3 "various." Only 50 of the partridges were of the red-legged species, often called French partridges, which today is the predominant partridge on most shoots for the reason that they are reared.

Most Expensive Game

The red grouse (*Lagopus scoticus*) is considered the most challenging game bird in the world due to its low and extremely speedy flight over the open terrain covering much of Scotland and northern England. Tradition dictates that the number of grouse killed on a shoot is counted in braces, and the

The Scottish grouse is capable of flying more than 80 miles per hour.

bird shooting in the world, but also the most expensive.

Most Successful Grouse Shoot

The opening day of grouse season in Great Britain is 12 August, better known as The Glorious Twelfth. It is also on this date that the record bag of driven grouse was made in 1915 on Littledale and Abbeystead Beat in Lancashire, England. Eight guns were shooting during six beats and killed 2,929 of the speedy birds. The next day, an additional 236 birds were picked up.

On day two the eight guns killed 1,763 grouse on a neighboring moor, and on day

value of these heather-covered areas is actually determined by the number of grouse you can expect to shoot annually. Currently the price is £3,000 to £4,000, or roughly $5,000 to $6,500, per brace of grouse. A good moor needs to be quite large, so an attractive grouse moor will typically sell for between $15 and $30 million.

As grouse cannot be reared like other gallinaceous birds, the only way to increase the population is to optimize its habitat and keep the number of predators down. This is quite costly as it takes a lot of effort from skilled managers. As a rule of thumb you'll need to employ one gamekeeper for every 3,500 acres of grouse moor. In addition there are the taxes and maintenance costs for roads, bridges, et. al. On top of this, beaters will cost around $3,500 per day's shooting. Accordingly, the cost of shooting driven grouse currently is up to $180 per bird, making this not only the most exclusive and challenging

Incredible but True!

Grouse hunting on the moors in Scotland and northern England is expensive. Currently it costs $180 per bird to shoot grouse, and with all the other expenses involved, grouse hunting is the most expensive, exclusive, and challenging bird shooting in the world.

In 1915, three days of shooting by a party of eight guns resulted in almost 6,000 grouse bagged.

three, an additional 1,279 birds. The total for the three days of shooting was 5,971 grouse, or according to the traditional way of counting, 2,985½ brace.

By the end of October 1915, the area had yielded a total of 17,078 grouse, which says a lot about the effort put in by the game managers on this 17,000 acres of moor.

Most Grouse

In terms of total number of grouse bagged, the most successful hunter the world has seen is Lord Ripon (1852–1923), who is mentioned numerous times throughout this book.

From 1867 until his death in 1923, Ripon annually killed between 90 (in 1874) and 3,435 grouse (in 1916)—and he had six seasons when he killed more than 3,000 grouse. His largest bag in one day was 12 August 1894, when Ripon killed 650 birds. During his 56 seasons Ripon bagged 97,503 red grouse.

Shooting with three guns and coordinating your movements with two loaders is far from a simple matter, and it was after a grouse shoot that Ripon had to make a note in his game book: *"Blew the top off my No. 2 gun!"* A too-fast swing after a bird had resulted in a load of shot hitting the end of the barrels of the Purdey gun that his loader held ready to hand Ripon after he had emptied the gun he was shooting with. The story doesn't reveal what happened to the unfortunate loader who was holding the barrels a little too high.

As described above, red grouse is the most expensive flying game in the world to shoot, with current prices exceeding $180 per bird killed. It is thought-provoking that if you wanted to copy Lord Ripon's bag of grouse today, it

Lord Ripon is the most successful grouse shot the world has seen.

would cost you almost $18 million for this dubious pleasure.

Largest Solo Bag

In spite of his enormous totals, it is not Lord Ripon who shot the most grouse in one day. That record belongs to his contemporary and fellow contestant to the title of being the best shot in England ever, Lord Thomas Walsingham (1843–1919), who made it at his hunting grounds, Blubberhouse Moor in Yorkshire, England.

Walsingham's rather bizarre record is reputed to have been made because the Prince of Wales turned down an invitation to shoot at Walsingham's estate and because Walsingham later heard that the cause of the prince's refusal was that he didn't consider Walsingham's grounds sufficiently large and game-rich to make the trip up there worthwhile. This seems surprising, as Walsingham in the record grouse year of 1872 had killed 842 grouse in one day, but several of the leading hunters of the time questioned whether this enormous bag was

Lord Walsingham killed the largest number of grouse in one day.

The red grouse (Lagopus lagopus scotica).

factual, so there might be some truth to the story.

Regardless of his motive, Lord Walsingham was ready at 5:12 AM on 30 August 1888, when his forty beaters began the first of the day's twenty drives. Walsingham used a quartet of guns and two loaders, and when he walked home at 7:30, he had killed 1,070 grouse with 1,550 cartridges, including 40 used for signal shots. This was an average of 2.33 birds per minute, or a bird for each 26 seconds during the 20 drives.

During a 23-minute drive, Lord Milbank killed a grouse every 7 seconds.

The hit rate was over 70 percent, the equivalent of 1.41 shots per bird killed. Part of this great tale is that Walsingham claimed to be not the least bit tired or have the slightest headache after the day's shoot, and his claim was substantiated by the fact that he played cards with his guests all night.

Most Grouse in One Drive

Considering his record, one would suspect that Walsingham was also the man who shot the most grouse in one drive, but that is not the case. The highest number of birds killed in any of Walsingham's twenty drives on the day he shot his record bag yielded 93 grouse. Sixteen years earlier, on 20 August 1872, this had been doubled. Sir Frederick Milbank (1820–1898) hosted a party of five guests and managed to kill 728 grouse in one day, including 190 shot during a sin-gle drive lasting 23 minutes. Milbank used a trio of pinfire guns loaded with blackpowder cartridges without ejectors, but that didn't prevent him from killing one grouse every seven seconds during this drive.

As it was in many other places, 1872 was the best grouse year ever on Milbank's estate, and the season total was an astonishing 17,064 of the brown heather-dwelling birds, of which the host shot 5,099.

Grouse and Pointing Dogs

As the red grouse is considered one of the most difficult birds to hit, it is hardly surprising that England's most famous shooters are each represented with some sort of grouse record. While Lord Walsingham shot the most in one day and Lord Ripon the most overall, it was another of the top guns of their time who made a third record. Maharaja Duleep Singh (1838–1893) was for a while

Maharaja Duleep Singh.

the holder of the record for bagging the most grouse over pointing dogs in one day. On the Glorious Twelfth in 1871 he was shooting at the Grandtully Estate in Perthshire, Scotland.

The maharaja had become rather obese, and in order to be able to hunt with pointing dogs he was mounted on a very reliable horse so he could cover as much ground as possible.

With no less than three teams of dogs and handlers, the maharaja would ride from one pointing dog to the next, dismount, shoot, and ride on to the next pointing dog. His assistants took care of retrieving and, as up to three dogs often were pointing at the same time, the mounted prince was often quite busy.

At the end of the day he had bagged 440 grouse in this extraordinary way.

Sixteen years later, a Captain Tomasson broke the maharaja's record. He went out on the Glorious Twelfth, 1887, with his pointing dogs at a Scottish estate appropriately named Hunt Hill. When it got dark Captain Tomasson had shot 458 grouse.

Pheasants

The pheasant was probably first introduced to Western Europe by the Roman conquerors who brought them north when they occupied the British Isles in 52 B.C. Pheasants were primarily ornamental birds for gardens

Today, shooting driven pheasants is more about quality than quantity.

and an exotic dish for the wealthy. While the descendants of birds that escaped into the wild were hunted to a very limited extent, rearing pheasants for shooting purposes did not take place until the late eighteenth century.

Around 1825, large-scale rearing of pheasants took place at the English estate Hewell Grange and the duke of Buccleuch's estate in Scotland. This practice became widespread as the development of hunting guns made it possible not only to shoot at birds flying at any angle but also to fire many shots in a short time. Instead of having the hunters walking up the birds the traditional way, it soon became common practice to have beaters drive the birds toward the guns, not only to spare the shooters the trouble of walking, but also because this resulted in more varied and challenging shots.

From Britain, this kind of hunting spread to the European continent and by the turn of the century, bird shooting was producing bags of a size most people would consider inappropriate today. The large bags were possible because the pheasant has an enormous reproductive rate if it lives in good conditions. If there are no predators a population will become extremely dense very quickly.

(On the island of Pelee in Canada, 36 pheasants were released in 1927 and the habitat must have suited the long-tailed birds as there were 20,000 on the island only five years later.)

The first recorded bag of over 1,000 pheasants shot in one day's driven shooting was made in 1845 at Lord Ashburton's estate, Buckenham, in England. From then on things developed quickly and the bags increased steeply both in Britain and in Central Europe. As late as 1933 a party of ten guns in Czechoslovakia shot 21,698 head of game in only five days of shooting, and 5,089 of these were pheasants, although only cocks were shot.

The French had a different outlook on the large bags. They called this kind of shooting *La Maladie Anglaise*—the English Disease, which in French was also the popular name for syphilis.

Largest Bag in One Day

At his estate, Tót Megyer, in the northwestern part of the former Austria-Hungary, Count Louis Karolyi kept an enormous number of wild pheasants. On 10 December 1909, eight guns killed 6,125 pheasants—in addition to 150 hares and 50 partridges. On a date that

The estate Tót Megyer in Hungary.

At his estate, Tót Megyer, in Hungary, Count Louis Karolyi hosted the largest recorded shoot for pheasants ever recorded.

Lord Ashburton was one of the guns at the famous drive at Beeches Corner, where he killed 300 birds in about 45 minutes.

Most Pheasants in One Drive

As far as I have been able to establish, the largest bag of pheasants shot in one drive was made at Lord Nunburnholme's estate, Warter Priory, where he had a beat that surpassed all others in the country and was called "Golden Valley." The source of this information is one of the relatively few female hunters of the period leading up

unfortunately is not recorded, another shoot on Tót Megyer resulted in what is probably the largest-ever bag of cocks only: 4,274 birds were displayed when the day was over.

The largest bag of pheasants in one day's shooting, however, was made almost a year later at the Hungarian estate Keszthely. On 13 November 1910, the owner, Prince Tasziló Festetics (1850–1933), hosted a shoot for nine guns. The day's bag was a total of 6,381 pheasants (both hens and cocks).

The largest bag of pheasants in one drive was made at the English estate Warter Priory.

Lord Nunburnholme hosted the shoot where the most pheasants were shot in a single drive.

tween 1,300 and 1,400 pheasants on 29 November 1895. Both Lord Ripon and Lord Ashburton got some 300 birds during the exactly 45 minutes it took the beaters to go through it.

A more precise record was made at Elveden Estate in England. Here there was a shoot on 17 December 1895, and one of the drives was known as Contract Rise. In only 46 minutes, 1,006 pheasants were killed, which was more than a third of the day's total of 2,554 birds.

Quantity vs. Quality

The enormous bags of birds in the years leading up to World War I are difficult to defend by present standards, and people who are opposed to hunting and shooting for sport are still critical of today's much smaller bags.

Misgivings about shooting ethics before the turn of the nineteenth century were expressed by one of the

to World War I, Mrs. Florence Hwfa Williams.

According to her memoirs, she watched a drive where "more than 1,500 pheasants" were killed, and she added: "The birds were flying very high and it really was most tiring work to shoot them. The men were tired out, when they came back."

The date of this shoot is unfortunately not recorded in Mrs. Williams' memoirs but it seems likely it was 5 December 1909, as this is the day a new record of game bagged in one day was recorded at Warter Priory: 4,406 birds, of which 3,824 were pheasants.

Another famous pheasant drive was Beeches Corner at Lord Carnarvon's estate, Highclere, in England. Depending on which source you choose to believe, Beeches Corner yielded something be-

While King George V had second thoughts about the number of birds killed at the driven shoots of his time, his father, Edward VII, was less scrupulous. When he was the host of a shoot at his estate Sandringham in November 1905, he and his fellow guns killed 7,256 head of game.

In Great Britain great numbers of birds are still presented during some shoots but it is bad style to shoot at birds that are not difficult targets.

most privileged sportsmen of the time, King George V of England (1865–1936). On 18 December 1913, the king was a guest of Lord Burnham at his estate, Hall Barn, in England. During this short December day, which was even further shortened by an opulent 5-course, 1½-hour lunch, the seven shooters killed 3,937 pheasants and King George shot more than 1,000 himself, achieving the still-standing British record bag of pheasants in one day. That evening, the king was very quiet, and reportedly said, "I think Burnham rather overdid it today."

In spite of the absurd numbers bagged on shoots before World War I, we should credit the British for still conducting driven shoots as they did then, but now focusing on quality instead of quantity. The pheasants in the days of the enormous bags were not nearly as difficult to hit as they are now at the best shoots, and fortunately the

development in shooting has moved away from an obsession with the size of the bag. Today the bag of a British shoot is typically 150 to 200 birds divided between 6 or 10 guns, and the hunters will only shoot the challenging birds and forgo birds that are flying low and slow, as opposed to many other places in the world.

Black Grouse

The (second?) largest bag of black grouse (*Tetrao tetrix*) in one day is 252, killed during a driven shoot at Cannock Chase in Staffordshire, England, around 1860. As the exact date is not known, many think that the proper record is 247 killed at the estate Glenwharrie in Dumfriesshire, Scotland, on 4 October 1869. Among the guns were Prince Christian and the famous author Sir Walter Scott. More than 200 of the grouse were cocks.

There is little doubt regarding the largest bag of black grouse recorded for one man in a day. It belongs to Lord Berkeley Paget (1844–1913),

Black grouse populations are rarely so dense that driven shoots for this species have been arranged, but there are a few examples of this, especially from Great Britain.

Few hunters in history have had the experience of shooting driven capercaillie.

Capercaillie

After the native Scottish population of capercaillie (*Tetrao urogallus*) became extinct in 1762, a number of Swedish capercaillie were released several places in the country from 1827 onward. The species profited so much from the game management of the time (e.g., the eradication of predators) that seven guns on the estate of Dunkeld on 4 November 1910, killed 69 capercaillies, a number that apparently has never been surpassed anywhere else in the world.

A bag of 60 capercaillies was made several times at the same estate in the beginning of the twentieth century, while the record for a season was set in 1903–1904 with a total of 136 of the large turkeylike forest birds.

Making a double on capercaillies is very rare and only reported to have happened once in Great Britain, at the Lawers Estate in Perthshire, Scotland.

The largest total bag of capercaillies ever was probably made by an anonymous Scandinavian or Russian hunter, just as with black grouse.

who owned the estate Cannock Chase and who killed 126 black grouse over pointing dogs. It has, however, not been established whether these 126 birds were part of the total of 189 black grouse that were shot there on 7 November 1865.

The most successful hunter of black grouse I have been able to find records of is the Danish Count J. H. E. Bernstorff-Gyldensteen (1815–1898), who killed a total of 557 cocks during his lifetime, all of them in neighboring Sweden. The true holder of the record is probably an anonymous Scandinavian or maybe Russian hunter who never kept records or told of his exploits.

Prince Victor Duleep Singh in action during a rabbit shoot.

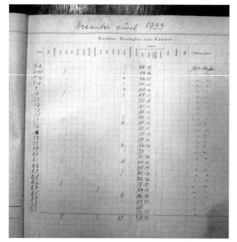

The game books of Vegeholm Castle contain page after page showing around 1,000 rabbits killed each month.

distribution was over 1.5 million square miles and the population numbered more than 10 billion rabbits. In spite of traps, poison, and increasingly more advanced diseases, which have limited the number of rabbits dramatically, it does not seem possible to completely eradicate this species from any environment that suits it once it is introduced.

In Europe the rabbit's stronghold was and still is Great Britain, albeit today the populations are only a tiny fraction of their former immense size. For instance, the English estate Elveden had a record season in 1921–1922 when a total of 128,856 rabbits were shot or captured. Elveden had

Rabbits

Today it is hard to imagine how huge the populations of rabbits (*Oryctolagus cuniculus*) were many places in the world before the deliberate introduction of the disease myxomatosis in 1938 and subsequently other diseases in an attempt to control the number of animals. Why the following enormous bags could be made on rabbit hunts in Europe and especially Great Britain is probably best explained by describing what happened in Australia.

Around 150 years ago somebody released 24 rabbits from England near Geelong in the state of Victoria. As a female rabbit will give birth to 18 to 30 young ones annually, it was hoped that it soon would be possible to hunt rabbits in Australia.

The attempt was successful: As early as the 1920s the area of the rabbit's

Incredible but True!

About 150 years ago somebody released 24 rabbits from England near Geelong, Victoria. It was hoped that it soon would be possible to hunt rabbits in Australia. As early as the 1920s the population of rabbits numbered more than 10 billion animals!

several seasons with a total bag over 100,000 rabbits, whereas the average annual bag in the beginning of the century was around half these record numbers. Probably due to the less demanding shots, rabbit hunting wasn't as highly regarded as bid shooting in those days (or now, for that matter).

A good example of the multitude of rabbits before the introduction of myxomatosis comes from the estate Highland in the southeast of England. Here Mr. Charles Eley (the famous cartridge maker) hunted rabbits with a friend on 19 November 1894. The two men were using a pair of guns and had a loader. Although the rabbit warrens only covered an area of 40 acres, the two hunters managed to kill 900 rabbits in one day.

The record for one day of rabbit shooting, however, was set at the English estate Blenheim on 7 October 1898. The estate's many gamekeepers had blocked the entrance holes of the burrows in order to prevent the rabbits from taking shelter and that enabled the beaters to drive the animals toward the line of five guns. The hunt started at 9:10 AM and

continued with seven drives until 5:40 PM, only interrupted by a short lunch break lasting 35 minutes.

The result of the day's efforts was a total bag of 6,943 rabbits, in addition to 26 hares and 13 partridges. The host was the duke of Marlborough, and he even claimed that had the daylight lasted a little longer the party would have shot

In Central Europe, hare shoots with enormous bags were once common.

500 more rabbits. The five guns used 10,810 cartridges, an average of 1.46 shots per rabbit. On average, each hunter killed 2.6 rabbits per minute.

This extraordinary number of rabbits killed per minute had actually been exceeded the year before. The largest recorded bag of rabbits shot by one man in a day was made near the village of Fonthill in England when Mr. J. A. Morrison killed 1,878 rabbits, 14 hares, and one partridge on 18 December 1897. Under the presumption that in late December Mr. Morrison could not have had more than eight hours of daylight to shoot, he must have killed 4 rabbits every minute from dawn till dusk.

A similar monstrous bag was made by Lord Carnarvon and his friend, Prince Victor Duleep Singh, who on 19 October 1895, shot 3,082 rabbits, 6 pheasants, 5 partridges, and 1 "various." Lord Carnarvon fired a total of 1,880 shots and killed 1,559 rabbits, an average of 1.2 cartridges per rabbit. The prince's average was slightly better, 1.17 cartridges per rabbit, but he had to settle for a total bag of "only" 1,523 head of game.

Hares

Historically the hare has never garnered as much attention from hunters as other game species. One reason probably is that the hare rarely offers very difficult shooting.

The largest bag of hares in one day I have been able to find records of was made at Frederick Wenckheim's estate in Hungary on 28 December 1898. The host and his guests killed a total of 3,094 hares, in addition to 1 roe deer, 5 pheasants, 59 partridges, 1 bustard, 2 foxes, and 1 "various." Although I have read thousands of pages of hunting stories, I never cease to be astonished by the amount of game you

The Austro-Hungarian Archduke Franz Ferdinand is the person who killed the most hares during one day.

could find at the best estates in Europe before World War I. The hare record above was made during one of six consecutive days of shooting at Wenckheim's estate where the total bag made by the 12 guns was 10,405 head of game.

Baron Hirsch (1831–1896) had numerous estates in Europe, including one in Hungary called Schloss St. Johann. In 1894 he had a five-day shoot where the hunters killed "7,500 hares and 2,500 rabbits." It is astonishing, too, that 11 guns at the English estate Holkham in Norfolk killed 1,215 hares on 19 December 1877, only 5 days after the same number of guns had killed 1,039 hares.

The former Central European country of Czechoslovakia could also boast an amazing density of game. Here even the enormous bag from Schloss St. Johan was surpassed in 1933 during a six-day hunt with a party of 10 guns who reportedly killed 9,359 hares, about 1,560 per day on average. The rest of the bag wasn't bad either: 7,245 partridges and 5,089 pheasants (cocks only)—a total of 21,698 head of game.

The largest record bag of hares in one year and from one area I have been able to find was made at the princely Bohemian house of Schwartzenberg. During the 1908 season the total bag of game on the family's estates was 23,921 of the long-eared rodents.

The largest personal bag of hares I have been able to find is in the records of Lord Ripon (1852–1923). From 1867 to 1923 no less than 31,934 hares were killed by this trigger-happy hunter.

The Archduke Franz Ferdinand of Austria-Hungary (1863–1914) prob-

ably holds the record of most hares bagged in one day. During one hunting day in 1911 he shot 1,277 hares.

Jack Rabbits

North America is home to numerous species of rabbits and hares but unfortunately I have not been able to find any systematic documentation of organized hunts nor bags made.

Most "hunts" really were organized vermin control and consisted more of trapping than of hunting in the recreational sense of the word, as the jack rabbits were driven into pens and killed with sticks.

One of the largest of these "hunts" I have been able to find records of took place on 13 March 1892, near Fresno, California. According to the newspapers around 8,000 people participated in the hunt and killed, depending on the

When the estates began rearing pheasants and other game birds in Europe, fox hunting became one of the gamekeeper's most important tasks. Here is Albin Svensson from Lystrup Estate, Denmark, photographed in 1925.

As early as 2,500 years ago, the Greek historian Xenophon described the fox as a problematic species.

Xenophon considered hunting an important part of a cultivated man's education and wrote that foxes should be killed as vermin since they distracted the dogs from hunting the hares.

Starting in the Middle Ages, the status of the fox changed and became a noble species that was hunted from horseback. This became an English tradition that was maintained for the next 700 years. It was banned in Great Britain in 2005.

The most successful fox hunter I have found records of is the Elector Johann Georg I of Saxony (1586–1656). If you leaf through the old elector's many beautifully bound game books, which are today kept at Sächsische Landesbibliothek in Dresden, you will find that during his more than 60 years of hunting he killed 19,015 foxes.

source, somewhere between 20,000 and 30,000 jack rabbits.

Foxes

Hunting the red fox (*Vulpes vulpes*) has been a common sport of the European elite from very early times. The earliest known report of a fox hunt was made by Alexander the Great (356–323 B.C.), and a Persian seal depicting a rider impaling a fox is from about the same period of time.

That there is not much new under the sun when it comes to hunting is well documented by the Greek philosopher and historian, Xenophon (430–354 B.C.). His work *Kynegetikos* ("On Hunting") is the earliest known literary work about hunting.

Elector Johann Georg I of Saxony is the most successful fox hunter in history.

Chapter 13

Shotguns

The first weapons for small game were throwing sticks, as depicted on this ancient Egyptian temple wall.

Earliest Hunting Arm

The earliest known implements used for hunting flying or running small game were undoubtedly the throwing sticks used in ancient Egypt. When the sticks were thrown they rotated in the air and killed or maimed the game so it could be dispatched. The pharaoh Tutankhamen (c. 1340–1323 B.C.), was an avid duck hunter and used throwing sticks for this sport.

The next step in the early stages of development was the boomerang, used not just in Australia but in numerous cultures all over the world. The Hopi Indians of Arizona, for instance, used boomerangs for hunting jack rabbits long before Europeans arrived to the continent. The lighter types of boomerangs will describe an arc after being thrown and at least partially return to the thrower if they do not hit something. The heavier, non-returning types were preferred for hunting.

Modern Arms

It was not until the beginning of the seventeenth century that firearms

Although over/under guns were made in the middle of the eighteenth century, it was not until after World War II that this type of shotgun became popular.

Due to the long time needed to ignite the powder in a muzzleloader, it was far more difficult to shoot moving game with these guns than it is with their modern counterparts.

became sufficiently light and balanced enough to give a hunter a fair chance of hitting flying game. With flintlock shotguns, considerable time elapsed from when the trigger was pulled until the shot was in the air. The long period of time before the shot reached the game made it much more difficult to achieve the proper lead than it is with the shotguns we use today.

The many difficulties of shooting flying game with flintlock guns led to the invention of guns with two barrels in order to increase the chance of bagging game. The earliest double-barreled shotguns appeared in the late seventeenth century.

The earliest guns did not have their barrels situated side-by-side but on top of each other, and it took rather a long while before the latter type of guns became popular with hunters. From the moment the first side-by-side gun with the barrels soldered together appeared around 1750, this type of shotgun dominated the market for almost two hundred years. It was not until the American gun designer John Moses Browning (1855–1926) made his legendary Model B25 Superposed that shotguns with stacked barrels again became popular, first for clay pigeon shooting and later for hunting.

Recent Inventions

Although breechloading shotguns had existed for centuries, it was not until the appearance of cartridges that this invention had any significance to hunters. The first breechloader using a cartridge was made by the Frenchman Samuel Pauly in 1812; it used a primitive cartridge made of a metal shell with a primer inside.

Via several other designs, the first modern breechloading gun was invented in 1841 by another Frenchman, Casimir Lefaucheux (1802–1852). When the breech was opened, the two barrels dropped down allowing you to insert two pinfire cartridges, which apart from the ignition system look similar to the ones we are still using. From then on a breathless race of developing and perfecting the modern shotgun took place, especially in Britain. Practically all of the inventions behind the modern shotgun were made in the latter half of the nineteenth century. Apart from

The first modern shotgun was made by the French gunmaker Casimir Lefaucheux in 1840.

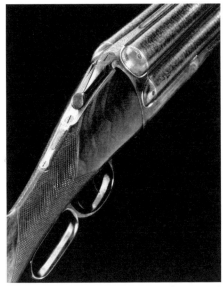

Although several gunmakers designed guns with three barrels and both Purdey and Lancaster (above) made guns with four barrels, none of these ever became a success.

better materials and different designs, there have been only a few significant developments related to shotguns in the last century.

In 1861 the German François Eugéne Schneider made a gun with extractors as we know them today. In 1863 James Purdey invented the double bolt, a principle which is still used on the majority of break-open shotguns made ever since. Two years later William M. Scott designed the top lever, which also reigns supreme today on all break-open guns.

In 1866 William Pape of Newcastle launched the first guns with choked bores and a year later the American Sylvester Roper made the first interchangeable chokes. In 1871 Theophi-

lus Murcott made the first shotgun with internal hammers and in 1874 John Needham made the first ejector gun. One year later two employees of Westley Richards in Birmingham designed the first boxlock gun.

The first "magazine shotgun" was a pump gun invented in 1882 by American Christopher Miner Spencer (1833–1922). Sixteen years later, John Moses Browning (1855–1926) designed the first truly successful semiautomatic shotgun, called the Auto-5. Unlike Spencer's pump gun, the Auto-5 became a great success and more than a million were produced. The production of the Auto-5 continued until 1998, exactly one century after it was introduced.

First Boxlock

Most mechanical designs developed gradually over time but one exception to this rule is the most successful shotgun action ever, the boxlock. It was invented by William Anson (1840–1895) and John Deeley (1825–1913), both employed by the famous gunmaker Westley Richards of Birmingham, England.

The first boxlock gun was made in 1875.

John Moses Browning with his Auto-5.

Most Popular Shotgun

Although boxlock shotguns are numerous, it is a pump gun that holds the record of being the most popular model of shotgun. The American gun manufacturer Remington introduced the Model 870 Wingmaster in 1949, and it has since been made in a vast number of variations from .410-bore to 12-gauge. On 13 April 2009, the total production of Wingmasters exceeded 10 million, and this makes Remington's Model 870 by far the most popular shotgun ever.

One Gun for Everything

Ever since rifled barrels were invented, designers have tried to make firearms that could be used for both shot and ball. In Europe, multiple-barreled guns were made with different combinations of rifled and smooth barrels. However, this implied so many compromises regarding weight and balance that the

happy new owner the equivalent of roughly $18,000.

As this first boxlock had internal hammers and the safety button placed on the tang, any hunter of today could easily use this gun without any instruction.

As the boxlock gun was designed to be produced by machine and was accordingly far cheaper to make than any sidelock gun, more than 90 percent of all break-open hunting firearms have been built on this principle ever since.

Westley Richards was so certain that its new "hammerless gun" would be a great success that they had these words engraved on the first one: "The First Anson & Deeley Hammerless Gun, Patented 11 May 1875." This gun was sold at Bonhams Auction in London in December 2007. It cost the

More Remington 870s have been sold than any other model of shotgun ever made.

Nitro "Paradox" Gun (12-Bore)

The "Paradox" Gun has the following advantages:

Holland & Holland's Paradox, a gun for all types of hunting.

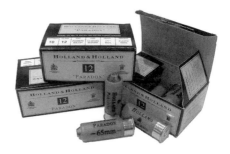

Slugs for a Holland & Holland Paradox gun.

solution, especially with three or more barrels, never became practical.

This situation changed on 1 May 1886, when the British gunmaker Holland & Holland introduced the Paradox, a gun with bores that were rifled only in the last three inches before the muzzle. This ingenious design came from British Lt. Col. G. V. Fosbery (1832–1907), and it meant the guns could use shotshells but also fire a single projectile with sufficient precision for use at normal distances.

The new "combination gun" was immediately put to the test by the gunwriters of the time. The tests were all very positive; one of the most successful was made on 20 May 1886, and later reported in *Badminton Library's Shooting*. At 100 yards, the Paradox put six shots fired alternately from each barrel into a rectangle measuring 1½ x 4½ inches. With a load of 1⅛ oz. No. 6 shot, the gun also patterned well, placing 144 and 165 pellets respectively within a 30-inch circle at 40 yards.

The Paradox guns were soon copied by other manufacturers and enjoyed

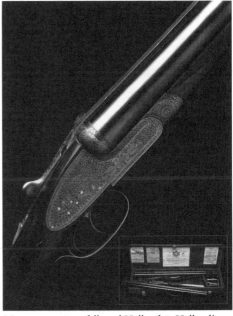

Many competitors followed Holland & Holland's lead but today this concept is almost forgotten.

some popularity until World War I when production gradually decreased as big-game hunters became more specialized in their requirements and demand dwindled. But the last was not heard of the Paradox. After a pause of almost seventy years, Holland & Holland again started production of the Paradox and you can now purchase one—provided you can afford the current cost of $92,000.

The action of a Purdey gun is very complex and difficult to make. Some joke that it does not work due to its design, but in spite of it.

Longest Continuous Production

No model of shotgun has been in longer continuous production than James Purdey & Sons' side-by-side gun. It was designed and patented by the British gunmaker Frederick Beesley in 1880 after he had left Purdeys'. Beesley sold the patent to

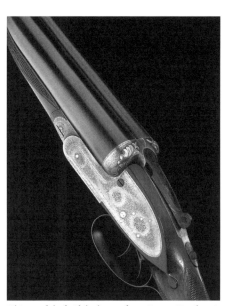

This model of sidelock gun from James Purdey & Sons has been made since 1880.

his former employer, James Purdey the Younger, who immediately recognized its potential, and the company's side-by-side guns and rifles have been built on this action virtually unaltered for 133 years.

What makes Beesley's action special is that it is self-opening. After having driven the tumblers forward, the mainsprings will force the barrels down as the action is opened. Accordingly, when the top lever is activated the gun is pushed open and the empty cartridges thrown out by the ejectors, greatly increasing the speed of reloading—a very important feature for the shooting elite of the time with their focus on enormous bags.

The drawback is that both the mainsprings and the ejector springs must be cocked upon closing the gun after reloading it, and this takes a little practice to get used to. When the gun was introduced and tested by the shooting magazines, a reporter asked James Purdey, "Doesn't this feature make the gun rather hard to close?" Purdey's answer was, "Our clients never close their guns!"—a reference to the fact that any shooting gentleman who could afford a Purdey would certainly have at least one loader.

Most Expensive Shotgun

When comparing costs of shotguns it is necessary to disregard specially made guns with extreme engraving or ornamentations of gold and jewels. These guns can be interesting, but for a comparison to make sense the guns must be made according to a standard, be in ongoing production, and be on a maker's price list.

By these prerequisites, the most expensive shotgun on the market is an over/under in 28-gauge or .410-bore from the famous gunmaker Boss & Co. in London. The company was founded in 1812 and still prides itself on being "Builders of Best Guns Only."

Not surprisingly, their production has always been very limited in size and in spite of the longevity of the company the total number of Boss guns probably does not exceed 7,500 shotguns and rifles in total—an average of forty a year. In the years leading up to the

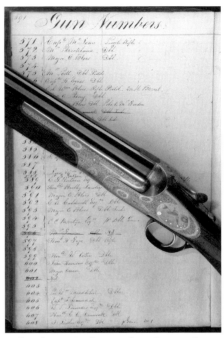

A bespoke over/under gun from Boss & Co. in London is the most expensive shotgun on the market.

If you want a bespoke gun from Boss and can settle for a side-by-side instead of an over/under you'll save the cost of a medium-priced car, or roughly $35,000.

new millennium, production was as low as five guns per year.

A standard model over/under in 28-gauge or .410-bore with basic engraving will, according to the Boss & Co. price list for 2013, cost you $150,000—plus 20 percent VAT if it is not exported from Britain. For $10,000 less, you can get a 12- or 20-gauge. If you settle for a side-by-side, you will save the cost of a nice car, as prices for these models are around $32,000 lower than for the over/under.

Should you decide to invest in a pair of guns, you expect to pay more than twice the price of a single gun, as the highly figured stocks must be made from matching walnut blanks.

Lightest Guns

Shotgun barrel length and weight has varied over time as popular tastes changed. At the end of the nineteenth century, when side-by-side guns were fully developed, a standard 12-gauge shotgun had 30-inch barrels and weighed around seven pounds.

But soon lightweight guns became popular. From the year 1900 onward, numerous gunmakers made lightweight models. These were often made in 12-gauge and chambered for 2-inch cartridges, which had a moderate load and eased the larger recoil from lighter guns.

Until World War II the general perception was that a shotgun for hunting was a 12-gauge, or if you were small, a 16-gauge. Guns in 20-gauge or less were generally considered useful for women and children only.

The most famous lightweight gun was probably Charles Lancaster's "Twelve-Twenty," indicating that the gun was a 12-gauge but handled like a 20-gauge. Other makers shortened the barrels of their guns to reduce weight, including Robert Churchill's Model XXV with 25-inch barrels or Holland & Holland's Model Brevis with 26- or 28-inch barrels. These lightweight guns, and many similar ones, were quite popular until the 1970s, but today's fashion is more akin to that of the end of the nineteenth century: 30-inch barrels and a weight close to 7 pounds.

The most extreme exponent of lightweight guns was the gunmaker Thomas Turner of London, who specialized in this field. In order to save weight he reduced the thickness of practically everything on his guns apart from the walls of the barrels. The action was shortened and the wood on both sides of the stock was removed, giving the guns a rather unusual appearance.

Today most hunters would probably consider a Beretta Model 687 Silver Pigeon in 20-gauge a light gun, as it weighs slightly over 6 pounds, while a similar gun in 12-gauge is a pound heavier.

But back in the 1880s, Thomas Turner made two lightweight models in 12-gauge with different barrel lengths.

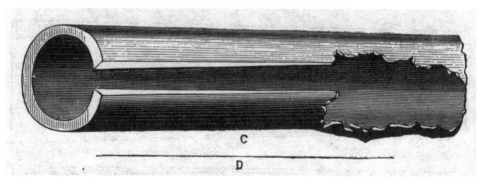

The British gunmaker W. W. Greener made a working gun barrel which in the middle part had a wall thickness of only .010 inch, the thickness of the line beneath the drawing of the barrel.

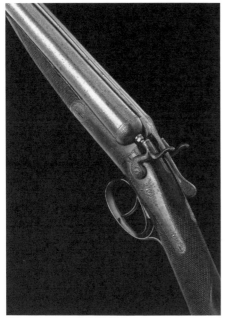

British gunmaker Thomas Turner specialized in lightweight guns. Notice the very short fore-end.

His Featherweight model had 28-inch barrels and weighed 5¾ pounds. His Levissimus model could be had with either 27- or 24-inch barrels, reducing the weight to 5 and 4¾ pounds respectively.

Shortest Barrels

From the dawn of modern shotguns the standard barrel length was 30 inches, partly due to the combustion rate of the blackpowder used, and partly in order to obtain a proper balance and weight distribution.

When smokeless powder became standard at the end of the nineteenth century, the normal barrel length was gradually reduced to 28 inches, but as late as 1925 it caused outrage among hunters

and gunwriters of the day when Robert Churchill introduced his Model XXV with 25-inch barrels. Churchill claimed that you could make a gun with this barrel length that was just as well balanced as any other and that the difference in muzzle velocity would be negligible when using modern gunpowder.

One believer in short barrels was Arthur Guinness (1876–1949), brother of the famous Lord Iveagh (Edward Guinness), who was the proprietor of one of the largest estates in England, Elveden in northwest Suffolk.

Arthur Guinness became widely known in Britain when, in France during World War I, he arrested a cyclist in a British uniform for being a spy. In Arthur Guinness's opinion, it was not possible for such a young person to have earned the number of medals that adorned the man's chest. It turned out that he had arrested the Prince of Wales!

After the war Arthur Guinness devoted his time to the pleasures of shooting and hunting, most often at his brother's estate. However, he wasn't happy with his shooting and thought that his gun barrels were too long.

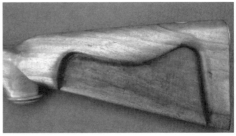

Even the stock was trimmed down on the lightweight guns from Thomas Turner.

Accordingly he had the barrels of his pair of 20-gauge guns shortened every season for a number of years. Starting with 28-inch barrels, he went down to 26, 24, 20—and ended up with the barrels of his shotguns measuring only 17 inches!

The head keeper of Elveden, Thomas Turner, commented that he personally would have worried about his left hand sliding out over the muzzles during shooting with these guns, and said that they reminded him more of pistols than shotguns. They were nevertheless very efficient in the hands of Arthur Guinness, who made many long shots and killed numerous high pheasants with these unusual guns.

That Arthur Guinness was not the only advocate of short barrels is proved by the fact that Boss & Co. made a set of 17-inch barrels. But both of these barrels had full-choke bores, so they couldn't be the ones Arthur Guinness gradually shortened, since shortening the barrels removed any choke boring.

Most Hopeless Firearm

George Sitwell (1860–1943) was a famous British eccentric who was so preoccupied with the Middle Ages that he decorated his home in the style of the fourteenth century and gave his children pocket money converted from the currency of the time. In the same spirit, Sitwell also tried to pay their school fees with produce from his farm.

Sitwell had many other odd notions. A sign on his house warned guests: "I must ask anyone entering the house never to contradict me or differ from

The British eccentric George Sitwell invented the most hopeless firearm ever.

me in any way, as it interferes with the functioning of my gastric juices and prevents my sleeping at night."

Sir George was not a great hunter but among his many hopeless inventions (such as a musical toothbrush), was a miniature gun for shooting hornets in the air. Unfortunately no prototype of this firearm has survived, and it remains unclear if anyone ever hit a flying hornet with it.

Oddest Gauge

Shotgun gauge numbers were derived from a measurement of how many lead spheres of a diameter equal to the inside of the barrel could be cast from a pound of lead. Obviously, the smaller the balls were, the more you could cast from one pound of lead, so a 20-gauge (bore diameter .614 inch) is smaller than a 12-gauge (diameter .729 inch).

The smallest shotgun cartridge for sport hunting is the .410-bore, which for unknown reasons is the only shotgun size measured in inches. If it were named like the other shotguns, it would be a 67-gauge, but to add confusion it is often called a 36-gauge in Europe. The .410 is not very widely used in Europe but is popular in the U.S. for training purposes and for shooting small birds like quail and doves. Larger shotgun gauges still in common use are 28, 20, 16, and 12. Shotguns have been made as large as 4-gauge, but today it is quite rare to see even a 10-gauge in practical

The most bizarre shotgun gauge ever was developed by the British gunmakers Cogswell & Harrison.

use. Other now-obsolete gauges include the 11, 14, 15, 18, 24, and 32.

The most bizarre gauge (or unsuccessful marketing gimmick) was made by the English gunmaker Cogswell & Harrison in the early part of the twentieth century. At the time, hunters wanted lighter shotguns, but guns in 20-gauge or smaller were considered useful only for ladies or boys. So there were a number of different attempts to produce lighter versions of the more accepted 12-gauge.

In order to meet this demand for lightweight guns, Cogswell & Harrison came up with the bizarre 14¾-gauge. The designers claimed that this gauge was ideal for a load of 1¹⁄₁₆ oz. of shot and patterned as well or better than a standard 12-gauge. The load was claimed to have a greater velocity, deeper penetration, and longer range, and the gun weighed 6 ounces less than an equivalent gun in 12-gauge.

Part of the idea was probably also to increase the customer's loyalty to the brand, as the cartridges for this odd gauge could only be bought from Cogswell & Harrison. Unfortunately these wonder guns were 10 percent more expensive than the same company's guns in 12-gauge and very few were ever made. Shotguns in 14¾-gauge are extremely rare today.

Unfortunate Design

In the middle of the 1890s the English gunmaker Charles Lancaster introduced a cartridge that was purportedly 2 inches long and accordingly named

The smallest traditional shotgun cartridges on the market were 353-gauge or 6mm. Today the equivalent cartridges are made in the same dimensions as a .22 LR caliber, the so-called rat shot.

Rat shot is also known as snake shot.

Smallest Gauge

Apart from very special cartridges made for indoor use, the smallest cartridge with shot is a 6mm, or 353-gauge by traditional measurement. This cartridge was formerly made in both Germany and Great Britain and used for shooting rats and other "vermin" such as thrushes in orchards.

A modern version of this cartridge is still made and often called rat-shot or snake-shot. It is actually a .22 LR with a shot-filled plastic hood that shatters when the cartridge is fired and allows the shot to spread in a small pattern. The effective range of these cartridges is extremely short—typically three to five yards.

Large Gauges

The largest shotgun that is possible to fire from your shoulder at moving game is an 8-gauge—equivalent to a

Pygmie. In spite of its shorter length, the cartridge had a load of 1¹⁄₁₆ oz. of shot and was designed to be fired in guns with the then-standard length of 2½ inches or longer. The name was mainly a marketing stunt, as the true length of the cartridge was 2¼ inches.

The design of the cartridge unfortunately often caused the pellets to lump together and act almost as a single ball. Obviously this made the cartridge dangerous to use, and several beaters were killed by shots which normally would have left them unharmed. Not surprisingly, the Pygmie cartridge was soon described "rather unfavorably" in the press and soon it disappeared from the market. One correspondent to *The Field* magazine, Mr. H. Cumberland Bentley, put it this way: "The Beater is worthy of his hire; why, then, drive a hole through him that would stop a rhinoceros?"

The British gunmaker Charles Lancaster developed a short cartridge for his lightweight guns that turned out to have very unfortunate characteristics.

diameter of .835 inch, as opposed to a 12-gauge's .729 inch. Although you can find shoulder guns from 4-gauge all the way up to 1-gauge, these were not made for hunting running or flying game but were intended as smooth-bored big-game guns firing lead bullets.

Adding to the confusion, the bore diameter of these large calibers was rarely consistent with that of their designation. Cartridges stamped "2" were in reality often the size of a 4-gauge, and cartridges stamped "4" were really 5- or 6-gauge.

The weight of a double in 8-gauge was typically between 12 and 15 pounds, which is close to the practical limit of how heavy a gun a person can efficiently handle. In addition, the cartridges have a load of only 2 ounces, which equals a heavy load of a 12-gauge with 3-inch chambers. Both these factors probably contributed to the fact that the 8-gauge is no longer a standard cartridge anywhere in the world.

Shotguns in 4-gauge are the largest which can be practically used for moving targets.

Largest and Smallest Pellets

Apart from slugs intended for use in smoothbore guns, the largest lead shot made is size TriBall (buckshot) having a diameter of .60 inch and weighing 315 grains. However, this size is so rare that the largest size commonly made is 000 buck, with a diameter of .38 inch and a weight of 95 grains per pellet. This means that a standard load of 1 oz. contains 6 or 7 pellets depending on the percentage of antimony used to harden the lead.

At the other end of the scale we find No. 13 shot, often called dust shot in Britain. With a diameter of .040 inch, a standard cartridge with 1 oz. of shot contains between 4,610 and 4,799 pellets, again depending on the percentage of antimony.

With steel shot the variation in size is less, as the largest have a diameter of .23 inch while the smallest are around .079

A case for a 4-gauge next to a 12-gauge cartridge.

The world's smallest working shotguns are in 2,600-gauge.

inch. One ounce of shot will contain around 35 pellets of the largest size and 892 of the smallest.

Smallest Shotguns

The smallest working shotguns ever made are a trio that James Purdey & Sons Ltd. finished in 1935 as a gift for King George V's Silver Jubilee. The guns are exact replicas of the king's matched pair of guns, but at one-sixth of the original size. Under the supervision of Purdey's factory manager, Harry Lawrence, it took the company's gunmaker three years to finish the minute guns for the king, which were numbered 25,000 and 25,001. The third gun is still with the company as it was made just in case of an accident during the making of the king's pair.

The guns are made of 69 parts each and had 4¾-inch barrels with ⅖-inch chambers. The barrels were cylinder bored, like the king's pair in 12-gauge. The length of the guns was 7 inches and the weight ⅘ of an ounce.

The cartridges had a diameter of ⅛ inch, or 2,600-gauge. They were specially made by Imperial Chemical Industries and contained 2.02 grains of shot propelled by 1.62 grains of powder. The shot was around dust size with a diameter of 0.04 inch and each cartridge contained 21 pellets.

The guns were presented to the king in a silver case with gold embellishment made by the well-known jeweler Garrard & Co. in London. The case contained a complete set of miniature fittings, turn screws, oil-bottles, snap-caps, etc. Whether the king ever fired the guns remains unknown.

Purdey's made the world's smallest working shotguns for King George V's Silver Jubilee.

The smallest working shotgun cartridges ever were made by Eley Cartridge Co. Ltd. for the king's miniature guns. Here is a box and a single cartridge compared with an ordinary round in 12-gauge.

Largest Shotguns

The largest shotguns ever made were too heavy for a man to lift and could not be fired from the shoulder. Instead they were mounted in a punt, with which the hunter could slowly approach and fire at flocks of seabirds resting on the water.

The calibers of these guns were often individually designed by the makers but became more standardized as breechloaders appeared. Most often the caliber was 1½ inches, but all sizes from 1¼ to 2 inches could be found. The entire gun was typically 9 feet long and weighed around 100 pounds. The paper cartridges were 8 to 10 inches long and typically loaded with 1 to 1½ pounds of shot. The efficiency of these monster guns was not proportional to their size. The maximum efficient range was only 80 or 90 yards.

Although punt guns have been made in gauges up to AA (4 inches), I have not been able to find useful records of a gun larger than "Irish Tom." It had a caliber of 2¹⁄₁₆ inches, was 14 feet, 1½ inches long, and weighed 300 pounds. Its load was 3 pounds of shot fired with 10 ounces of blackpowder.

A punt gun. These enormous shotguns were made to be used from punts able to float on very shallow water.

Several British makers made punt guns, especially Holland & Holland, Thomas Bland, Moore & Grey, W. W. Greener, and J&W Tolley.

Punt gunning undeservedly got a bad reputation among those who condemned the mere thought of "mass murder" via a "floating cannon." It is true that some punt gunners occasionally made impressive bags with a single shot, but small bags and large frustrations

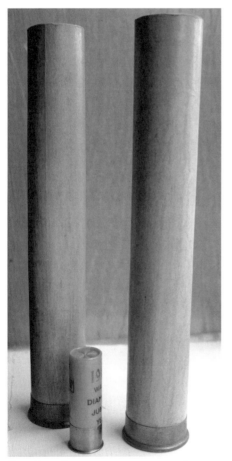

Cartridges for a punt gun compared to an ordinary 12-gauge cartridge.

were much more common results for a punt gunner. In rare instances the bags reached 50 to 100 birds in one shot, but these cases were definitely exceptions as the average bag was between 6 and 12 birds per shot fired.

In Great Britain punt gunning is still legal. The maximum caliber allowed is 1¾ inch. A survey shortly before World War II documented 186 punt guns still in active use, a number that had been reduced to around 100 when the Wildfowler's Association of Great Britain and Ireland (WAGBI) made a count in 1967. By 1979 there were less than 50 punt guns in regular use and the number today is probably less than half of that.

A survey by British Association for Shooting and Conservation (BASC) showed that the average punt gunner of recent years went out on the sea seven times per season, fired four shots, and had a total bag of 16 birds. The record bag with one shot for the last 50 years was 23 birds.

The largest recorded bag in something approaching one shot was made during a hunt in 1860 in England. At least 32 hunters went out with a fleet of punt guns during a clear night with a full moon. Their prey was a flock of brant geese on the mud banks of an estuary. When the punts were all in range, a signal to fire was given and all the guns went off almost at the same time. When the smoke from the many blackpowder loads lifted, there were 705 dead geese on the water. In the morning an additional 250 were picked up or finished off by hunters walking along the shoreline.

Holland & Holland was the only company that made double-barrel punt guns like this one being tested on the shooting range.

Most punt gunners were professionals hunting for the market but there were others who took an interest in this kind of hunting. The king of Portugal, Carlos I (1863–1908), for instance, ordered a punt gun from Holland & Holland in 1896 and used it often.

Holland & Holland sold another punt gun to the Maharaja of Kolhapur (1874–1922) when he was in England in 1902 for the coronation of Edward VII. The maharaja took the gun back to India, had it mounted in a small boat, and commanded an unfortunate *shikari* (hunting guide) to skipper the vessel. The boat was then pushed out on the lake in front of the palace where a large number of ducks were resting. When the maharaja thought it was the right moment, he raised his hand and the skipper fired the gun, and the boat, gun, and poor *shikari*, who couldn't

The Maharaja of Kolhapur, Shahaji II, was the original owner of the world's probably least-used punt gun.

Charles Gordon.

He was the son of a British officer who put him in the care of his uncle and aunt in Scotland when his mother died shortly after his birth. When Gordon reached the age of fourteen, the uncle, aunt, and father had all died too, and Gordon inherited the large estate of Halmyre and a huge annual income.

The boy was from then on left on his own to administer his life. He developed a mania for collecting and bought enormous amounts of wine bottles, fishing equipment, shooting paraphernalia, and especially guns.

I have sometimes jokingly diagnosed some of my gun-collecting friends as having a typical case of *Armas numeralitis*. If such a disease were ever recognized by doctors there is

swim, promptly sank to the bottom of the lake. The man was rescued, as was the gun the following day, but it was never fired again.

Armas numeralitis

If you ask a collector how many guns a man needs, you are likely to get this answer: One more than he's already got!

The most eccentric gun collector the world has ever seen was probably Charles Ferrier Gordon (1853–1918).

Charles Gordon had his guns made by John Dickson and other gunmakers. This muzzleloader was made for him by James Purdey & Sons.

absolutely no doubt that Charles Gordon suffered from it. In the year 1896, for instance, Gordon ordered a total of twenty-six bespoke guns from John Dickson & Son—that's one gun every two weeks.

Although the exact number cannot be established due to the loss of the gunmakers' records, Gordon had around 300 bespoke guns and pistols of the very highest quality built for him, mostly from the Scottish gunmaker John Dickson & Son, but also a number from other famous makers such as Alexander Henry, Joseph Harkom, and James Purdey & Sons. All the firearms were delivered in handmade cases with all kinds of tools and paraphernalia.

On top of this, Gordon had an obsession with flintlock and percussion guns. Many of the breechloaders he ordered were made with these types of locks and the majority of his guns were never fired.

Naturally the costs of this hobby were enormous, just as they would be today, when a bespoke gun from John Dickson costs roughly $62,500. If made today Gordon's collection would be worth something in the neighborhood of $20 million or more.

In 1908 Gordon's inherited fortune was gone and all his properties were sold. He died at the age of sixty-five in a humble cottage on the estate that was formerly his own.

Hammer Gun Bags

James Purdey & Sons introduced the first hammerless gun as early as 1880; it had the desirable feature that it was self-opening, and the fall of the barrels automatically cocked the gun as the spent cartridges were thrown out by the ejectors. All this greatly increased the speed of reloading. Although hunters traditionally were (and still are) quite conservative, the advantages of the hammerless guns were so obvious that it took only six years before Purdey received more orders for hammerless guns than for their models with external hammers.

Nevertheless, a number of the most famous shots of the time stuck with hammer guns for the rest of their lives, although they were quick to adopt other novelties such as ejectors. These famous shots were not particularly concerned

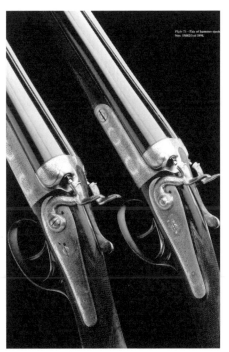

A pair of hammer guns made by James Purdey & Sons for King George V.

Unlike his father, King George V preferred to use hammer guns throughout his life, although hammerless guns for many years had been the standard within the shooting fraternity.

manship represented by high-quality hammer guns, especially those made in Great Britain, which are recognized by their exquisite balance and the extraordinary quality of the work. In the United States there is an official and quite prestigious club for users of fine British guns called The Order of Edwardian Gunners (usually referred to as "The Vintagers"). As the members only use guns made between 1880 and 1914, many hammer guns are in evi-

about reloading speed as all used a pair, a trio, or sometimes even a quartet of guns while shooting, and were assisted by the equivalent number of loaders.

Unlike his father, Edward VII, who quickly adopted hammerless guns, King George V (1865–1936) claimed that a gun without hammers looked "like a spaniel without ears!"

King George V and the two most famous shots in England, Lord Walsingham (1843–1919) and Lord Ripon (1852–1923) continued to use hammer guns throughout their lives, all made by James Purdey & Sons. Ripon's total bag of more than half a million head of game was made with hammer guns only and the same goes for King George V's almost 250,000 head of game.

Although a few hammer guns are still made, they are quite a rare sight on a shoot nowadays. In recent years, an increasing number of shotgun aficionados around the world have enthusiastically embraced the crafts-

In some respects it is only fair to designate Lord Walsingham as a gun nerd.

Damascus barrels have their name from the technique by which they are made, which originates from the swordmakers of Damascus during the Crusades.

dence during the club's events, and the participants' clothing and accessories also must be appropriate to the English sportsman of the period.

Gun Nerd

Sometimes it can be hard to define the difference of being enthusiastic and being a bit of a nerd but most people would probably place the following observations and conclusions in the latter category.

When Lord Walsingham (1843–1919) on 30 August 1888 achieved his record bag of 1,070 grouse shot by one man in a day (as described in chapter 12), he also had the presence of mind to make detailed notes on the different qualities of the guns and the cartridges he used that day.

During the record day, Walsingham used exactly 1,550 cartridges, including the forty shots fired as a signal to the beaters. His Blubberhouse grouse moor was shaped like an hourglass, and Walsingham placed himself in the middle

while the birds were driven over him from each side alternately.

For the shoot he used a quartet of hammer guns made by James Purdey & Sons in London. All four guns had 30-inch barrels and none had any choke. Three of the guns had Damascus barrels, handmade by forge-welding three twisted steel and iron rods in a coil around a mandrel of the caliber wanted. The last gun, however, had barrels made of cast steel. This had been made possible by a new casting process invented by Sir Joseph Whitworth; the casting was made under high pressure (6 tons per square inch), which drove out the small pockets of gas and blowholes in the material. By the beginning of the twentieth century, steel barrels of different qualities became standard and the noble art of forge-welding Damascus barrels died with the barrel makers of the time.

Lord Walsingham wrote in his notes that his ordinary cartridges were loaded by Johnson of Swaffham with 3⅛ drams of Hall's Field Blackpowder

Few people ever have been as happy for a dud cartridge as Lord Walsingham.

from that given off by Damascus barrels: there is more ring about it, and I can imagine that this might prove a serious annoyance to anyone who minds the noise of shooting. I have no recollection myself of ever having had a headache from gun-firing.

Moreover, the Whitworth barrels become hot much more rapidly than the Damascus barrels, and this is a serious drawback, especially to a man who shoots without gloves. I can well imagine that they last much longer, and are in many ways suited for ordinary light work; but I am now replacing them with Damascus, as in all my other guns.

A True Safety

For obvious reasons gunmakers want us to buy more guns and often extol the features of their latest model regardless how useful it really is. In the early days of gun development, however, you could find a very good example of how useful it could be to have the latest novelty in guns.

On 31 March 1887, a British colonial administrator with a great name for a hunter—Killingsworth Hedges—sent a letter to the British magazine *The Field* about an unexpected advantage of having one of the then-new hammerless guns. Hedges wrote:

behind 1⅛ ounces of No. 5 Derby shot, while the cartridges for the birds that were flying upwind (and therefore not as fast) only had a load of 3 drams of the same powder.

Walsingham concluded that if he was to repeat the record day he would have used a 1-oz. load of shot, not because of the recoil but because he had noticed that the lighter of his two loads penetrated better at longer distances (undoubtedly due to its greater velocity). Walsingham continued:

> I distinctly remember firing three barrels at one bird, striking well in the body every time, but killing dead only with the last shot; the powder seemed to burn too slow.
>
> Another thing I learned was that Whitworth steel barrels are not desirable for a heavy day's shooting. The explosion in them makes quite a different sound

> Sir: It may interest your readers to know that the British officers, who were recently attacked by Arabs, when shooting near the Pyramids, owe their lives to the fact that the Arabs could not fire the officers' hammerless guns. The English papers omit to state that the Arabs intended to shoot their prisoners at once with the officers'

breechloaders. Fortunately the safety bolt had been turned, so that, not understanding the action, they gave up the idea, determining to hang the officers, from which fate they were providentially rescued just in time.

A Quality Cartridge

At the other end of the safety scale it was a common practice to use several loaders to increase the speed a hunter could shoot and collect enormous bags. In order to save even more time, some hunters ordered their reloaded guns handed to them with cocked hammers, which greatly increased the risk of accidents during the fast exchange of guns. Some prominent hunters were killed, among them the well-known Colonel Buckley, who was hit in the leg during a shoot at a Norfolk estate.

During a later shoot at the same estate, Lord Walsingham (1843–1919) had the very same post and the situation with an unintended discharge repeated itself. When the gun barrels were only fifteen inches from Walsingham's back, the loader accidentally pressed the trigger of the gun. The hammer dropped, the firing pin dug deep into the primer, but the gun didn't fire, which undoubt-

Nine European kings photographed at the burial of England's King Edward VII in 1910. They all used shotguns made by James Purdey & Sons.

James Purdey & Sons was without comparison the most popular gunmaker for the world's crowned heads.

edly saved Walsingham's life. To be sure, the quality of cartridges was not quite as high in those days, but nevertheless Walsingham was lucky. Of the many hundreds of cartridges he fired that day, only five were duds.

Royal Guns

No gunmaker in the world has made both rifles and shotguns for as many royal courts as James Purdey & Sons in London. Most of the royal and princely houses in Europe had residents who used shotguns from the famous maker. At the burial of Edward VII in 1910, a photo was taken of nine kings gathered in one place: King Haakon VII of Norway, King Ferdinand of Bulgaria, King Manuel II of Portugal, Emperor Wilhelm II of Germany, King George I of Greece, King Albert of Belgium, King Alphonso XIII of Spain, King George V of England, and King Frederik VIII of Denmark. James Purdey & Sons had made guns for them all—and also for the Swedish King Gustaf V, who was not present that day.

Oldest Gunmaker

The oldest existing maker of hunting firearms is the Italian company Pietro Beretta in the Trompia Valley near Gardone. This area was a center

In the Beretta collection you can find guns from almost 500 years of continuous production.

Pietro Beretta and his brother, Carlo, with family, photographed in 1906.

leading small arms makers of the world. Even more unusual, the family has managed to keep control of the company for more than half a millennium. Today Gussalli Beretta as well as his two sons, Pietro and Franco, are part of the management. Beretta also owns a host of other companies including Benelli, Franchi, Sako, Stoeger, Tikka, Uberti, and Burris.

Staunch Workers

In the gunmaking business, long terms of employment are not unusual. James Purdey & Sons had a gunmaker,

for making metal products as early as the Middle Ages, and from the Renaissance onward it became famous for its production of arms. We know from the archives of the company that in 1526 Bartolomeo Beretta delivered 185 barrels for matchlock guns to the Arsenal of Venice.

The company continued to grow, and in 1698 Beretta was the second-largest barrel maker in Gardone. The company managed to continue its production after Napoleon invaded the country in 1797 and during Austrian-Hungarian rule.

The company got its present name, Fabbrica d'Armi Pietro Beretta, in 1832. After Pietro Beretta died in 1850 and his son, Guiseppe, took over, the company began to design and produce its own firearms. In 1860 the production was around 300 firearms annually, and it increased to more than 8,000 in the 1880s. Today the company makes 1,500 firearms per day.

Today, more than 500 years after its founding, the company is one of the

Tony Lokatis with a Boss over/under. In the rear left you can see the very loyal Mr. Oliver. People familiar with the company at the time would be able to tell that the picture was taken shortly after 10:30 am due to the half-empty glass of Guinness at the desk.

Ebenezer Hands at work ca. 1960.

Abbe Robins, who hardened the metal parts of the actions. According to the company's archives, Robins was employed "about 1825" and continued until he retired in 1901 at an age of 92. If 1825 is the correct year, Robins was employed by Purdey's for 76 years. Several other Purdey gunmakers were employed for more than 60 years.

Fred Oliver began with Boss & Co. in 1922 as a boy loading cartridges, and continued with the company for more than 70 years until he retired in the early 1990s.

The gunmaker who was active within his trade for the longest time is probably Ebenezer Hands (1871–1962). His father, who had the same name, was a stockmaker in Birmingham and took his son on as an apprentice, probably when Ebenezer Jr. was 12 years old, as that was the norm in those days. After his

7-year apprenticeship, Ebenezer Jr. was employed in his father's shop until 1918 when he was persuaded by Watson Bros. of London to become their stockmaker. Although this company was later sold and became part of the Atkin, Grant & Lang group in 1935, the now very skilled Hands continued as stockmaker in the new company until his death at the age of 91, after 79 years in the same trade.

Rarest Production Gun

By the end of the nineteenth century, the development of the modern shotgun was at its peak in Great Britain. The intense competition between the gunmakers led them to build light, elegant, perfectly balanced guns and today, well over a century later, many hunters still consider English side-by-side guns the most distinguished in the world.

Although the British gunmakers perfected side-by-side guns, they never really got good at making over/under guns in spite of numerous attempts in the years up to and especially right after World War I. The first (and in some critics' opinions, the only) really good British over/under was made by Boss & Co. in 1909. But even this top-grade maker produced a total of only 396 over/under guns before 1950, or fewer than seven a year on average. London's most famous gunmaker, James Purdey & Sons, only managed to make 27 during the same period.

In spite of this, as early as 1888 the leading Scottish gunmaker John Dickson of Edinburgh made the first British over/under that was a commercial prop-

John Dickson designed and built the world's rarest shotgun.

osition. Dickson received an order for an over/under from a client who was used to single-shot rifles and accordingly wanted a shotgun with a single sight plane.

In those days the only thing that counted was to shoot as many birds a day as possible. Hence gunmakers were encouraged to develop guns that would enable the hunter to fire as many shots as quickly as possible with the aid of one or several loaders. Clever gun designer that he was, John Dickson realized that it takes longer to open and reload an over/under than a side-by-side because, as the barrels are placed on top of each other, you need twice the opening angle in order to allow the cartridge to eject from the lower chamber.

Dickson chose the unusual solution of making the action on his new over/under open in the horizontal direction instead of vertically like a side-by-side. In his catalog Dickson described the model: "12 bore round action under and over gun with our unique side opening action."

The price was the enormous sum of £475 at a time when a side-by-side gun from James Purdey & Sons cost £65. This was probably the reason why only four of these guns were ever made: three 12-gauge guns and one 20-gauge.

The gun illustrated here belonged to a Danish collector who sold it in August 2006 through Sotheby's. The new owner paid roughly $128,000 for the privilege of owning the world's rarest production shotgun.

This Dickson over/under with the so-called side-opening-action is one of only four ever made.

Chapter 14

Hunting and Shooting

Fact and Fiction

It can sometimes be hard to determine how much a story has been "improved" through numerous retellings. The most successful small-game hunter in history, Lord Oliver Ripon (1852–1923), has been credited with a number of feats; some of them true, some that have been proven impossible, and others that belong in a gray zone between fact and fiction.

An example of the first case is the oft-quoted anecdote of Lord Ripon being such a marvelous and fast shot that he once had seven dead birds in the air at the same time. This story has been retold numerous times, but it is simply impossible for even the fastest and most dexterous marksman to perform the feat.

Even if you presume that a bird is killed forty yards above the gun, it will take only 2¾ seconds to hit the ground. Having seven dead birds in the air means that the shooter of a side-by-side shotgun must, in those 2¾ seconds, not only swing and fire his gun six more times, but also change guns

three times. This is simply impossible unless the hunter kills more than one bird with each shot or one or several of the birds is actually gliding toward the ground (and therefore not dead, but merely wounded).

An example of a "gray zone" feat is that Ripon is said to have killed twenty-eight pheasants in one minute. This was determined by an onlooker who had a stopwatch and timed the great shooter. To kill one pheasant every two seconds is perhaps technically possible, but it takes a very steady stream of incoming birds. The story, however, was confirmed by Ripon himself shortly before his death in an interview with the well-known shooting author Sir Hugh Gladstone.

It is in fact true that Ripon is the only person ever recorded to have killed all the grouse in a covey of five. Normally it would be an extraordinary feat to make one double in front of the grouse butt and another behind it. To get all five, the very experienced Ripon chose to shoot the first grouse far ahead of the butt and instantly exchange the half-empty gun for a fully loaded one. With this, he made a double in front of the butt, exchanged guns again, and made a double on the remaining two birds after they had passed him.

It is also known that Ripon won a wager during a shoot at the English estate Panshanger by killing 52 out of 54 birds using only one hand when shooting. This

Lord Ripon was without any doubt the best marksman of his time.

The Portuguese King Carlos I was a very competitive person and an excellent shot.

might have been because of some practice he'd had on a very rainy September day at his own estate, Studley Royal, in 1881. On that day Ripon killed three out of five birds driven over him although he shot with his right hand only, and used his left for his umbrella.

Even Handed

Some people are ambidextrous or able to use their hands equally well. Some are even capable of shooting equally well regardless whether they shoot from their right or left shoulder.

The Portuguese King Carlos I (1863–1908) was a very good shot and anxious to be the best in everything he did, whether he was painting, playing billiards, or engaging in any of his other numerous hobbies. Carlos I was a regular guest of the king of England at Windsor Castle and at Elveden Estate owned by Sir Edward Guinness, and if he thought that there was an interested audience close enough to his post, he would sing arias from the opera *La Traviata* while waiting for the pheasants, and then shoot the birds from both shoulders alternately. Low birds he shot with his gun held in one hand with the arm stretched out in front of him, also using the left and right hand alternately.

One of the most impressive feats of shooting from both shoulders was made by Sir Victor Brooke (1843–1891) at his estate, Colebrooke, in Ireland. During a shoot in 1885 he bagged a total of 740 rabbits in one day and used 1,000 cartridges to do it. Sir Brooke shot from his right shoulder in the morning and from his left in the afternoon.

Danish shooter Allan Christensen was one of the leading target shots of his time and had the same astonishing capacity. Christensen mastered sporting clays as well as skeet and trap shooting.

Danish Allan Christensen was a legendary shot who managed to win the national championship shooting from both his right and left shoulder.

Neighboring guns would hardly get away with stealing a bird from Lord Balfour during a driven shoot.

Very few hunters in history have had the same combination of luck and shooting skill as the English Lord Balfour of Burleigh (1849–1921). When he was a guest at a shoot on the estate of Clackmannan in 1890 he was posted in front of a small oak scrub. When the beaters went through it, four woodcock rose at the same time, and Lord Balfour killed all four with his pair of guns. Reputedly he kept "a stiff upper lip" in the classic British tradition and showed absolutely no emotion after the remarkable feat.

Lord Balfour's exceptional shooting was in sharp contrast to an unfortunately undated event at the estate of Shouldham in Norfolk, England. According to the then well-known shooting author L. H. De Visme Shaw, a woodcock took wing during a driven shoot and flew right down the line of five guns firing at it—only to turn around and try the same experience in the opposite direction. The death-defying bird was finally killed by the seventeenth shot fired at it.

When he won the Danish Championship in the 1940s, he shot from his right shoulder but as he gradually lost the sight in his right eye, he started shooting from his left, and a few years later he won the championship again.

A Double Double

Only when percussion guns appeared in the 1840s did it become possible to make a double on woodcock. Since then, hundreds of hunters have been lucky and skilled enough to accomplish this feat. It takes a good deal of luck just to get the chance to shoot at more than one of the nimble, forest-dwelling birds at the same time, and even more skill to kill them both.

It takes great skill and coordination to react to a covey of partridges suddenly sweeping over a fence.

Eight for Eight

Two of the best game shots the world has seen were Lord Walsingham (1843–1919) and Lord Ripon (1852–1923), both of whom are mentioned numerous times in this book. During a pheasant shoot at Holkham Estate in England where both were guests, they got a chance to prove their skill at the noble art of shooting driven birds. According to the unwritten rules you may never "steal" a bird by shooting at one that is nearer to or presents a better target for another gun in the party. If there are many birds, the decision to shoot or not must often be made in a fraction of a second.

In one drive during the Holkham shoot, the two famous shooters were situated at the edge of a hedgerow and waiting for the pheasants to arrive when a covey of ten partridges suddenly and very quickly swept over the hedgerow. The partridges instantly spotted the two guns and the covey broke up in all directions.

As a result of the great marksmanship skills of both men and their ability to choose the right birds, not a single one of the eight shots from their two pairs of Purdeys were wasted—eight birds dropped dead to the ground.

Lord Dorchester, who witnessed the feat, claimed to never have seen "such a wonderful display of harmony and judgment" as the two had exercised when deciding which of the birds to shoot.

Cormorant Marksmanship

The famous ivory hunter Walter D. M. Bell (1880–1954) was known for his outstanding shooting skills, which were

Walter Dalrymple Maitland Bell shot flying cormorants at a height of 100 yards with his rifle.

demonstrated many times during his safaris in East Africa between 1902 and 1914. On one of these trips, Bell had bought a batch of 6,000 rifle cartridges in caliber .318 Westley Richards, but unfortunately it turned out that a large number of them were duds and not suited for hunting dangerous game. Accordingly Bell decided to get rid of the cartridges and at the same time get some practice.

Bell's camp was situated near Jinja in southeastern Uganda, close to Lake Victoria. Every evening there was a flight of cormorants returning from the lake to the trees where they spent the night. Cormorants are fast flyers but normally fly in a straight line, which makes them less difficult to hit. In spite of the faulty ammunition and the fact that he was shooting a rifle with open sights at a distance of some 100 yards, Bell managed to kill an average of six out of every ten cormorants he fired at, and his best evening yielded an average of eight dead birds out of ten. One evening Bell noticed two civil servants from the local government office watching his shooting.

One of them politely asked, "What a marvelous shotgun you have, sir. It works far better than ours! May we have a look at it?"

The facial expressions of the two clerks must have been a sight to behold when Bell unloaded and handed over his rifle.

The tenth Earl of Southesk was an eminent shot who during a single drive managed to kill more than one bird every five seconds.

Difficult Debut

The Danish Count Kresten Scheel (1915–1975) was one of the best target and game shots in his country, and he was also interested in air guns. His debut as an air gun hunter was far from promising; his records show that he fired more than 2,000 shots before ever killing anything—and that was a blue tit he had not even aimed at. Later he got the hang of it, and during the winter of 1941 he shot more than 1,000 house sparrows to reduce the damage they caused to the grain stores. Scheel did not keep a record, but wrote that a conservative estimate of his total bag of house sparrows was "more than 5,000."

Dead Certain Shot

The tenth Earl of Southesk, Charles Noel Carnegie (1854–1941), was an avid hunter who killed thousands of head of game during his long career. He demonstrated on many occasions that he was an excellent shot. One of the best examples was during a shoot in North England when he killed 48 grouse with 48 shots. He actually did miss one, but later in the day he killed two birds with one shot and hereby "corrected" the statistics.

At another occasion Lord Carnegie killed 63 partridges in 63 shots and 79 pheasants in 79 shots. In other instances he was close to a "full house" by killing 98 pheasants in 101 shots and 103 in 107 shots. Even more remarkable, perhaps, he once shot 228 pheasants with 238 shots in only 17 minutes, an average of more than one bird every 5 seconds!

Not Empathetic

In the early days of driven shooting the attitude toward safety was much more relaxed than today. As a guest of John Trollope, the first baron of Kesteven (1800–1874), the Englishman Teddy Chaplin learned this the hard way during a shoot. As he was walking down a road his host peppered him. Shocked and bleeding, the guest cried out, "Do you know, my Lord, that you shot me?"

The aging baron, hardly wracked with guilt, laconically answered, "Then why don't you get into the cart with the rest of the game?"

A Long Shot

As firearms and ammunition improved, even the titled hunters had to start paying more attention to safety when shooting as one of a party of hunters. One of the longest recorded accidental shots with a shotgun was made during a shoot in England in the early 1860s. George Stanhope, the seventh Earl of Chesterfield (1831–1871), fired a shot that hit his friend, James Innes-Ker, the seventh duke of Roxburghe (1839–1892), so hard in the face that blood poured down over his shirt. The distance was 180 yards.

Longest Shots

Few subjects are as eagerly discussed among shotgunners as how far away a given person has managed to kill a bird. The record is not possible to establish as the exact distance to a live, flying target can rarely be measured.

The British world-champion target shooter, George Digweed, is also the man who has broken a clay target with his shotgun at the longest range.

On the other hand, it is relatively easy to establish the distance when you shoot clay targets. The current record belongs to the Englishman George Digweed (b. 1964), the many-time world champion of several disciplines of sporting clays. At the 2011 Bisley Live Shooting Show

Incredible but True!

The tenth Earl of Southesk, Charles Noel Carnegie, once killed 228 pheasants with 238 shots in only 17 minutes, averaging more than one bird every 5 seconds. He also once killed two grouse with one shot.

in England, Digweed shot a clay pigeon at a distance of 130 yards.

When it comes to shots at living targets the only reliable ones I have been able to find are from the famous British naturalist and hunter Lord Walsingham (1843–1919). He carefully measured and recorded the distances of four extraordinarily long shots which he quite properly characterized as "flukes." The four birds were killed by Walsingham and his gamekeeper within only half an hour.

First, two wild ducks were killed by Walsingham at a distance of 84 and 84½ yards, respectively. Half an hour later, the gamekeeper killed two mallards at a distance of 89 and 114 yards respectively. The drake, which was hit in the head at the distance of 89

yards, rose again and required one more shot to bring it to bag. The load used was in all four instances 1⅛ oz. of shot and the guns used were Lord Walsingham's hammer guns made by Purdey, all with barrels that were cylinder choked.

High Pheasants

Among dedicated pheasant hunters, particularly on estates in Great Britain, it is prestigious to shoot high-flying birds, which obviously are more difficult to bring down than ones that are closer to the guns. Strangely, in discussions about the difficulty of these shots, there is a lot of attention given to the height of the incoming pheasant but little to its speed, in spite of the fact that a pheasant gliding down toward the ground is

Extremely high pheasants are a British specialty.

By utilizing the terrain, it is possible to make the birds fly very high over the shooters.

shooters are placed in a deep ravine with tall trees on the edges. The tops of these trees are 80 yards above the bottom of the ravine and the birds passing over the trees are accordingly at least 77 yards above the muzzles of the guns. At this range it is not possible to achieve acceptable hits with ordinary guns and loads. Most hunters use special guns with 34-inch barrels and extra-full-choked bores. Although most of the shooters are extremely experienced, it is normal that they kill one bird for every ten shots fired. I think it is fair to say that from an ethical point of view it is worrying to purposely go this close to (or past) the effective range of a shotgun when shooting at living creatures.

moving much faster than when flying horizontally.

This fact is useful if you combine it with knowledge of the pheasant's biology. The British Game Conservancy has demonstrated that a pheasant in good condition has emptied the reserves of energy in its muscles after about eight seconds of flying, after which it has to start gliding.

The knowledge of the pheasant's flight and flying capacity is used by skillful gamekeepers in combination with the proper terrain. Partly by using the terrain and placing the guns at the bottoms of slopes and ravines, and partly by making the birds rise at a distance where they will reach their maximum speed and height when over the guns, they can ensure the pheasants are as high and difficult to shoot as possible.

One example is from the Whitfield Estate in Northumberland. Here the

Dropping Birds

Unless you have ever killed a bird in the air and had it fall and hit another hunter, it can be difficult to imagine how powerful a blow this can inflict. When a bird hits someone from great height, apart from physical damage from the blow, there is a grave risk of an accidental discharge from the hunter's shotgun when the unfortunate hunter is hit or falls to the ground. This happened quite often during the driven shoots around the turn of the nineteenth century.

Even the most experienced shot of all, the famous Lord Ripon, committed this cardinal sin, and the victim was the worst possible: King Edward VII of England. The shoot took place at Windsor Castle and some weeks earlier the king had been unfortunate enough to step in a rabbit hole and not only break the stock and dent the barrels of his Purdey gun, but he also injured his Achilles' tendon. For this reason the king was shooting from a wheelchair when the next accident happened. Fortunately for the king (and probably Ripon, too), the famous shot's pheasant did not hit the king himself, but the armrest of the chair.

The speed of the dropping bird was such that the carcass exploded upon impact, covering King Edward VII in blood, intestines, and feathers. According to eyewitnesses it looked for a while like the king was going to explode, too.

Francis Greville, the fifth Earl of Warwick (1853–1924), was not as lucky. During a grouse shoot at Cawdor Moors near Nairn in Scotland, there was a strong wind blowing the birds toward the guns. Lord Warwick shot a bird high in front of him, and without waiting to see the result of his shot, he turned halfway around in an attempt to make a double. He never succeeded

A caricature of Lord Warwick who was not very lucky in avoiding a falling bird during a grouse shoot in Scotland.

With the large number of shoots Edward VII participated in, it is not strange that he sometimes was in jeopardy of being hit by a dead and falling bird.

as the moment he pulled the trigger, he felt a terrific blow to the side of his face, which knocked him to the ground. His loader quickly got his lordship back on his feet and it was only then that it dawned upon Warwick that he had been hit by the grouse he had shot first and "which came with the speed of an Express train."

Dazed and a bit angry, Lord Warwick asked his loader, "Didn't you see that bird coming?"

The loader responded, "Yes, m'Lord, I did see it coming, so I hid behind your Lordship!"

A Fair Sharing

The two best game shots in Edwardian England, Lord Ripon and Lord Walsingham, were often invited to the same shoots all over the country. In one case, where Lord Ripon was the host at his estate, Studley Royal, in northern England, the two famous shots had drawn pegs next to each other. In order to increase the sport, they agreed to shoot alternately so both would get more challenging birds. The result was that they killed forty-nine

Lord Ripon shot so much game that it today would cost well over $40 million to reproduce his bag.

pheasants each, and each spent fifty cartridges to do so.

Shooting Costs

As Lord Ripon is the man who killed the most small game in Edwardian times, he is not surprisingly most likely also the person who spent the most money on this hobby.

Today it would cost something in the neighborhood of $18 million to kill the number of grouse that Lord Ripon did in his long career. He shot pheasants worth about the same amount. Today a pheasant at a shoot in England costs between $50 and $80, depending on the quality. As he killed a total of no less than 241,224 pheas-

Before the start of a drive, the two leading shots in Edwardian England agreed to take turns shooting in order not to ruin each other's chances by mistake. The result was quite impressive.

ants, the equivalent cost of shooting the same number today would be close to $18 million.

Lord Ripon's total bag was no less than 557,688 head of game, which for many reasons is not likely ever to be surpassed. By subtracting the bag of pheasants and grouse from the total, we end up with 338,727 head of game, primarily partridges and rabbits. If we presume the average cost of these today is around $30 per head, the cost of reproducing Ripon's complete bag today would be well over $40 million. There are many sound reasons not to reproduce a slaughter of this scale, but if somebody ever wanted to he would need deep pockets.

Rabbits Galore

In October 1898 Sir Robert Gresley (1866–1936) was shooting rabbits at Blenheim Estate in England. He killed 1,430 rabbits in exactly 1,700 shots, a success rate of 84 percent, or less than 1.2 shots per rabbit killed.

Sir Robert Gresley.

Meticulous Records

The second Earl of Malmesbury, James Edward Harris (1778–1841), was a very meticulous keeper of shooting records through all his forty seasons as a hunter. The records contain not only the date, species, and number of game animals he killed, but also the weather, the amount of time spent in the field, the distance he walked, and the amount of powder and shot he spent.

At his estate, Heron Court in England, a total of 56,001 head of game were killed during the years 1801–1840, primarily by Malmesbury himself as this was before the days of the large shooting parties. In total Malmesbury killed exactly 38,221 head of game consisting of 10,744 partridges, 8,862 pheas-

Incredible but True!

*L*ord Ripon's total bag would cost well over $40 million to reproduce today!

ants, 4,694 snipe, 1,080 woodcock, and 12,841 other birds and animals.

He hunted 3,645 days in total during his thirty-nine years as a hunter—very close to ten full years of hunting. On average, he walked 2.5 miles an hour and covered a distance equal to roughly one and a half times around the earth at the equator. Malmesbury was never bedridden for as much as a single day due to sickness or accidents during his hunting career, and in total he fired 54,987 shots, of which 16,766 were misses—a success rate close to 70 percent. He used up 750 pounds of gunpowder and 8,951.5 pounds of shot.

The second earl of Malmesbury, James Edward Harris, kept a very detailed game book throughout his life.

Practice Makes Perfect

The Irish hunter Patrick Halloran (1862–1927) killed over 40,000 snipe, and this naturally gave rise to some unusual incidents. His best "series" without misses was twenty-three snipe, of which ten were killed in doubles. One day in 1924, Halloran's last season, was even more unusual. First he made two doubles, and then three snipe flew up together and he felled all three in one shot. Shortly after, he shot two more with one shot, making a total of nine snipe killed in six shots.

Worst Shot Ever?

In spite of being the owner of Chatsworth, one of England's finest shooting estates, the eighth duke of Devonshire, the marquis of Hartington (1833–1908), was never a keen sportsman and was definitely not a good shot. According to the shooting gossip he was more likely to hit something if he didn't even try to aim at it. He was nicknamed "Harty Tarty" and was an unflagging optimist who never stopped trying in spite of his disastrous lack of skill. His shooting guests were therefore all very surprised when Hartington killed a very high partridge during a shoot at his estate, Creswell Crags. The shot was so phenomenal that his friends spontaneously and loudly applauded it. After the drive, Hartington said to one of the other guns, "I wonder why Harry Chaplin and the other guns applauded when I fired two shots at the pheasant which I didn't get?"

The eccentric Marquis of Hartington, better known as Harty Tarty, was infamous as the worst shot in England.

connection with the shoot would have been ruined if the chef had been seriously wounded!"

Surefire

Col. Peter Hawker (1786–1853) was a famous author who published a number of books on shooting, angling, and firearms. His *Advice to Young Sportsmen* from 1814 earned almost Biblelike status among sportsmen in the nineteenth century. Hawker was an excellent shot; in front of witnesses he killed 14 snipe in 15 shots and 77 pheasants in 78 shots, all with flintlock guns made by the Manton Brothers of London where James Purdey had his apprenticeship. When shooting with even the best flintlock gun, it took roughly 15 times as long from when

When he was told that he had killed the highest partridge of the day he answered: "Did I? I didn't even know it was there. But now it is done so please don't tell anyone and let me keep the honor."

But discretion is a rare thing among shooting friends, as most hunters know, and the place has ever since been called "Hartington's Post."

During another shoot, Harty Tarty shot at a pheasant so low that it was being chased by a retrieving dog. He not only killed the bird, but also the dog, which was in hot pursuit. In addition, the dog handler was hit in the leg and the duke's chef, who was an onlooker, got hit by pellets.

The duke instantly expressed his main concern over the possible consequences of his shot: "All the dinners in

Peter Hawker was an eminent shot and the first popular author of books related to hunting and guns.

the hammer fell to when the load of shot was in the air as it takes with a modern shotgun.

Show, Don't Tell

The Danish Baron Eiler Holck (1913–1975) was a keen hunter and an excellent shot who considered it a bad day if he used more than 1.5 cartridges per head of game killed. But in his younger years he had great trouble hitting snipe, and so he was invited for a shoot in 1930 by his older friend, Count Erik Bernstorff-Gyldensteen (1883–1968) who was one of the most successful snipe hunters in the country. The idea was that the young baron should try to pick up some of the techniques of the noble art of snipe shooting from his older mentor.

Gyldensteen Estate was then known for its many snipe, and it didn't take long before the first snipe rose in front of the two sportsmen. Holck fired two quick shots in succession but both missed the bird. Bernstorff-Gyldensteen didn't say anything and the two men continued their hunt. Soon another snipe rose, and it too survived Holck's two shots. He looked despairingly at Bernstorff-Gyldensteen, who soothed him and said, "Now I'll show you how to do it!"

The two men continued and when the next snipe rose, Bernstorff-Gyldensteen put his gun down on the ground only to pick it up again, put it to his shoulder, and killed the snipe with a beautiful shot. Then he turned toward the flabbergasted Holck and said, "Now

Eiler Holck was one of Denmark's most successful hunters but nevertheless had problems with snipe in his younger years.

you see. There is plenty of time to shoot a snipe!"

Good Start

After World War I many gun factories had to find new markets, and one of them, Birmingham Small Arms (B.S.A.), introduced a simple and relatively cheap side-by-side boxlock shotgun. In order to increase sales, the company offered buyers the option of paying in installments, but hardly anyone in the company imagined what this would lead to.

A seventeen-year-old British boy by the name of John Edgar Johnson (1915–2001) was able to get a gun by paying in installments with the profits from his rabbit shooting. A rabbit would earn him one shilling at the market, and the boy calculated that provided he could shoot two rabbits for every three shots, this would pay his installments and make him the owner of the gun.

As fate would have it, "Johnnie" became the most successful Spitfire pilot during World War II, with a total

Johnnie Johnson was Britain's most successful fighter ace during World War II.

of thirty-four enemy airplanes shot down. His own plane was only hit once during his five years in the war and the following conflict in Korea. Like his German counterpart in World War I, Baron von Richthofen (the "Red Baron"), Johnnie credited his success to his shooting experience as a boy, which taught him the necessary lead for shooting at moving targets.

Most Birds with One Shot

It is not difficult to find records of more than one bird killed with one shot, whether it was intentional or not. The largest number I have been able to find in the literature was, not surprisingly, made with a shot from a punt gun. However, this particular gun was not mounted in a punt and the target was not waterfowl.

One of the earliest gunwriters in history was Col. Peter Hawker (1786–1853). With his double-barreled punt gun loaded with 30 ounces of shot, the colonel fired at a flock of starlings near Whittlesea Mere in Cambridgeshire

Johnnie's very simple but well balanced boxlock gun made by B.S.A.

on 26 October 1825. After the shot a total of 234 starlings were picked up, but as many of the birds had fallen in a reed-covered area, a staff of workers was ordered to cut the reeds next morning. During this process "between 200 and 300 more were found dead among the reeds."

Big Double

On 15 January 1922 it snowed heavily around Bylaugh in Norfolk, England, but this did not prevent Michael Mclean from going shooting. As a flight of snipe passed him in the snowy weather, he fired both barrels, killing seven and then four snipe in a rather voluminous double.

The unfortunate Masséná was shot by Napoleon.

Change of Consequence

Obviously you must be more safety conscious as a member of a party where the game is driven toward you by dogs and beaters than when you hunt alone. In Great Britain, hunters jokingly say: "Better to kill a fellow gun than wing a beater!" Protocol dictates, in other words, that hitting a beater or a keeper is unforgivable. This, however, hasn't always been the case, as you can tell from the reports below.

A combination of elitist arrogance and lack of safety consciousness led to many shooting accidents during the great shoots in Europe.

Both the famous nineteenth-century European generals, Napoleon and Wellington, were careless shots. During a partridge shoot where three of the guns were Napoleon Bonaparte (1769–1821), his Field Marshal André Masséná (1758–1817), and his chief of staff, Louis Alexandre Berthier (1753–1815), a covey of low-flying birds passed between Napoleon and Masséná.

Napoleon fired and hit Masséná. Eager to absolve himself of any guilt, Napoleon turned to Berthier and said, "Berthier, it is you who have wounded Masséná!" In all fairness, however, it must be said that Napoleon regretted this and in compensation gave Masséná command of the army in Portugal.

The man who finally defeated Napoleon at the battle of Waterloo in 1815 was the duke of Wellington (1769–1852). It was often said that he was more dangerous in the shooting field than in the theater of war. When he was a guest at Lord Granville's shoot in 1823, Wel-

The English prince George Augustus Frederick, better known as Prinny.

Fortescue, the second Viscount Clermont (1764–1829), with a load of shot.

The incident was described in *The Times*: "Lord Clermont, who had enjoyed a robust meal, was resting in a sitting position behind a furze. Two of the prince's dogs got wind of the highly noble gentleman and pointed. The crown prince fired . . . and wounded Lord Clermont in the most defenseless part of his body." The crown prince regretted the incident but did not alter his future conduct.

The change in what is considered acceptable behavior of an English hunter of the upper class is illustrated by the very different reaction of the conservative politician and home secretary of England, William Whitelaw (1918–

lington accidentally shot at his host and several pellets hit him in the face. This incident, however, did not prompt any further caution, and the duke later shot a beater. A few years later, Wellington was shooting at Lady Shelley's place and hit one of the maids while she was putting the laundry out to dry.

Lady Shelley was standing next to the duke when the accident happened and the victim cried out, "Milady, I'm hit!"

Lady Shelley answered, "You have received a rare honor today, Mary; you have the distinction of having been shot by the duke of Wellington!"

The oldest son of the English King George III was named George Augustus Frederick (1762–1830), but was better known by his nickname, Prinny. During a shoot close to the outskirts of London in the first years of the nineteenth century, Prinny hit one of the other hunters, William Charles

The duke of Wellington was reputed to be just as dangerous on a shoot as he was on the battlefield.

Napoleon Bonaparte was not grand enough to acknowledge his guilt in a shooting accident. That was wiped off on his chief of staff.

William Whitelaw.

1999), to a shooting accident. Whitelaw fired a shot during a grouse shoot in 1984 where he managed to hit both the gamekeeper and another guest, Sir Joseph Nickerson, the most successful and famous shooter in England at the time. Although Nickerson treated the incident with good humor, Whitelaw took it very seriously and never participated in a shoot again.

The unfortunate episode of Lord Clermont was illustrated like this in a satirical magazine of the time.

Safe Sport

Today hunting is one of the least dangerous activities you can engage in. A survey from 2011 compared the number of accidents to the number of people involved in different activities. In 2010 the number of active hunters in the USA was 16.3 million and in total they suffered 8,122 accidents.

Compared to hunting, the risk of having an accident is:

Incredible but True!

Hunting *accidents occur annually with approximately one per 2,000 participants, which makes hunting safer than golf, volleyball, snowboarding, riding a bike or a skateboard, or playing soccer.*

In addition it is interesting that by far most of the hunting accidents in the United States are caused by falls from tree stands. The number of accidents related to the use of tree stands amounts to more than 80 percent of all hunting accidents involving injury.

3x82

Sir Horatio Ross (1801–1886) was known as one of the best shots in Britain with gun, rifle, and pistol, as described earlier in this book. According to tradition the Scottish landowner always celebrated his birthday shooting grouse over pointing dogs in the heather-clad hills surrounding his home. On his eighty-second birthday, 5 September

+ 11 times higher if you play volleyball
+ 19 times higher if you go snowboarding
+ 25 times higher if you ride a bike
+ 34 times higher if you play soccer or ride a skateboard
+ 105 times higher if you play American football

Today hunting is the third safest of 28 pastimes surveyed. Only billiards and camping are safer. With approximately one accident annually per 2,000 participants (0.05 percent), hunting is far safer than golf (0.16 percent), whereas the risk of having an accident while playing American football is as high as 1 in every 19 participants (5.27 percent).

Horatio Ross was one of Great Britain's best shots.

1883, Ross very suitably killed eighty-two grouse in eighty-two shots.

Shooting Economics

Shooting rights were not cheap around the turn of the nineteenth century. The extremely wealthy German Baron Hirsch rented the shooting rights to Merton Estate in England for £4,500—roughly $500,000 in today's money—for the period of 1 December to the end of the season on 1 February, which implies that the owner had already shot there at least once in November.

While the landowners in the agricultural districts had to balance the number of birds reared with the yield of the crops, most Scottish landowners had no such problems.

At one time, the value of the game bagged was much greater than it is today.

When the railroads made access to Scotland's vast moorlands easy, it became fashionable among elite to travel there to shoot grouse and deer. This development was very profitable for the larger landowners, especially those in areas that so far had been

In Scotland, most of the land is of such poor agricultural quality that it is more profitable to use it for grouse shooting than for farming.

difficult to reach. From his estates in Perthshire, Sir Robert Menzies (1817–1893) had an annual farming income of £600 during the latter half of the nineteenth century. When the railroad reached Perthshire, the shooting rights gave him an income of £6,000.

Grouse shooting is still an important source of income in most parts of Britain where the bird is distributed. In total the economic value of the gamekeeping, land management, hotel accommodations for visitors, etc., represents more than $165 million. If you calculate this into full-time jobs, more than 2,000 people are employed because of grouse shooting.

Rearing pheasants on a grand scale is a costly affair.

Chapter 15

Remarkable Shots and Shoots

Precise Prince

Queen Victoria's husband, Prince Albert of Saxe-Coburg and Gotha (1819–1861), was a keen hunter and turned the royal estate of Windsor into a hunting grounds dotted with glades and set-asides, enabling him

Prince Consort Albert of Saxe-Coburg and Gotha in 1842.

to entertain foreign dignitaries in a suitable way. Pheasants were reared and released and hares were stocked. In the 1840s the prince's friends began to follow his example and create similar hunting estates so they could return one of the coveted invitations to shoot at Windsor.

In 1846, after having returned from his annual stag hunt in Scotland, the prince accepted an invitation to shoot at the Marquise of Salisbury's estate Hatfield in Hertfordshire. Here he set a new record. Using four muzzleloading guns and three loaders, he killed 150 pheasants in 150 minutes, a number that was completely unheard of at the time.

Master Monarch

The Spanish King Alfonso XIII (1886–1941) was a very enthusiastic hunter. He was married to a niece of Edward VII and was accordingly a regular guest at the royal estates. If there was any doubt of the royal guest's skill at the shoots, it was quickly swept away. The year he was married, Alfonso

The Spanish King Alfonso XIII.

been on the verge of ordering a pair of pigeon guns—but now he just wanted to order one to match the gun he just won! To soothe Purdey, however, the king ordered another gun as a present for a friend.

Old Friends

On 16 December 1933, a party of very experienced hunters gathered for a shoot at Kinnaird Castle in Scotland. The party consisted of the oldest member, W. Shaw Adamson (83), Maj. Lindsay Carnegie (82), the Earl of Southesk (80), Capt. W. H. Burn (80), and Col. W. Stuart Fotheringham, a mere boy of 71. In total the party was 396 years old, but still managed to kill 114 pheasants, 9 hares, 1 teal, 3 partridges, and 36 rabbits. The gentlemen were all using guns from James Purdey & Sons.

visited Britain for the first time and won the clay target championship on the Isle of Wight.

The famous British gunmaker, James Purdey, called Alfonso XIII "one of the best friends Purdey ever had." Through the years he bought scores of guns in different bores/gauges, including a set of four guns in 14-gauge to shoot driven partridges in Spain. In 1922, James Purdey & Sons offered a specially made pigeon gun as first prize for the competition *Tir au Pigeon* (for live pigeons) held at San Sebastian in Spain. Alfonso entered the competition and won it hands-down. After his victory the king told Athol Purdey that he had

These well-seasoned hunters were a total of 396 years when they killed 163 head of game in one day.

Francis Denzil Edward Baring, the fifth baron of Ashburton, waiting for the birds. He was one of the best shots in England and always good for a biting comment about (or to) his fellow guns.

Uneven Distribution

Anyone who has taken part in a driven shoot knows that some shooting pegs provide a lot more chances than others. One of the worst cases of this I have found occurred at the Grange in England. The estate belonged to Lord Ashburton (1866–1931), who invited six friends for a partridge shoot 18–21 October 1887. The seven guns bagged a total of 4,109 wild partridges, and the daily bag varied from 732 to 1,344 birds. The second-largest bag was made on 19 October with a total of 1,093 partridges killed—but on that same day, one of the seven guns only killed five birds.

Avid Huntress

While numerous female hunters have distinguished themselves hunting large game, they are almost absent from written sources when it comes to hunting small game with a shotgun. One remarkable exception was the Danish Countess Agnes Louise "Sophie" Bernstorff-Gyldensteen (1892–1975).

Sophie, as she was called, accompanied her father from an early age hunting all over the world, and she was only thirteen when she killed her first head of big game, a red stag. She later said, "I was raised to consider the red deer as a sort of shrine."

On her fourteenth birthday in 1906, a fallow buck was added to her game book, and before she was sixteen she killed two more red stags, a wild boar, and 11 roebucks. As a teenager, Sophie was a good shot and in 1910 she killed a total of 387 head of game, including 6 red stags, 10 fallow bucks, and 12 roebucks. Within a month she made doubles on both fallow bucks and

Incredible but True!

The most successful Danish huntress ever, Danish Countess Agnes Louise "Sophie" Bernstorff-Gyldensteen, had a bag total larger than her name, killing her first red stag when she was only thirteen.

Agnes "Sophie" Bernstorff-Gyldensteen and her husband Erik, photographed in front of Frijsenborg estate after a hunt in 1916.

red stags. The following year she made a double on axis deer in Ceylon before killing a rogue elephant bull.

On the day that World War I broke out in 1914, she married the Danish Count Erik Bernstorff-Gyldensteen; he was an eager hunter, too. Just days after the wedding Sophie killed 20 ducks during a morning's flight at Gyldensteen Estate. A month after giving birth to a son in 1917, she killed 9 roebucks in five days. The following year she killed 10 ducks on an evening flight just one month before giving birth to a daughter.

In 1920 she killed roebuck number 100 and killed four moose from the same post during a hunt in Norway. In 1921 she killed 999 head of game, mainly ducks, geese, and snipe. Three years later she killed duck number 1,000 and in 1935 duck number 2,000.

Sophie was a good shot with both rifle and shotgun. During a duck flight she killed 23 birds in 26 shots, and during a pheasant shoot she killed 18 birds in 23 shots. In 1955 she killed duck number 5,000 and was later invited to a shoot with the Danish King Frederik IX. She killed 9 deer out of the total bag of 56.

As Sophie got older she didn't hunt as much, and in 1968 she declined an invitation to a shoot at Gyldensteen Estate, which was now the property of her son. However, when she heard the shots, she regretted her decision and drove out to her son's post where she sat and watched the proceedings. Although she had her gun with her, she told her son she did not intend to shoot. However, when the son emptied his gun at a covey of birds, two flew directly over her. She then rose from her place, turned around, and elegantly made a double—at the tender age of 76!

During her long career as a huntress she killed several hundred head of big game in addition to 3,531 hares, 7,779 pheasants, 437 geese, 1,578 snipe, and 5,476 ducks. She was the most successful Danish huntress ever.

James Booth's ashes were loaded into cartridges similar to these.

An Unusual Farewell

In 2001 the British gunwriter James Booth (1951–2001) died tragically from food poisoning. In accordance with his will, his body was cremated. His widow, Joanna, following his wishes, arranged for the ashes to be filled into shotgun cartridges loaded by the Caledonian Cartridge Company in Brechin near Angus in Scotland. The cartridges were 12-gauge with one ounce of shot, and the ashes were used as a filler between the pellets. In total, 275 cartridges were loaded.

On 31 January 2004, the last day of the season, Joanna Booth invited twenty of her late husband's closest friends for a shoot at Brucklay Estate in Aberdeen-shire, Scotland. Before the first drive commenced, Reverend Alistair Donald, of the Church of Scotland, blessed the cartridges. He said that he had no qualms about the ceremony. "It was a perfectly normal scattering of ashes, a few words and prayers. After all, he had a lifelong interest in ballistics."

The shoot yielded 70 partridges, 23 pheasants, 7 ducks, and 1 fox. Remarkably, one of the Booth couples' female friends got four partridges although she had never shot before. James Booth's unusual farewell has since inspired a number of hunters to add similar requests to their wills.

Largest Bag

As described earlier in this book, the most successful hunters ever were

Emperor Frans I of Austria was host at a shoot in 1753 with the largest bag ever recorded.

two German electors using methods we would not consider even remotely sporting by today's standards. This probably also was the case during the most successful "hunt" ever recorded, which took place in Bohemia and was arranged for the Austrian Emperor Frans I (1708–1765) in 1753.

Over a period of 20 days, a party of 23 hunters killed 19 red stags, 77 roe deer, 10 wild boars, 10 foxes, 18,272 hares, 19,545 partridges, 9,499 pheasants, 114 larches, 353 quail, and 54 various species including thrushes and pigeons. In total the bag was 47,950 head of game, or 104 per hunter per day. Some 116,231 shots were fired, roughly 2.4 shots per head of game killed. Princess Charlotte fired 9,010

shots while the emperor modestly only made 1,798 shots.

Modern Record

When it comes to hunting in a (slightly) more modern sense, it is not surprising that the record bag was made in Britain.

Although driven shooting was a European invention, the British were quick to adopt it once Queen Victoria married the German Prince Albert. It wasn't long before the British elite did everything possible to improve the game population on their estates in order to enable shoots that lasted three to five days and resulted in enormous bags of small game.

If you take into account both the number of guns and the shoot's duration, the largest bag I have been able to find records of took place 26, 27, and 29 November 1895 at Lord Carnarvon's Highclere Estate. Lord Carnarvon, who would later become famous for finding the tomb of the pharaoh Tutankhamen in Egypt, invited five of England's best shots to his estate, including the

Lord Carnarvon in a relaxed moment.

Incredible but True!

*L*ord Carnarvon, known for finding the tomb of the pharaoh Tutankhamen in Egypt, hosted a hunting party with five of England's best shots at his estate, Highclere Estate. The shoot would produce a bag of 10,807 heads of small game.

the quality of the food rather than the quality of the shooting.

During his own shoots a small white donkey with panniers filled with ice-cooled drinks was taken around to ensure no one was thirsty—especially not the host. No detail seemed to be too small for Chaplin's dedication to hedonism. After an opulent lunch where one of the courses was ortolans (sparrow-size songbirds), he complained to a fellow guest that the accompanying grapes ought to have been pitted.

Later in life, Chaplin announced that he had always lived according to a very simple plan: "To have whatever I want, whenever I want it, and as much of it as I wanted!"

brothers Victor and Frederick Duleep Singh and Lord Ripon.

The total bag of the shoot was 10,807 head of game, of which 5,671 were pheasants. The rest consisted of 5,033 rabbits, 4 woodcock, 16 partridges, 43 hares, 2 ducks, and 38 "various."

Shooting Gourmand

A famous shot in Edwardian England, Sir Harry Chaplin (1840–1923), owner of Blankney Estate in Lincolnshire, England, prided himself on the epicurean meals that accompanied his shoots. There are many indications that he primarily accepted invitations to shoots according to

Harry Chaplin was not only fond of shooting but also the pleasures of the table, as you can tell from the picture here.

The Danish King Christian X was a keen hunter and very self-conscious.

It was hardly a surprise that Chaplin's lifestyle had consequences. Due to the size of his body later in his life he could no longer walk between drives but used a horse for transport. He also contracted gout, which is said to be caused by too much red meat, claret, and especially port. However, Chaplin knew his limitations. He once said, "My gout is very bad, but I have earned every twinge of it!"

Noblesse Oblige?

In the archives of the Danish estate Lerchenborg, it is recorded that King Christian X (1870–1947) was a guest on a two-day shoot in 1913 where His Majesty personally killed 240 pheasants and 101 hares, which for Denmark was an unusually large bag. However, the king was not above using his rank and position to get the chance of bagging more game than the other hunters. This became evident at another shoot in the early 1920s. Naturally the king was given the post considered the best in every drive, and on one of them he killed 65 hares. He proudly told his host, Count Lerche, about this bag when the hunters met again after the drive. Moments later, another gun, Mr. Sass, arrived and said he had shot 68 of the long-eared rodents. This made the king snort and exclaim, "What the hell is this? I thought I was supposed to have the best posts!"

The result was that the host told the other guests that they could not shoot more than His Majesty and that the king's bag in the future would be placed apart from the others when it was displayed at the end of the day. Although the king was out of old nobility, his behavior obviously wasn't always noble.

Count Manfred von Clary-Aldringen was for a time the prime minister of Austria-Hungary.

Tolerable Otium

Count Manfred von Clary-Aldringen (1852–1928), the 28th prime minister of Austria, was born into a very wealthy and influential Bohemian family that held a lot of political and diplomatic positions.

After the collapse of the Austro-Hungarian Empire in 1918, Clary-Aldringen retired from all official duties and spent the rest of his life at the family's numerous estates where his main activity was hunting and shooting. However, Clary-Aldringen must also have found time to hunt when he was younger as his game books begin in 1876 and end with his death in 1928.

He killed immense numbers of game, and none of it was reared. In his game book, he entered 122,316 pheasants, 68,587 partridges, 50,218 rabbits, 17,937 hares, 5,881 grouse, 4,875 ducks, 3,399 larches, 1,705 thrushes, 1,657 quail, and 41,271 "various." In total the retired prime minister shot 338,484 head of game—an average of 8,059 every season of the 52 years covered by his game books.

Keen Sportsman

One of the most eager European nonprofessional hunters in the years leading up to World War II was Danish chamberlain and landowner Holger Collet (1864–1943). From 1890 to 1920 Collet managed to shoot an average of 98 days a year with an all-time high in the year 1900 of 133 days. This means that Collet spent more than a quarter of each year in the shooting fields.

The size of his total bag reflects the fact that reared game was then rare in the Danish shooting fields, unlike in Central Europe and Britain. In spite of his enormous number of active hunting days during more than 60 years as a hunter, Collet "only" killed a total of 68,000 head of game, including 6,442 hares and 16,939 pheasants.

Greatest Shoot

Measured by the size of the bag and the number of guns, the largest driven

Holger Collet (right) was Denmark's most successful hunter between the two world wars. He was photographed with the Danish King Christian X in 1920.

Count Hieronymus Colloredo.

guest was the Austrian emperor Franz I (1708–1765).

The arrangement demanded the participation of 300 gamekeepers, who were assisted by 1,750 porters and an equivalent number of beaters. The latter were summoned from 19 villages in the area. The result of all this effort materialized during the 18 days into a bag of 29,545 partridges, 9,004 pheasants, 3,320 snipe, 746 larches, 13,243 hares, 1,710 wild boars, 3,216 red stags, 932 foxes, and 630 "various." In total, 62,337 head of game were killed during the hunt—or 76 per gun per day.

Driven Geese

shoot I have been able to find records of took place during 18 days in September 1758. Count Hieronymus von Colloredo (1732–1812) was the owner of a large estate in Bohemia and invited 45 guests to shoot. The most prominent

Many goose hunters are ingenious people who are constantly developing new methods to get within range of the timid birds. One of the most outlandish examples of this was one of Great Britain's most eager wildfowlers, Stan-

Stanley Duncan tried to arrange a shoot for driven geese by the aid of an airplane.

William Scott-Elliot is the hunter who participated in the most opening days of grouse season, better known as The Glorious Twelfth.

ley Duncan, who hunted in northeastern England. Duncan was author of several books on wildfowling and co-founded the Wildfowler's Association of Great Britain and Ireland in 1908.

Duncan conducted all sorts of experiments in his quest for the best hunting method. One of the most absurd took place between the two world wars, when Duncan decided to try a goose drive with the aid of an airplane and found a pilot who was willing to assist. Duncan had access to a field near the coast where the geese were feeding, and he left them in peace for several weeks before the drive. The plan was for the pilot to fly low over the terrain with the idea that the sudden appearance of the plane from behind the hedge surrounding the field would make the geese fly toward the blind

at the opposite end of the field where Duncan and a friend were waiting.

The first try was a flop. The geese heard the noise of the engine long before the plane arrived, and they took wing and swung left over the hedge, away from the disappointed hunters.

The pilot landed a few miles away and waited for the geese to return, which they did a few hours later. Now the wind was howling, and this was probably the reason the geese did not hear the plane until it came roaring over them.

Instead of trying to escape, the geese just pressed their bodies into the ground. A few shots made them reconsider, and shortly the air was full of geese.

The geese flew in front of the plane and the flock went over the hunters, who both managed to make several doubles. Although this elaborate and costly hunting method was considered a success, it was never repeated, which is a good thing considering the very questionable ethics of the practice.

Most Opening Days

William Scott-Elliot of Arkelton, Dumfriesshire, Scotland (1810–1901), probably participated in the most opening days of the grouse season (or Glorious Twelfths).

He started in 1824 at the age of 14 and was in the field on every one of the succeeding 73 opening days. On his last opening day he was 88 years old.

Female Gamekeepers

The profession of gamekeeping has existed since the Middle Ages and

Ann Holland.

but wore a keeper's hat." She was known as an accomplished horse breaker and an exceptional shot, but most of all for being the terror of poachers. Polly Fishburne left Holkham in 1822 to work for John Stanhope at Cannon Hall

for centuries it has been dominated by males. The earliest female gamekeeper was probably Mary "Polly" Fishburne (1793–1873), who worked on Holkham Estate in northern England in the early years of the nineteenth century. She was called "Black-eyed Polly" and was "a formidable figure with bright red cheeks, fine white teeth, with a man's haircut. She dressed in female clothing,

Incredible but True!

Gamekeeper Ann Holland once shot the heel off the boot of a fleeing poacher with her police carbine so she would have no difficulty catching up to him.

One of Polly Fishburne's anonymous colleagues.

estate in Yorkshire, where she remained until her death.

Ann Holland was another female gamekeeper who was employed by the fifth baron Rossmore, Derrick Westenra (1853–1921), to manage his 10,000-acre grouse moor at Mountain Lodge in County Monaghan, Ireland. Maybe the poachers at the estate briefly thought that they would have an easy time avoiding a female gamekeeper, but this was not to be. Ann Holland was a very good keeper and soon brought poaching to a halt. She once shot the heel off the boot of a fleeing poacher with her police carbine so she would have no difficulty catching up to him.

Costly Bags and Books

In Great Britain as well as in Central Europe, several hunters shot around a quarter million head of game or more. Among them are King George V who shot 246,000, the Archduke Franz Ferdinand with almost 275,000, and Count Manfred von Clary-Aldringen, who killed no less than 338,484 head of game. As late as at the end of the twentieth century, Sir Joseph Nickerson's total bag was close to 300,000.

The largest total bag of one individual hunter, however, was made by Lord Frederick Oliver Ripon (1852–1923). His game books listed no less than 557,688 heads of game from snipe to rhinoceros. And this comprehensive material did not even cover his entire bag, as all the game he killed during his many trips to Europe is not included.

In Great Britain the shooting season was then, as now, 12 August to 1

Erzherzog Franz Ferdinand d'Este
Jugendbildniss.

The Austro-Hungarian Archduke Franz Ferdinand was a passionate but unscrupulous hunter whose behavior was criticized by his contemporaries in spite of his position.

February, or about 175 days. Obviously not even Lord Ripon was shooting on every one of the approximately 10,000 possible days of his 57 seasons as a hunter, although one easily could get that impression. However, if we presume that he did so, he would have shot 56 head of game each day. Obviously, as he did not shoot every day, his actual bag per shooting day is somewhat higher. Unfortunately I have not had access to his game books, but as far as I have been able to establish, he shot an average of four days a week during the season,

Franz Ferdinand's castle Konopiste in the Czech Republic, where you still can see some of his more than 100,000 trophies.

which raises his average bag per day to almost 98 head of game.

Lord Ripon's game books, which consisted of 53 volumes, were sold in 1985 at one of Sotheby's auctions for around $100,000.

More Socializing, Less Shooting

The tradition of driven shoots developed during the latter half of the nineteenth century and soon society's elite were trying to outdo each other in terms of shooting the largest bags and providing the most luxurious dinners and evening entertainments during the shoots. It was

Trophies in Franz Ferdinand's castle Konopiste.

Lord Ripon awaiting the arrival of the birds.

Lord Ripon's game books—53 volumes in total.

Sir Edward Guinness loved to attend shoots, but he preferred the social aspect to the shooting itself.

One guest who did this frequently was Sir Edward Guinness (1847–1927). After having inherited half of the shares in his father's small Irish brewery, Edward managed it very well and was able to buy the other half from his brother when he was twenty-nine. Over the next decade he turned his company into the largest brewery in the world. It caused quite a stir in the British business world when Guinness sold two-thirds of his shares in the brewery for £6 million and became the richest man in England at the young age of forty. Not surprisingly he decided to enjoy life, including by going shooting with the rest of society's elite.

However, the richest man in England often bribed the head keeper to give him a post where there would be very few or no birds at all. Sir Edward was perfectly happy to be placed at the bottom of a valley or at the edge of a glade where he wouldn't have to fire many shots. Although the keepers considered him crazy (or eccentric, as it is called when you are rich), the reason was that Guinness loved the social aspects of the shoots but didn't much like the noisy shooting part.

not unusual for a guest to fire up to 1,500 shots a day at these events, which would make many of them so hard of hearing they had to stop shooting.

As the gamekeepers' pay at many estates was partially financed by gratuities from guests, it was not unheard of that a guest tried to get his post "rearranged" by giving large tips.

In 1894 Sir Edward Guinness bought Elveden Estate in order to be able to return invitations to shoots.

GENᴸ GEORGE HANGER.

Pubᵈ 14ᵗʰ March 1816 by J.J.Stockdale 41 Pall Mall.

The eccentric Baron George Hanger depicted in a caricature.

Poacher Paranoia

The fourth baron Coleraine, George Hanger (1751–1824), was a famous British officer, author, and eccentric. He loved to hunt and organized spectacular pheasant shoots, but never allowed anyone else to shoot with him. To keep his pheasants for himself became an obsession and he used a number of bizarre methods to achieve this goal.

Hanger designed a number of large cannons and had them mounted behind the parapet of the estate's main building,

Driven shoots around the turn of the nineteenth century often involved the firing of several thousand cartridges per day.

301

which was situated above the forests surrounding it. He fired these cannons at the slightest indication that anyone was disturbing his pheasants. The cannonballs were made of clay and contained marbles. The hissing sound of these huge clay balls in the air and sound they made when they hit the ground was said to be sufficient to scare off even the most determined poacher.

The estate's employees, especially the gamekeeper, lived in constant fear of Hanger's bizarre ideas. Hanger had built a house for the keeper that had neither doors nor windows at ground level. The idea was that the keeper would be safe from poachers who might want to get even with him after a controversy. Once the keeper had crawled up a ladder to enter the house, he was

William Higgin was a very active hunter who, while on leave during World War II, shot down a German Dornier plane with two shots from his service rifle.

William Higgin started to hunt at the age of eight.

supposed to pull it up behind him. A footbridge led from the house to a 30-foot-high tower where one of Hanger's cannons was placed; this allowed the gamekeeper to defend himself against even a determined attack. What the gamekeeper thought of the entire setup is unfortunately not recorded.

Successful Shooter

Capt. William Higgin (1922–2002) was one of England's most successful hunters of recent times. He belonged to a family of hunters and kept careful records from the time he was eleven years old, although not everything he shot was entered. You will, for instance, look in vain for the two peacocks he shot as a soldier in India. He didn't

The plane shot down by Higgin.

realize that the birds were sacred to the locals, who caught and almost lynched him. He managed to get smuggled out of the village with the aid of a native assistant.

Another "bird" not entered in his game book was a German Dornier bomber that Higgin shot down with his .303 Lee-Enfield service rifle during a leave in 1940. In an interview Higgin said, ". . . the plane came quite low in order to hit the steel works at Queensferry, so it was actually quite easy to put a bullet in each engine."

After the war, Higgin managed three farms in Cheshire, North Wales, and Shropshire, but still managed to shoot five days a week, and often six.

When a friend at a party once said to Higgin that he had spent a fortune shooting, Higgin said, "I have used three!"

This was probably true, as Higgin's game books reveals that his total bag was 357,000 head of game.

As an officer in Burma during World War II, Higgin contracted polio and never recovered entirely. At an age

of seventy-five he was hospitalized after a severe attack of asthma, but had his doctor give him an injection so he could participate in a great shoot the following day. The injection worked to a certain extent as Higgin felt all right, but it did not solve all his health problems.

When he fired his first shot, he fell over backward. Fortunately he had brought his keeper along as a loader, a large and powerful man who was told to hold Higgin upright by the collar every time he shot. In this unorthodox way, Higgin managed to kill 102 birds this day. At the age of seventy-eight, however, Higgin had to stop shooting. He was a guest at Altcar Estate on the last day of the season but found that he could no longer raise his gun. His right shoulder had worn out.

Lord Francis Hope.

Henry Hope.

Foot Faults

The eighth duke of Newcastle, Lord Francis Hope (1866–1941), was a well-known eccentric who loved shooting. He is most famous for his ownership of the Hope Diamond, which is said to put its owners under a curse. During a pheasant shoot, Lord Hope accidentally shot himself in the foot, probably while closing his gun. With the characteristic British "stiff upper lip," he ignored the accident and kept shooting, standing on one leg. Later his foot had to be amputated. This is quite remarkable, but it is even more amazing that his brother, Henry Hope (1864–1928), had shot himself in the foot at an earlier shoot and had also had it amputated. The two accidents did not stop the brothers from

shooting. They both stoically stated that they would have to hop—and they did.

Serious Shooting

Few hosts ever took shooting as seriously as 2nd Lord Leicester, Thomas William Coke (1822–1909). His father had the foresight to cultivate bird habitat at his Holkham Estate in the first half of the nineteenth century and accordingly Lord Leicester had outstanding numbers of birds at Holkham as early as the 1870s.

Lord Leicester did not wish to spend time on the social pastimes with his guests. To him shooting was a serious matter, and his guests had to conform to the shooting, not the other way round. Their reward, however, came in the shape of immensely game-rich drives. It was said that no man in England knew better than Lord Leicester how to make pheasants do what he wanted them to; he was reputed to be able to drive birds into his billiard room. However, the lunches at his shoots were very Spartan and usually consisted of a few sandwiches.

There was no room for excesses like a seated lunch during Lord Leicester's shoots, as opposed to most other places where opulent meals were served.

You did not get anything to drink unless you had the foresight to bring a flask. The "meal" was normally eaten standing while the birds were driven into the next beat. You were allowed to sit if you had to, but talking was frowned upon by the host as this might disturb the birds.

Lord Leicester watching the drive.

It says a lot about Lord Leicester's efforts—or that of his keepers—that during a shoot at Holkham in 1898 the three lines of guns were able to bag more than 1,000 birds in a single drive, including 760 pheasants.

A cassowary can reach a height of more than six feet.

The Greek Aeschylus died in a very unusual way.

Fatal Birds

While there are countless examples of men killing birds, the opposite is quite rare, but it does happen. On 6 April 1943, Phillip McClean (1926–1943) and his brother spotted a cassowary (*Casuarius casuarius*), a heavy Australian bird related to the ostrich and emu. Cassowaries can be up to 7 feet tall and weigh as much as 150 pounds and can be aggressive when threatened.

The two boys tried to bag the bird with their clubs but when they got close, the cassowary turned around and kicked the brother and he fell. Phillip McClean hit the bird with his club, but it spun around and kicked Phillip to the ground before kicking

him again. Phillip ended up with a cut in his throat, and although he managed to escape, he unfortunately bled to death soon after.

Another example of a bird killing a man comes from ancient Greece. Aeschylus (525–455 B.C.), considered the father of tragedy, died in a remarkable way by being hit by a falling tortoise dropped by an eagle. Eagles habitually drop tortoises from a great height in order to crack the shell so they can eat the contents. In his advanced

Lord Walsingham was not only an eccentric and an outstanding shot, he was also an avid naturalist, ornithologist, and etymologist.

306

Wales has never been home to many black grouse, which makes the hunter Arwel Morgan's experience even more unusual.

age Aeschylus had become bald, and it was supposed that the eagle mistook his bald scalp for a rock.

Mixed Bag

Even for Lord Walsingham, one of Britain's best shots, the last day of the season, 31 January 1889, was an unusually good day at his Merton Estate. At the end of the day he put an unusual number of species on display—a so-called mixed bag. He had killed 39 pheasants, 5 gray partridges, 1 red-legged partridge, 23 mallards, 6 gadwalls, 4 pochards, 7 teal, 3 swans, 1 woodcock, 1 common snipe, 2 jack snipe, 1 wood pigeon, 2 herons, 65 coots, 2 moorhens, 9 hares, 16 rabbits, 1 otter, 1 pike (shot!), and 1 "various," which, when you study his game book, turns out to be "a very large rat." That's 191 head of game in total, and 21 different species.

Walsingham noted that he also saw, but did not try to shoot, several additional species, including long-tailed duck, tufted duck, widgeon, shoveler,

Incredible but True!

Mr. Arwel Morgan, of the island of Anglesey in Wales, was after a rabbit when he slipped and fell, causing his gun to shoot two shots. When he got up he discovered the shots had gotten two black grouse.

water rail, kingfisher, and several species of seagulls.

Blessing in Disguise

In the early 1920s Mr. Arwel Morgan was hunting on the island of Anglesey in Wales. In spite of having walked almost fifteen miles that morning, the eager hunter had only managed to shoot two wood pigeons.

Shortly after he decided to turn back, Morgan saw a rabbit sitting on its rear legs and watching him from the top of a small grassy slope some distance away. Morgan spent ten minutes making a detour in the hope of stalking within range of the rabbit. When he finally got up to the bush, he had kept in line between him and the spot where he had seen the rabbit, he was quite

"Mad" Jack Mytton.

disappointed to see that the rabbit had vanished.

He tried to lower the hammers on his old shotgun, but as he did he slipped and fell, and both barrels of the gun went off. Morgan realized that this was not going to be his day and decided to go home. As he crossed the open area in front of him he found two dead black cocks—stone dead and still warm. This coincidence is made even more remarkable by the fact that black grouse were quite rare at Anglesey then, and still are today.

The Naked Hunter

One of the most eccentric hunters the world has ever seen was John "Mad Jack" Mytton (1796–1834) of Britain. Mytton's father died when Jack was only two years old and left his son properties with a value equivalent to $7.5 million of today's dollars. The income from his father's additional 132,000 acres of land gave Mytton an annual income of another million dollars.

In spite of his enviable economic situation, Mytton did not do very well in life. He was expelled from two private schools and accordingly he must not have accomplished much in the academic field before he was admitted to the University of Cambridge. He arrived for the first term with 2,000 bottles of port to help him through his studies.

The academic world soon bored Mytton, who went on a tour of Europe before attempting a military career. As this was no success either, Mytton decided to become a politician. He got people to vote for him by running through town and encouraging them to pinch the £10 notes he had put under the band of his hat. In this rather unorthodox way Mytton managed to get elected to the British Parliament at a cost of more than £10,000. The money was not well spent, however, as he had the least glorious parliamentary career in British history. He arrived for his first meeting, found the room hot and uncomfortable, and after half an hour he left the parliament and never returned.

Mytton is said to have arrived at a dinner at his estate, Halston Hall, riding on a bear. However, the animal bit him in the calf when he tried to make it gallop around the dining table using spurs.

Jack Mytton often went shooting in the middle of the night and the middle of winter, undressed. Here is a contemporary illustration of one of his hunts; for the sake of decorum he is wearing a nightshirt.

Mytton was known for his fondness for alcohol and sometimes drank eight bottles of port a day, in addition to a few large glasses of brandy. He accidentally killed one of his horses by making it drink a bottle of port.

He was also a great prankster who on one occasion exchanged the local vicar's Sunday sermon with pages from a shooting magazine. His greatest passion, however, was hunting. At the age of ten he was already a keen fox hunter, and in the wintertime he arranged rat hunts where he and a small army of servants would skate around trying to kill the rodents with hockey sticks.

Mytton showed little sensitivity to cold and went shooting in all kinds of weather wearing only a light jacket, light shoes, breeches, and silk stockings. If he got too warm during a hunt he was famous for stripping and continuing the hunt stark naked. In the winter he would often lie naked in snowdrifts. Most remarkable, however, was Mytton's fondness for getting up in the middle of the night to go duck hunting.

He would remove his nightshirt and walk naked over the frozen fields with his favorite gun. He would sneak up to the ducks, fire a shot or two, and then return home. Often he would then rise again half an hour later and repeat the performance. One night, when Mytton got tired of waiting for the ducks to swim within range, he decided to crawl naked over the ice until he was close enough to shoot. The trip over the ice took more than an hour, but Mytton never caught so much as a cold during his hunts.

Incredible but True!

Mad Jack Mytton owned 150 trousers, 700 pairs of boots, 1,000 hats, and 3,000 shirts for hunting purposes. His wardrobe preference for hunting: nothing. He preferred to hunt naked—even in winter!

Despite his fondness for hunting naked, he owned a vast wardrobe of 150 hunting trousers, 700 pairs of boots, 1,000 hats, and 3,000 shirts—for hunting purposes only.

Mytton also owned more than 2,000 hunting dogs for different purposes—hounds for fox hunting as well as spaniels, retrievers, and pointers for bird shooting. His favorite dogs were served steaks and champagne. Some dogs wore a livery while others had more specialized costumes. His favorite horse, Baronet, had free access to the entire mansion at Mytton's estate, Halston Hall. The horse would often lie with Mytton in front of the fireplace in the great hall.

A vermin line photographed in England around 1900.

to kill any predators they thought would decimate or harass the game. In England it was customary for the keeper to demonstrate his zealousness by making a so-called vermin line, which was a rope tied between two trees with the killed predators suspended from it. Every month the head keeper would inspect the bag in order to calculate the bonus the underkeeper was to receive; this often made up a large part of his wages.

In the latter half of the 1890s such an inspection was made, with the British landlord accompanying his head keeper. Among all the dead crows, hawks, stoats, and foxes, the two men to their great surprise saw a songbird hanging from the vermin line. The landlord asked the underkeeper what kind of bird it was, and he replied, "A nightingale, sir!"

Amazed, the landlord asked, "What harm can a nightingale possibly do?"

The underkeeper's indignant reply was, "Harm, sir? I'm not going to have my young pheasants kept awake at night!"

Mytton's eccentric behavior got him into all kinds of trouble. His lifestyle and spending on gambling exceeded even the huge income he had. His estate manager tried to help him and calculated that if Mytton would limit his spending to £6,000 annually for six years he would not have to sell the properties that had been in his family for almost 500 years.

Mytton would not consider this for a moment, saying, "I couldn't care less for a life with only £6,000 a year."

From then on Mytton's fate was sealed. In 1831 he had to flee to France in order to avoid his creditors and when he later returned to England he ended up in the debtor's prison, where he died at the age of only thirty-eight.

Zealous Keeper

A lot has changed since the nineteenth century when one of the gamekeeper's most important tasks was

The Austro-Hungarian Archduke Franz Ferdinand (center with gun on shoulder) photographed during the fateful shoot in England.

Incredible but True!

William O'Malley of Galway, Ireland, was on a walk-up shoot along the river Ballinahinch. He aimed at a grouse and shot. Just as he shot, a hare jumped up from the grass into the line of the shot, and behind the hare and the grouse in the river was a salmon which also jumped into the line of fire.

Three in One

William O'Malley (1853–1939) was a reporter, the business manager of a number of newspapers, and a member of the British parliament for the Irish district of Connemara in Galway. In August 1886 he was on a walk-up shoot along the River Ballinahinch.

A grouse rose, and as O'Malley shot it, a hare ran into his line of fire. While O'Malley was discussing the strange incident with his two fellow guns, a man shouted at them from down the riverbank.

"That is a great shot, sir!"

"What is a great shot?" O'Malley asked.

"Sir, you have made a great shot and have killed the salmon!"

It turned out that O'Malley, in one shot, had not only killed a grouse and a hare but also a jumping salmon!

The ghillie swam for the salmon, which weighed close to 10 pounds.

For obvious reasons O'Malley said that if this incident had not happened in the presence of two witnesses he would never have been believed by any hunter—or angler for that matter. He was probably right.

Fatal Miss

The Austro-Hungarian heir to the throne, Archduke Franz Ferdinand (1863–1914), was a frequent guest at British shooting estates and a good shot who quickly learned the noble art of shooting high pheasants.

In December 1913 he was visiting the duke of Portland. He was posted on a spot where there was snow on the ground. The heir to the throne was using a trio of guns and as the drive went well for him he quickly got into a good rhythm of exchanging guns with his two loaders. However, suddenly one of the loaders slipped and fell to the ground. The gun he had held in his hands hit the ground and both shots went off, passing within a foot of Franz Ferdinand's head.

When the Serbian student Gavrilo Princip assassinated the Archduke the

Maharaja Duleep Singh photographed with Lord Huntingfield, Lord Ripon, and Lord Walsingham at Elveden Estate. Together they were called "The Great Four" and were the elite of the British shots at the time.

Prince Victor Duleep Singh ready for action.

following July, he indirectly caused the outbreak of World War I and the deaths of 10 million people. But few people would have ascribed any political motives to the death of Franz Ferdinand due to a shooting accident, so perhaps the world would look very different today if the shots from his own shotgun had hit him that day in December.

Headless

Some of the best and most famous shots around the turn of the nineteenth century were Maharaja Duleep Singh (1838–1893) and his two sons, Victor (1866–1918) and Frederick (1868–1926), who were often called "The Black Princes of Perthshire." The Maharaja's state, Punjab, was annexed by the British government in 1849, and in 1854

Duleep Singh was exiled to Britain. As compensation he was granted an annual sum of £50,000, the equivalent of $6 million in today's money.

Duleep soon became one of Queen Victoria's favorites and decided to live the life of a British landlord, just like the rest of the elites surrounding the queen. He bought Elveden Estate in Suffolk and soon it was turned into a sportsman's paradise by a staff of gamekeepers.

The maharaja single-handedly shot 780 partridges on 8 September 1876, and his two sons almost outdid this on 23 September 1895, when the two of them shot 846 partridges before lunch.

Victor Duleep Singh was a good shot but not always very social.

The maharaja and his sons often shot at Britain's largest and most game-rich estates with other members of the shooting elite of their time. The two brothers were guests at the famous shoot at Highclere Estate in November 1895 when almost 11,000 head of game was killed by only six guns. They were also two of the five guns who set the British record bag of 6,943 rabbits killed in one day at Blenheim Estate on 7 October 1898.

Victor Duleep Singh, especially, was an eccentric man and sometimes difficult to have as a neighboring gun at a shoot. He was an excellent shot and used guns with full choke, not to increase his range but in order to be able to shoot low pheasants without ruining the meat by shooting them in the body. He was reputed to decapitate these birds and if true, this tells a lot about how close they were to him.

Victor's single-mindedness also became evident during a shoot at Lord Carnarvon's Estate Highclere, where the birds were driven up through a long narrow covert that ran along the top of a steep hill. From here they were intended to rise and fly over the valley toward another covert. Victor was placed at the end of the covert to shoot any birds that broke out and veered to the right, while the rest of the guns were in the valley below, expecting high and challenging birds. But the first two birds that tried to fly over the valley were killed by Victor when they were almost at the muzzle of his guns, and the next two met the same fate.

This proved too much for one of the other guns, Lord Ripon, who shouted out, "Oh, Singh, Singh!"

This had no visible effect on Singh, who continued shooting with great speed. He did not stop until he had killed 81 pheasants. One of the guns in the valley was Lord Ashburton, who demonstrated his contempt by putting his gun on the ground and turning his back to the spectacle. Afterward, the infuriated host had to admit that 76 of the birds killed by Victor were fit for the market as they had all been shot in the head. The feat was both a display of extraordinarily good marksmanship and very poor sportsmanship.

Victor did not always fare this well with his marksmanship. During a later shoot at Lord Ashburton's estate, The Grange, Victor had a bad day and missed a lot. After the last drive he

Mary Russell had many talents and a very unusual life. Here she is as a newly wedded duchess.

Mary Russell was an active pilot.

a recognized photographer, and a talented painter—in addition to being a skilled mechanic.

She was also said to be capable of training animals to do almost anything, except for her spoiled Pekinese dog, Chee Foo. At the age of sixty, Mary Russell decided to learn how to fly an airplane and four years later she beat the record of flying from London to Karachi, then in India. The following year she beat the record time flying from London to Cape Town.

In addition to all these remarkable feats, Mary Russell was a keen huntress and considered the best female shot in England. During her most successful season she killed 4,823 head of game with her pair of 16-gauge guns. Her best hit rate over an entire season was when she killed 2,392 head of game with 4,861 cartridges, or slightly more than two per bird.

threw both his guns into a hedgerow and told his loader to leave them there! What the often very sarcastic Lord Ashburton thought of this is, sadly, not recorded.

Active Duchess

Although very few huntresses were to be found in the shooting fields, there were still some who excelled in the noble art of shooting driven birds. One of the best examples is the Duchess of Bedford, Dame Mary Russell (1865–1937). She was a very active woman even by today's standards.

Her most successful day as a fly fisher yielded no less than 18 salmon weighing a total of 200 pounds. Mary Russell was also a dedicated mountaineer, an adventurous sailor, an excellent skater,

Lord Cardigan.

A contemporary portrait of Lord Cardigan.

Her record for partridges was 115 birds in one day and 40 grouse killed with 70 shots. Her highest hit rate of the very swift grouse, however, was 67 birds in 96 shots, or 1.43 shots per bird killed.

At her estate, Woburn, in Bedfordshire, England, on 31 January 1928, she killed 273 "remarkably tall pheasants" and two jays with a total of 366 cartridges, or 1.33 per bird killed.

At another occasion she made a hit rate of no less than 89 percent as she killed 84 pheasants in 94 shots, or 1.12 per bird. The Duchess ended her very active life at the age of seventy-one when her airplane went down over the North Sea. Neither the wreck of the airplane nor her body were ever found.

Pride

During a driven shoot you can compare the head gamekeeper with a general who is leading his troops into battle. If the owner of the shoot does not agree with the tactics of the head keeper, very awkward situations will arise. Only a very knowledgeable and dedicated landowner should question his keeper's plans for a shoot.

This was proved to a very embarrassing extent by the British Lord Cardigan (1797–1868), whose name is not only linked to a type of button-front sweater, but also to incompetent and arrogant behavior throughout his life. It was Lord Cardigan who, during the Peninsular War in 1854, ordered the disastrous cavalry charge of the Light Brigade that was almost completely wiped out by the Russian cannons.

Cardigan's arrogance was demonstrated during a shoot he hosted in the 1850s. Cardigan was unhappy with the number and height of the birds presented to him in a drive and shouted to his gamekeeper while pointing to a distant copse, "I want you to beat through that wood. And if there aren't far more birds you will be dismissed!"

"But, Your Grace . . ." the keeper tried to object.

"Not a word, sir! Do as I tell you!"

The poor keeper went off with his beater and began driving the wood. It produced a large number of high-flying birds and Cardigan was delighted.

Thomas Turner photographed shortly before his death in 1963.

paradise when Maharaja Duleep Singh bought it in 1863, and it continued to be when Lord Iveagh (formerly Sir Guinness) took over in 1894. As Lord Iveagh was the richest man in England, he did not care much about the farming aspects of the estate but wanted his friends to enjoy some of the best shooting available. Accordingly farming was secondary to game management, and Turner became head keeper with more than seventy employees.

In addition to the large population of breeding wild pheasants, another 20,000 pheasants were bred and released annually, and it was not unusual to have a bag of 1,000 birds for every shooting day.

Later in the day, in front of his guests, Cardigan took great pleasure in pointing out to his keeper that he had been right all along.

The keeper politely waited for his master to stop boasting about his knowledge of how to drive birds before saying, "But my lord, I questioned your decision regarding the wood for the simple reason that it is not yours. It belongs to your neighbor!"

Faithful Keeper

Few hunters ever had as long and active a life as gamekeeper Thomas Turner (1868–1963) did at Elveden Estate in Suffolk, England. The 17,000-acre estate was turned into a game

Lord Walsingham.

Shooter and loader changing guns—Position No. 1.

Shooter and loader changing guns—Position No. 2.

Shooter and loader changing guns—Position No. 3.

Lord Walsingham demonstrates the correct handling of a pair of guns when exchanging them with the loader.

The record was set in 1899, when the total bag reached 21,053 pheasants out of a grand total of 103,392 head of game.

Thomas Turner left school in 1876 at the age of eight and went to work for one of the beat keepers before working his way up to head keeper. He died 87 years later at the age of 95, three weeks before his planned retirement.

At a celebration of Turner's 80th anniversary of gamekeeping in 1956, he was asked what he thought was the secret of his advanced age.

Turner instantly replied with the old joke, "The speed I could duck when somebody shouted 'woodcock.' "

Shooting for Every Penny

Lord Thomas Walsingham (1843–1919), who is mentioned many times in this book, was born Thomas de Grey, but when his father died in 1870 he became the sixth baron of Walsingham. He began his career as a hunter in December 1852, at the tender age of nine. That year the following was recorded in the family's game book: "The Hon. Thomas de Grey killed one pheasant (with a stone)."

Forty-seven years later, when Thomas had become Lord Walsingham, he added: "roosting on the walnut tree, since blown down near the back yard gate.—*Walsingham 1899.*"

In his time he was one of the most famous game shots in England, but also a highly influential politician and a very keen amateur naturalist with a special interest in ornithology and etymology. Walsingham collected a vast number of bird species for the British Museum, and donated not only his library of 2,600 books on natural history but also his collection of butterflies and moths, which constituted 260,000 specimens.

Walsingham's rather eccentric nature showed via his clothes: He normally wore a genuine moleskin coat actually made from skins of moles. In addition, he would wear a waistcoat of snakeskin and a hat made from hedgehog skins, complete with quills and two large glass eyes.

His friend Lord Huntley claimed that Walsingham was never outdoors without his butterfly net, not even when shooting, and "at any lull in proceedings of the shoot he could be seen careering after insects."

When it came to women and money, Walsingham wasn't exactly orthodox either. He was married three times but was notoriously unfaithful to his wives, especially with the maids, which made the scandals that surrounded him even juicier.

Perhaps worst of all was his total lack of ability to balance his escapades with his income, which was far from modest. In 1870, Walsingham inherited the family estate, Merton, from his father, and when his aunt Lady Frankland-Russell died, he inherited two more estates in Yorkshire.

In addition to this came a number of separate possessions in London and other places, including the site of the famous Ritz Hotel. In 1876 the income from the Norfolk estates alone was the equivalent of almost $900,000 in today's money. Nevertheless, Walsingham managed to spend his entire fortune.

He did not have a lucky hand with investments, and agriculture became less profitable in his lifetime, but the major cause of his economic downfall was his excessive spending on shooting. When the Prince of Wales (later Edward VII) became a regular shooting guest at Merton in the late 1890s, Merton's wine cellar, which had been painstakingly built through generations, was exhausted in just one shooting season.

Around the turn of the century, the cost of game management at his estates and the decline in revenues forced Walsingham to borrow money.

Lord Wemyss.

Emperor Wilhelm II in the official hunting uniform of his court.

especially good form and soon began a competition for who could kill the most birds by the end of the day. On the last drive, Lord Wemyss drew the better position and he was almost sure to end as the "grouse king" of the day.

As he stood dropping birds from the sky, unburned blackpowder residue started glowing in the heather in front of him. Being far too occupied with winning the competition, he did not step on the small coals but continued shooting. The peat earth in front of him smoldered for a long time and suddenly a gust of wind made the flames rise and set the heather ablaze so that the lord eventually had to leave his post.

For the next two weeks, the entire local workforce had to carry water buckets up in the hills to stop the fire from spreading. But Lord Wemyss was happy—he shot more grouse than Ripon on that day.

Later, he said, "A piece of burned moor means nothing, but to beat the best shot in England means a whole lot!"

Fox Hunting Monarchs

Many of the world's crowned heads were keen fox hunters. In spite of not having any mobility in his left arm, Kaiser Wilhelm II of Germany (1859–1941) managed to kill 439 foxes from his debut as a hunter until 1910. His total bag is unfortunately not recorded, but it seems unlikely that the kaiser spent much time hunting foxes during World War I (1914–1918), and after the war he was living in exile in Holland where it is doubtful that he did much fox hunting.

In 1912 his debts had become so large that he had to sell all his possessions apart from Merton, which was subject to an entail. Presumably for this reason, Walsingham spent the last seven years of his life abroad.

Hot Competition

When shooting grouse at the duke of Cleveland's estate, High Force, in the late 1890s, both Lord Ripon and Lord Wemyss (1857–1937) were in

Danish King Christian X and his fox number 200.

The Danish King Christian X (1870–1947) was probably the second most successful fox-hunting monarch in Europe. Unfortunately, the court has not allowed access to the late king's shooting records so the precise total bag is not available, but the king's 200th fox was mounted and can be seen at the National Danish Museum of Hunting and Forestry in Hørsholm, Denmark.

Impudence Rewarded

In October 1904, the following advertisement in *The Times* created considerable excitement in shooting circles:

SHOOTING

Gentleman, educated Eton and Cambridge, first class all-round shot, is prepared to consider INVITATIONS TO SHOOT, having a few days still free this season; highest references, and terms strictly moderate.

Apply 'R.S.'
17 Pont Street
Belgravia
London, S.W.

Allegedly the advertisement was a hoax, but much to his astonishment the author received more than one genuine reply in addition to the many insulting letters he had expected.

Q.E.D.?

The eighth baron of Middleton, Lord Henry Willoughby (1817–1877), was one of the many eccentric noblemen of the Victorian era of Great Britain's history. As an avid hunter, the baron once boasted to the gamekeeper of his estate, Birdsall, that he was the better shot of the two, in spite of the latter being a professional. This immediately

Ripon in his younger years.

caused an argument, and in order to get the question settled the two men decided to go hunting.

In order to shorten the competition, it was agreed that each hunter should carry what the other shot during the day in order to give the most successful hunter an advantage. However, as time passed, the situation did not develop favorably for Lord Middleton, and when the two men walked past a field where a donkey was grazing peacefully, Middleton decided to increase his odds of winning. He shot the donkey

Lord Ripon at his favorite pastime.

Lord Ripon, with his back to the camera, counting grouse he shot.

tame pigeons on the roof of the barn. When Olly had shot the first two, he turned around and said, "Oh! This is far too tame. Make them fly, Hymes."

Hymes did as he was ordered, and the result was the same each time: one shot and a dead pigeon.

When he was thirteen, Olly shot for the first time on the Glorious Twelfth. Olly's bag for the three-day shoot was 20, 65, and 51 grouse respectively, and the result of his second day was the second-largest bag of all the guns in the party. The opening day for partridges was 1 September and before Olly returned to school at Eton on 26 September, the boy managed to shoot for 15 days, killing almost 500 birds in total.

Apart from being lucky enough to be the only son in a wealthy family, Olly was fortunate enough to have a father who was very interested in hunting and shooting. Due to his father's title and large fortune, Olly's shooting was almost a career in itself. His shooting skills were so extraordinary that he

and insisted that the unfortunate gamekeeper carry it along with the rest of his bag!

Olly

What better way to end this book than with a treatise on the most dedicated game shot the world has ever seen? We have met him repeatedly throughout this book, but as one of the most extraordinary shots in history, he merits a more in-depth examination.

Frederick Oliver Robinson, the second Marquis of Ripon (1852–1923), was known as "Olly" to his friends. He began his career as a hunter with a 28-gauge muzzleloader at the tender age of nine when he was taken out by one of the gamekeepers who taught him to shoot songbirds sitting in the trees. It soon became obvious that the boy had an extraordinary talent for shooting. A few days later the bailiff at Newby Hall, Mr. Hymes, asked the boy to shoot some

Ripon ready for action.

soon became a coveted guest on all the leading British shooting estates.

Ripon's unique skills with his shotguns made him an icon in the shooting fraternity, and it was not unusual for him to shoot twice or three times as many birds as the other guns in a shooting party. At a driven shoot at the British estate Croxteth Hall on 20–23 November 1883, six guns made a bag of 7,691 head of game of which Ripon, with 2,800 shots, accounted for 2,105 head, more than double the average of the other five guns.

On the second day of the shoot at Croxteth Hall, he killed 781 pheasants, which at the time was his personal record. The record stood until 25 November 1896, when Ripon killed 894 pheasants at Lambton Estate out of a total of 2,984 birds.

Ripon liked rabbit shooting, too. On 7 October 1885, Ripon participated in the most successful rabbit shoot ever held in Great Britain, which took place at the Rhiwlas Estate in Wales. The result of the day for the five guns was 5,096 rabbits, in addition to 6 pheasants, 1 grouse, and 3 snipe. Ripon killed 920 rabbits, for once slightly less than the average. Even at the end of his career he was an avid rabbit shooter.

In 1922, the year before his death, he was rabbit shooting at Mackershaw Park and set another personal record by shooting 920 rabbits in just two hours. The year before he had killed 345 rabbits in three hours.

During Ripon's frequent visits to Baron von Hirsch's estates, St. Johann and Eichhorn, he and other guests shot enormous numbers of partridges, as mentioned previously. Ripon's best year in this respect was 1893, when he shot 7,807 partridges.

Ripon would normally have a 70 percent success rate (1.4 shots per kill) when shooting, but in spite of his phenomenal skills, he was not above "improving" his statistics a little after the drive. This caused an especially embarrassing situation during a shoot at Gopsall Estate, where Ripon had not been able to bring his own loaders and accordingly had borrowed one from a fellow guest, Sir John Willoughby.

After the drive, when the host asked Ripon how many birds he had shot, the answer was, "124, and I fired 127 shots."

However, Sir Willoughby, who was not known to show excessive respect for rank or title, broke in and said, "That is not correct because my man told me that you fired over 150!"

After a very brief pause, the host suggested that the gentlemen should join the ladies.

However, there is absolutely no doubt that Ripon was an exceptional shot. On 3 September 1884, he killed 278 grouse in 350 shots, or 1.25 shots per bird, a feat which few will ever come even close to.

In all fairness, it must also be added that Ripon was a sufficiently passionate hunter to go shooting on his own and in places where the number of birds killed certainly never would be anything near the huge bags made on the driven shoots. In October 1910, he shot alone for three days at Coombes Estate, and the best day

A portrait of Ripon at the peak of his career.

yielded 8 partridges and 28 pheasants. Two years later he shot at the same place with two friends and the bag of the day was "only" 67 head of game.

Nevertheless, it is hard to describe Ripon's "trigger-happiness" as anything else than an obsession bordering on the pathological. There was hardly any live target which he would not shoot. For instance, under the category "various" he added the following note to his game book after a shoot in 1873: "1 Waxwing. Very rare."

In the off-season, he would shoot bumblebees, butterflies, and dragonflies "to keep the eye in shape"—as well as many other flying targets such as sparrows, starlings, and swallows. As a guest at Ferdinand de Rothschild's English estate Waddesdon, Lord Ripon had to spend a day alone as his host had to go to London to take care of an urgent matter.

When the host returned, he was met by an obviously proud Ripon who led Rothschild over to rows of songbirds—chaffinches, linnets, bullfinches, etc.—all carefully laid out with males in front and females behind, just like in an ordinary game parade. For some reason, Ripon was never invited to Waddesdon again.

When he visited his friend Sir Henry Gore Booth at his Irish Lissadell Estate, Ripon would often shoot hares out of his bedroom window with his service revolver on the lawn in front of the mansion.

Throughout his life Ripon stuck to hammer guns from James Purdey & Sons and had a total of six trios built for him by the famous London gunmaker.

Ripon's two loaders were instructed to hand him the guns with hammers cocked, a practice not without danger and for which he was criticized several times by other shooters.

Hammerless guns never impressed Ripon but he was not opposed to other developments in gunmaking. As soon as ejectors appeared, Ripon realized how much they raised the rate of fire and later he had all his guns built with ejectors. When chokes appeared in the 1870s, he had his guns built with full-choked barrels, but later returned to the usual combination of cylinder bore in the right barrel and modified or three-quarter choke in the left. In his later years the degree of choke was reduced as he realized that heavy choking did not improve his shooting.

Naturally Ripon did not achieve his results without practicing. The art of exchanging a trio of guns with two loaders took a lot of practice. At his home, Studley Royal in Yorkshire, he would practice exchanging guns for hours in the hall before going outside to practice with live ammunition. In those days it was considered finer to have natural skills for a given pastime than to learn it, so Ripon always pretended that his shooting skills were innate. Accordingly he must have been very displeased when Lady Edith Balfour could not sleep during a stay at Panshanger Estate and went to the library to find a book—only to surprise Ripon practicing with his two loaders.

But the practice paid off. During one drive at Blankney Estate as early

GAME KILLED by MARQUIS of RIPON
FROM 1867 TO 1923

Date	Rhinoceros	Tiger	Buffalo	Sambur	Pig	Deer	Red Deer	Grouse	Partridges	Pheasants	Woodcock	Snipe	Wild Duck	Black Game	Capercailzie	Hares	Rabbits	Various	Total
1867							8	265	1179	741	20	22	10			719	934	115	4013
1868							35	201	1418	1601	28	67	23			690	543	1 13	4719
1869							35	135	1659	1431	26	133	37			547	443	122	4568
1870							21	498	2309	2117	36	53	30			833	626	137	6660
1871							55	1408	1598	1859	80	244	42			1093	341	225	6945
1872							38	1498	2083	2835	27	60	31			1108	756	235	8671
1873							25	248	2417	3050	95	263	85			1027	450	591	8251
1874						3	5	90	2878	2345	229	462	131	5	4	1200	302	1200	8854
1875							3	287	2882	3225	176	461	208			1376	576	743	9937
1876								1551	3394	4110	30	25	37			1245	890	266	11.551
1877						2	4	2032	2359	4235	35	45	33	11	11	1496	1044	309	11,616
1878						4	9	1669	3378	4679	43	44	55	5	6	2157	662	503	13.214
1879							4	1344	630	3140	132	92	62	9	11	1125	287	215	7051
1880	9	6	18	31		73	12	1131	682	531	9	47	54	26	5	501	141	408	3684
1881							5	1566	3465	5014	26	14	43			1058	791	166	12,148
1882	2	2	6	1	66	104	10	3025	2123	2370	14	21	44			464	1122	117	9491
1883							5	2896	1845	6119	157	84	155			918	1386	319	13.884
1884							10	3073	3523	4347	134	70	70	38	8	713	1896	407	14.289
1885							5	2015	2788	4620	104	23	31			589	2547	108	12,830
1886							20	1989	1463	3383	105	87	72			357	786	349	8611
1887							57	2258	3785	3387	104	3	12			415	2328	237	12.586
1888							4	3060	853	5072	31	151	10			307	1523	85	11,096
1889							5	3081	5751	6182	100	109	14			1747	1069	181	18,239
1890								2006	7002	6498	172	105	28			1446	1120	123	18,500
1891								2277	1699	5794	34	13				711	406	271	11,205
1892							1	1412	6784	5580	7	10	5			453	1233	281	15,766
1893								2611	8732	5760	66	7	42			837	914	166	19,135
1894							1	2567	7261	5034	76	7	12			935	580	222	16,695
1895							1	1272	3461	6101	11	13	17			352	1040	210	12,478
1896								2649	2613	8514	13	11	4			314	557	177	14,852
1897							1	2797	1914	7850	67	10	47			358	828	152	14,024
1898								1693	1200	3432	18	3	6			169	298	144	6963
1899								823	1309	4605	16	2	57			205	609	137	7763
1900								1033	1322	6762	24	8	95			223	819	141	10.427
1901								2037	1991	8478	8	11	141			262	595	114	13,637
1902								1706	1701	4998	11	3	166			268	479	280	9612
1903								1890	462	4709	16	3	213			206	647	111	8257
1904								1355	1794	5032	17	13	127			186	173	114	8811
1905								1636	2292	6939	15	11	111			258	582	206	12.050
1906								2179	2019	8647	22	12	268			230	416	212	14,005
1907								1268	477	4386	15	7	111			88	152	144	6648
1908								1523	364	5764	29	9	129			159	183	176	8316
1909								2036	653	6374	25	15	115			155	195	195	9763
1910								1923	770	6115	24	12	155			150	89	234	9472
1911								2036	978	6463	23	5	59			158	143	191	10,056
1912								1810	518	7539	18	1	103			251	409	45	10,694
1913								1461	820	5179	13	11	172			243	223	121	8233
1914								2385	1628	4434	6	7	42			178	709	78	9467
1915								3078	2576	2598	17	6	5			341	594	96	9311
1916								3435	613	875	8	3				116	474	105	5629
1917								2087	1159	1990	15	4	9	1		168	584	36	6053
1918								1445	878	1279	10	3	1			128	564	184	4492
1919								1097	1151	1185	9		13			156	619	262	4492
1920								765	685	1527	16	6	19			144	899	111	4172
1921								1984	1242	2081	16	7	18			190	793	82	6413
1922								992	1307	2289	7	4	10			182	438	134	5363
1923								1080	356		2	5				51	346	200	2040
	2	11	12	19	97	186	382	97,668	124,193	241,234	2560	2927	3569	95	45	31934	40138	12616	557,688

A summary (albeit incomplete) of Lord Ripon's bag showing the absurd numbers of birds he killed.

327

as 4 December 1875, Ripon killed 95 pheasants in only 10 minutes. It was said that there was no noticeable difference in time between the second and third shot from two guns, and Ripon claimed that "A fast shot will fire two guns and four barrels almost as if they were placed on the same stock!"

When his loaders could not keep up with him they received the following comment, "Three empty guns! You might as well bring walking sticks if you cannot reload the guns faster than this!"

Ripon ended his seventy-one years of life rather suitably. On 22 September 1923, he was shooting driven grouse at Studley Royal's Dallowgill Moor. While the 51 grouse shot in the drive were being picked up, Lord Ripon dropped dead in the heather.

Entirely in accordance with Ripon's spirit, the head keeper recorded the bag of the day in Ripon's game book with the following line: "166 grouse and one snipe. Missed the snipe with the first two shots but killed it with the first shot from gun No. 2."

Bibliography

This work is based upon a review of a large number of sources, including databases, newspaper archives, and articles in a vast number of magazines. As the purpose of this work was never intended to be scientific, I have only included the most important sources published in books and magazines.

Ahlefeldt-Laurvig-Bille, Gregers & Vitus Gay. *Dansk Jagtleksikon*. Copenhagen: Standardforlaget, 1944.

Ahlefeldt-Laurvig-Bille, Gregers. *Impala*. Copenhagen: Nordisk Forlag, 1937.

——. *Jæger, Jagt & Vildt Verden Over*. Copenhagen: Chr. Erichsens Forlag, 1954.

Akehurst, Richard. *Sporting Guns*. London: Octopus Books, 1972.

Anderson, George H. *African Safaris*. Nairobi: Nakura Press, 1946.

Anderson, Kenneth. *Nine Man-Eaters and One Rogue*. New York: E. P. Dutton & Co. Inc, 1954.

Andrews, R. C. *Across Mongolian Plains*. New York and London: D. Appelton & Co. 1921.

Aschan, Ulf. *Baron Blixen*. Malmö, Sweden: Förlags AB Wiken, 1986.

Attenbury, Richard. *Hunting the American West*. Missoula, Montana: Boone and Crockett Club, 2008.

Baillie-Grohman, W. A. *Big Game Shooting*. Badminton Library, London: Longmans Green & Co., 1894.

Baillie-Grohman, W. A. *Sport in the Alps*. London: Adam & Charles Black, 1896.

Baker, J. & R. Lake. *Paradox*. Ceredigion, Wales, and Livermore, California: Printed by the authors, 2010.

Baker, Sir Samuel W. *Wild Beasts and their Ways*. London: MacMillan & Co., 1890.

Barclay, Edgar N. *Big Game Shooting Records*. London: H. F. & G. Witherby, 1932.

Barnes, Frank C. *Cartridges of the World*. 3rd & 8th eds. Chicago: Follett Publishing Co. 1972 & 1997.

Bayern, A.u.J.v. *Über Rehe*. München, Wien & Zürich: BLV Verlagsgesellschaft, 1975.

BB. *The Shooting Man's Bedside Book*. London: Eyre and Spottiswoode, 1948.

Beaumont, R. *Purdey's*. London: David & Charles, Newton Abbott, 1984.

Bell, W. D. M. *Bell of Africa*. London: Neville Spearmann, 1960.

——. *Wanderings of an Elephant Hunter*. London: Neville Spearman, 1923.

Bennet, E. *Shots and Snapshots in British East Africa*. London: Longmans, Green & Co., 1914.

Biermann & Odenfeldt. *Illustriertes Jadgbuch*. Rødovre, Denmark: Askholms Forlag, 1870.

Blaine, Delabere P. *Encyclopædia of Rural Sports*. London: Longmans, Orme, Brown, et al., 1840.

Blunt, David Enderby. *Elephant*. London: East Africa London Publications, 1933.

Booth, Martin. *Carpet Sahib*. London: Constable, 1986.

Boothroyd, G. *Shotguns and Gunsmiths*. London: A & C Black, 1986.

Brander, Michael. *The Big Game Hunters*. London: Sportsman's Press, 1988.

Brander, Michael. *The Perfect Victorian Hero*. Edinburgh: Mainstream Publishing Co., 1982.

Brandt, John H. *Asian Hunter*. Mesilla, New Mexico: Wild Sheep and Goat International, 1989.

Brown, Monty. *Hunter Away*. London: Privately printed, 1993.

Buchanan, Minor Ferris. *Holt Collier*. Jackson, Mississippi: Centennial Press of Mississippi, Inc., 2002.

Buckley, William. *Big Game Hunting in Central Africa*. London: C. Palmer, 1930.

Bull, Bartle. *Safari—A Chronicle of Adventure*. London: Viking, 1988.

Bulpin, T. V. *The Ivory Trail*. Cape Town: Books of Africa Ltd., 1954.

Burger, John F. *My Forty Years in Africa*. London: Robert Hale Ltd., 1960.

Burger, John. *Horned Death.* Huntington, West Virginia: Standard Publications, 1947.

Burrard, Gerald. *Big Game Hunting in the Himalayas and Tibet.* London: Herbert Jenkins Ltd., 1925.

Cameron, Kenneth M. *Into Africa.* London: Constable, 1990.

Capstick, Fiona C. *The Diana Files.* Johannesburg: Rowland Ward Publications, 2004.

Carruthers, D. *Unknown Mongolia.* London: Hutchinson, 1913.

Cederlund, Göran & Wiberg, Olof. *Rådjuret.* Stockholm: Svenska Jägereförbundet, 1995.

Chandler, Davis. *Legends of the African Frontier.* Long Beach, California: Safari Press, 2008.

Christensen, B. *Jagtkonger.* Ørbæk, Denmark: Forlaget Montrose, 1995.

Clark, James L. *The Great Arc of the Wild Sheep.* Norman, Oklahoma: University of Oklahoma Press, 1964.

——. *Trails of the Hunted.* Boston: Little, Brown & Co., 1928.

Cooley G. & Newton, J. *Cogswell & Harrison.* London: The Sportsman's Press, 2000.

Corbett, Jim. *The Leopard of Rudraprayag.* Oxford: Oxford University Press, 1947.

Czech, Kenneth. *With Rifle and Petticoat.* New York: Derrydale Press, 2002.

Dallas, D. *Boss & Co.* Wykey, England: Quiller Publishing Ltd., 2005.

Dallas, D. *Charles Gordon.* Wykey, England: Quiller Publishing Ltd., 2009.

Dallas, D. *Holland & Holland—The Royal Rifle Maker.* Wykey, England: Quiller Publishing, Ltd., 2003.

——. *Purdey—Gun & Rifle Makers.* Wykey, England: Quiller Publishing Ltd., 2000.

——. *The British Sporting Gun and Rifle.* Wykey, England: Quiller Publishing Ltd., 2008.

Dansk Jagttidende (Denmark). Various issues.

De Haas, Frank. *Bolt Action Rifle.* Northfield, Illinois: DBI Books Inc., 1971.

De Watteville, Vivienne. *Out in the Blue.* London: Methuen & Co., 1927.

Drastrup, Elmar. *Blandt Danske og Norske Fangstmænd i Nordøstgrønland.* Copenhagen: Aschehough, 1932.

Eastman, M. *Browning, 1903–1992.* Long Beach, California: Safari Press, 2008.

Egdal, Margit (ed.). *Schultz & Larsen.* Næstved, Denmark: Forlaget Devantier, 2007.

Engell, M. C. *Om Elefantens Udbredelse i Afrika.* Copenhagen: Copenhagen University, 1899.

Espersen, M. *Bomskud og Pletskud.* Copenhagen: Gyldendal, 1998.

Foran, Robert. *Kill or Be Killed.* London: Hutchinson, 1933.

——. *The Elephant Hunters of the Lado.* Long Beach, California: Safari Press, 2007.

Géza, Count Széchényi. *Sport in Europe.* London: Sands & Co., 1901.

Gladstone, H. S. *Record Bags and Shooting Records.* London: H. F. & G. Witherby, 1930.

Godfrey, R. *Olly.* Wiltshire, England: Privately printed, 2012.

Greener, W.W. *The Gun and its Development 9th edn.* London: Cassell & Co. Ltd., 1910.

Harding, C. W. *Eley Cartridges.* Wykey, England: Quiller Publishing Ltd., 2006.

Hastings, M. *Scattered Shots.* London: Pan MacMillan, 1999.

Heiberg, Th. *Jaktjournal 1892–1951.* Haga, Norway: Heiberg private archives.

Hemsing, Jan. *Encounters With Lions.* Agoura, California: Trophy Room Books, 1994.

Herbert, Agnes. *Casuals in the Caucasus.* London: The Bodley Head, 1912.

Herbert, Agnes. *Two Dianas in Alaska.* London: The Bodley Head, 1909.

——. *Two Dianas in Somaliland.* London: The Bodley Head, 1908.

Holman, Dennis. *Inside Safari Hunting.* New York: G. P. Putnam's Sons, 1969.

Holmberg, Andrew. *Out in Africa.* Agoura, California: Trophy Room Books, 2000.

Houze, Herbert G. *Winchester Repeating Arms Company.* Iola, Wisconsin: Krause Publications, 1996.

Huntchinson, Horace G. *Big Game Shooting, I & II.* London: The Country Life, 1905.

Hunter, John A. *Hunter.* New York: Harper & Brothers, 1951.

Illustrierter Zeitung (Germany). Various issues.

Jagt & Fiskeri (Denmark). Various issues.

Jagtvennen (Denmark). Various issues.

Jakt og Fiske (Norway). Various issues.

Jenkins, M. *Sport and Travel in Both Tibets.* London: Blades, East & Blades, 1909.

Jones, D. *Gamekeeping Past & Present.* Fovant, England: Polraen Publications, 2009.

Bibliography

Keith, Elmer. *Hell, I Was There*. Los Angeles: Petersen Publication Co., 1979.

Kemp, Kenneth. *Tales of the Big Game Hunters*. London: The Sportsman's Press, 1986.

King, P. *The Shooting Field*. Wykey, England: Quiller Publishing Ltd., 1985.

Kingsley-Heath, John. *Hunting the Dangerous Game of Africa*. Boulder, Colorado: Sycamore Island Books, 1998.

Laursen, J. *Herregårdsjagt i Danmark*. Copenhagen: Gads Forlag, 2009.

Lee Rue III, Leonard. *The Deer of North America*. New York: The Lyons Press, 1997.

Lloyd, L. *Scandinavian Adventures*. London: Richard Bentley, 1854.

Lyell, Denis D. *The African Elephant and Its Hunters*. London: Heath Cranton Ltd., 1924.

Macdonald, H. *The Shotgun*. London: David & Charles, 1981.

Manners, Harry. *Kambaku*. London: Frederick Muller Ltd., 1980.

Manniche, A. *Haandbog for Jægere*. Copenhagen: Gyldendal, 1933.

Marcot, R. *Remington*. Peoria, Illinois: Primedia, 1998.

Martin, B. *The Great Shoots*. London: David & Charles, 1987.

Masters, D. A. *Atkin, Grant & Lang*. Long Beach, California: Safari Press, 2006.

Maydon, H. C. *Big Game Shooting in Africa*. London: Seeley, Service & Co. Ltd., 1932.

Mellon, James. *African Hunter*. Long Beach, California: Safari Press, 1985.

Merfield, Fred G. *Gorilla Hunter*. New York: Ferrar, Straus & Cudahy, 1956.

Mikkelsen, Peter S. *Nordøstgrønland 1908–1960*. Copenhagen: Aschehough, 1994.

Montbel, Sascha de. *Grande Chasses*. Johannesburg: Rowland Ward Ltd., 1995.

Morden, William J. *Across Asia's Snows and Deserts*. New York: G. P. Putnam & Sons, 1927.

Morkel, Bill. *Hunting in Africa*. Cape Town: Howard Timmins Ltd., 1980.

Murray-Smith. T. *Safari Trail*. London: Robert Hale Ltd., 1965.

Neumann, A. *Elephant Hunting in East Equatorial Africa*. London: Rowland Ward, 1899.

Nickerson, J. *A Shooting Man's Creed*. London: Sidgwick & Jackson Ltd., 1989.

Pakenham, V. *The Noonday Sun*. York, England: Methuen, 1985.

Pappas, Cal. *The .600 Nitro Express*. Willows, Alaska: Privately printed, 2009.

Pardal, José. *Elephant Hunting in Portuguese East Africa*. Long Beach, California: Safari Press, 1990.

Parker, Ian. *Ivory Crisis*. London: Hogarth Press, 1983.

Pease, Alfred E. *The Book of the Lion*. London: J. Murray Ltd., 1909.

Pfizenmayer, E. W. *Siberian Man and Mammoth*. London: Blackie & Son Ltd., 1939.

Prior, Richard. *The Roe Deer*. Shrewsbury, England: Swan Hill Press Ltd., 1995.

Quinn, Tom. *The World's Greatest Shooting Stories*. Wykey, England: Quiller Publishing Ltd., 2010.

Read, Tony. *Kings of the Trigger*. New York: Read Book Design, 2007.

Renau, Jack & Justin Spring (editors). *Records of North American Big Game 13th edn.* Missoula, Montana: Boone and Crockett Club, 2011.

Roosevelt, K. & T. *Trailing the Giant Panda*. New York: Scribner's Publishing, 1929.

Ruffer, J. *The Big Shots*. London: Quiller Press, 1989.

Rusby, George G. *No More The Tusker*. London: W. H. Allen, 1965.

San Francisco Cronicle. Various issues.

Sánchez-Ariño, Tony. *Claws & Fangs*. Long Beach, California: Safari Press, 2011.

———. *Elephant Hunters, Men of Legend*. Long Beach, California: Safari Press, 2005.

———. *On the Trail of the African Elephant*. Long Beach, California: Safari Press, 1987.

Sand, Rudolf. *Afrika—stadig vildt*. Copenhagen: Hasselbalchs Forlag, 1962.

———. *Those Were The Days*. Long Beach, California: Safari Press, 1992.

Scheel, K. *På Jagtstien*. Copenhagen: Høst & Søn, 1953.

Schneider, Eberhard et al. *Jagdlexikon*. München, Wien & Zürich: BLV Verlagsgesellschaft, 1996.

Sedgwick, N. *The Shooting Times Anthology*. London: Percival Marshall & Co., 1963.

Selous, F. C. *Travel & Adventure in South-East Africa*. London: Rowland Ward & Co. Ltd., 1893.

Setterblad, Oscar m. fl. *Djur och Jakt Jorden Runt.* Gothenburg, Sweden: Gothia Aktiebolag, 1951.

Siemel, Sasha Jr. *Sashino.* Engelwood Cliffs, New Jersey: Prentice Hall, 1965.

Solli, S. *Jægeren Fridtjof Nansen.* Oslo: Gyldendal Norsk Forlag, 2002.

Solli, Svein. *Ikke bare troféer.* Oslo: Naturforlaget, 1999.

Speed, Jon et. al. *Mauser Original Oberndorf Rifles.* Cobourg, Ontario: Collector Grade Publications, 1997.

Sporon-Fiedler, Ivar. *I Afrikas Kløer.* Copenhagen: Nordisk Forlag, 1934.

Stebbins, Henry M. *Rifles.* Harrisburg, Pennsylvania: The Stackpole Company, 1958.

Stigand, C. H. *Hunting the Elephant in Africa.* New York: The Macmillan Company, 1913.

Stockley, C. H. *Stalking in the Himalayas and Northern India.* London: Herbert Jenkins Ltd., 1936.

———. *Big Game Shooting in the Indian Empire.* London: Constable, 1928.

Stonehenge [pseud.] (J. H. Walsh). *British Rural Sports.* London: Warne, 1871.

Sutherland, James. *The Adventures of an Elephant Hunter.* London: Macmillan & Co. Ltd., 1912.

Svensk Jakt (Sweden). Various issues.

Taylor, John. *African Rifles & Cartridges.* Georgetown: Small Arms Technical Publishing Company, 1948.

———. *Last of the Ivory Hunters.* New York: Simon & Schuster, 1955.

Taylor, Stephen. *The Mighty Nimrod.* London: Collins, 1989.

Temple-Perkins, E. A. *Kingdom of the Elephant.* London: Andrew Melrose, 1955.

The Field (England). Various issues.

The New York Times. Various issues.

The Shooting Times (England). Various issues.

The Times (England). Various issues.

Truesdell, S. R. *The Rifle and its Development.* Long Beach, California: Safari Press, 1992.

Bibliography

Trzebinsky, Errol. *The Kenya Pioneers*. London: W. W. Norton, 1985.

Turner, T. W. *Memoirs of a Gamekeeper*. London: Geoffery Bles, 1954.

Undheim, M. *Njardarheim*. Kvæven Bygdetun, Norway, 1999.

Wallace, H. F. *The Big Game of Central and Western China*. Penrith, England: David Grayling, 1992.

Walsh, Harry M. *The Outlaw Gunner*. Cambridge, Maryland: Tidewater Publishers, 1971.

Ward, Rowland. *Records of Big Game, 8th and 9th eds*. London: Rowland Ward & Co. Ltd. 1922 & 1935.

Watson, J. N. *Victorian & Edwardian Fieldsports*. London: Batsford, 1978.

Weismann, C. *Vildtets og Jagtens Historie i Danmark*. Copenhagen: C. A. Reitzels Forlag, 1931.

Weitemeyer, Aage & Frithiof Hansen. *Nyt Dansk Jagtleksikon*. Copenhagen: Branner & Korch, 1973.

Whitehead, Kenneth. *Encyclopedia of Deer*. London: Swan Hill, 1993.

Wild und Hund (Germany). Various issues.

William, Prince of Sweden. *Among Pygmies and Gorillas*. New York: E. P. Dutton & Co., 1922.

Wilson, D. & P. Ayerst. *White Gold*. London: Heinemann, 1976.

Wilson, R. L. *The World of Beretta*. Edison, New Jersey: Chartwell Books Inc., 2000.

Wolhuter, H. *Memoires of a Game Ranger*. Johannesburg: The Wildlife Protection Society, 1948.

Woods, Gregor. *Rifles for Africa*. Long Beach, California: Safari Press, 2002.

Zwilling, Ernst. A. *Jungle Fever*. London: The Travel Book Club, 1951.

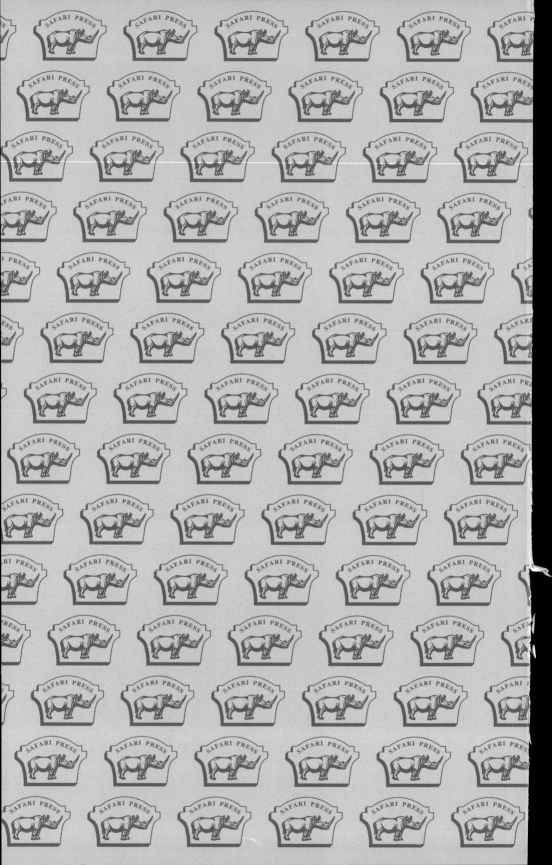